Hidden Hawaii
Winner of
The Lowell Thomas Travel Journalism Award
for
Best Guidebook

Hidden Hawaii is a winner of the coveted Lowell Thomas Award. Presented by the Society of American Travel Writers Foundation, the prize is the most prestigious honor in the field of travel writing.

A national team of judges from the University of Missouri Journalism School selected the winners from among all American and Canadian travel journalists. In naming it Best Guidebook, the awards committee said *Hidden Hawaii* "reveals so much detail on the state's natural wonders that a reader will have no trouble planning and executing an extraordinary trip or just adding a few unusual sights to the usual tour . . . . This guidebook makes good reading before, during and after the trip."

HIDDEN HAWAII
The Adventurer's Guide

"Great."   *Library Journal*

"A bible."   *Honolulu Advertiser*

"Thorough."   *Publishers Weekly*

"Don't leave home without it."   *Los Angeles Herald Examiner*

"Will make a fine traveling companion."   Stephen Birnbaum,
Nationally-syndicated columnist

"Riegert deserves high marks for solid and basic research."
Oakland Tribune

"Offers the best of all worlds to the Hawaii visitor."
Dallas Morning News

"History, low cost lodging, eating, intriguing nightspots, shell hunting, much more."   *Mademoiselle*

"Exotic destinations are described in intimate and encyclopedic detail. . . . A view no travel agent can offer. Riegert's adventures are crammed with fascinating insider's advice."   *Los Angeles Times*

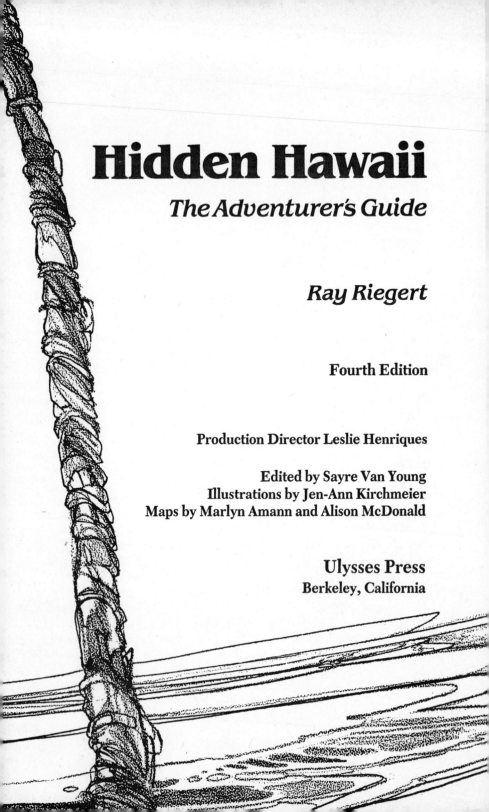

Hidden Hawaii

The Adventurer's Guide

Ray Riegert

Fourth Edition

Production Director Leslie Henriques

Edited by Sayre Van Young
Illustrations by Jen-Ann Kirchmeier
Maps by Marlyn Amann and Alison McDonald

Ulysses Press
Berkeley, California

Copyright © 1979, 1982, 1985, 1987 Ray Riegert. All rights reserved, including the right to reproduce this book or portions thereof in any form whatsoever, except for use by a reviewer in connection with a review.

Published by: Ulysses Press
Sather Gate Station
Box 4000—H
Berkeley, CA 94704

Library of Congress Cataloging in Publication Data

Riegert, Ray, 1947–
    Hidden Hawaii.

        Fourth edition
        Bibliography: p. 359
        Includes index.

Library of Congress Catalog Card Number 87-050717
ISBN 0-915233-04-5

Printed in the U.S.A. by the George Banta Company

First Edition: 1979
Second Edition: 1982
Third Edition: 1985
Fourth Edition: 1987

20 19 18 17 16 15 14 13

Cover Design: Tim Lewis
Text Design: Carlene Schnabel
Research Assistance: Claire Chun
Typesetting: Lindsay Mugglestone and Boyd Hunter
Proofreading: Leslie Henriques and Sayre Van Young
Cover Photography: Rita Ariyoshi
Map Research: Sayre Van Young
Paste-up: Phil Gardner, Angela Gennino, and Patricia Fostar
Index: Sayre Van Young

To Jim Chanin,
for years of friendship

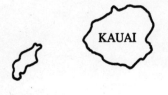

THE HAWAIIAN ISLANDS

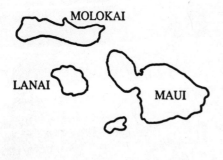

MOLOKAI

LANAI

MAUI

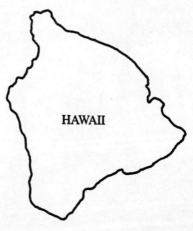

HAWAII

Preface

Hawaii. What images does the word bring to mind? Crystal blue waters against a white-sand beach. Palm trees swaying in a soft ocean breeze. Volcanic mountains rising in the hazy distance. Bronzed beach boys and luscious Polynesian women. Serenity. Luxury. Paradise.

To many it conjures still another dream—the perfect vacation. There is no more beautiful hideaway than this spectacular chain of tropical islands. For over a century Hawaii has been the meeting place of East and West, a select spot among savvy travelers. These adventurers are attracted not by Hawaii's famed tourist resorts—which are usually crowded and expensive—but by the opportunity to travel naturally and at low cost to an exotic locale.

As you'll find in the following pages, it is possible to tour economically through Hawaii's major sightseeing centers. It's even easier to explore the archipelago's more secluded realms. Few people realize that most of Hawaii's land is either rural or wilderness, and there's no price tag on the countryside. You can flee the multitudes and skip the expense by heading into the islands' endless backcountry. And if you venture far enough, you'll learn the secret that lies at the heart of this book: the less money you spend, the more likely you are to discover paradise.

Quite simply, that's the double-barreled purpose of *Hidden Hawaii*—to save you dollars while leading you to paradise. Whatever you're after, you should be able to find right here. When you want to relax amid the comforts of civilization, this book will show you good restaurants, comfortable hotels, quaint shops, and intriguing nightspots.

When you're ready to depart the beaten track, *Hidden Hawaii* will guide you to untouched beaches, remote campsites, underwater grottoes, and legendary fishing holes. It will take you to the Pacific's greatest surfing beaches, on hiking trails across live volcanoes, into flower-choked jungles, through desert canyons, and up to the top of the world's most massive mountain.

Hidden Hawaii is a handbook for living both in town and in the wild. The first chapter, covering Hawaii's history and language, will familiarize you with the rich tropical culture. Chapter Two describes how to get to the islands, what to bring, and what to expect when you arrive. The third chapter prepares you for outdoor life—swimming, hiking, camping, skin diving, and living off the land.

The last six chapters describe individual islands. Unlike other tour books, which begin with Oahu and concentrate on Honolulu, this volume starts on the Big Island at the southeastern end of the chain and moves northwest to Maui, Lanai, Molokai, Oahu, and Kauai. Honolulu is just another stop along the way.

Each island chapter is divided into three parts. When you want to find a car, hotel, or restaurant, check out the "Easy Living" section. "The Great Outdoors" segment will take you to beaches, parks, hiking trails, and isolated regions. The last section, "Travelers' Tracks," returns to the beaten path and leads to many sightseeing, shopping, and entertainment spots.

This book is not intended for those tourists in plastic *leis* who plop down on a Waikiki beach, toast for two weeks, then claim they've seen Hawaii when all they've really seen is some bizarre kind of Pacific Disneyland. No, *Hidden Hawaii* is for adventurers: people who view a vacation not as an escape from everyday routine, but rather as an extension of the most exciting aspects of their daily lives. People who travel to faraway places to learn more about their own homes. Folks like you and me who want to sit back and relax, but also seek to experience and explore.

Ray Riegert
Honolulu, 1979

NOTE: Throughout the text, hidden beaches, remote locales, and points of particular interest are marked with a star (★).

Acknowledgments

Since this book is now entering its fourth edition, there are several generations of people to thank. The person to whom I owe the deepest gratitude has been working on the project since the very beginning. I met my wife Leslie when I first arrived in the islands to write *Hidden Hawaii*. Since then she has contributed to the book as an editor, writer, researcher, and innovator. Her energy and spirit have been an inspiration throughout.

The current edition results from the efforts of several people. Sayre Van Young once again lent her skills as editor, proofreader, and indexer; Lindsay Mugglestone and Claire Chun skillfully shepherded the book through many stages; Tim Lewis devoted his talents to the cover design; Boyd Hunter ably handled the typesetting; Miki Demarest was particularly helpful; Phil Gardner, Angela Gennino, and Patricia Fostar contributed their expertise on the paste-up table. In Hawaii, Rita Ariyoshi provided outstanding cover photos while Auntie Lisa and Auntie Sheila made me feel at home. My son Keith and daughter Alice also merit a warm note of thanks for their encouraging smiles and infectious energy.

I want to convey a special thanks to those people in the publishing industry who rarely receive credit for the vital work they do. Foremost are the distributors. Charlie Winton, Randy Fleming, Mike Winton, Julie Bennett, Bill Hurst, Cherlyn Oto, Rob Jameson, Bonnie Beren, and all the other folks at Publishers Group West have contributed invaluable assistance and advice in nearly every phase of publishing and marketing. Randy Beek at Bookpeople, the folks at Quality Books and Raincoast, and Bill Julius and Pat Nowell at Banta Company have also been particularly helpful over the years.

People to whom I am indebted for prior work on *Hidden Hawaii* include Carlene Schnabel, the project coordinator for the earlier editions; Jen-Ann Kirchmeier, who contributed her boundless enthusiasm as well as a collection of marvelous drawings; Marlyn Amann and Alison McDonald, who complemented the text with a series of excellent maps; and Ed Silberstang, who offered expert assistance with the manuscript. I want to express my gratitude to Ronn Ronck, Doug Brown, Gail Brown, Beryl Shaw, and Linda Lyons for assistance above and beyond the call of friendship.

To everyone, I want to extend a *mahalo nui loa*—thank you a thousand times for your *kokua*.

CONTENTS

MAPS

Introduction

Reading *Hidden Hawaii* brought back memories of my long and frustratingly unconsummated love affair with the islands. Throughout my childhood I listened spellbound as my father and uncles swapped tales of sun-washed beaches far across the Pacific. Like millions of other sailors and GIs, they had toured distant lands courtesy of that great travel agent, Uncle Sam. Between battles they recuperated under swaying coco palms, swilling warm beer and bartering with the natives. Stale Lucky Strikes were traded for hand-forged bolo knives and intricately carved hardwood spears. And though their travels took them far beyond "Pearl," to me the atolls, jungles, and magical reefs of which they spoke all spelled Hawaii.

"Hawaii Granted Statehood," the headline ran. I folded the damp newspaper, hurled it toward my customer's front porch, and pedaled angrily along my paper route. *They* had done it, by a simple stroke of an administrative pen. My dream of retiring to the islands at age fifteen gave a violent lurch. Hawaii suddenly shifted from the distant edge of the unknown Orient to just another state. The Iowa of the Pacific. Offshore California. No more need for a passport or an interpreter. No gorging on exotic *mahimahi* and *poi*—the fabled Sandwich Islands would now feed me on McBurgers and cola.

I survived the disillusionment of statehood and though, two years later, I squandered my meager savings (earmarked for passage to the islands) on a battered motorbike, the dream did not fade entirely. Friends-of-friends returned from two-week Hawaiian idylls, faces and arms tanned to an improbable richness. Wilted *leis* would be casually draped over lampshades and mantlepieces, a not-so-subtle reminder of their brief fling in the sun. I could only wait.

Later, the islands subverted my college career. In the storm clouds gathering above the campus, I saw the foam of a turquoise wave curling around a slender surfer. Rain-washed ivy dissolved into frangipani and bougainvillea. The neo-Gothic monstrosity of the campus library became a battered volcanic grotto, rumbling with echoes of ocean rollers. My instructors, unable to see beyond the tips of their umbrellas, rewarded my visions of paradise with neat lines of zeroes.

Flunking out of college, however, almost brought me my dream. I found myself low man on the totem pole on a disabled fishing boat, drifting helplessly across the Gulf of Alaska. There seemed little promise of sunburns and coco palms in those cold, relentless waves. And then the captain took a close look at the charts.

"Well, boys, if this keeps up, we'll just have to head for Hawaii," he muttered. It had already been two endless weeks. Given the force of wind and current, we would hail the islands' sparkling shores within a month.

But it was just another lost chance, thwarted by an annoyingly efficient Norwegian chief engineer who dreamed of cod and boiled salmon heads rather than pineapple and passion fruit. The ancient engine coughed to life and took us north, back into the Big Grey.

Like many early explorers before me, I now took the only reasonable alternative left in my unsuccessful quest for the islands: I gave up. I went south instead, to a land where coconuts and tequila create a dream of their own. I traded my vision of a Polynesian outrigger for a ticket on the Greyhound, drawn to the irresistible warmth of a Mexican sun. Hawaii receded over the horizon.

A few years later, returning north through California, land of surprises, the dream suddenly reappeared. My partner Lorena and I were invited to a birthday *luau* honoring King Kamehameha, father of the islands. In the shade of a redwood forest we feasted on rich, greasy barbecued pork, delicate raw fish, tropical fruits, palm hearts, and that exotic beverage, Budweiser-on-tap. Frustrated Hawaiians weaving another year's dream from Maui smoke, we lay back on soft aromatic pine needles, lulled into fantasies of graceful sea canoes, the melancholy summons of conch shell trumpets, the rhythmic sweep of the paddles . . . carrying us off to the islands.

We could resist no longer; we determined to make the big break with the mainland. Having already written a travel book on Mexico, I now had the ultimate justification. We would go to Hawaii and return with knowledge and advice to pass on to others—while also earning a royalty that would guarantee a long rest on a hidden beach. Lorena was enthusiastic; between the native herbs and tropical sunsets, she could pass many many days. The final lure was thrown to us by our publisher: the promise of an advance to finance the journey. "But only when you've finished your camping book on Mexico," he warned.

●　　　●　　　●

"Hey, Carl, remember the book you were going to do on Hawaii?" I held the phone in a white-knuckled grip. Publishers are notorious for their twisted humor. Surely "remember" and "were going to do" were just sad attempts to cheer me toward my deadline.

"Yeah," I answered, "I have my Hawaiian shirt on right now. The one you bought me at Goodwill. *Remember?*"

There was a short, cynical laugh.

"Well, Ray Riegert just wrote it for you. Looks like it's time to play spin-the-globe again."

I slammed the phone down. Moments later I was trudging through the dusty Mexican streets, snarling at burros and stray dogs. At least my new recipe for *mai tais* wouldn't be wasted!

•   •   •

Good travel writers must constantly walk a tightrope between telling too much and not telling enough. The lazy tourist demands to be led by the nose to a comfortable yet inexpensive hotel and from there to a tasteful, quaint cafe. Nothing can be left to the demons of Surprise and Chance. Restless natives laboring over tom-toms in the middle of the night must be courtesy of the local tourist bureau, a civic contribution to amuse the traveler, rather than an inconvenient rebellion.

And with the distance between the islands and the continental U.S. reduced to nothing more than a quick lunch and a few drinks on a passenger jet, the pressures of tourism have become enormous. Hawaii's very lure is in danger of becoming its downfall.

This has created a situation in which a responsible and imaginative writer can perform a service both to adventurers and to the places they travel to see. A sensitive and aware guidebook like *Hidden Hawaii* helps educate and, in so doing, creates sensitive and aware travelers. The vast majority of guidebooks are not actually guides but consumer directories: where to spend your money with a minimum of distraction. That type of book actually steers us away from the heart of a place and an under-standing of its peoples, on to nothing more than a superficial tour of the "sights." Ray Riegert shows us a Hawaii blessed with an incredible richness of cultures, history, topography, and climates.

Hidden Hawaii not only points out attractive and inexpensive alter-natives in meals, lodging, entertainment, and shopping, but also takes us beyond Hawaii's often overdeveloped facade: where to watch whales; how to find the best parks, trails, and campsites; how to live on the beach, foraging, fishing, and diving; where to go shell collecting, marijuana sampling, volcano gazing... a variety of information as broad as the interests of travelers who want a lot out of a trip without going bankrupt.

Hidden Hawaii demonstrates a very encouraging trend: I like guide-books that are starting points for my own explorations, not addictive crutches. A little help can, and should, go a long way. Travel is a creative activity, one that should enhance the traveler as well as the places and people visited.

This is a book with an underlying attitude of respect and an awareness that it is more often one's attitude, rather than physical presence, that can be destructive. The hiker's motto, "Walk softly on the Earth," is just as valid to the traveler strolling the streets of Lahaina as it is to the explorer on the trails of Kauai or the hidden beaches of Molokai.

It's up to *us* to keep hidden Hawaii unspoiled and enjoyable for everyone.

Carl Franz
San Miguel de Allende, 1979

HIDDEN HAWAII
The Adventurer's Guide

No alien land in all the world has any deep, strong charm for me but that one, no other land could so longingly and so beseechingly haunt me, sleeping and waking, through half a lifetime, as that one has done. Other things leave me, but it abides; other things change, but it remains the same . . . . In my nostrils still lives the breath of flowers that perished twenty years ago.

Mark Twain, 1889

CHAPTER ONE

Paradise Lost
Hawaii's History and Culture

Hawaii, B.C. (Before Cook)

GEOLOGIC TIME

More than twenty-five million years ago a fissure opened along the Pacific floor. Beneath tons of sea water molten lava poured from the rift. This liquid basalt, oozing from a hot spot in the earth's center, created a crater along the ocean bottom. As the tectonic plate which comprises the ocean floor drifted over the earth's hot spot, numerous other craters appeared. Slowly, in the seemingly endless procession of geologic time, a chain of volcanic islands, stretching almost two thousand miles, emerged from the sea.

On the continents it was also a period of terrible upheaval. The Himalayas, Alps, and Andes were rising, but these great chains would reach their peaks long before the Pacific mountains even touched sea level. Not until a few million years ago did these underwater volcanoes break the surface and become islands. By then, present-day plants and animals inhabited the earth, and apes were rapidly evolving into a new species.

For a couple of million more years, the mountains grew. The forces of erosion cut into them, creating knife-edged cliffs and deep valleys. Then plants began germinating: mosses and ferns, springing from wind-blown spores, were probably first, followed by seed plants carried by migrating birds and on ocean currents. The steep-walled valleys provided natural greenhouses in which unique species evolved, while transoceanic winds swept insects and other life from the continents.

Some islands never survived this birth process; the ocean simply washed them away. The first islands that did endure, at the northwestern end of the Hawaiian chain, proved to be the smallest. Today these islands, with the exception of Midway, are barren uninhabited atolls. The volcanoes which rose last, far to the southeast, became the mountainous archipelago generally known as the Hawaiian Islands.

POLYNESIAN ARRIVAL

The island of Hawaii, the Big Island, was the last land mass created in this dramatic upheaval but the first to be inhabited by humans. Around the eighth century, Polynesians sailing from the Marquesas Islands, and then later from Tahiti, landed near Hawaii's southern tip. In Europe, mariners were rarely venturing outside the Mediterranean Sea, and it would be centuries before Columbus happened upon the New World. Yet in the Pacific, entire families were crossing 2,500 miles of untracked ocean in hand-carved canoes with sails woven from coconut fibers. The boats were awesome structures, catamaran-like vessels with a cabin built on the platform between the wooden hulls. Some were a hundred feet long and could do twenty knots, making the trip to Hawaii in a month.

The Polynesians had originally come from the coast of Asia about three thousand years before. They had migrated through Indonesia, then pressed inexorably eastward, leapfrogging across archipelagoes until they finally reached the last chain, the most remote—Hawaii.

These Pacific migrants were undoubtedly the greatest sailors of their day, and stand among the finest in history. When close to land they could smell it, taste it in the seawater, see it in a lagoon's turquoise reflection on the clouds above an island. They knew 150 stars. From the water color, they determined ocean depths and current directions. They had no charts, no compasses, no sextants; sailing directions were simply recorded in legends and chants. Yet Polynesians discovered the Pacific, from Indonesia to Easter Island, from New Zealand to Hawaii. They made the Vikings and Phoenicians look like landlubbers.

HAWAIIAN CULTURE

Hawaii, according to Polynesian legend, was discovered by Hawaii-loa, an adventurous sailor who often disappeared on long fishing trips. On one voyage, urged along by his navigator, Hawaii-loa sailed toward the planet Jupiter. He crossed the "many-colored ocean," passed over the "deep-colored sea," and eventually came upon "flaming Hawaii," a mountainous island chain that spewed smoke and lava.

History is less romantic. The Polynesians who found Hawaii were probably driven from their home islands by war or some similar calamity. They traveled in groups, not as lone rangers, and shared their canoes with dogs, pigs, and chickens with which they planned to stock new lands. Agricultural plants such as coconuts, yams, taro, sugar cane, bananas, and breadfruit were also stowed on board.

Most important, they transported their culture, an intricate system of beliefs and practices developed in the South Seas. After undergoing the stresses and demands of pioneer life, this traditional lifestyle was transformed into a new and uniquely Hawaiian culture.

It was based on a caste system that placed the *alii* or chiefs at the top and the slaves, *kauwas,* on the bottom. Between these two groups were the priests, *kahunas,* and the common people or *makaainanas.* The chiefs, much like feudal lords, controlled all the land and collected taxes from the commoners who farmed it. Each island was divided like a pie into wedge-shaped plots, *ahupuaas,* which extended from the ocean to the mountain peaks. In that way, every chief's domain contained fishing spots, village sites, arable valleys, and everything else necessary for the survival of his subjects.

Life centered around the *kapu,* a complex group of regulations which dictated what was sacred or profane. For example, women were not permitted to eat pork or bananas; commoners had to prostrate themselves in the presence of a chief. These strictures were vital to Hawaiian religion; *kapu* breakers were directly violating the will of the gods and could be executed for their actions. And there were a lot of gods to watch out for, many quite vindictive. The four central gods were *Kane,* the creator, *Lono,* the god of agriculture, *Ku,* the war god, and *Kanaloa,* lord of the underworld. They had been born from the sky father and earth mother, and had in turn created many lesser gods and demigods who controlled various aspects of nature.

It was, in the uncompromising terminology of the West, a stone-age civilization. Though the Hawaiians lacked metal tools, the wheel, and a writing system, they managed to include within their short inventory of cultural goods everything necessary to sustain a large population on a chain of small islands. They fashioned fish nets from coconut fibers, made hooks out of bone, shell, and ivory, and raised fish in rock-bound ponds. The men used irrigation in their farming. The women made clothing by pounding mulberry bark into a soft cloth called *tapa,* dyeing elaborate patterns into the fabric. They built peak-roofed thatch huts from native *pili* grass and *lauhala* leaves. The men fought wars with spears, slings, clubs, and daggers; the women used mortars and pestles to pound the roots of the taro plant into *poi,* the islanders' staple food.

The West labeled these early Hawaiians "noble savages." Actually, they often lacked nobility. The Hawaiians were cannibals who sometimes practiced human sacrifice and often used human bait to fish for sharks. They constantly warred among themselves and would mercilessly pursue a retreating army, murdering as many of the vanquished soldiers as possible.

But they weren't savages either. The Hawaiians developed a rich oral tradition of genealogical chants and created beautiful lilting songs to accompany their hula dancing. Their musicians mastered several instruments including the *ukeke* (a single-stringed device resembling a bow), an *ohe* or nose flute, conch shells, rattles, and drums made from gourds, coconut shells, or logs. Their craftsmen produced the world's finest featherwork, weaving thousands of tiny feathers into golden cloaks and ceremonial helmets. The Hawaiians helped develop the sport of surfing.

They also swam, boxed, bowled, and devised an intriguing game called *konane*, a cross between checkers and the Japanese game of *go*. They built hiking trails from coral and lava, and created an elemental art form in the images—petroglyphs—which they carved into rocks along the trails.

They also achieved something far more outstanding than their varied arts and crafts, something which the West, with its awesome knowledge and advanced technology, has never duplicated. The Hawaiians created a balance with nature. They practiced conservation, establishing closed seasons on certain fish species and carefully guarding their plant and animal resources. They led a simple life, without the complexities the outside world would eventually thrust upon them. It was a good life; food was plentiful, people were healthy, and the population increased. For a thousand years the Hawaiians lived in delicate harmony with the elements. It wasn't until the West entered the realm, transforming everything, that the fragile balance was destroyed. But that is another story entirely.

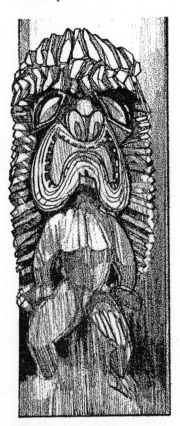

Hawaii, A.D. (After Discovery)

CAPTAIN COOK

They were high islands, rising in the northeast as the sun broke across the Pacific. First one, then a second, and finally, as the tall-masted ships drifted west, a third island loomed before them. Landfall! The British crew was ecstatic. It meant fresh water, tropical fruits, solid ground on which to set their boots, and a chance to carouse with the native women. For their captain, James Cook, it was another in an amazing career of discoveries. The man whom many call history's greatest explorer was about to land in one of the last spots on earth to be discovered by the West.

He would name the place for his patron, the British earl who became famous by pressing a meal between two crusts of bread. The Sandwich Islands. Later they would be called Owhyhee, and eventually, as the Western tongue glided around the uncharted edges of a foreign language, Hawaii.

It was January, 1778. The English army was battling a ragtag band of revolutionaries for control of the American colonies, and the British Empire was still basking in a sun that never set. The Pacific had been opened to Western powers over two centuries before when a Portuguese sailor named Magellan crossed it. Since then the British, French, Dutch, and Spanish had tracked through in search of future colonies.

They happened upon Samoa, Fiji, Tahiti, and the other islands which spread across this third of the globe, but somehow they had never sighted Hawaii. Even when Cook finally spied it, he little realized how important a find he had made. Hawaii, quite literally, was a jewel in the ocean, rich in fragrant sandalwood, ripe for agricultural exploitation, and crowded with sea life. But it was the archipelago's isolation that would prove to be its greatest resource. Strategically situated between Asia and North America, it was the only place for thousands of miles to which whalers, merchants, and bluejackets could repair for provisions and rest.

Cook was forty-nine years old when he shattered Hawaii's quiescence. The Englishman hadn't expected to find islands north of Tahiti. Quite frankly, he wasn't even trying. It was his third Pacific voyage and Cook was hunting bigger game, the fabled Northwest Passage that would link this ocean with the Atlantic.

But these mountainous islands were still an interesting find. He could see by the canoes venturing out to meet his ships that the lands were inhabited; when he finally put ashore on Kauai, Cook discovered a Polynesian society. He saw irrigated fields, domestic animals, and high-towered temples. The women were bare-breasted, the men wore loin-cloths. As his crew bartered for pigs, fowls, and bananas, he learned that the natives knew about metal and coveted iron like gold.

If iron was gold to these "Indians," then Cook was a god. He soon realized that his arrival had somehow been miraculously timed, coinciding with the *Makahiki* festival, a wild party celebrating the roving deity Lono whose return the Hawaiians had awaited for years. Cook was a strange white man sailing monstrous ships—obviously he was Lono. The Hawaiians gave him gifts, fell in his path, and rose only at his insistence.

But even among religious crowds, fame is often fickle. After leaving Hawaii, Cook sailed north to the Arctic Sea, where he failed to discover the Northwest Passage. He returned the next year to Kealakekua Bay on the Big Island, arriving at the tail end of another exhausting *Makahiki* festival. By then the Hawaiians had tired of his constant demands for provisions and were suffering from a new disease which was obviously carried by Lono's archangelic crew—syphilis. This Lono was proving something of a freeloader.

Tensions ran high. The Hawaiians stole a boat. Cook retaliated with gunfire. A scuffle broke out on the beach and in a sudden violent outburst, which surprised the islanders as much as the interlopers, the Hawaiians discovered that their god could bleed. The world's finest mariner lay face down in foot-deep water, stabbed and bludgeoned to death.

Cook's end marked the beginning of an era. He had put the Pacific on the map, his map, probing its expanses and defining its fringes. In Hawaii he ended a thousand years of solitude. The archipelago's geographic isolation, which has always played a crucial role in Hawaii's development, had finally failed to protect it, and a second theme had come into play— the islands' vulnerability. Together with the region's "backwardness," these conditions would now mold Hawaii's history. All in turn would be shaped by another factor, one which James Cook had added to Hawaii's historic equation. The West.

KAMEHAMEHA AND KAAHUMANU

The next man whose star would rise above Hawaii was present at Cook's death. Some say he struck the Englishman, others that he took a lock of the great leader's hair and used its residual power, its *mana,* to become king of all Hawaii.

Kamehameha. A tall, muscular, unattractive man with a furrowed face, a lesser chief on the powerful island of Hawaii. When he began his career of conquest a few years after Cook's death, he was a mere upstart, an ambitious, arrogant young chief. But he fought with a general's skill and a warrior's cunning, often plunging into the midst of a melee. He had an astute sense of technology, an intuition that these new Western metals and firearms could make him a king.

In Kamehameha's early years the Hawaiian islands were composed of many fiefdoms. Several kings or great chiefs, continually warring among themselves, ruled individual islands. At times a few kings would carve up one island or a lone king might seize several. Never had one monarch controlled all the islands.

But fresh players had entered the field: Westerners with ample firepower and awesome ships. During the decade following Cook, only a handful had arrived, mostly Englishmen and Americans, and they had not yet won the influence which they soon would wield. However, even a few foreigners were enough to upset the balance of power. They sold weapons and hardware to the great chiefs, making several of them more powerful than any of the others had ever been. War was imminent.

Kamahameha stood in the center of the hurricane. Like any leader suddenly caught up in the terrible momentum of history, he never quite realized where he was going or how fast he was moving. And he cared little that he was being carried in part by Westerners who would eventually want something for the ride. Kamehameha was no fool. If political expedience meant Western intrusion, then so be it. He had enemies among chiefs on the other islands; he needed the guns.

When two white men came into his camp in 1790, he had the military advisers to complement a fast expanding arsenal. Within months he cannonaded Maui. In 1792 Kamehameha seized the Big Island by inviting his main rival to a peaceful parley, then slaying the hapless chief. By 1795 he had consolidated his control of Maui, grasped Molokai and Lanai, and begun reaching greedily toward Oahu. He struck rapidly, landing near Waikiki and sweeping inland, forcing his enemies to their deaths over the precipitous cliffs of the Nuuanu Pali.

The warrior had become a conqueror, controlling all the islands except Kauai, which he finally gained in 1810 by peaceful negotiation. Kamehameha proved to be as able a bureaucrat as he had been a general. He became a benevolent despot who, with the aid of an ever-increasing number of Western advisers, expanded Hawaii's commerce, brought peace to the islands, and moved his people inexorably toward the modern age.

He came to be called Kamehameha the Great, and history first cast him as the George Washington of Hawaii, a wise and resolute leader who gathered a wartorn archipelago into a kingdom. Kamehameha I. But with the revisionist history of the 1960s and 1970s, as Third World people questioned both the Western version of events and the virtues of progress, Kamehameha began to resemble Benedict Arnold. He was seen as an opportunist, a megalomaniac who permitted the Western powers their initial foothold in Hawaii. He used their technology and then, in the manner of great men who depend on stronger allies, was eventually used by them.

As long a shadow as Kamehameha cast across the islands, the event which most dramatically transformed Hawaiian society occurred after his death in 1819. The kingdom had passed to Kamehameha's son Liholiho, but Kamehameha's favorite wife, Kaahumanu, usurped the power. Liholiho was a prodigal son, dissolute, lacking self-certainty, a drunk. Kaahumanu was a woman for all seasons, a canny politician who combined brilliance with boldness, the feminist of her day. She had infuriated Kamehameha by eating forbidden foods and sleeping with other chiefs, even when he placed a taboo on her body and executed her lovers. She drank liquor, ran away, proved completely uncontrollable, and won Kamehameha's love.

It was only natural that when he died, she would take his *mana*, or so she reckoned. Kaahumanu gravitated toward power with the drive of someone whom fate has unwisely denied. She carved her own destiny, announcing that Kamehameha's wish had been to give her a governmental voice. There would be a new post and she would fill it, becoming in a sense Hawaii's first prime minister.

And if the power, then the motion. Kaahumanu immediately marched against Hawaii's belief system, trying to topple the old idols. For years she had bristled under a polytheistic religion regulated by taboos, or *kapus*, which severely restricted women's rights. Now Kaahumanu urged the new king, Liholiho, to break a very strict *kapu* by sharing a meal with women.

Since the act might help consolidate Liholiho's position, it had a certain appeal to the king. Anyway, the *kapus* were weakening: these white men, coming now in ever greater numbers, defied them with impunity. Liholiho vacillated, went on a two-day drunk before gaining courage, then finally sat down to eat. It was a Last Supper, shattering an ancient creed and opening the way for a radically new divinity. As Kaahumanu had willed, the old order collapsed, taking away a vital part of island life and leaving the Hawaiians more exposed than ever to foreign influence.

Already Western practices were gaining hold. Commerce from Honolulu, Lahaina, and other ports was booming. There was a fortune to be made dealing sandalwood to China-bound merchants, and the chiefs were forcing the common people to strip Hawaii's forests. The grueling labor might make the chiefs rich, but it gained the commoners little more than a barren landscape. Western diseases struck virulently. The Polynesians in Hawaii, who numbered 300,000 in Cook's time, were extremely susceptible. By 1866 their population would dwindle to less than 60,000. It was a difficult time for the Hawaiian people.

MISSIONARIES AND MERCHANTS

Hawaii was not long without religion. The same year that Kaahumanu shattered tradition, a group of New England missionaries boarded the brig *Thaddeus* for a voyage around Cape Horn. It was a young company—many were in their twenties or thirties—which included a doctor, a printer, and several teachers. They were all strict Calvinists, fearful that the Second Coming was at hand and possessed of a mission. They were bound for a strange land called Hawaii, 18,000 miles away.

Hawaii, of course, was a lost paradise, a hellhole of sin and savagery where men slept with several wives and women neglected to wear dresses. To the missionaries, it mattered little that the Hawaiians had lived this way for centuries. The churchmen would save these heathens from hell's everlasting fire whether they liked it or not.

The delegation arrived in Kailua on the Big Island in 1820 and then spread out, establishing important missions in Honolulu and Lahaina. Soon they were building schools and churches, conducting services in Hawaiian, and converting the natives to Christianity.

The missionaries rapidly became an integral part of Hawaii, despite the fact that they were a walking contradiction to everything Hawaiian. They were a contentious, self-righteous, fanatical people whose arrogance toward the Hawaiians blinded them to the beauty and wisdom of island lifestyles. Where the natives lived in thatch homes open to the soothing trade winds, the missionaries built airless clapboard houses with New England–style fireplaces. While the Polynesians swam and surfed frequently, the new arrivals, living near the world's finest beaches, stank from not bathing. In a region where the thermometer rarely drops much below seventy degrees, they wore long-sleeved woolens, ankle-length dresses, and claw-hammer coats. At dinner they preferred salt pork to fresh beef, dried meat to fresh fish. They considered coconuts an abomination and were loath to eat bananas.

And yet the missionaries were a brave people, selfless and God-fearing. Their treacherous voyage from the Atlantic had brought them into a very alien land. Many would die from disease and overwork; most would never see their homeland again. Bigoted though they were, the Calvinists committed their lives to the Hawaiian people. They developed the Hawaiian alphabet, rendered Hawaiian into a written language, and, of course, translated the Bible. Theirs was the first printing press west of the Rockies. They introduced Western medicine throughout the islands and created such an effective school system that by the mid-nineteenth century eighty percent of the Hawaiian population was literate. Unlike almost all the other white people who came to Hawaii, they not only took from the islanders, they also gave.

But to a missionary, *giving* means ripping away everything repugnant to God and substituting it with Christianity. They would have to destroy Hawaiian culture in order to save it. Though instructed by their church elders not to meddle in island politics, the missionaries soon realized that heavenly wars had to be fought on earthly battlefields. Politics it would be. After all, wasn't government just another expression of God's bounty?

They allied with Kaahumanu and found it increasingly difficult to separate church from state. Kaahumanu converted to Christianity, while the missionaries became government advisers and helped pass laws protecting the sanctity of the Sabbath. Disgusting practices such as hula dancing were prohibited.

Politics can be a dangerous world for a man of the cloth. The missionaries were soon pitted against other foreigners who were quite willing to let the clerics sing hymns but were damned opposed to permitting them a voice in government. Hawaii in the 1820s had become a favorite way station for the whaling fleet. As the sandalwood forests were decimated, the island merchants began looking for other industries. By the 1840s, when over 500 ships a year anchored in Hawaiian ports, whaling had become the islands' economic lifeblood. More American ships visited Hawaii than any other port in the world.

Like the missionaries, the whalers were Yankees, shipping out from bustling New England ports. But they were a hell of a different cut of Yankee. There were rough, crude, boisterous men who loved rum and music, and thought a lot more of fornicating with island women than saving them. After the churchmen forced the passage of laws prohibiting prostitution, the sailors rioted along the waterfront and fired cannons at the mission homes. When the smoke cleared, the whalers still had their women.

Religion simply could not compete with commerce, and other Westerners were continuously stimulating more business in the islands. By the 1840s, as Hawaii adopted a parliamentary form of government, American and British fortune hunters were replacing missionaries as government advisers. It was a time when anyone, regardless of ability or morality, could travel to the islands and become a political powerhouse literally overnight. A consumptive American, fleeing the mainland for reasons of health, became chief justice of the Hawaiian Supreme Court while still in his twenties. Another lawyer, shadowed from the East Coast by a checkered past, became attorney general two weeks after arriving.

The situation was no different internationally. Hawaii was subject to the whims and terrors of gunboat diplomacy. The archipelago was solitary and exposed, and Western powers were beginning to eye it covetously. In 1843, a maverick British naval officer actually annexed Hawaii to the Crown, but the London government later countermanded his actions. Then, in the early 1850s, the threat of American annexation arose.

Restless Californians, fresh from the gold fields and hungry for revolution, plotted unsuccessfully in Honolulu. Even the French periodically sent gunboats in to protect their small Catholic minority.

Finally the three powers officially stated that they wanted to maintain Hawaii's national integrity. But independence seemed increasingly unlikely. European countries had already begun claiming other Pacific islands, and with the influx of Yankee missionaries and whalers, Hawaii was being steadily drawn into the American orbit.

THE SUGAR PLANTERS

There is an old Hawaiian saying that describes the nineteenth century: the missionaries came to do good, and they did very well. Actually the early evangelists, few of whom profited from their work, lived out only half the maxim. Their sons would give the saying its full meaning.

This second generation, quite willing to sacrifice glory for gain, fit neatly into the commercial society which had rendered their fathers irrelevant. They were shrewd, farsighted young Christians who had grown up in Hawaii and knew both the islands' pitfalls and potentials. They realized that the missionaries had never quite found Hawaii's pulse, and they watched uneasily as whaling became the lifeblood of the islands. Certainly it brought wealth, but whaling was too tenuous—there was always a threat that it might dry up entirely. A one-industry economy would never do; the mission boys wanted more. Agriculture was the obvious answer, and eventually they determined to bind their providence to a plant that grew wild in the islands—sugar cane.

The first sugar plantation was started on Kauai in 1835, but not until the 1870s did the new industry blossom. By then the Civil War had wreaked havoc with the whaling fleet, and a devastating winter in Arctic whaling grounds practically destroyed it. The mission boys, who prophesied the storm, weathered it quite comfortably. They had already begun fomenting an agricultural revolution.

Agriculture, of course, means land, and in the nineteenth century practically all Hawaii's acreage was held by the king and the chiefs. So in 1850, the mission sons, together with other white entrepreneurs, pushed through the Great Mahele, one of the slickest real estate laws in history. Rationalizing that it would grant chiefs the liberty to sell land to Hawaiian commoners and white men, the mission sons established a Western system of private property.

The Hawaiians, who had shared their chiefs' lands communally for centuries, had absolutely no concept of deeds and leases. What resulted was the old $24-worth-of-beads story. The benevolent Westerners wound up with the land, while the lucky Hawaiians got practically nothing. Large tracts were purchased for cases of whiskey; others went for the cost of a hollow promise. The entire island of Niihau, which is still owned by the same family, sold for $10,000. It was a bloodless coup, staged more than forty years before the revolution that would topple Hawaii's monarchy. In a sense it made the 1893 uprising anticlimactic. By then Hawaii's future would already be determined: white interlopers would own four times as much land as Hawaiian commoners.

Following the Great Mahele, the mission boys, along with other businessmen, were ready to become sugar planters. The *mana* once again was passing into new hands. Obviously, there was money to be made in cane, a lot of it, and now that they had land, all they needed was labor. The Hawaiians would never do. Cook might have recognized them as industrious, hardworking people, but the sugar planters considered them shiftless. Disease was killing them off anyway, and the Hawaiians who survived seemed to lose the will to live. Many made appointments with death, stating that in a week they would die; seven days later they were dead.

Foreign labor was the only answer. In 1850, the Masters and Servants Act was passed, establishing an immigration board to import plantation workers. Cheap Asian labor would be brought over. It was a crucial decision, one that would ramify forever through Hawaiian history and change the very substance of island society. Between 1850 and 1930, 180,000 Japanese, 125,000 Filipinos, 50,000 Chinese, and 20,000 Portuguese immigrated. They transformed Hawaii from a chain of Polynesian islands into one of the world's most varied and dynamic locales, a meeting place of East and West.

The Chinese were the first to come, arriving in 1852 and soon outnumbering the white population. Initially, with their long pigtails and uncommon habits, the Chinese were a joke around the islands. They were poor people from southern China whose lives were directed by clan loyalty. They built schools and worked hard so that one day they could return to their native villages in glory. They were ambitious, industrious, and — ultimately — successful.

Too successful, according to the sugar planters, who found it almost impossible to keep the coolies down on the farm. The Chinese came to Hawaii under labor contracts which forced them to work for five years. After their indentureship, rather than reenlisting as the sugar bosses had planned, the Chinese moved to the city and became merchants. Worse yet, they married Hawaiian women and were assimilated into the society.

These coolies, the planters decided, were too uppity, too ready to fill social roles that were really the business of white men. So in the 1880s they began importing Portuguese. But the Portuguese thought they already *were* white men, while any self-respecting American or Englishman of the time knew they weren't.

The Portuguese spelled trouble, and in 1886 the sugar planters turned to Japan, with its restricted land mass and burgeoning population.

The new immigrants were peasants from Japan's southern islands, raised in an authoritarian, hierarchical culture in which the father was a family dictator and the family was strictly defined by its social status. Like the Chinese, they built schools to protect their heritage and dreamed of returning home someday; but unlike their Asian neighbors, they only married other Japanese. They sent home for "picture brides," worshipped their ancestors and Emperor, and paid ultimate loyalty to Japan, not Hawaii.

The Japanese, it soon became evident, were too proud to work long hours for low pay. Plantation conditions were atrocious; workers were housed in hovels and frequently beaten. The Japanese simply did not adapt. Worst of all, they not only bitched, they organized, striking in 1909.

So in 1910 the sugar planters turned to the Philippines for labor. For two decades the Filipinos arrived, seeking their fortunes and leaving their wives behind. They worked not only with sugar cane but also with pineapples, which were becoming a big business in the twentieth century. They were a boisterous, fun-loving people, hated by the immigrants who preceded them and used by the whites who hired them. The Filipinos were given the most menial jobs, the worst working conditions, and the shoddiest housing. In time another side of their character began to show—a despondency, a hopeless sense of their own plight, their inability to raise passage money back home. They became the niggers of Hawaii.

REVOLUTIONARIES AND ROYALISTS

Sugar, by the late nineteenth century, was king. It had become the center of island economy, the principal fact of life for most islanders. Like the earlier whaling industry, it was drawing Hawaii ever closer to the American sphere. The sugar planters were selling the bulk of their crops in California; having already signed several tariff treaties to protect their American market, they were eager to further strengthen mainland ties. Besides, many sugar planters were second-, third-, and fourth-generation descendants of the New England missionaries; they had a natural affinity for the United States.

There was, however, one group which shared neither their love for sugar nor their ties to America. To the Hawaiian people, David Kalakaua was king, and America was the nemesis that had long threatened their independence. The whites might own the land, but the Hawaiians, through their monarch, still held substantial political power. During Kalakaua's rule in the 1870s and 1880s, anticolonialism was rampant.

The sugar planters were growing impatient. Kalakaua was proving very antagonistic; his nationalist drumbeating was becoming louder in their ears. How could the sugar merchants convince the United States to annex Hawaii when all these silly Hawaiian royalists were running around pretending to be the Pacific's answer to the British Isles? They had tolerated this long enough. The Hawaiians were obviously unfit to rule, and the planters soon joined with other businessmen to form a secret revolutionary organization. Backed by a force of well-armed followers, they pushed through the "Bayonet Constitution" of 1887, a self-serving document which weakened the king and strengthened the white landowners. If Hawaii was to remain a monarchy, it would have a Magna Carta.

But Hawaii would not be a monarchy long. Once revolution is in the air, it's often difficult to clear the smoke. By 1893 Kalakaua was dead and his sister, Liliuokalani, had succeeded to the throne. She was an audacious leader, proud of her heritage, quick to defend it, and prone to let immediate passions carry her onto dangerous ground. At a time when she should have hung fire, she charged, proclaiming publicly that she would abrogate the new constitution and reestablish a strong monarchy. The revolutionaries had the excuse they needed. They struck in January, seized government buildings and, with four boatloads of American marines and the support of the American minister, secured Honolulu. Liliuokalani surrendered.

It was a highly illegal coup: legitimate government had been stolen from the Hawaiian people. But given an island chain as isolated and vulnerable as Hawaii, the revolutionaries reasoned, how much did it really matter? It would be weeks before word reached Washington of what a few Americans had done without official sanction, then several more months before a new American president, Grover Cleveland, denounced the renegade action. By then the revolutionaries would already be forming a republic. They would choose as their first president Sanford Dole, a mission boy whose name eventually became synonymous with pineapples.

Not even revolution could rock Hawaii into the modern age. For years an unstable monarchy had reigned; now an oligarchy composed of the revolution's leaders would rule. Officially Hawaii was a democracy; in truth, the Chinese and Japanese were hindered from voting, and the Hawaiians were encouraged not to bother. Hawaii, reckoned its new leaders, was simply not ready for democracy. Even when the islands were finally annexed by the United States in 1898 and granted territorial status, they remained a colony.

More than ever before, the sugar planters, alias revolutionaries, held sway. By the early twentieth century they had linked their plantations into a cartel, the Big Five. It was a tidy monopoly composed of five companies which owned not only the sugar and pineapple industries, but the docks, shipping companies, and many of the stores as well. Most of these holdings, happily, were the property of a few interlocking, inter-marrying mission families—the Doles, Thurstons, Alexanders, Baldwins, Castles, Cookes, and others—who had found heaven right here on earth. They golfed together and dined together, sent their daughters to Wellesley and their sons to Yale. All were proud of their roots, and as blindly paternalistic as their forefathers. It was their destiny to control Hawaii, and they made very certain, by refusing to sell land or provide services, that mainland firms did not gain a foothold in their domain.

What was good for the Big Five was good for Hawaii. Competition was obviously not good for Hawaii. Although the Chinese and Japanese were establishing successful businesses in Honolulu and some Chinese were even growing rich, they posed no immediate threat to the Big Five. And the Hawaiians had never been good at capitalism. By the early twentieth century they had become one of the world's most urbanized groups. But rather than competing with white businessmen in Honolulu, unemployed Hawaiians were forced to live in hovels and packing crates, cooking their *poi* on stoves fashioned from empty oil cans.

Political competition was also unhealthy. Hawaii was ruled by the Big Five, so naturally it should be run by the Republican Party. After all, the mission families were Republicans. Back on the mainland, the Democrats had always been cool to the sugar planters, and it was a Republican president, William McKinley, who eventually annexed Hawaii. The Republicans, quite simply, were good for business.

The Big Five set out very deliberately to overwhelm any political opposition. When the Hawaiians created a home-rule party around the turn of the century, the Big Five shrewdly co-opted it by running a beloved descendant of Hawaii's royal family as the Republican candidate. On the plantations they pitted one ethnic group against another to prevent the Asian workers from organizing. Then, when labor unions finally formed, the Big Five attacked them savagely. In 1924, police killed sixteen strikers on Kauai. Fourteen years later, in an incident known as the "Hilo massacre," the police wounded fifty pickets.

The Big Five crushed the Democratic Party by intimidation. Polling booths were rigged. It was dangerous to vote Democratic—workers could lose their jobs, and if they were plantation workers, that meant losing their houses as well. Conducting Democratic meetings on the plantations was about as easy as holding a hula dance in an old missionary church. The Democrats went underground.

Those were halcyon days for both the Big Five and the Republican Party. In 1900, only five percent of Hawaii's population was white. The rest was comprised of races that rarely benefited from Republican policies. But for the next several decades, even during the Depression, the Big Five kept the Republicans in power.

While the New Deal swept the mainland, Hawaii clung to its colonial heritage. The islands were still a generation behind the rest of the United

States—the Big Five enjoyed it that way. There was nothing like the status quo when you were already in power. Other factors which had long shaped Hawaii's history also played into the hands of the Big Five. The islands' vulnerability, which had always favored the rule of a small elite, permitted the Big Five to establish an awesome cartel. Hawaii's isolation, its distance from the mainland, helped protect their monopoly.

THE JAPANESE AND THE MODERN WORLD

All that ended on December 7, 1941. The Japanese bombers which attacked Pearl Harbor sent shock waves through Hawaii that are still rumbling today. World War II changed all the rules of the game, upsetting the conditions that had determined island history for centuries.

Ironically, no group in Hawaii would feel the shift more thoroughly than the Japanese. When the Emperor declared war on the United States, 160,000 Japanese-Americans were living in Hawaii, fully one-third of the islands' population. On the mainland, Japanese-Americans were rounded up and herded into relocation camps. But in Hawaii that was impossible; there were simply too many, and they comprised too large a part of the labor force.

Many were second-generation Japanese, *nisei*, who had been educated in American schools and assimilated into Western society. Unlike their immigrant parents, the *issei*, they felt few ties to Japan. Their loyalties lay with America, and when war broke out they determined to prove it. They joined the U.S. armed forces and formed a regiment, the 442nd, which became the most frequently decorated outfit of the war. The Japanese were heroes, and when the war ended many heroes came home to the United States and ran for political office. Men like Dwight Eisenhower, Daniel Inouye, John Kennedy, and Spark Matsunaga began winning elections.

By the time the 442nd returned to the home front, Hawaii was changing dramatically. The Democrats were coming to power. Leftist labor unions won crucial strikes in 1941 and 1946. Jack Burns, an ex-cop who dressed in tattered clothes and drove around Honolulu in a beat-up car, was creating a new Democratic coalition.

Burns, who would eventually become governor, recognized the potential power of Hawaii's ethnic groups. Money was flowing into the islands—first military expenditures and then tourist dollars, and non-whites were rapidly becoming a new middle class. The Filipinos still constituted a large part of the plantation force, and the Hawaiians remained disenchanted, but the Japanese and Chinese were moving up fast. Together they all comprised a majority of Hawaii's voters.

Burns organized them, creating a multiracial movement and thrusting the Japanese forward as candidates. By 1954, the Democrats controlled the legislature, with the Japanese filling one out of every two seats in the capital. Then, when Hawaii attained statehood five years later, the voters elected the first Japanese ever to serve in Congress. Today both U.S. senators and the governor are Japanese. On every level of government, from municipal to federal, the Japanese predominate. They have arrived. The *mana,* that legendary power coveted by the Hawaiian chiefs and then lost to the sugar barons, has passed once again—to a people who came as immigrant farmworkers and stayed to become the leaders of the fiftieth state.

The Japanese and the Democrats were on the move, but in the period from World War II until the present day, everything was in motion. Hawaii was in upheaval. Jet travel and a population boom shattered the islands' solitude. While in 1939 about 500 people flew to Hawaii, now more than five million land every year. The military population escalated as Oahu became a key base not only during World War II but throughout the Cold War and the Vietnam War as well. Hawaii's overall population exploded from a half-million just after World War II to one million today.

No longer did the islands lag behind the mainland; they rapidly acquired the dubious quality of modernity. Hawaii became America's fiftieth state in 1959, Honolulu grew into a bustling high-rise city, and condominiums mushroomed along Maui's beaches. Outside investors swallowed up two of the Big Five corporations, and several partners in the old monopoly began conducting most of their business outside Hawaii. Everything became too big and moved too fast for Hawaii to be entirely vulnerable to a small interest group. Now, like the rest of the world, it would be prey to multinational corporations. Hawaii had arrived; it was fully a part of the modern world. An island chain which had slept for centuries had been rudely awakened by the forces of change.

Hawaii Today

THE LAND

Hawaii is an archipelago that stretches more than 1,500 miles across the North Pacific Ocean. Composed of 132 islands, it has eight major islands, clustered at the southeastern end of the chain. Together these larger islands are about the size of Connecticut and Rhode Island combined. Only seven are inhabited; the eighth, Kahoolawe, serves as a bombing range for the U.S. Navy. Another island, Niihau, is privately owned and off-limits to the public. So in planning your trip, you'll have six islands to choose from.

They're located 2,500 miles southwest of Los Angeles, on the same 20th latitude as Hong Kong and Mexico City. It's two hours earlier in Hawaii than in Los Angeles, four hours before Chicago, and five hours earlier than New York. Since Hawaii does not practice daylight-saving, this time difference becomes one hour greater during the summer months.

Each island, in a sense, is a small continent. Volcanic mountains rise in the interior, while the coastline is fringed with coral reefs and white-sand beaches. The northeastern face of each island, buffeted by trade winds, is the wet side. The contrast between this side and the island's southwestern sector is sometimes startling. Kauai, for instance, contains the wettest spot on earth, but its southwestern flank resembles Arizona. Dense rain forests in the northeast are teeming with exotic tropical plants, while across the island you're liable to see cactus growing in a barren landscape!

THE PEOPLE

Because of its unique history and isolated geography, Hawaii is truly a cultural melting pot. It's the only state in the union in which white people are a minority group. Whites, or *haoles* as they're called in the islands, comprise only about twenty-seven percent of Hawaii's one million population. Japanese constitute twenty-three percent, Hawaiians and part-Hawaiians account for seventeen percent, Filipinos eleven percent, Chinese about five percent, and other racial groups seventeen percent.

It's a very young, vital society. Almost half the community is under thirty, and over one-quarter of the people were born of racially mixed parents. Four out of every five residents live on the island of Oahu, and almost half of those live in the city of Honolulu.

One trait characterizing many of these people is Hawaii's famous spirit of *aloha*, a genuine friendliness, an openness to strangers, a willingness to give freely. Undoubtedly, it is one of the finest qualities any people has ever demonstrated. *Aloha* originated with the Polynesians and played an important role in ancient Hawaiian civilization. When Western colonialists arrived, however, they viewed it not as a Hawaiian form of graciousness, but rather as the naivete of a primitive culture. They turned *aloha* into a tool for exploiting the Hawaiians, taking practically everything they owned.

Today, unfortunately, the descendants of the colonialists are being repaid in kind. The *aloha* spirit is still present in the islands, but another social force has arisen—racial hatred. There is growing resentment toward white people and other mainlanders in Hawaii.

Sometimes this hatred spills into ripoffs and violence. Therefore, mainland visitors must be very careful, particularly when traveling in heavily touristed areas. Try not to leave items in your car; if you absolutely must, lock them in the trunk. Don't leave valuable gear unattended in a campsite. And try not to antagonize the islands' young people.

It's exciting to meet folks, and I highly recommend that you mix with local residents, but do it with forethought and consideration. A lot of locals are eager to make new acquaintances; others can be extremely hostile. So choose the situation. If a local group looks bent on trouble, mind your own business. They don't need you, and you don't need them. For most encounters, I'd follow this general rule—be friendly, but be careful.

THE ECONOMY

For years sugar was king in Hawaii, the most lucrative part of the island economy. Today tourism is number one. Over four million Americans, and five-and-a-half million travelers worldwide, visit the Aloha State every year. It's now a five billion dollar business that has expanded exponentially during the 1970s and 1980s.

With 125,000 personnel and dependents stationed in Hawaii, the U.S. military is another large industry. Concentrated on Oahu, where they control one-quarter of the land, the armed forces pour about two billion dollars into the local economy every year.

Marijuana is now Hawaii's foremost cash crop (one leading authority estimates that the market totals over one billion dollars). *Pakalolo* flourishes on Maui, Hawaii, and Kauai. Nurtured under ideal growing conditions, Hawaiian dope is especially potent and commands high prices all across the continental United States. It's a very interesting product, one which has created an underground economy.

Of course, no Chamber of Commerce report will list the demon weed as Hawaii's prime crop. Officially, sugar is still tops. While the $340 million sugar industry is small potatoes compared to tourism and the military, Hawaii remains one of America's largest sugar-producing states. But sugar, like everything else in the islands, is threatened by urban development. A ton of water is required to produce a pound of sugar. Since the construction industry is now a one-and-two-fifths billion dollar business, new housing developments are competing more and more with sugar cane for the precious liquid.

Pineapple is another crop that's ailing. Stiff competition from the

Philippines, where labor is cheap and easily exploitable, has reduced Hawaii's pineapple plantations to a few relatively small operations.

Hawaii is still the only place in the United States that grows coffee. The islands do a booming business in macadamia nuts, orchids, anthuriums, guava nectar, and passion fruit juice. Together these industries have created a strong economy in the fiftieth state. The per capita income is greater than the national average, and the standard of living is generally higher.

Important note: Hawaii has a higher cost of living than almost any state in the union. As in the rest of the country, inflation is no stranger here; price increases are common. Therefore, don't be surprised if the prices quoted in this book are sometimes lower than those you'll actually be paying.

THE CUISINE

Nowhere is the influence of Hawaii's melting pot population stronger than in the kitchen. While in the islands, you'll probably eat not only with a fork, but with chopsticks and fingers as well. You'll sample a wonderfully varied cuisine. In addition to standard American fare, hundreds of restaurants serve Hawaiian, Japanese, Chinese, Korean, Portuguese, and Filipino dishes. There are also fresh fruits aplenty—pineapples, papayas, mangoes, bananas, and tangerines—plus native fish such as *mahimahi,* marlin, and snapper.

The prime Hawaiian dish is *poi,* made from crushed taro root and served as a pasty purple liquid. It's pretty bland fare, but it does make a good side dish with roast pork or tripe stew. You should also try *lau lau,* a combination of fish, pork, and taro leaves wrapped in a *ti* leaf and steamed. And don't neglect to taste baked *ulu* (breadfruit) and *opihi* (limpets). A good way to try all these dishes at one sitting is to attend a *luau.* I've always found the tourist *luaus* too commercial, but you might watch the newspapers for one of the special *luaus* sponsored by civic organizations.

Japanese dishes include sukiyaki, teriyaki, and tempura, plus an island favorite—*sashimi,* or raw fish. Similarly, Chinese menus usually feature the dishes you've sampled at home as well as some less common treats. Among these are *saimin,* a noodle soup filled with meat and vegetables, and crack seed, a delicacy made from dried fruits.

You can count on the Koreans for *kim chi,* a spicy salad of pickled cabbage, and *kun koki,* barbecued meat prepared with soy and sesame oil. The Portuguese serve up some delicious sweets including *malasadas* (donuts minus the holes) and *pao doce,* or sweet bread. For Filipino fare, I recommend *adobo,* a pork or chicken dish spiced with garlic and vinegar, and *pochero,* a meat entree cooked with bananas and several vegetables.

As the Hawaiians say, *"Hele mai ai."* Come and eat!

THE LANGUAGE

The language common to all Hawaii is English, but because of its diverse cultural heritage, the archipelago also supports several other tongues. Foremost among these are Hawaiian and pidgin.

Hawaiian, closely related to other Polynesian languages, is one of the most fluid and melodious languages in the world. It's composed of only twelve letters: five vowels—*a, e, i, o, u* and seven consonants—*h, k, l, m, n, p, w.*

At first glance, the language appears formidable: how the hell do you pronounce *humuhumunukunukuapuaa?* But actually it's all quite simple. After you've mastered a few rules of pronunciation, you can take on any word in the language.

The first thing to remember is that every syllable ends with a vowel, and the next to last syllable receives the accent.

The next rule to keep in mind is that all the letters in Hawaiian are pronounced. Consonants are pronounced the same as in English (except for the *w,* which is pronounced as a *v* when it introduces the last syllable of a word—as in *ewa* or *awa.* Vowels are pronounced the same as in Latin or Spanish: *a* as in *among, e* as in *they, i* as in *machine, o* as in *no,* and *u* as in *too.* Hawaiian has four vowel combinations or diphthongs: *au,* pronounced *ow, ae* and *ai,* which sound like *eye,* and *ei,* pronounced *ay.*

By now you're probably wondering what I could possibly have meant when I said Hawaiian was simple. I think the glossary which follows will simplify everything while helping you pronounce common words and place names. Just go through the list, starting with words like *aloha* and *luau* that you already know. After you've practiced pronouncing familiar words, the rules will become second nature; you'll practically be a *kamaaina.*

Just when you start to speak with a swagger, cocky about having learned a new language, some young Hawaiian will start talking at you in a tongue that breaks all the rules you've so carefully mastered. That's pidgin. It started in the nineteenth century as a lingua franca among Hawaii's many races. Pidgin speakers mix English and Hawaiian with several other tongues to produce a spicy creole. It's a fascinating language with its own vocabulary, a unique syntax, and a rising inflection that's hard to mimic.

Pidgin is definitely the hip way to talk in Hawaii. A lot of young Hawaiians use it among themselves as a private language. At times they may start talking pidgin to you, acting as though they don't speak English; then if they decide you're okay, they'll break into English. When that happens, you be one *da kine brah.*

So *brah,* I take *da kine* pidgin words, put 'em together with Hawaiian, make one big list. Savvy?

aa (**ah**-ah) - a type of rough lava
ae (eye) - yes
aikane (eye-**kah**-nay) - friend
akamai (ah-**kah**-my) - wise
alii (ah-**lee**-ee) - chief
aloha (ah-**lo**-ha) - hello; greetings; love
aole (ah-**oh**-lay) - no
auwe (ow-**way**) - ouch!
brah (bra) - friend; brother; bro'
bumby (**bum**-bee) - after awhile; by and by
dah makule guys (da mah-**kuh**-lay guys) - senior citizens
da kine (da kyne) - whatdyacallit; thingamajig; that way
duh uddah time (duh **uh**-duh time) - once before
diamondhead - in an easterly direction
ewa (**eh**-vah) - in a westerly direction
hale (**hah**-lay) - house
haole (**how**-lee) - Caucasian; white person
hapa (**hah**-pa) - half
hapa-haole (**hah**-pa **how**-lee) - half-Caucasian
heiau (hey-ee-**ow**) - temple
hele on (**hey**-lay own) - hip; with it
holo holo (**ho**-low **ho**-low) - to visit
howzit? (hows-it) - how you doing? what's happening?
hukilau (**who**-key-lau) - community fishing party
hula (**who**-la) - Hawaiian dance
imu (**ee**-moo) - underground oven
ipo (**ee**-po) - sweetheart
jag up (jag up) - drunk
kahuna (kah-**who**-nah) - priest
kai (kye) - ocean
kaka-roach (**kah**-kah roach) - ripoff; theft
kamaaina (kah-mah-**eye**-nah) - longtime island resident
kane (**kah**-nay) - man
kapu (**kah**-poo) - taboo; forbidden
kaukau (**cow**-cow) - food
keiki (**kay**-key) - child

kiawe (key-**ah**-vay) - mesquite tree
kokua (ko-**coo**-ah) - help
kona winds (**ko**-nah winds) - winds that blow against the trades
lanai (lah-**nye**) - porch; also island name
lauhala (lau-**hah**-lah) or *hala* (**hah**-lah) - a tree whose leaves are used in weaving
lei (lay) - flower garland
lolo (low-low) - stupid
lomilomi (**low**-me-**low**-me) - massage; also raw salmon
luau (**loo**-ow) - feast
mahalo (mah-**hah**-low) - thank you
mahalo nui loa (mah-**hah**-low new-ee **low**-ah) - thank you very much
mahu (**mah**-who) - gay; homosexual·
makai (mah-**kye**) - toward the sea
malihini (mah-lee-**hee**-nee) - newcomer; stranger
mauka (**mau**-kah) - toward the mountains
nani (**nah**-nee) - beautiful
ohana (oh-**hah**-nah) - family
okole (oh-**ko**-lay) - rear; ass
okolemaluna (oh-ko-lay-mah-**loo**-nah) - a toast: bottoms up!
ono (**oh**-no) - tastes good
pahoehoe (pah-**hoy**-hoy) - ropy lava
pakalolo (pah-kah-**low**-low) - marijuana
pakiki head (pah-**key**-key head) - stubborn
pali (**pah**-lee) - cliff
paniolo (pah-nee-**oh**-low) - cowboy
pau (pow) - finished; done
pilikia (pee-lee-**key**-ah) - trouble
puka (**poo**-kah) - hole
pupus (**poo**-poos) - hors d'oeuvres
shaka (**shah**-kah) - great; perfect
swell head - angry
tapa (**tap**-ah) - a tree bark which is used as a fabric
wahine (wah-**hee**-nay) - woman
wikiwiki (wee-key-**wee**-key) - quickly; in a hurry
you get stink ear - you don't listen well

CHAPTER TWO

Rediscovering Paradise
The How, Where, When and What
of
Traveling in Hawaii

How to Go
GETTING TO THE ISLANDS

During the nineteenth century, sleek clipper ships sailed from the West Coast to Hawaii in about eleven days. Today you'll be traveling by a less romantic but far swifter conveyance—the jet plane. Rather than days at sea, it will be about five hours in the air from California, nine hours from Chicago, or around eleven hours if you're coming from New York.

There's really nothing easier, or more exciting, than catching a plane to Hawaii. No fewer than seven major airlines—**United, Hawaiian, Continental, American, TWA, Delta,** and **Northwest Orient**—fly regular schedules to Honolulu. United also flies direct to the Big Island, Maui, and Kauai. American and Delta fly direct to the island of Maui. This non-stop service is particularly convenient for travelers who are interested in visiting the outer islands while bypassing Honolulu.

Whichever carrier you choose, ask for the economy or excursion fare, and try to fly during the week; weekend flights are usually about 25 percent higher. To qualify for lower price fares, it is sometimes necessary to book your flight two weeks in advance and to stay in the islands at least one week. Generally, however, the restrictions are minimal. Children (two to eleven years) can usually fly for three-quarters the regular fare. Each passenger is permitted two large pieces of luggage plus a carry-on bag. Shipping a bike or surfboard will cost extra.

In planning a Hawaiian sojourn, one potential moneysaver is the package tour, which combines air transportation with a hotel room and other amenities. Generally it is a style of travel that I avoid. However, if you can find a package that provides air transportation, a hotel or condominium accommodation, and a rental car, all at one low price—it might be worth considering. Just try to avoid the packages that preplan your entire visit, dragging you around on air-conditioned tour buses. Look for the package that provides only the bare necessities, namely transportation and lodging, while allowing you the greatest freedom.

However you decide to go, be sure to consult a travel agent. They are professionals in the field, possessing the latest information on rates and facilities, and their service to you is usually free.

GETTING BETWEEN ISLANDS

Since cruise ships are the only commercial boats serving Hawaii's six islands, most of the transportation is by plane. **Aloha Airlines** and **Hawaiian Air**, the state's major carriers, provide frequent inter-island jet service. If you're looking for smooth, rapid, comfortable service, this is certainly it. You'll be buckled into your seat, offered a low-cost cocktail, and whisked to your destination within about twenty minutes. You might also consider flying via **Mid Pacific Air**, a smaller and younger firm that has gained popularity.

Without doubt, the best service aboard any inter-island carrier is on Aloha Airlines. They have an excellent reputation for flying on time. For the last three years running the U.S. Department of Transportation has named them the top airline *in the country* for having the fewest passenger complaints. I give them my top recommendation.

Now that you know how to fly quickly and comfortably, let me tell you about the most exciting way to get between islands. Several small airlines—such as **Reeves Air, Princeville Airways,** and others—fly twin-engine propeller planes. These small, eight-passenger airplanes travel at low altitudes and moderate speeds over the islands. Next to chartering a helicopter, they are the finest way to see Hawaii from the air.

The service is very personalized; often the pilot will point out landmarks along the route, and sometimes he'll fly out of his way to show you points of particular interest. I often fly this way when I'm in the islands and highly recommend these small planes to anyone with a sense of adventure.

Let me describe a typical flight I took between Honolulu and Kona. So that I'd get a better view, the captain suggested that I sit up front in the co-pilot's seat. After taking off in a wide arc around Honolulu, we passed close enough to Diamond Head to gaze down into the crater, then headed across the Kaiwi Channel to Molokai. Since we had to pick up passengers at Molokai's lonely airstrip, the pilot gave me a tour of the island. We paralleled the island's rugged north face, where sharp cliffs laced with waterfalls drop thousands of feet to the sea. Then we swept in toward Maui for a view of Haleakala Crater, and continued past the Big Island's snowtipped volcanoes before touching down in Kona.

Rates for these twin-engine propeller planes are very competitive when compared with the inter-island jets. Coupled with the fact that your ticket on the smaller carriers is worth a guided tour as well as a trip between islands, you really can't do better than booking your flights on these sturdy little planes.

Hawaii's grand oceanliner tradition is carried on today by **American Hawaii Cruises** (550 Kearny Street, San Francisco, CA 94108; 800-227-3666). Sailing the S.S. *Independence* and the S.S. *Constitution,* they sail the inter-island waters, docking at Kauai, Maui, the Big Island, and near Aloha Tower in Honolulu. The cruises are week-long affairs which evoke memories of the old steamship era.

Where To Go

Deciding to take a vacation in Hawaii is easy; the hard part comes when you have to choose which islands to visit. All six are remarkably beautiful places, each with unique features to offer the traveler. Eventually you should try to tour them all, but on a single trip you'll probably choose only one, two, or three.

To help you decide which to see, I'll briefly describe the key features of each. For more detailed information, you can turn to the introductory notes in each of the island chapters.

My personal favorites are the Big Island and Kauai, and I often recommend to friends unfamiliar with Hawaii that they visit these two islands. That way they manage to travel to both ends of the chain, experiencing the youngest and most rugged, and the oldest and most lush, of all the islands. The two offer a startling contrast, one that quickly shatters any illusion that all the islands are alike.

The island of **Hawaii,** or the **Big Island,** is true to its nickname. Located at the southeastern end of the Hawaiian chain, and dominated by two 13,000-foot volcanoes, this giant measures over twice the size of all the other islands combined. It's a great place to mountain climb and explore live volcanoes, to swim along the sun-splashed Kona Coast, or to tour orchid farms in the verdant city of Hilo.

Maui, the second largest island, is rapidly becoming Hawaii's favorite destination for young visitors. Haleakala alone, the extraordinary crater which dominates the island, makes the Valley Isle worth touring. The island also sports many of Hawaii's prettiest beaches, produces some of the world's most potent marijuana, and provides an offshore breeding ground for rare humpback whales.

Directly to the west, lying in Maui's wind-shadow, sits the smallest and most secluded island. **Lanai** is an explorer's paradise, with a network of jeep trails leading to hidden beaches and scenic mountain ridges. There are only 2,000 people and about twenty miles of paved road here. If you're seeking an idyllic retreat, this is the place.

Molokai, slightly larger but nearly as remote, provides another extraordinary hideaway. With white-sand beaches, a mountainous interior, and a large population of Hawaiians, the friendly isle retains a unique sense of old Hawaii. Here you can visit a leper colony on the windswept

Kalaupapa Peninsula, a pilgrimage that could prove to be the most awesome of all your experiences in Hawaii.

Seemingly a world away, across the Kaiwi Channel, sits **Oahu,** Hawaii's most populous island. Dominated by the capital city of Honolulu, and featuring the Waikiki tourist center, this is the most heavily touristed island. It's too crowded for many visitors. But Oahu *is* a prime place to mix city living with country exploring. It's also rich in history, culture, and beautiful beaches.

Hawaii's prettiest, most luxuriant island lies at the northwestern end of the chain. **Kauai,** with its jewel-like beaches and uninhabited valleys, is a place you shouldn't miss. Along the north shore are misty cliffs that fall precipitously to the sea; from the island's center rises a mountain that receives more rainfall than any place on earth; and along Kauai's southern flank there's a startling desert region reminiscent of the Southwest. With its wildly varied climates and terrain, this island is like a small continent.

When To Go

SEASONS

There are two types of seasons in Hawaii, one keyed to tourists and the other to the climate. The peak tourist seasons run from mid-December until Easter, then again from mid-June through Labor Day. Particularly around the Christmas holidays and in August, the visitor centers are crowded. Prices increase, hotel rooms and rental cars become harder to reserve, and everything moves a bit more rapidly.

If you plan to explore Hawaii during these seasons, make reservations several months in advance; actually, it's a good idea to make advance reservations whenever you visit. Without doubt, the off-season is the best time to hit the islands. Not only are hotels more readily available, but campsites and hiking trails are also less crowded.

Climatologically, the ancient Hawaiians distinguished between two seasons—*kau*, or summer, and *hoo-ilo*, or winter. Summer extends from May to October, when the sun is overhead and the temperatures are slightly higher. Winter brings more variable winds and cooler weather.

The important rule to remember about Hawaii's beautiful weather is that it changes very little from season to season but varies dramatically from place to place. The average yearly temperature is about 75°, and during the coldest weather in January and the warmest in August, the thermometer rarely moves more than 5° or 6° in either direction. Similarly, sea water temperatures range comfortably between 74° and 80° year-round.

A key aspect to this luxurious semitropical environment is the trade wind, which blows with welcome regularity from the northeast, providing a natural form of air-conditioning. When the trades stop blowing, they are sometimes replaced by *kona* winds carrying rain and humid weather from the southwest. These are most frequent in winter, when the islands receive their heaviest rainfall.

While summer showers are less frequent and shorter in duration, winter storms are sometimes quite nasty. I've seen it pour for five consecutive days, until hiking trails disappeared and city streets were awash. If you visit in winter, particularly from December to March, you're risking the chance of rain.

A wonderful factor to remember through this wet weather is that if it's raining where you are, you can often simply go someplace else. And I don't mean another part of the world, or even a different island. Since the rains generally batter the northeastern sections of each island, you can usually head over to the south or west coast for warm, sunny weather. Or if you seek cooler climes, head up to the mountains; for every thousand feet in elevation, the temperature drops about 3°. If you climb high enough on Maui or the Big Island, you might even encounter snow!

Sometimes nasty weather engulfs the entire chain, but there's usually a sunny refuge somewhere. I once spent a strenuous period along the Kona Coast working on a suntan. Across the island near Hilo, flood warnings were up. Twenty-five inches of rain dropped in twenty-four hours; five feet of water fell in seven days. Toward the end of the week, when my major problem was whether the tan would peel, officials in Hilo declared a state of emergency.

CALENDAR OF EVENTS

Something else to consider in planning when to visit Hawaii is the amazing lineup of annual cultural events. For a thumbnail idea of what's happening when, check the calendar below. You might just find that special occasion to climax an already dynamic vacation.

JANUARY

Mid-January or February: The month-long **Narcissus Festival** begins with the Chinese New Year. During the weeks of festivities there are open houses, street parties, and parades in Honolulu's Chinatown.

FEBRUARY

During February: If weather conditions permit, the **Mauna Kea Ski Meet** is held on the 13,000-foot slopes of the Big Island volcano.

Mid-February: *Paniolos* from all islands come to Waikoloa on the Big Island to compete in the **Great Waikoloa Horse Races and Rodeo.**

Late February through March: The Japanese community celebrates its **Cherry Blossom Festival** in Honolulu with tea ceremonies, *Kabuki* theatre presentations, martial arts demonstrations, and crafts exhibits.

MARCH

During March: Island musicians perform at Waikiki's Kapiolani Park in the **Hawaiian Song Festival and Song Composing Contest.** Hawaiian school children also compete in Honolulu in the **Kamehameha Schools Song Annual Contest.** For tickets to the latter, write in advance to Kamehameha Schools, Kapalama Heights, Honolulu, Oahu, HI 96817.

March 26: Major festivities on Kauai and Oahu mark the **Prince Kuhio Festival,** commemorating the birthdate of Prince Jonah Kuhio Kalanianaole, Hawaii's first delegate to the U.S. Congress.

APRIL

Early April: The four-day **Merrie Monarch Festival** on the Big Island pays tribute to David Kalakaua, Hawaii's last king. Festivities include musical performances, pageants, and a parade.

Early April: Buddhist temples on all the islands mark **Buddha Day,** the luminary's birthday, with special services. Included among the events are pageants, dances, and flower festivals.

MAY

May 1: **Lei Day** is celebrated on all the islands by people wearing flower *leis* and colorful Hawaiian garb. In Oahu's Kapiolani Park there are pageants and concerts.

Mid-May: **Fiesta Filipina,** a month-long celebration of Filipino culture—songs, folk dances, and craft exhibits—begins on Oahu and Kauai.

JUNE

During June: International bicyclists compete in the four-day **Great Waikoloa Bike Race** on the Big Island. Canoeists vie on Oahu in the 100-mile **Around-the-Island Canoe Race.**

June 11: **Kamehameha Day,** honoring Hawaii's first king, is celebrated on all six islands with parades, chants, hula dances, foot races, and exhibits.

JULY

During July and August: On Oahu and the other islands, Buddhists perform colorful **Bon Dances** every weekend to honor the dead.

Fourth of July: In addition to fireworks, Hawaii celebrates Independence Day with the **Makawao Rodeo** on Maui, and with the **Hilo Orchid Society Flower Show** on the Big Island.

During July: Ethnic groups from all islands come to the Big Island for the **International Festival of the Pacific.** This week-long program features a lantern parade, ethnic foods, and cultural presentations. On Maui, the **Kapalua Music Festival** is staged at the Kapalua Bay Hotel.

AUGUST

During August: The **Annual Macadamia Nut Augustfest** celebrates the harvest at Honokaa on Hawaii: horseracing, carnival, bakeoff.

During August, on consecutive Sundays: Local artists perform at the **Hula Festival** and the **Ukelele Festival** in Waikiki's Kapiolani Park.

During August: The dramatic **Hawaii State Surfing Championships** and **Bodysurfing Championships** are held on Oahu. The **Queen Liliuokalani Canoe Regatta** is staged on the Big Island.

SEPTEMBER

Mid-September: The **Hawaii County Fair** in Hilo on the Big Island features an orchid show, steer show, *lei* contest, agricultural displays, plus exhibits of Hawaiian arts and crafts.

Late September and during October: The highlight of Hawaii's cultural season is the **Aloha Week** festival, a series of week-long celebrations featuring parades, street parties, and pageants. Each week a different island stages the festival, and the entire sequence ends with a **Molokai-to-Oahu Canoe Race**.

OCTOBER

During October: The **Orchid and Flower Show** in Honolulu presents thousands of orchids and other tropical plants.

Early October: The **Maui County Fair** features agricultural exhibits and arts-and-crafts displays; later is the **Na Mele O Maui** music and dance festival, and the **Iron Man Triathlon** on the Big Island.

NOVEMBER

Mid-November: The Big Island's **Kona Coffee Festival** celebrates the coffee harvest with a parade, international food bazaar, and musical entertainment.

Mid-November: *Paniolos* on the Big Island turn out for the **Bull and Horse Show**.

Late November and early December: The world's greatest surfers compete on Oahu's north shore in a series of contests including the **Smirnoff Pro-Am Surfing Championship, Men's World Cup, Women's World Cup,** and the **Duke Kahanamoku Surfing Classic.** With thirty-foot waves and prize money topping $50,000, these are spectacular events.

DECEMBER

Early December: Buddha's enlightenment is commemorated on all the islands with **Bodhi Day** ceremonies and religious services.

Early December: Runners by the thousands turn out for the **Honolulu Marathon**.

Mid-December: The **Kamehameha Schools Christmas Song Festival** is staged in Honolulu.

Late December: The **Makaha Surfing Championships,** with events for top men and women surfers, are held on Oahu.

What to Take

When I get ready to pack for a trip, I sit down and make a list of everything I'll need. It's a very slow, exact procedure: I look in closets, drawers, and shelves, and run through in my mind the activities in which I'll participate, determining which items are required for each. After all the planning is complete and when I have the entire inventory collected in one long list, I sit for a minute or two, basking in my wisdom and forethought.

Then I tear the hell out of the list, cut out the ridiculous items I'll never use, halve the number of spares among the necessary items, and reduce the entire contents of my suitcase to the bare essentials.

Before I developed this packing technique, I once traveled overland from London to New Delhi carrying two suitcases and a knapsack. I lugged those damned bundles onto trains, buses, jitneys, taxis, and rickshaws. When I reached Turkey I started shipping things home, but by then I was buying so many market goods that it was all I could do to keep even.

I ended up carrying so much crap that one day when I was sardined in a crowd pushing its way onto an Indian train, someone managed to pick my pocket. When I felt the wallet slipping out, not only was I unable to chase the culprit—I was so weighted down with baggage that I couldn't even turn around to see who was robbing me!

I'll never travel that way again, and neither should you. Particularly when visiting Hawaii, where the weather is mild, you should pack very light. The airlines permit two suitcases and a carry-on bag; try to take one suitcase and maybe an accessory bag that can double as a beach bag. Dress styles are very informal in the islands, and laundromats are frequent, so you don't need a broad range of clothing items, and you'll require very few extras among the essential items.

Remember, you're packing for a semitropical climate. Take along a sweater or light jacket for the mountains, and a poncho to protect against rain. But otherwise, all that travelers in Hawaii require are shorts, bathing suits, lightweight slacks, short-sleeved shirts and blouses, and summer dresses or *muumuus*. Rarely do visitors require sport jackets or formal dresses. Wash-and-wear fabrics are the most convenient.

For footwear, I suggest soft, comfortable shoes. Low-cut hiking boots or tennis shoes are preferable for hiking; for beachgoing, there's nothing as good as sandals.

There are several other items to squeeze in the corners of your suitcase—suntan lotion, sunglasses, a towel, and of course, your copy of *Hidden Hawaii*. You might also consider packing a mask, fins, and snorkel, and possibly a camera.

If you plan on camping, you'll need most of the equipment required for mainland overnighting. In Hawaii you can get along quite comfortably with a lightweight tent and sleeping bag. You'll also need a knapsack, canteen, camp stove and fuel, mess kit, first-aid kit (with insect repellent, water purification tablets, and Chapstick), toilet kit, a pocket knife, hat, waterproof matches, flashlight, and ground cloth.

How to Deal With . . .

CAR RENTALS

Renting a car is as easy in Hawaii as anywhere. Every island supports at least several rental agencies, which compete fiercely with one another in price and quality of service. So before renting, shop around: check the listings in this book, and also look for the special temporary offers that many rental companies sometimes feature.

There are several facts to remember when renting a car. First of all, a major credit card is very helpful; if you lack one, you'll often have to leave a cash deposit on the car. Also, some agencies don't rent at all to people under twenty-five. Regardless of your age, many companies charge several dollars a day extra for insurance. The insurance is optional, but if you don't take it you're liable for the first several thousand dollars in accident damage. So before leaving home, check to see how much coverage your personal insurance policy provides for rental cars.

Rates fluctuate with the season; slack tourist seasons are great times for good deals. Also, three-day, weekly, and monthly rates are almost always cheaper than daily rentals; cars with standard shifts are generally less than automatics; and sedans are more economical than the larger four-door models. You may also be given the option of a flat daily rate or a rate keyed to the number of miles driven. Take the flat rate.

Other than on the island of Lanai, I don't recommend renting a jeep. They're more expensive and less comfortable than automobiles, and won't get you to very many more interesting spots. Except in extremely wet weather when roads are muddy, all the places mentioned in this book, including the hidden (★) locales, can be reached by car. Since many rental agencies have "no camping" restrictions, it's wise to keep backpacks and other gear out of sight when first renting a car.

CONDOMINIUM LIVING

Many people visiting Hawaii, especially those traveling with families, find that condominiums are often cheaper than hotels. While some hotel rooms come equipped with kitchenettes, few provide all the amenities of condominiums. A condo, in essence, is an apartment away from home. Designed as studio, one-, two-, or three-bedroom apartments, they come equipped with full kitchen facilities and complete kitchenware collections. Many also feature washer-dryers, dishwashers, air-conditioning, color televisions, telephones, lanais, and community swimming pools.

Utilizing the kitchen will save considerably on your food bill; by sharing the accommodations among several people, you'll also cut your lodging bill. While the best way to see Hawaii is obviously by hiking and camping, when you're ready to come in from the wilds, consider reserving a place that provides more than a bed and night table.

HOTELS

Accommodations in Hawaii range from funky cottages to highrise condominiums. You'll find inexpensive family-run hotels, middle class tourist facilities, and world class resorts.

Whichever you choose, there are a few guidelines to help save money. Try to visit during the off-season, avoiding the high rate periods during the summer and from Christmas to Easter. Rooms with mountain views are less expensive than ocean view accommodations. Generally, the further a hotel is from the beach, the less it costs. Another way to economize is by reserving a room with a kitchen. In any case, try to reserve far in advance.

Throughout this book hotels are described according to price category. *Budget* hotels have rooms starting from $30 or less per night for two people. *Moderate* facilities begin somewhere between $30 and $60. *Deluxe* hotels offer rates starting from $60 to $100. *Ultra-deluxe* establishments rent accommodations at prices above $100.

RESTAURANTS

A few guidelines will help you chart a course through Hawaii's countless dining places. Within a particular chapter, the restaurants are categorized geographically, with each restaurant entry describing the establishment as budget, moderate, deluxe, or ultra-deluxe in price. Dinner entrees at *budget* restaurants usually cost $7 or less. The ambience is informal cafe style and the crowd is often a local one. *Moderately* priced restaurants range between $7 and $14 at dinner and offer pleasant surroundings, a more varied menu, and a slower pace. *Deluxe* establishments tab their entrees above $14, featuring sophisticated cuisines, plush decor, and more personalized service. *Ultra-deluxe* restaurants generally price above $20.

Breakfast and lunch menus vary less in price from restaurant to restaurant. Even deluxe kitchens usually offer light breakfasts and lunch sandwiches which place them within a few dollars of their budget-minded competitors. These early meals can be a good time to test expensive restaurants.

MAIL

If you're staying in a particular establishment during your visit, you can usually have personal mail sent there. Otherwise, **American Express** will hold mail for no charge at its Honolulu office for 30 days, and will provide forwarding for cardholders. I've always found their service terrible, but they are the only organization with such a program. If you do decide to use their facilities, have mail addressed to American Express, Client Mail, 2424 Kalakaua Avenue, Honolulu, Oahu, HI 96815 (922-4718). If you don't use this service, your only other recourse is to have mail sent to a particular post office in care of general delivery.

VISITOR INFORMATION

The **Hawaii Visitors Bureau,** a privately-funded agency, is a valuable resource from which to obtain free information on Hawaii. With offices nationwide and branches on each of the four largest islands, the Bureau can help plan your trip and then offer advice once you reach Hawaii.

Details concerning the island offices appear in the "Addresses" section at the end of the Hawaii, Maui, Oahu, and Kauai chapters. On the mainland, you can contact the Hawaii Visitors Bureau at the following offices: on the West Coast—at 3440 Wilshire Boulevard, Los Angeles, CA 90010 (213-385-5301), or at 50 California Street, Suite 450, San Francisco, CA 94111 (415-392-8173); in the Midwest—at 180 North Michigan Avenue, Chicago, IL 60611 (312-236-0632); and on the East Coast—at 441 Lexington Avenue, New York, NY 10017 (212-986-9023).

Another excellent resource is the **Hawaii State Library Service.** With a network of libraries on all the islands, this government agency provides facilities that can be used by residents and non-residents alike. The libraries are good places to find light beach-reading material as well as books on Hawaii. Visitors can check out books by simply applying for a library card with a valid identification card.

BEING DISABLED

The **Commission on the Handicapped** is publishing a survey of the city, county, state, and federal parks in Hawaii that are accessible to disabled people. For information, contact the Commission at 335 Merchant St. #353, Honolulu, Oahu, HI 96813 (548-7606). They have a handy guide available, "The Aloha Guide to Accessibility," with information on Maui and the Big Island. They also have "Traveler's Guides" to Oahu, Maui, Kauai, and the Big Island which give information on various hotels, shopping centers, and restaurants that are accessible.

A federal pamphlet provides helpful information for disabled travelers. "Access Travel" is available from the **U.S. Printing Office** (Washington, DC 20402) for a nominal fee. The **Society for the Advancement of Travel for the Handicapped** (26 Court Street, Brooklyn, NY 11242; 718-858-5483) also offers information.

Be sure to check in advance when making room reservations. Some hotels feature facilities for those in wheelchairs.

TRAVELING WITH CHILDREN

Hawaii is an ideal vacation spot for family holidays. The pace is slow, the atmosphere casual. A few guidelines will help ensure that your trip to the islands brings out the joys rather than the strains of parenting, allowing everyone to get into the *aloha* spirit.

Use a travel agent to help with arrangements; they can reserve spacious bulkhead seats on airlines and determine which flights are least crowded. They can also seek out the best deals on inexpensive condominiums, saving you money on both room and board.

Planning the trip with your kids stimulates their imagination. Books about travel, airplane rides, beaches, whales, volcanoes, and Hawaiiana help prepare even a two-year-old for an adventure. This preparation makes the "getting there" part of the trip more exciting for children of all ages.

And "getting there" means a long-distance flight. Plan to bring everything you need on board the plane—diapers, food, toys, books, and extra clothing for kids and parents alike. I've found it helpful to carry a few new toys and books as treats to distract my son and daughter when they get bored. I also pack a few snacks.

Allow extra time to get places. Book reservations in advance and make sure that the hotel or condominium has the extra crib, cot, or bed you require. It's smart to ask for a room at the end of the hall to cut down on noise. And when reserving a rental car, inquire to see if they provide car seats and if there is an added charge. Hawaii has a strictly enforced car seat law.

Besides the car seat you may have to bring along, also pack shorts and T-shirts, a sweater, sun hat, sun dresses, and waterproof sandals. A stroller with sunshade for little ones helps on sightseeing sojourns; a shovel and pail are essential for sandcastle building. Most importantly, remember to bring a good sunblock. The quickest way to ruin a family vacation is with a bad sunburn. Also plan to bring indoor activities such as books and games for evenings and rainy days.

Most towns have stores that carry diapers, food, and other essentials. However, prices are much higher in Hawaii. To economize, some people take along an extra suitcase filled with diapers and wipes, baby food, peanut butter and jelly, etc., etc. If you're staying in Waikiki, **ABC** stores carry a limited selection of disposables and baby food. Shopping outside Waikiki in local supermarkets will save you a considerable sum: **Star**

Market (2470 South King Street; 941-0913) is open twenty-four hours a day.

A first-aid kit is always a good idea. Also check with your pediatrician for special medicines and dosages for colds and diarrhea. If your child does become sick or injured in the Honolulu area, contact **Children's Hospital** (947-8623). On the Windward Coast of Oahu call **Castle Medical Center** (261-0841); on the North Shore, **Kahuku Hospital** (293-9221); and on the leeward side, **Wahiawa General Hospital** (621-8411). On the Big Island's east side there's **Hilo Hospital** (961-4211); in Kona, **Kona Hospital** (322-9311); Maui, **Maui Memorial Hospital** (242-2343); Lanai, **Lanai Community Hospital** (565-6411); Molokai, **Molokai General Hospital** (553-5331); and Kauai, **Wilcox Memorial Hospital and Health Center** (245-1100). There's also a **Poison Control Center** in Honolulu which can be reached from the outer islands at 1-800-362-3585 or from Oahu at 941-4411.

Hotels often provide access to babysitters. On Oahu a licensed and bonded babysitting agency is also available: **Aloha Babysitting Service** (732-2029). In the Lahaina-Kaanapali area of Maui you can try **Babysitting Services of Maui** (661-4118).

Some resorts and hotels have daily programs for kids during the summer and holiday seasons. Hula lessons, *lei* making, story telling, sandcastle building, and various sports activities keep *keikis* (kids) over six happy while also giving Mom and Dad a break. As an added bonus these resorts offer family plans, providing discounts for extra rooms or permitting children to share a room with their parents at no extra charge. Check with your travel agent.

When choosing the island to visit, consider how many diversions it will take to keep your children happy. Oahu offers numerous options, from the Honolulu Zoo to theme parks to museums, while the outer islands have fewer attractions. It might be helpful to read the "Sightseeing" and "Sporting Life" sections of this book before selecting your family vacation spot.

CHAPTER THREE

Paradise for Free
Natural Living in Hawaii

With its luxurious parks, mountain retreats, and deserted beaches, Hawaii is a paradise for campers and backpackers. Because of the varied terrain and the islands' microenvironments, it's possible to experience all kinds of outdoor adventures. One day you'll hike through a steaming rain forest filled with tropical flowers; the next night you'll camp atop a volcanic crater in a stark, windblown area that resembles the moon's surface; then you'll descend to a curving white-sand beach populated only by shorebirds and tropical fish.

Paradise means more than physical beauty, however. It also involves an easy life and a bountiful food supply. The easy living is up to you; just slow down from the frantic pace of mainland life and you'll discover that island existence can be very relaxing. As for wild food—you'll find it hanging from trees, swimming in the ocean, and clinging to coral reefs. With the proper techniques and a respect for conservation needs, it's yours to take.

In this chapter I'll detail some of the outdoor skills necessary to camp, hike, and live naturally in Hawaii. This is certainly not a comprehensive study of how to survive on a Pacific island; I'm just passing along a few facts I've learned while exploring Hawaii. I don't advise that you plan to live entirely off the land. Hawaii's environment is too fragile to support you full-time. Anyway, living that way is a hell of a lot of work! I'll just give a few hints on how to supplement your provisions with a newly-caught fish or a fresh fruit salad. That way, not only will you save on food bills, you'll also get a much fuller taste for the islands.

Camping and Hiking

Camping in Hawaii usually means pitching a tent, reserving a cabin, or renting a camper. Throughout the islands there are secluded spots and hidden beaches, plus numerous county, state, and federal parks. All these campsites, together with hiking trails, are described in the individual island chapters; it's a good idea to consult those detailed listings when

43

planning your trip. You might also want to obtain hiking maps; they are available from the Hawaii Geographic Society, 217 South King Street, Suite 308, Honolulu, HI 96813 (538-3952). The camping equipment you'll require is listed in the preceding chapter.

Before you set out, there are a few important matters that I want to explain more fully. First, bring a campstove: firewood is scarce in most areas and soaking wet in others. It's advisable to wear long pants when hiking in order to protect your legs from rock outcroppings and spiny plants. Also, if you're going to explore the Mauna Kea, Mauna Loa, or Haleakala volcanoes, bring cold-weather gear; all these peaks occasionally receive snow.

Most trails you'll be hiking are composed of volcanic rock. Since this is a very crumbly substance, be extremely cautious when climbing rock faces. In fact, you should avoid steep climbs if possible. Stay on the trails: Hawaii's dense undergrowth makes it very easy to get lost. If you get lost at night, stay where you are. Because of the low latitude, night descends rapidly here; there's practically no twilight. Once darkness falls, it can be very dangerous to move around. You should also be careful to purify all drinking water. And be extremely cautious near streambeds as flash-flooding sometimes occurs, particularly on the windward coasts.

Another problem that you're actually more likely to encounter are those nasty varmints that buzz your ear just as you're falling asleep—mosquitoes. Hawaii contains neither snakes nor poison ivy, but it has plenty of these dive-bombing pests. Like me, you probably consider that it's always open season on the little bastards.

With most of the archipelago's other species, however, you'll have to be a careful conservationist. You'll be sharing the wilderness with pigs, goats, tropical birds, deer, and mongooses, as well as a spectacular array of exotic plants. They exist in one of the world's most delicate ecological balances. There are more endangered species in Hawaii than in all the rest of the United States. So keep in mind the maxim that the Hawaiians try to follow. *Ua mau ke ea o ka aina i ka pono:* The life of the land is preserved in righteousness.

Fishing and Gathering

While you're exploring the islands, the sea will be your prime food source. Fishing in Hawaii is good all year round, and the offshore waters are crowded with many varieties of edible fish. For deep-sea fishing you'll have to charter a boat, and fresh-water angling requires a license; so I'll concentrate on surf-casting. It costs nothing to fish this way.

In the individual island chapters, you'll find information on the best spots to fish for different species; in the "Addresses" section of those chapters, you'll see a fishing supply store listed. For information on seasons, licenses, and official regulations, check with the Fish and Game Division of the State Department of Land and Natural Resources. This agency has offices on most of the major islands.

The easiest, most economical way to fish is with a hand-held line. Just get a fifty- to one-hundred-foot line, and attach a hook and a ten-ounce sinker. Wind the line loosely around a smooth block of wood, then remove the wood from the center. If your coil is free from snags, you'll be able to throw-cast it easily. You can either hold the line in your hand, feeling for a strike, or tie it to the frail end of a bamboo pole.

Beaches and rocky points are generally good places to surf-cast; the best times are during the incoming and outgoing tides. Popular baits include octopus, eel, lobster, crab, frozen shrimp, and sea worms. You can also fish with lures. The ancient Hawaiians used pearl shells to attract the fish, and hooks, some made from human bones, to snare them. Your friends will probably be quite content to see you angling with store-bought artificial lures.

TORCHFISHING AND SPEARFISHING

The old Hawaiians also fished at night by torchlight. They fashioned torches by inserting nuts from the *kukui* tree into the hollow end of a bamboo pole, then lighting the flammable nuts. When fish swam like moths to the flame, the Hawaiians speared, clubbed, or netted them.

Today, it's easier to use a lantern and spear. (In fact, it's all *too* easy and tempting to take advantage of this willing prey: take only edible fish and only what you will eat.) It's also handy to bring a facemask or a glass-bottomed box to aid in seeing underwater. The best time for torch-fishing is a dark night when the sea is calm and the tide low.

During daylight hours, the best place to spearfish is along coral reefs and in areas where the bottom is a mixture of sand and rock. You can use a speargun or make your own spear with heavy rubber bands and a piece of metal. Then, equipped also with mask, fins, and snorkel, you can explore underwater grottoes and spectacular coral formations while seeking your evening meal.

CRABBING

For the hungry adventurer, there are two important crab species in Hawaii—Kona crabs and Samoan crabs. The Kona variety are found in relatively deep water, and can usually be caught only from a boat. Samoan crabs inhabit sandy and muddy areas in bays and near river mouths. All you need to catch them is a net fastened to a round wire hoop and secured by a string. The net is lowered to the bottom; then, after a crab has gone for the bait, the entire contraption is raised to the surface.

SQUIDDING

Between June and December, squidding is another popular sport. Actually, the term is a misnomer: squid inhabit deep water and are not usually hunted. What you'll really be after are octopuses. There are two varieties in Hawaii, both of which are commonly found in water three or four feet deep: the *hee*, a greyish-brown animal which changes color like a chameleon, and the *puloa*, a red-colored mollusk with white stripes on its head.

Both are nocturnal and live in the holes along coral reefs. At night by torchlight you can spot them sitting exposed on the bottom. During the day, they crawl inside the holes, covering the entrances with shells and loose coral.

The Hawaiians used to pick the octopus up, letting it cling to their chest and shoulders. When they were ready to bag their prize, they'd

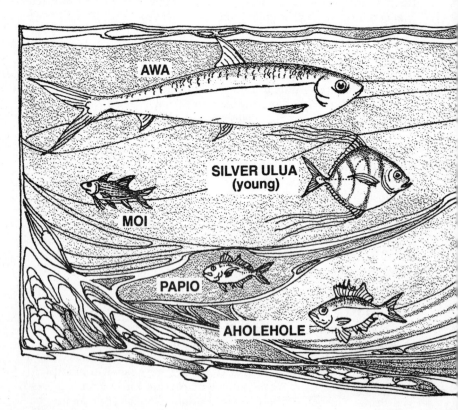

dispatch the creature by biting it between the eyes. You'll probably feel more comfortable spearing the beast.

SHELLFISH GATHERING

Other excellent food sources are the shellfish that inhabit coastal waters. Oysters and clams, which use their muscular feet to burrow into sand and soft mud, can be collected along the bottom of Hawaii's bays. Lobsters, though illegal to spear, can be taken with short poles to which cable leaders and baited hooks are attached. You can also gather limpets, though I don't recommend it. These tiny black shellfish, locally known as *opihi*, cling tenaciously to rocks in areas of very rough surf. The Hawaiians gather them by leaping into the water after one set of waves breaks, then jumping out before the next set arrives. Being a coward myself, I simply order them in Hawaiian restaurants. (Text continued on page 52.)

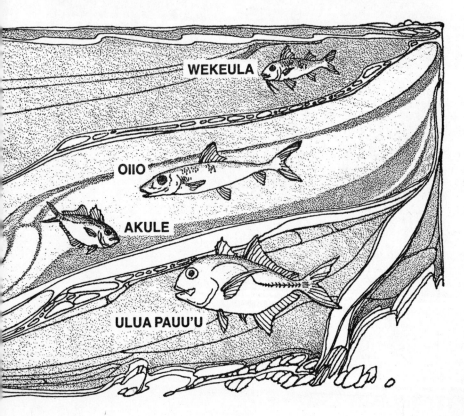

WEKEULA

OIIO

AKULE

ULUA PAUU'U

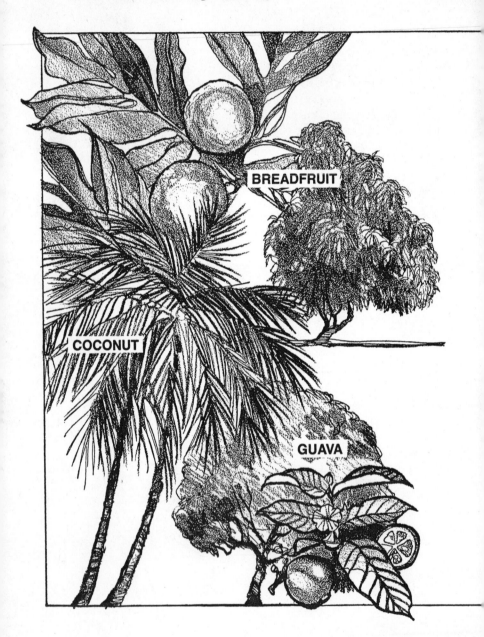

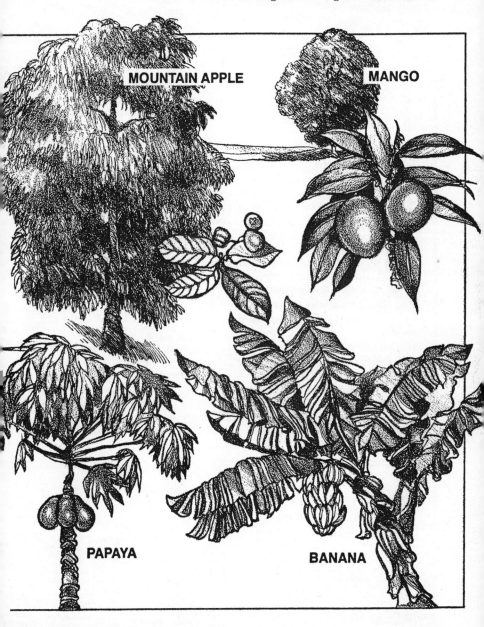

Relating to the Ocean

For swimming, surfing, and skin diving, there's no place quite like Hawaii. With endless miles of white-sand beach, the islands attract aquatic enthusiasts from all over the world. They come to enjoy Hawaii's colorful coral reefs and matchless surf conditions.

Many water lovers, however, never realize how awesome the sea can be. Particularly in Hawaii, where waves can reach thirty-foot heights and currents flow unobstructed for thousands of miles, the ocean is sometimes as treacherous as it is spectacular. Over thirty people a year drown in Hawaii, many others are dragged from the crushing surf with broken backs, and countless numbers sustain minor cuts and bruises.

These accidents can be entirely avoided if you relate to the ocean with a respect for its power as well as an appreciation of its beauty. All you have to do is heed a few simple guidelines. First, never turn your back on the sea. Waves come in sets: one group may be small and quite harmless, but the next set could be large enough to sweep you out to sea. Never swim alone, and don't swim for at least an hour after eating.

Don't try to surf, or even bodysurf, until you're familiar with the sports' techniques and precautionary measures. Be extremely careful when the surf is high.

If you get caught in a rip current, don't swim *against* it: swim *across* it, parallel to the shore. These currents, running from the shore out to sea, can often be spotted by their ragged-looking surface water and foamy edges.

Around coral reefs, wear something to protect your feet against coral cuts. Particularly good are the inexpensive Japanese *tabis,* or reef slippers. If you do sustain a coral cut, clean it with hydrogen peroxide, then apply an antiseptic or antibiotic substance. This is also a good procedure for octopus bites.

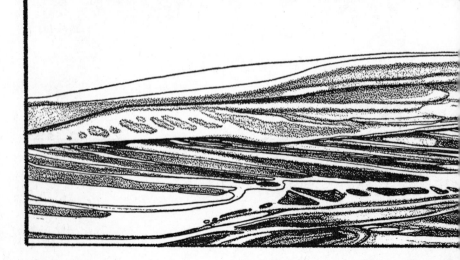

When stung by a Portuguese man-of-war or a jellyfish, mix unseasoned meat tenderizer with alcohol, leave it on the sting for ten or twenty minutes, then rinse it off with alcohol. The old Hawaiian remedies, which are reputedly quite effective, involve applying urine or green papaya.

If you step on the sharp, painful spines of a sea urchin, soak the affected area in very hot water for fifteen to ninety minutes. Another remedy calls for applying urine or undiluted vinegar. If any of these preliminary treatments do not work, consult a doctor.

Oh, one last thing. The chances of encountering a shark are about as likely as sighting a UFO. But should you meet one of these ominous creatures, stay calm. He'll be no happier to see you than you are to confront him. Simply swim quietly to shore. By the time you make it back to terra firma, you'll have one hell of a story to tell.

SEAWEED GATHERING

Few people think of seaweed as food, but it's very popular today among the Japanese, and it once served as an integral part of the Hawaiian diet. It's extremely nutritious, easy to gather, and very plentiful.

Rocky shores are the best places to find the edible species of seaweed. Some of them float in to shore and can be picked up; other species cling stubbornly to rocks and must be freed with a knife; still others grow in sand or mud. Low tide is the best time to collect seaweed: more plants are exposed, and some can be taken without even getting wet.

Picking Fruit

There's a lot more to Hawaii's tropical wonderland than gorgeous flowers and overgrown rain forests. The islands are also teeming with edible plants. Roots, fruits, vegetables, herbs, and spices grow like weeds from the shoreline to the mountains. By learning to identify key species you can add numerous dishes to your table.

Here's a brief list of some of the islands' more common fruits. They can be picked by hand, poked with a stick, or plucked with a fruit-picker. This last device is easily made by threading a wire loop through a small sack, then fastening it to the end of a bamboo pole.

Banana: The Polynesians use banana trees not only for food, but also for clothing, roofing, medicines, dyes, and even alcohol. The fruit, which grows upside down on broad-leaved trees, can be harvested as soon as the first banana in the bunch turns yellow.

Coconut: The coconut tree is probably the most important plant in the entire Pacific. Every part of the towering palm is used. You'll probably be concerned only with the hard brown nut, which yields delicious milk as well as a tasty meat.

Climbing a coconut palm is a task for the daring or foolhardy; personally, I wait for the nuts to fall and then pick them up off the ground. If the coconut is still green, the meat is a succulent jelly-like substance. Otherwise it's a hard but delicious white rind.

Papaya: These delicious fruits, which are picked as they begin to turn yellow, grow on unbranched trees. Summer is the peak harvesting season.

Guava: Roundish yellow fruits which grow on a small shrub or tree, these are extremely abundant in the wild. They ripen between June and October.

Mango: Known as the king of fruits, the mango grows on tall shade trees. The oblong fruit ripens in the spring and summer.

Breadfruit: These large round fruits grow on trees that reach up to sixty feet high. Breadfruit must be boiled, baked, or fried.

Mountain apple: This sweet fruit grows in damp, shaded valleys at an elevation of about 1,800 feet. The flowers resemble fluffy crimson balls; the fruit, which ripens from July to December, is also a rich red color.

Passion fruit: This delicious yellow fruit, oval in shape, grows to a length of about two or three inches. It's produced on a vine and ripens in summer or fall.

Avocado: Covered with a tough green or purple skin, this pear-shaped fruit sometimes weighs as much as three pounds. It grows on ten-to forty-foot-high trees, and ripens from June through November.

Relating To Drugs

For decades Hawaii has been known for its sparkling beaches and lofty volcanoes. Agriculturally, the islands have grown famous by producing sugar cane and pineapples. But during the last several years, the fiftieth state has become renowned for another crop, one which some deem a sacrament and others consider a sin.

In the islands it's commonly referred to as *pakalolo*. Mainlanders know it more familiarly by the locales in which it grows—Maui Wowie, Kona Gold, Puna Butter, and Kauai Buds. Because of Hawaii's lush tropical environment, marijuana grows year-round and has become the state's number one cash crop. Plants easily reach ten- or twelve-foot heights; colas as thick as bottle brushes drip with resin.

Now that marijuana is big business, ripoffs have become a harrowing problem in Hawaii. Growers often guard their crops with guns and booby traps. Because of this armed protection, it can be very dangerous to wander through someone's dope patch. It might be on public land far from the nearest road, but in terms of the explorer's personal safety, a marijuana plantation should be treated as the most private property imaginable. In the words of the islanders, it is strictly *kapu*.

CHAPTER FOUR

Hawaii

The Big Island, they call it, and even that is an understatement. Hawaii, all 4,030 square miles, is almost twice as large as the other Hawaiian islands combined. Its twin volcanic peaks, Mauna Kea and Mauna Loa, dwarf most mountains. Mauna Kea, rising 13,796 feet, is the largest island-based mountain in the world. Mauna Loa, the world's largest active volcano, looms 13,680 feet above sea level. This is actually 32,000 feet from the ocean floor, making it, by one system of reckoning, the tallest mountain on earth, grander even than Everest. And in bulk it is the world's largest. The entire Sierra Nevada chain could fit within this single peak. Kilauea, a third volcano whose seething firepit has been erupting with startling frequency, is the world's most active crater. This is a place of geologic superlatives.

But size alone does not convey the Big Island's greatness. Its industry, too, is expansive. Despite the lava wasteland which covers large parts of its surface, the Big Island is the state's greatest producer of sugar, papayas, vegetables, anthuriums, macadamia nuts, and cattle. Its orchid industry, based in rain-drenched Hilo, is the world's largest. Over 22,000 varieties grow in the nurseries here.

Across the island in sun-soaked Kona, the nation's only coffee industry operates. Just off this spectacular western coast lie some of the finest deep-sea fishing grounds in the world. Between Hilo and Kona sits the Parker Ranch, sprawling across 225,000 acres, one of the world's largest independently owned cattle ranches.

Yet many of these measurements are taken against island standards. Compared to the mainland, the Big Island is a tiny speck in the sea. Across its broadest reach it measures a scant ninety-three miles long and seventy-six miles wide, smaller than Connecticut. The road around the island, including several secondary sightseeing loops, totals only 300 miles, and can be driven in a day, though I'd recommend taking at least five. The island's 106,000 population comprises a mere ten percent of the state's citizens. Its lone city, Hilo, has a population of only 35,000.

But large or small, numbers alone cannot fully describe the Big Island, for there is a magic about the place which transcends statistics. Hawaii, also nicknamed the Orchid Island and Volcano Island, is the home of Pele, the goddess of volcanoes. Perhaps her fiery spirit is what infuses the Big Island with an unquantifiable quality. Or maybe the island's comparative youth (still growing in size from two active volcanoes, it is geologically the youngest spot on earth) is what makes the elements seem nearer, more alluring, and strangely threatening here. Whatever it might be, the Big Island has always been where I feel closest to the Polynesian spirit. Of all the Hawaiian islands, this one I love most.

It was here that Polynesian explorers first landed when they discovered the island chain around 750 A.D. Until the advent of the white man, it was generally the most important island, supporting a large population and occupying a vital place in Hawaii's rich mythology. Little wonder then that Kamehameha the Great, the chief who would become Hawaii's first king, was born here in 1753. He established the archipelago's first capital in Kailua and ruled there until his death in 1819.

Within a year of the great leader's passing, two events occurred in Kailua which jolted the entire chain far more than any earthquake. First the king's heir, Liholiho, uprooted the centuries-old taboo system upon which the island religion rested. Then, in the spring of 1820, the first missionaries dropped anchor offshore, bringing a new faith to the island which would fast supplant the old.

It was also near here that Captain James Cook, history's greatest discoverer, was slain in 1779 by the same people who had earlier welcomed him as a god. Across the island another deity, Pele, was defied in 1824 when the high chieftess Kapiolani, a Christian, ate *kapu* fruit on the rim of Kilauea crater.

As stirring as the Big Island's story might be, much of its drama still awaits the visitor. For the land—the volcanoes, beaches, and valleys—is as vital and intriguing today as in the days of demigods and kings. This is a place for the adventurer to spend a lifetime.

On the east coast, buffeted by trade winds, lies Hilo, a lush tropical town that soaks up 140 inches of rain annually. Just to the south— smoking, heaving, and sometimes erupting—sits Volcanoes National Park. In the northwest, from the Hamakua Coast to the Kohala Peninsula, heavy erosion has cut through jutting cliffs to form spectacular valleys such as the Waipio.

In startling contrast to these verdant mountains is the desert-like Kau district at the southern tip of the island (and, for that matter, the southernmost point in the United States). Along the west coast stretches the Kona district, a vacationer's paradise. Suntan weather, sandy beaches, and coral reefs teeming with tropical fish make this an ideal area to just kick back and enjoy. And for something unique to the Big Island,

(Text continued on page 62.)

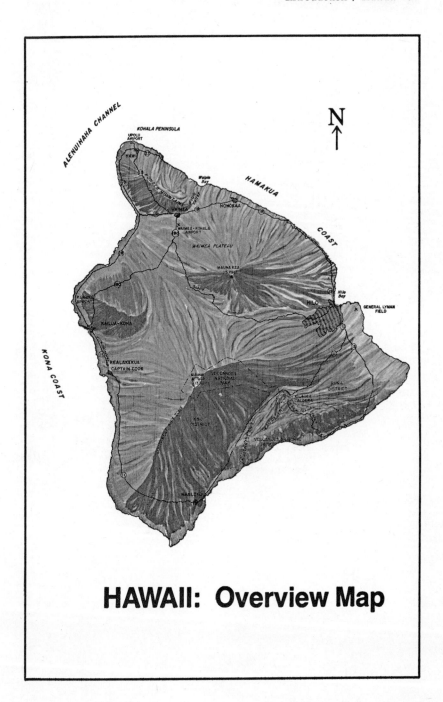

HAWAII: Overview Map

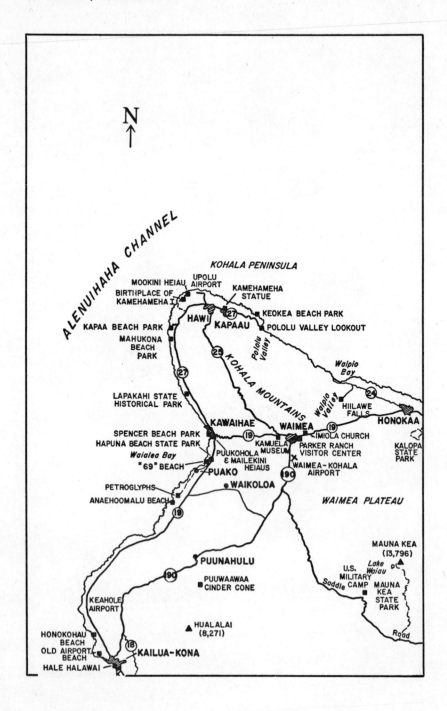

N
↑

ALENUIHAHA CHANNEL

KOHALA PENINSULA

UPOLU
AIRPORT
MOOKINI HEIAU
BIRTHPLACE OF
KAMEHAMEHA I
KAMEHAMEHA
STATUE
HAWI
KAPAAU
KEOKEA BEACH PARK
POLOLU VALLEY LOOKOUT
KAPAA BEACH PARK
MAHUKONA
BEACH
PARK
Pololu
Valley
Waipio
Bay
LAPAKAHI STATE
HISTORICAL PARK
KOHALA MOUNTAINS
Waipio
Valley
HIILAWE
FALLS
HONOKAA
SPENCER BEACH PARK
HAPUNA BEACH STATE PARK
KAWAIHAE
WAIMEA
IMIOLA CHURCH
KAMUELA
MUSEUM
PARKER RANCH
VISITOR CENTER
KALOPA
STATE
PARK
Waialea Bay
"69" BEACH
PUUKOHOLA
& MAILEKINI
HEIAUS
PUAKO
WAIMEA-KOHALA
AIRPORT
PETROGLYPHS
ANAEHOOMALU BEACH
WAIKOLOA
WAIMEA PLATEAU
MAUNA KEA
(13,796)
PUUNAHULU
Lake
Waiau
PUUWAAWAA
CINDER CONE
U.S.
MILITARY
Saddle CAMP
MAUNA
KEA
STATE
PARK
KEAHOLE
AIRPORT
HUALALAI
(8,271)
HONOKOHAU
BEACH
OLD AIRPORT
BEACH
KAILUA-KONA
HALE HALAWAI
Road

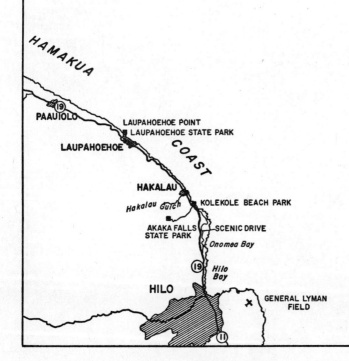

HAWAII: Travel Map

(see following pages for southern half)

HAMAKUA

19
PAAUIOLO

LAUPAHOEHOE POINT
LAUPAHOEHOE STATE PARK
LAUPAHOEHOE

COAST

HAKALAU
Hakalau Gulch
KOLEKOLE BEACH PARK
AKAKA FALLS
STATE PARK
SCENIC DRIVE
Onomea Bay

19
*Hilo
Bay*
HILO
GENERAL LYMAN
FIELD

11

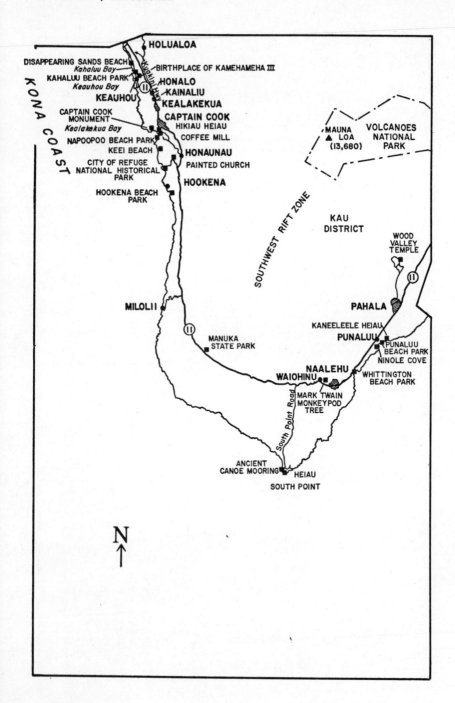

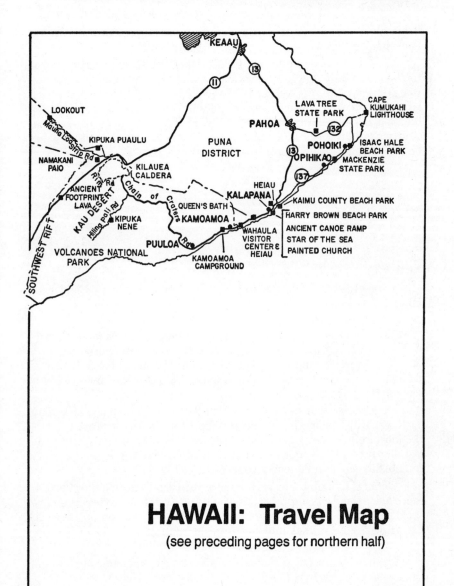

HAWAII: Travel Map
(see preceding pages for northern half)

there's Waimea with its rolling grasslands, cattle herds, and *paniolos,* the Hawaiian-style cowboys.

It's an island I don't think you should miss, an island that's beginning to change rapidly due to its growing popularity among tourists, but one that still retains its original charm. To geologists the Big Island is a natural laboratory in which the mysteries of volcanic activity are a fact of everyday life; to many Hawaiians it is the most sacred of all the islands. To everyone who visits it, Hawaii is a place of startling contrasts and unspeakable beauty, an alluring and exotic tropical island.

Easy Living

Transportation

ARRIVAL

Four airports serve the Big Island—**General Lyman Field** near Hilo, Kailua-Kona's **Keahole Airport, Upolu Airport** on the Kohala peninsula, and **Waimea-Kohala Airport** near Waimea.

The main landing facility is **Keahole Airport.** Many mainland visitors fly here rather than to Honolulu to avoid Oahu's crowds. **United Airlines,** which provides the most frequent service to Hawaii, is the only carrier flying from the mainland to Kailua-Kona. United provides several flights daily to this airport.

Passengers flying between the islands use **Aloha Airlines, Hawaiian Airlines, Mid-Pacific Air,** and **Princeville Airways.** The first two provide the most frequent jet service from Oahu and the other islands, while the last flies prop planes. Personally I prefer Aloha Airlines because of their punctuality and excellent service record.

General Lyman Field in Hilo, once the island's main jetport, is now more like a small city airport. Here you'll find a cafeteria-style restaurant, cocktail lounge, gift shop, newsstand, and lockers, but no bus service. Covering the two miles into town means renting a car, hailing a cab, hitching, or hoofing.

Keahole Airport near Kailua-Kona is served by the same inter-island carriers as General Lyman Field. This windswept facility has snack bars, cocktail lounges, and souvenir shops, but no lockers or bus service. A nine-mile cab ride into town costs about $11.

Upolu Airport is a desolate landing strip on the Kohala peninsula along the island's northwest coast. There are no facilities whatever, not even a telephone, and only prop planes land here.

Waimea-Kohala Airport, two miles outside the cowboy town of Waimea, is served by **Princeville Airways.** There are waiting rooms, but no shops of any kind here. Both airline and car rental offices are often closed unless a flight is scheduled, so it's best to make all reservations in advance.

CAR RENTALS

Big Island rental agencies generally charge slightly more than is charged on the other islands because of the longer distances traveled. Also, they often charge a fee ($20 or so) for cars rented in Hilo or Kona and dropped off in the other city. It's wise to remember that you will be driving farther on Hawaii, sometimes through quite rural areas; it may sound obvious, but remember to watch your gas gauge.

When choosing a rental agency, check whether they permit driving on the Saddle Road across the island and on South Point Road, both good paved roads with few potholes and many points of interest. I think it's quite unfair, even irrational, that some rental companies revoke insurance coverage if you drive these thoroughfares. But my protests will be of little benefit in case of an accident. So check first or be prepared to take your chances!

That said, my favorite car rental operations are the smaller companies. Like the nationally known firms, they generally have booths either in Hilo or Kona, or both. (The first phone number listed here is for Hilo, the second for Kona.) Generally, the lesser-known outfits tend to be easier on the purse than nationally acclaimed companies. I have always found Hawaii's small, independent car rental agencies provide comparable service, and therefore I generally recommend them. So with your budget in mind, consider the following companies: **Phillip's U-Drive** (935-1936; 329-1730); **Robert's Hawaii Rent-A-Car** (935-2858); and **United Car Service** (935-2115; 329-3411).

Several of the big national companies have franchises at the Hilo and Kailua-Kona airports. Among these are **American International Rent-A-Car** (935-1108; 329-2926), **National Rent-A-Car** (935-0891; 329-1674), **Dollar Rent-A-Car** (961-6059; 329-2744), **Avis** (935-1290; 329-1745), **Hertz** (935-2896; 329-3566), and **Budget Rent-A-Car** (935-6878; 329-8511).

Many outfits located outside General Lyman Field and Keahole Airport feature competitive rates. These include **Tropical Rent-A-Car** (935-3385; 329-2437), which is located near both airports, and **Ugly Duckling** (329-2113) and **Rent and Drive Inc.** (329-3033), which serve the Kailua-Kona area. These companies often provide free service to and from the airport.

Hertz (882-7006) serves the Waimea-Kohala Airport. Since the office is located at the Mauna Kea Beach Hotel, it's advisable to make reservations in advance.

(See Chapter 2 for a complete explanation of car rentals in the islands.)

JEEP RENTALS

Dollar Rent-A-Car (961-6059; 329-2744) and **Budget Rent-A-Car** (935-6878; 329-8511) rent 4-wheel drives.

MOTOR SCOOTER RENTALS

Honda scooters are available for rent from **Kona Fun 'n Sun** (329-6068), located in World Square in the heart of Kona.

PUBLIC TRANSPORTATION

The **Hele-On Bus** provides cross-island service Monday through Saturday between Hilo and Kailua-Kona. There are also frequent intracity buses serving Hilo, and an hourly shuttle which travels the length of Kailua's Alii Drive. Other buses drive to the Kona and Kau coasts. The Hele-On runs Monday through Saturday; fares range from 75¢ for short rides to $6 for the Hilo-Kailua cross-island run.

The Hilo bus terminal is on Kamehameha Avenue at Mamo Street. You'll see few bus stops indicated on the island. The official stops are generally unmarked, and you can hail a bus anywhere along its route. Just wave your hand. When it's time to get off, the driver will stop anywhere you wish. For information and schedules, call Hele-On at 935-8241 or 961-8343.

BICYCLING

Hawaii offers very good roads and many unpopulated stretches which make it ideal for cyclers. Much of the island is mountainous with some fairly steep grades in the interior. Saddle Road, the roads to Waimea, and the road from Hilo up to Volcanoes National Park will all make a heavy breather of you, but the coast roads are generally flat or gently rolling. Most roads have shoulders and light traffic.

Keep in mind that the northeast side of the island receives heavy rainfall, and the Kona side is almost always sunny. But wet side or dry, the scenery is spectacular throughout.

RENTALS

In Kailua, try **Dave's Triathlon Shop** (74-55960 Pawai; 329-4522). They rent 10-speed, 12-speed, and mountain bikes and do repairs.

REPAIRS

These shops will do repair work and will cheerfully sell you bike accessories: **The Bike Shop** (258 Kamehameha Avenue, Hilo; 935-7588), **Mid-Pacific Wheels** (2100 Kanoelehua, Hilo; 959-7606), and **B & L Marine, Bike & Sports** (74-5504-A Kaiwi, Kailua; 329-3309).

HITCHHIKING

Thumbing is very popular in Hawaii. Like any place, your luck will vary here, depending on your location, looks, the time, the tides, what-all. Generally, populated areas and tourist attractions are good spots for a ride. If you venture from these beaten paths, remember that the Big Island has long stretches with nothing but macadam and lava.

Check the Hele-On bus schedule before setting out just in case you get stranded. If your luck fails, you can hail a bus from anywhere along the roadside.

TOURS

Kenai Helicopters (329-7424) and **Kona Helicopters** (329-0551) offer helicopter tours from their headquarters on the Kona coast. In the Volcanoes National Park area, contact **Volcano Heli-Tours** (967-7578) or **TMP Helicopters** (Hilo; 935-7000).

Hotels

Most Big Island hotels are located either in Hilo or the Kailua-Kona region, but there are others scattered in outlying areas all around the island.

HILO HOTELS

The fashionable hotel district in this rain-plagued city sits astride the bay along Banyan Drive. Most hotels here offer moderately priced accommodations, while a few are designed to fit the contours of a more slender purse.

Near the far end of beautiful Banyan Drive lies the **Hilo Hukilau Hotel** (126 Banyan Way; 935-0821). This charming place is actually on a side street fronting Reed's Bay, an arm of Hilo Bay. Owned by the Kimis, a Hawaiian family, it has the same friendly ambience that pervades their other hotels. There's a large lobby decorated with bamboo and woven *lauhala*. A carp pond complete with footbridges dominates the grounds. The rooms are small and plainly decorated. Most are wallpapered in unattractive stripes and equipped with telephone, television, and a combination shower-tub (perfect for soaking away a rainy day). The lanais overlook lush gardens and the hotel swimming pool. All in all, for friendly ambience and a lovely setting, the Hukilau is a prime choice. Budget to moderate.

Hilo Bay Hotel (87 Banyan Drive; 935-0861) is another economical oceanfront establishment. The theme here is Polynesian, and proprietor "Uncle Billy" carries it off with flair: wicker furniture, thatch, and *tapa* in the lobby, a bayside swimming pool, and several carp ponds dotted about the tropical gardens. Standard rooms have wall-to-wall carpeting, televisions, telephones, and air-conditioning, but are lacking in style and elegance. The walls are plaster, and the rooms are plainly furnished and located away from the water. They rent for a moderate price. Superior rooms (which overlook the gardens, are larger, more attractive, and come with kitchenettes) can be reserved for slightly more.

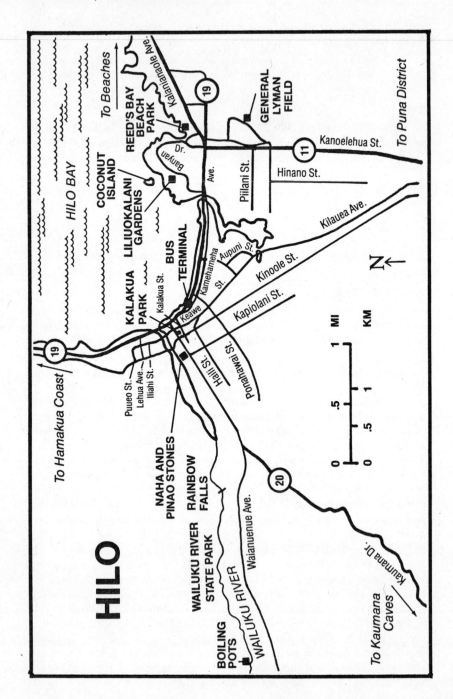

For luxurious living my favorite Hilo hostelry is the **Naniloa Surf** (93 Banyan Drive; 935-0831), a high-rise affair located right on the water. Rooms are comfortably furnished and nicely adorned. Restaurants, bars, and a nightclub are among the many amenities here, but the most alluring feature is the landscape—the tree-studded lawn is fringed with tidepools and volcanic rock. Add a swimming pool, spacious lobby, plus friendly staff and you have Hilo's premier hotel. With a price tag in the moderate range, it is also the area's best bargain.

To find more budget accommodations, you'll have to tote your bags up from the waterfront and closer to the town center. Here you'll find the **Hilo Hotel** (142 Kinoole Street; 961-3733), an oldtimer dating back to 1888 when the Spreckels sugar family built the original ten-room, two-bath hostelry. Fifteen years earlier, Princess Ruth reputedly planted the rubber tree which once towered more than 100 feet above the hotel's lush grounds. Time has left its traces on the hotel's older Kalakaua wing, where somewhat rundown rooms lack decoration. I prefer the newer, quieter Niolopa Wing with its wood-paneled walls and smaller rooms. Guests in both wings use the hotel swimming pool and television room, as well as the adjoining lounge and restaurant. Budget to moderate.

On a tree-lined residential street just across the Wailuku River sits the **Dolphin Bay Hotel** (333 Iliahi Street; 935-1466). This cozy two-story establishment has eighteen units, all equipped with kitchenettes. Studios are budget priced; one-bedroom apartments place in the moderate range but can accommodate up to four. Two-bedroom units house as many as six and are deluxe in price. Rooms upstairs have exposed beam ceilings; all units have cinder-block walls and are fairly attractive.

Not far away at **Lanikai Hotel** (100 Puueo Street; 935-5556) you'll find small, cozy rooms at budget prices. These are carpeted wall-to-wall and attractively furnished; some also have refrigerators and hotplates. There's a laundry room, rolling lawn out front, and a spacious though impersonal lobby with lounge and snack bar adjoining. Be prepared for some noise from the nearby highway. Special weekly rates.

KAILUA-KONA AREA HOTELS

The Kona Coast is as expensive as it is beautiful. Hawaiian royalty once resided here, and their former playground is still the haunt of well-heeled tourists. As a result, bargains are as rare as rainy days.

Kona Seaside Hotel (75-5646 Palani Road; 329-2455), a chunky six-story building, offers pretty ordinary rooms with televisions, telephones, and air-conditioning at moderate cost. Long dark corridors lead to the antiseptic rooms, which come with wall-to-wall carpeting and gaudy striped wallpaper. The lanais are small and lack privacy. But tackiest of all are the menus which the owners have inelegantly stapled on the walls to plug their restaurant.

I prefer the **Kona Hukilau** (75-5646 Palani Road; 329-2455), a sister hotel just down the street. Not only is it cheaper, but it's cozier. Most rooms look out on a pleasant central courtyard with lawn and swimming pool. A nearby sun deck overlooks Kailua Bay. There's a windswept lobby and adjacent restaurant and lounge. This 100-unit establishment shares outdoor facilities with the Kona Seaside: if it's a lazy day you can spend the morning at the Hukilau's pool, which catches the early sun, then shuffle over to the Seaside for an afternoon dip.

Hukilau rooms are cross-ventilated, partially carpeted, and sparsely decorated along their white stucco walls. Standard units have air-conditioning and price in the moderate range.

Kona Bay Hotel (75-5739 Alii Drive; 329-1393) is part of the old Kona Inn, the rest of which fell to Kailua developers who have perversely transformed it into yet another shopping mall. What remains is a four-story semicircular structure with a pool, bar, and restaurant in the center. The rooms are large, tastefully furnished, and quiet. Some have lava walls that provide a pleasant backdrop plus excellent soundproofing. Standard rooms as well as larger digs equipped with mini-kitchenettes are moderate in price. The staff is friendly, and the atmosphere is very appealing. I once spent a relaxing month here and highly recommend the place.

Kona Islander Inn (on Alii Drive; 329-3181) occupies several three-story buildings spread across a lush swath of land. Set between Alii Drive and Route 11 on Kailua's outskirts, this chain hotel has a large lobby and an oval pool flanked by MacArthur palms. All rooms have small lanais, cable televisions, refrigerators, carpets, and air-conditioning. Tastefully appointed, but lacking a good ocean view. Moderate.

Kona Tiki Hotel (on Alii Drive; 329-1425), a mile down the road, is a quaint hotel neatly situated on the ocean. The rooms are bright and clean. Despite the contrasting decorative themes and the noise from Alii Drive, I recommend this fifteen-unit establishment for its ocean view lanais, oceanfront pool, barbecue, garden, and complimentary continental breakfast. Rooms equipped with mini-kitchenettes (sink, refrigerator, and two-burner stove crowded into one unit) rent for moderate prices.

Also tabbed in the moderate range, but a better bargain still, are the rooms at **Kona White Sands Apartment Hotel** (on Alii Drive; 329-3210). Located just across the street from Disappearing Sands Beach (the nicest beach along Alii Drive), this ten-unit hotel offers both studios and one-bedroom apartments. Each comes with kitchenette; deluxe rooms have ceiling fans. The cinder-block and plasterboard walls are pretty plain, but who needs fancy interior decoration with that knockout ocean view? Rooms are cross-ventilated, and the cooling breeze will probably bring along noise from cars and sun revelers. That's the extra price for living this close to the Kona coast. Many people are willing to pay it, so you'll have to reserve a room far in advance. Write to Kona White Sands Apartment Hotel, P.O. Box 594, Kailua-Kona, Hawaii, HI 96745.

Anchoring one end of Kailua Bay is the town's most historic hotel. The **Hotel King Kamehameha** (75-5660 Palani Road; 329-2911), priced somewhat higher than its young neighbors, is nonetheless deserving of note. The lobby alone is worth the price of admission: it's a wood-paneled affair along which you can trace the history of ancient Hawaii.

For its guests, the "King Kam" has a pool, tennis courts, and jacuzzi, plus a host of other amenities ranging from an activities desk to room service. The rooms themselves are quite spacious, fashionably decorated, and equipped with positively everything. You'll find plush carpeting, color televisions, air-conditioning, refrigerators, and lanais with spectacular views of the ocean or mountains. Deluxe.

Of course, when money is no object the place to stay is **Kona Village Resort** (P.O. Box 1299, Kaupulehu, Kailua-Kona, HI 96745; 325-5555), a very plush, very private colony located several miles north of Kailua. Favored by movie stars and other celebrities seeking escape from autograph hounds and aggressive agents, this regal retreat is set along a white sand cove in an ancient Hawaiian fishing village. The individual guest cottages are thatched-roof structures (*hales*), variously designed to represent the traditional houses of Hawaiian, Tahitian, Fijian, Samoan, and other Polynesian groups. There are no televisions, radios, clocks, or front-door keys; but you will find serenity, solitude, and a well-heeled version of hidden Hawaii, not to mention tennis courts, sailboats, outrigger canoes, and glass-bottom excursion boats. Prices are in the ultra-deluxe class and are based on the American plan.

KAILUA-KONA AREA CONDOMINIUMS

Kona Alii (on Alii Drive next to the Islander Inn; 329-2076). One-bedroom, two-bath apartments run from $50 double (deduct ten percent during the off-season, April 1 to December 15). This seven-story building is just across the street from the ocean.

Alii Villas (on Alii Drive, one mile south of Kailua; 329-1288). A one-bedroom unit is $55 single or double; a two-bedroom, two-bath apartment is $90 for one to four people. Oceanfront, but with no beach.

The Sea Village (on Alii Drive, one mile south of Kailua; 329-1000). One bedroom units start at $40 single or double; two bedrooms, two baths, $56 for one to four people; prices increase from mid-December to mid-March. Jacuzzi and tennis courts. Oceanfront, but no beach.

Kona Bali Hai (76-6246 Alii Drive; 329-9381). Studio apartments are $55 single or double, one-bedroom apartments go for $70 for one to four people. Sauna, jacuzzi, and pool. One mile from Disappearing Sands Beach.

Kona Magic Sands (on Alii Drive; 329-9177). Studio apartment, $40 single or double. Located on the ocean, next to Disappearing Sands Beach. No one under sixteen years old permitted; four-night minimum.

HILO TO KONA HOTELS

If you're looking for an offbeat hotel or a halfway point on the long trek from Hilo to Kona, you'll find several places along both the northern and southern routes.

HILO TO KONA (NORTHERN ROUTE) HOTELS

Hotel Honokaa Club (on Route 24, Honokaa; 775-0678), perched on a hillside above the Hamakua Coast, has a boardinghouse atmosphere. The rooms upstairs are kept thoroughly scrubbed and freshly painted; they're quite adequate. A budget price buys a splendid ocean view through dirty plate-glass windows, color television, plus a tiny private bathroom. Or trade the trim carpets upstairs for a plain hardwood floor downstairs and you can have a small cubicle with community bathroom at even cheaper cost. These rooms are smaller and lack the view, but they're just as clean as the upstairs rooms.

One of the most primitive, secluded, and unusual lodgings anywhere in the islands is Tom Araki's five-room **Waipio Hotel** (★) (for reservations write to 25 Malana Place, Hilo, HI 96720 or call 775-0368 or 935-7466). Set deep in the luxurious Waipio Valley, this idyllic retreat is surrounded by waterfalls, sharp cliffs, and a black-sand beach. Don't expect too many amenities here in Eden—gas, electricity, and meal service are unheard of and the rooms are small and simple. But there are two kitchens available as well as a landscape filled with orchards. Accessible only by 4-wheel drive or by shuttle, it's the only commercial facility in an isolated and extraordinarily beautiful valley. The price of admission to paradise? A low-budget pittance.

Set amid the Kohala Mountains in the cowboy town of Waimea are two hotels, both within walking distance of local markets and restaurants. **The Lodge** (on Route 19, Waimea; 885-4100), a modern multi-unit motel, is owned by Parker Ranch, which seems to control most everything in these parts. Rooms are large, carpeted, and equipped with telephones, shower-tub combinations, color televisions, and small kitchenettes. The ceilings are exposed beam; from the walls hang textiles and oil paintings, some from Parker scion Richard Smart's private collection. Prices here run in the moderate range.

Kamuela Inn (on Route 19, Waimea; 885-4243), a poor neighbor just down the street, has modest rooms. These are clean and bright with wall decorations personally chosen by the manager. Each of the 19 units is equipped with a television and refrigerator. Guests are served a continental breakfast. Standard rooms and two-room units are moderately priced.

In the small rustic town of Hawi near Hawaii's northwestern tip, the **Old Hawaii Lodging Co.** (889-5577) and an adjacent restaurant are the hottest spots around. But there's still privacy and quiet aplenty out back in the sleeping quarters. Rooms in this refurbished establishment are tagged in the budget category. These tinroof accommodations feature handsome hardwood floors and face a small courtyard. The place is tidy, if less than elegant. The rooms in an adjacent building are priced the same.

You might try your luck down the road in Kapaau at the **Kohala Club Hotel** (on Route 27, Kapaau; 889-6793). I hope you fare better than I did. All I could discover was that the landlady rents mostly to local folks and doesn't talk to travel writers. But at the low budget prices she charges, rooms in those tinroof clapboard buildings could be a good buy. Let me know.

One of the Big Island's most gracious lodgings is the **Hawaiian Plantation House** (Route 27, Hawi; 889-5523). It's a magnificent old house which once served as the manager's home on a sugar plantation. Today the white clapboard sits on a four-acre spread surrounded by lush foliage and shade trees. The interior features four two-bedroom suites, each with sitting room and private bath. Guests share a dining room, kitchen, and a large living room with stone fireplace. The place has about it an old-time splendor that's rarely recaptured. Moderate to deluxe; reserve far in advance.

Condominiums are often synonymous with crowds and congestion. But the **Puako Beach Condominiums** (3 Puako Beach Drive, Puako; 882-7711) lie about thirty miles north of Kailua's traffic jams. Set across the street from a rocky shoreline, this condo is a short drive from some of the island's nicest beaches. One-bedroom apartments rent for a moderate cost; two-bedroom units are in the deluxe range; three-bedroom suites accommodating up to six people are also deluxe priced.

Waikoloa (883-9671), a townhouse-style condominium on the lower slopes of Mauna Kea, is another secluded resort. Located inland from the South Kohala coast, Waikoloa is a self-contained village with store, post office, pool, restaurant, tennis courts, golf course, and riding stables. Moderate.

For years the Kohala district was a placid region strewn with lava and dotted by several pearly beaches. A single resort stood along its virgin coastline. Today it's one of the fastest developing spots in Hawaii. The **Sheraton Royal Waikoloa Hotel** (Route 19, Waikoloa; 885-6789), a sprawling 543-unit resort, with rooms priced upward from the deluxe range, now stands along Anaehoomalu Beach. Several miles north, the **Mauna Lani Bay Hotel** (Route 19, Kawaihae; 885-6622), a 3,200-acre resort, rests on another white-sand beach; ultra-deluxe.

The Kohala Coast's original resort, the **Mauna Kea Beach Hotel** (Route 19, Kawaihae; 882-7222), is a world-class complex which still ranks as one of the very finest hotels in the islands. Set on a crescent beach, boasting an 18-hole golf course and 500 manicured acres, the hotel is lavishly decorated and enjoys an impeccable reputation. Room rates for a modified American plan (breakfast and dinner included) begin high in the ultra-deluxe category.

HILO TO KONA (SOUTHERN ROUTE) HOTELS

For a funky country place high in the mountains overlooking the Kona coast, try **Kona Hotel** (on Route 18, Holualoa; 324-1155). Catering primarily to workers, this eleven-unit hotel remains a real sleeper. It might be difficult to book a room during the week, but on weekends, the lunchpail crowd heads home and you can rent a small place at an unbelievable low-budget rate. No reservations, thank you. Shared bathroom facilities. It's five miles to the beaches and action around Kailua, but if you're after an inexpensive retreat, this is the place.

Down the road in Honalo, **Teshima's Inn** (on Route 11; 322-9140) has small, cozy rooms at similar rates. These are set in an L-shaped structure fronting a Japanese garden. The rooms have linoleum floors and wood-paneled walls decorated with Japanese art. Here you're 1,300 feet above sea level and seven miles from Kailua. This charming inn is run by Mrs. Teshima, a delightful Japanese woman who has operated the establishment for years.

Kona Sports Hostel (Route 11, Honalo; 322-8136) has dormitory accommodations as well as private rooms at budget prices. The facility sits hillside overlooking the ocean on an acre of land. The sundeck, hot tub, and kitchen are available to guests. Chores are required if you stay in the dorm; but unlike most hostels, you are permitted 24-hour use of the facilities.

At **H. Manago Hotel** (323-2642), on Route 11 in the town of Captain Cook, you'll have a varied choice of accommodations. Rooms with communal bath in the creaky old section are budget priced. The battered furniture, torn linoleum floors, and annoying street noise make for rather funky living here. Rooms in the new section rise in price as you ascend the stairs. First-floor accommodations are the cheapest and rooms on the ethereal third floor are the most expensive, but all reside in the budget range. The only advantage for the extra cost is a better view. All these rooms are small and tastelessly furnished—somehow orange carpets don't make it with pink naugahyde chairs. But you'll find visual relief in the marvelous views of mountain and sea from the tiny lanais. There's also a restaurant and television room back in the old section.

Shirakawa Hotel-Motel (on Route 11, Waiohinu; 929-7462), the country's southernmost hotel, sits on stunningly beautiful grounds.

There's a fruit farm out back and poinsettias lining the driveway. When I stopped by recently, a rainbow arched across the landscape and birds loudly rioted in the nearby hills. Located 1,000 feet above sea level, this corrugated-roof hostelry offers quaint rooms with faded furniture and functional kitchenettes at budget prices. Without cooking facilities, the bill is even less.

Sea Mountain at Punaluu (Route 11, Punaluu; 928-8301) is a welcome contradiction in terms—a secluded condominium. Situated in the arid Kau district south of Volcanoes National Park, it rests between volcanic headlands and a spectacular black-sand beach. A green oasis surrounded by lava rock and desert vegetation, the complex contains a golf course, pool, tennis courts, jacuzzi, restaurant, and store. The several dozen condos are multi-unit cottages pricing in the deluxe range. The condos are well decorated and include a bedroom, sitting room, kitchenette, and lanai; larger units available.

Volcano House (967-7321), a thirty-seven-room Sheraton hotel, perches 4,000 feet above sea level on the rim of Kilauea Crater. Situated in the heart of Volcanoes National Park, this country-style inn provides a unique resting place. You can watch the steam rise from Halemaumau Crater or study the rugged contours of slumbering Kilauea. Standard rooms are unfortunately located in a separate building behind the main hotel. For a view of Kilauea ask for a superior or deluxe room on the volcano side. The rooms are small and decorated in the Sheraton's ever tidy and cozy fashion. There's wall-to-wall carpeting but no television or radio. And you certainly won't need an air-conditioner at these breathless heights. Matter of fact, you'll probably be more interested in the hotel's steam bath, heated by the volcano. Well worth a one-night stand. Moderate.

In the beautiful Puna district, a volcanic region fringed with black-sand beaches, there's a marvelous place called the **Kalani Honua Culture Center and Retreat** (Box 4500, Kalapana, HI 96778; 965-7828). Situated six miles east of Kalapana, it sits just above the ocean on 20 acres. In addition to lodging, this New Age resort provides a lifestyle. There are classes in hula, weaving, carving, and *lei* making; lectures on the history and culture of Hawaii; plus programs in modern dance and aerobics. The facilities include a Japanese health spa with hot tub and sauna, a swimming pond, tennis courts, hiking trails, and ballcourts. Guests stay in multi-unit lodges, sharing a spacious living room and kitchen. Sleeping accommodations are basic but appealing, with pine walls, plain carpeting, foam rubber mattresses, and wallhangings crafted at the Center. For one, two, or three people, a room with shared bath or private bath runs in the budget to moderate range. Meals are $16 a day per person, or you can cook for yourself.

Restaurants

HILO RESTAURANTS

Hilo Budget Restaurants: Scattered throughout Hilo are numerous cafes, lunch counters, and chain restaurants serving low-cost meals. This is a great town for ethnic eating on a budget.

Vegetarians will do well to check out **Hilo Natural Foods** (306 Kilauea Avenue; 935-7002). Toward the back of the grocery section of the store, there's a snack bar featuring salads, sandwiches, and juices.

The **Coffee Shop** at Hilo Bay Hotel (87 Banyan Drive; 935-0861) provides a pennysaver's retreat from the more expensive restaurants along Banyan Drive's hotel row. There's nothing fancy about this cafe, but you can still enjoy a hearty breakfast out on the lanai. They also serve sandwiches, but no hot meals.

For those, hoof on over to **Gwen's** (96 Kalanianaole; 961-2044), near the edge of hotel row. The standard lunch menu consists of sandwiches (many at low, low cost) as well as Oriental and American platters. The menu's limited and the atmosphere nonexistent, but Gwen's place isn't bad for a quick meal. Breakfasts are served too; closed for dinner.

If you don't mind sharing the meal with a blaring jukebox and crackling pinball machine, try **K. K. Place** (413 Kilauea Avenue; 935-5216) in Kilauea Center. This cafe has complete breakfasts as well as plate lunches. A good bargain for both Oriental and American food.

Farther down Kilauea Avenue, across from Kaikoo Mall, sits one of the island's few delicatessens. The bill of fare at **Kawika's Deli** (804 Kilauea Avenue; 935-2141) is limited, but if you're dying for hot pastrami or other deli treats, this is the place.

Ever try *adobo?* Or *laoya?* They're pork and pig's feet dishes served Filipino-style at Asian cafes in the rundown center of Hilo. One of these, **Sophie's Place** (207 Kilauea Avenue; 935-7300), serves lunch plates for little money. A great way to go ethnic.

Hilo Moderately Priced Restaurants: Let's start with traditional and proceed to ethnic dining spots. **Ken's House of Pancakes** (1730 Kamehameha Avenue; 935-8711) has to top the list for all-American fare. If you've ever been to a Denny's or Howard Johnson's, you've been in Ken's. Endless rows of naugahyde booths, a long counter next to the kitchen, uniformed waitresses—the classic roadside America motif. The cuisine is on a par with the decorative taste: burgers and roast beef, mediocre in quality, moderate in cost. But when all else is closed, it's a good late-night option.

Another mediocre spot is **Hukilau Restaurant** (126 Banyan Way; 935-4222), adjacent to the popular Hilo Hukilau Hotel. Decorated in bamboo and *lauhala* weave, the Hukilau features a seafood menu complemented with meat 'n' potato favorites like pork chops, steak, and fried chicken. Dinners come with salad bar, soup, dessert, and beverage. For lunch, they offer sandwiches and other mid-day fare; also open at breakfast time.

Uncle Billy's (87 Banyan Drive; 935-0861) at nearby Hilo Bay Hotel also sports a typical Hawaiian decor. In addition to its classy rattan furnishings, this cozy club hosts Polynesian dinner shows nightly. The menu is filled with surf-and-turf dishes priced comfortably. There's no lunch here, but they do offer breakfast daily.

Situated across the street from the golf course, the **Red Carpet** (121 Banyan Drive; 961-6815) prepares breakfast, lunch, and dinner. The walls inside this restaurant-lounge are covered with unusual artworks and wrought iron fixtures, lending the place a medieval feel. The Red Carpet dinner is a buffet affair with such dishes as roast beef, short ribs, *mahimahi*, chicken, rice, and potatoes. You can also pay a visit to the salad bar. Prices range at the low end of the moderate category. For lunch you might be interested in the hot and cold sandwiches and homemade pie.

Or, better still, try one of Hilo's health food restaurants. At **Hilo Natural Foods** (306 Kilauea; 935-7002) there's a juice bar and sandwich shop. The folks here also serve fresh fruit freezes in every color from banana to papaya.

Hilo is a prime area for ethnic food. Here you'll find far more good Oriental restaurants than American restaurants. For example, **Sachi's Gourmet** (250 Keawe Street; 935-6255), a small cafe downtown, serves inexpensive Japanese meals. Sachi cooks several *donburi, udon,* and tempura dishes (priced very low) as well as several special seafood dishes.

For Chinese food, **Mun Cheong Lau Chop Suey Restaurant** (126 Keawe Street; 935-3040) is the Orient's answer to the greasy spoon (greasy chopstick?) cafe. The place is as big as a barn and gaudily decorated with magenta walls and plastic lanterns. If you can get past the interior devastation, there's an ample menu listing numerous seafood, fowl, pork, and rice dishes at chop suey prices. And in case of late-night munchie attacks, Mun Cheong stays open until the wee hours of the morning.

At **K. K. Tei Restaurant** (1550 Kamehameha Avenue; 961-3791) you can enjoy dinner while overlooking a lovely bonsai garden. The dining room offers an ample selection of both traditional Japanese dishes and unusual seafood plates. In addition to sukiyaki and tempura plates, the chefs prepare prawns, scallops, and shrimp. After dinner, stroll past the pagodas and arched bridges that ornament K. K.'s Japanese Garden.

Hilo Deluxe Restaurants: Hilo boasts a very fine Japanese restaurant which combines excellent cooking with private dining. At **Restaurant Fuji** (142 Kinoole Street; 961-3733), in the Hilo Hotel, you can dine on the poolside lanai where chefs fire up *teppanyaki* dishes right at your table. Or pass through the glass partitions indoors where the cooks prepare *uminoko*, the seafood counterpart of *teppanyaki*. There are also several *teishoku* (complete dinner) choices served with raw fish, vegetables, and soup, plus an elaborate lunch menu.

KAILUA-KONA AREA RESTAURANTS

Kailua-Kona Area Budget Restaurants: For anyone on a tight budget, Kailua would seem an unlikely place to find a decent meal. Most restaurants along the Gold Coast cater to gilded tourists and wealthy residents. If you work at it, though, you'll locate a few low-cost eating places.

Kona Coast Shopping Center houses several short-order joints. **Betty's Chinese Kitchen** (329-3770) serves tasty, nutritious meals at its cafeteria-style emporium. **Mr. Tonkatsu** (329-4677) has an assortment of low-priced Japanese dishes. The proprietor here takes great pride in his use of fresh foods and time-honored recipes. Open for lunch and dinner, he serves a deep-fried *menchi* burger (prepared Asian style), as well as chicken and pork cutlets and curry dishes. This mini-restaurant is definitely worth investigating.

If these places don't intrigue you, head downhill to the North Kona Shopping Center. **The Wurst Place** (329-1166) is not as bad as all that. Matter of fact, some people find the plate lunches and hot sandwiches downright *ono*.

For wholesome, tasteful meals at budget prices, the best bargain in all Kona is **Amy's Fine Food Factory** (75-5629-D Kuakini Highway; 329-2890) in the same shopping center. The accent here is on vegetarian and fresh fish entrees, but they also feature steaks, chicken, and turkey dishes. It's a perfect choice for pasta dishes, quiche, casseroles, soups, and salads. Open for lunch and dinner; recommended with gusto.

For budget dining in opulent surroundings, you should stop by the **Kona Veranda Coffee Shop** (329-2911) in the Hotel King Kamehameha. Open for breakfast as well as lunch, this pleasant cafe serves standard American fare as well as more imaginative island dishes. Of course the opulence comes not so much from the coffee shop as the hotel facilities. The "King Kam" is a famous hotel, featuring a lobby that contains a collection of ancient Hawaiian artifacts worthy of any museum. The hotel's beach and shopping mall also provide post-prandial opportunities.

Tolkien fans should stop by **Tom Bombadil's** (329-1292) quaint little place on Alii Drive across from the Hilton. The murals decorating this small cafe represent scenes from the Ring trilogy. In addition to pizza, Tom serves sandwiches straight from Goldberry's pantry. But take heed:

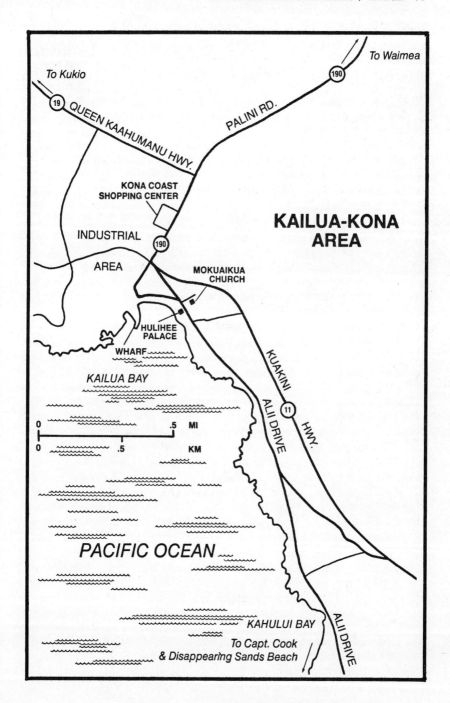

in these parts a roast beef sandwich translates as "The Pride of Gondor," turkey is a "Withywindle," and for ham and cheese read "Rivendell." Tom also serves fish and chicken dishes as well as salads. If you ever get past the menu, you'll find the food quite delicious.

Kailua-Kona Area Moderately Priced Restaurants: The best buys in this category are at the Oceanview Inn and at Stan's Restaurant. The **Oceanview Inn** (on Alii Drive; 329-9998), a large, informal hall opposite Kailua Bay, has a voluminous lunch and dinner menu. Chinese, Hawaiian, seafood, and meat dishes, served all day, comprise only part of the selection. This is a perfect opportunity to try fresh fish, caught several miles offshore in some of the world's finest fishing grounds. There's also a complete breakfast menu.

Right next door, at **Stan's Restaurant** (75-5687 Alii Drive; 329-4500), you can order from a unique menu which lists dinners by price. Tabbed in the moderate category are a number of steak and seafood concoctions. This open-air establishment overlooking Kona Bay offers significantly more atmosphere than the Oceanview. There are rattan furnishings, a cocktail lounge, and a windswept waiting area which was recently refurbished by the adjoining hotel's management. Lunch isn't served, but breakfast features coconut, macadamia nut, or banana hotcakes.

I've never eaten at **Kona Galley** (on Alii Drive; 329-3777), just down the street, but several friends have recommended it highly. It's an open-air dining room decorated in a nautical motif. The bill of fare, reflecting the porthole-studded surroundings, primarily features seafood. Among the selections are *mahimahi, ono, ahi,* and shellfish, plus such chef's specialties as seafood au gratin and crab newburg casserole. At lunchtime the galley serves sandwiches and a chef's salad.

The **Old Kailua Cantina** (75-5669 Alii Drive; 329-0788), on the same waterfront drive, specializes in south of the border cuisine. Here you'll dine out on a lanai overlooking Kailua Bay or in one of several rooms attractively paneled in *lauhala* and bamboo. Open for lunch and dinner, this moderate-priced restaurant offers several unique grill dishes. These include fresh fish, beef ribs, and chicken breast, each prepared with a tangy sauce. They also feature a complete selection of standard Mexican dishes.

Another popular oceanfront dining room is **Marty's Steak and Seafood** (Alii Drive; 329-1571). It's an open-air affair, with torches lighting the perimeter. The entire restaurant is situated on a balustraded balcony overlooking Kailua Bay, making it an enchanting place to dine (or simply enjoy a beer). Of course, that view is costly: the dinner menu rises from the moderate to the deluxe category; lunch is similarly priced. But I've always found Marty's dishes worth the asking price. So if you're in the mood for steak, chops, crab, lobster, or scampi, stop by.

Aesthetically speaking, **Kona Ranch House** (75-5653 Kuakini Highway; 329-7061) swings both ways. One section of the trimly appointed restaurant features informal dining in an understated and comfortable environment. On the other hand, in the adjoining Plantation Lanai facility you can treat yourself to a candlelight-and-linen-tablecloth experience. The menu is the same for both sections of this switchhitting establishment. Drop in for lunch or dinner and you'll find an inventory of entrees ranging from ribs to chicken and from New York steak to fresh fish. There are also inexpensive sandwiches and appetizer dishes. At breakfast Kona Ranch House offers an array of egg dishes. So take your pick of locales, easy or elegant, and enjoy good food at moderate prices.

For a touch of class at a reasonable price, consider **Eclipse Restaurant** (75-5711 Kuakini Highway; 329-4686). Open for dinner only, this sleek dining room offers filet mignon, prawns, seafood brochette, a vegetarian dish, and the catch of the day at moderate to deluxe prices. The place is finished in fine woods and decorated with original artworks, etched glass, and potted palms. You can gaze into the aquarium, lounge at the brass-rail bar, or stay after hours when it changes face to become a dance club. Appealing ambience, moderately good food, outstanding service.

The commemorative sign at the **Kona Inn** (75-5744 Alii Drive; 329-4455) tells the tale of the old inn—how it was built back in the steamship era when Kona was gaining fame as a marlin fishing ground. The bad news is that the original hotel was razed and replaced with a mall of which this contemporary namesake is part. The good news is that the restaurant is quite attractive—an open-air, oceanfront affair serving several fresh fish dishes daily, as well as steak, prime rib, and Hawaiian-style chicken. Open for lunch, dinner, and Sunday brunch, it's priced moderate to deluxe.

Jose's Mexican Restaurant (329-6931), on Route 11 several miles south of Kailua, also offers dining both indoors and out. Inside, piñatas and Spanish-style paintings lend a Latin flavor to this congenial cafe, but the slow-turning overhead fans betray its Polynesian locale. Outside, a stunning seascape reveals that this is most certainly the islands at their best. I also found the food quite satisfying when I sat down recently to an enchilada dinner. Open for lunch and dinner, Jose's has an adequate Mexican menu, but no American food, so come prepared to eat tangy dishes. *Mucho gusto!*

Kailua-Kona Area Deluxe Restaurants: **Dorian's** (on Alii Drive near Disappearing Sands Beach; 329-3195), a waterfront salon with continental cuisine, is *the* place to dine on the Kona Coast. Small, intimate, tucked unpretentiously into the corner of a large condominium, Dorian's conveys a modest sense of elegance: candlelight, high-backed chairs, linen tablecloths, a seascape through plate-glass doors, and good service. Choose from an enticing menu including scampi, lamb chops, roquefort steak, beef tournedos, seafood thermidor, baby lobster tails, and other gourmet delights.

For continental cuisine in a fashionable setting, consider **La Bourgogne French Restaurant** (Kuakini Plaza on Kuakini Highway, four miles south of Kailua; 329-6711). Open for dinner only, this French country dining room features beef bourguignon, roast saddle of lamb, veal sweetbreads with Madeira sauce, coquilles St. Jacques, and fresh fish selections. For appetizers there are escargots, truffled mousse, and steak tartar. Round off the meal with cherries jubilee or chocolate mousse and you have a French feast right here in tropical Hawaii.

For delicious food, pleasant surroundings, and a congenial staff, you might try **The Pottery** (75-5995 Kuakini Highway; 329-2277). Here is a candlelit inn gracefully decorated with ceramics tucked in the nooks and crannies of its wood-paneled walls. Pottery is sold on the premises, and after some meals you receive the pot in which your dinner was cooked. Most entrees come out of the Steak Kiln, but a few dishes, like *mahimahi* and Cornish game hen, are fired up for the less carnivorous.

HILO TO KONA (NORTHERN ROUTE) RESTAURANTS

Hilo to Kona (Northern Route) Budget and Moderately Priced Restaurants: Honokaa offers a convenient lunch stop for those making a day-trip between Hilo and Kona. The **Hotel Honokaa Club** (on Route 24, Honokaa; 775-0678) has a banquet-sized dining room that's large enough to play hockey on. The last time I was there, on a wet and miserable Sunday morning, it was cold enough inside to do just that. So don't expect a cozy hideaway. At least the food is hot, and priced well, too. At breakfast, lunch, or dinner you'll get by at modest cost. The menu is an interesting mix of Japanese and American food.

When in cowboy country do like the *paniolos* do. Up in the western-style town of Waimea the **Parker Ranch Broiler** (Parker Ranch Center, Waimea; 885-7366) serves steak, steak, and steak. At lunch and dinner there's also veal, pork chops, chicken, and seafood. The red brocade bar is right through them swinging doors and the dining room's mighty pretty. Moderate to deluxe.

Health-minded diners may be even more attracted to **Rainbow Mountain Natural Foods** (on Route 19, Waimea; 885-7202), a small restaurant serving soups, salads, and sandwiches. The house specialty is the vegieburger, prepared with vegetables and grains.

My favorite Waimea dining spot is the **Edelweiss** restaurant (Route 19, Waimea; 885-6800), a cozy club with a knockout interior design. The entire place was fashioned by a master carpenter who inlaid sugi pine, *koa,* and silver oak with the precision of a stonemason. Run by a German chef who gained his knowledge at prestigious addresses like Maui's plush Kapalua Bay Hotel, Edelweiss is a gourmet's delight. The dinner menu includes wienerschnitzel, roast duck, roast pork with sauerkraut, and a house specialty—sauteed veal, lamb, beef, and bacon with pfifferling. For lunch there is bratwurst and sauerkraut, turkey sandwiches, sauteed chicken breast, and club sandwiches. Priced moderate to deluxe.

Descending the Waimea plateau toward the Kohala coast, you'll find very few restaurants along Hawaii's northwestern shore. Sailors say that any port is good in a storm, and on such a sparsely settled coast any restaurant is probably worth heading for. But if you cast anchor at the **Harbor Hut** (882-7783) in Kawaihae, it may prove that necessity has blown you where you would have put ashore anyway. This backyard terrace serves inexpensive meals daily. Breakfast is a special treat; then at both lunch and dinner you can rest your weary sea legs and order a full-plate meal from the galley for a budget price. Or you can order a catch-of-the-day burger.

Up near Kohala's northern tip, in the timeworn town of Hawi, the **Kohala Inn** (889-5410) draws the crowds. Granted there's not much competition, and the crowds are pretty piddling, but the American and Oriental food at this spacious cafe is darned good. Full-course dinners, hearty lunches, and good breakfasts are all available at budget prices.

Generally, in outlying areas like the Kohala Peninsula, you'll find that although the restaurants are few and simple, they have a homey atmosphere about them that can never be captured in crowded urban areas. As I'm sure you're well aware, this fact sometimes makes dining in the outback almost as grand an adventure as hiking or camping.

Hilo to Kona (Northern Route) Deluxe Restaurants: With all the development that's been occurring along the Kohala Coast, it seems inevitable that gourmet restaurants would become an important part of the landscape. Thus far no independent dining rooms have opened; all are connected with one of the several resorts now dotting the shoreline.

For the ultimate luncheon buffet, try the **Cafe Terrace** (Route 11, Kawaihae; 882-7222) at the Mauna Kea Beach Hotel. This hotel, built on the south Kohala coast by Laurance Rockefeller, is rightly famous for its fabulous feasts. Every afternoon the staff spreads out assorted cold cuts and salads, plus steaming dishes such as hot sausages with sauerkraut and chicken paella, and a dessert table that resembles the window of a Parisian patisserie. The tab will be high, but this bounteous meal could be all you eat that day. In fact, you may want to skip breakfast if you plan on lunching here.

The Mauna Lani Bay Hotel (Route 19, Kawaihae; 885-6622) hosts some well-known, formal, deluxe-priced restaurants. The **Bay Terrace,** serving three meals, features an ever-changing dinner menu. The last time I stopped by, the offerings included poached wahoo, squab with herbs and truffles, sole amandine with hazelnut butter, and broiled lamb chops. At lunch there are cold sandwiches as well as specialties like *mahimahi*, quiche lorraine, and sauteed veal. If you'd prefer duck *a l'orange*, tournedos, rack of lamb, or scampi provencale, try **The Third Floor** restaurant; open for dinner only.

At the Sheraton Royal Waikoloa Hotel (Route 19, Waikoloa; 885-6789) there's a varied choice of restaurants. Depending on your purse, you can choose the moderate-priced **Garden Room,** a pleasant, open-air coffee shop; the wood-paneled **Tiara Room,** serving French cuisine and priced deluxe; or the similarly-tabbed **Royal Terrace,** a supper club featuring Hawaiian revues and other entertainment.

HILO TO KONA (SOUTHERN ROUTE) RESTAURANTS

From Kailua south, Route 11 heads up *mauka* into the mountains above the Kona Coast. There are numerous restaurants in the little towns which dot the first fifteen miles. All sit right on the highway.

Teshima's (322-9140), a pleasant restaurant in Honalo, is a good place to enjoy a Japanese meal or a drink in the lounge. Modestly decorated with lanterns and Oriental paintings, this busy cafe has a lunch menu priced in the moderate range. Dinner features several Japanese delicacies. Breakfast is also served.

There's a different mood entirely at the **Aloha Theatre Cafe** (322-3383) in Kainaliu. Here in the lobby of the town's capacious movie house, a young crew serves delicious breakfasts as well as sandwiches and Mexican dishes during lunch and dinner. So if for some bizarre reason you've always longed to dine in the lobby of a movie theatre. . . .(If not, you can eat out on the oceanview lanai.) Budget.

H. Manago Hotel (323-2642) in the town of Captain Cook, has a full-size dining room. Primarily intended for hotel guests, the menu is limited and the hours restricted to "meal times" (7 to 9 a.m., 11 a.m. to 2 p.m., and 5 to 7:30 p.m. Monday through Thursday). Lunch and dinner platters, consisting of a few daily specials, are moderately priced; sandwiches are also available.

Down in Naalehu, the nation's southernmost town, the central restaurant is **Naalehu Coffee Shop** (929-7238). Some people like the place. I was completely put off by all the tourist trappings: books, slides, knickknacks—even the wall decorations are for sale. But the banana bread is good and the menu is varied. There are several full-course breakfasts; at lunchtime they serve sandwiches with salad and garnishings; the dinner menu features beef, seafood, and chicken dishes.

Along the lengthy stretch from Naalehu to Volcanoes National Park, one of the few dining spots you'll encounter is the **Seamountain Golf Course & Lounge** (928-6222) in Punaluu. Situated a short distance from the black-sand beach, this moderate-priced restaurant serves a lunch (no breakfast or dinner) consisting of hot sandwiches plus a few platters. Topping the cuisine are the views, which range across the links out to the distant volcanic slopes.

If you'd like to dine amid comfortable accommodations overlooking a splendid lagoon, head to the nearby **Punaluu Black Sands Restaurant** (928-8528). Situated at Punaluu black-sand beach, it combines good food with spectacular views. At lunch they serve sandwiches and salads. Then for dinner there are chops, scampi, veal Oscar, pepper steak, and lobster tail. No breakfast but there's a full bar; moderate to deluxe in price.

Speaking of vistas, **Volcano House Restaurant** (967-7321)—perched on the rim of Kilauea Crater—affords extraordinary views. Located at the 4,000-foot elevation in Volcanoes National Park, this spacious dining room looks out on sheer lava walls and angry steam vents. If you can tear yourself away from the stunning scenery, there's an ample dinner menu highlighted by *mahimahi,* prime rib, roast pork, or a variety of seafood dishes. Some dinners are priced moderately, but others run in the deluxe range. Lunch is buffet style and there's a complete breakfast menu.

Out in the Puna district, you'll find slim pickings. Other than **Kalapana Restaurant** (965-9242), a take-out stand on Route 13 in Kalapana, there are few eating places. Luckily, however, this place is open all day and serves breakfast, sandwiches, and lunch plates at budget prices.

Up in the rustic town of Pahoa, there's **Luquin's Mexican Restaurant** (965-9990), a friendly Mexican eatery. Serving a variety of dishes from south of the border, it offers three meals daily at budget prices.

Grocery Markets

Hilo, Kailua-Kona, and Waimea are the best places on the island to shop. All have large supermarkets, as well as health food and specialty shops. Other than these population centers, you'll find the prices high and the inventory low at mom 'n' pop stores in the country. So stock up before heading into the outlying areas.

HILO GROCERY STORES

The island's largest city, Hilo, has several supermarkets. Foremost are **Sure Save** in Kaikoo Mall on Kilauea Avenue, **Sack-N-Save** at 250

Kinoole Street, and **Foodland** in the Puainako Shopping Center. After completing a limited price survey, I found Foodland generally to be the cheapest and Sack-N-Save the most expensive.

HILO HEALTH FOOD STORES

Hilo hosts two excellent natural food outlets—**Abundant Life Natural Foods**, 90 Kamehameha Avenue, and **Hilo Natural Foods**, 306 Kilauea Avenue. Both contain healthy supplies of vitamins, juices, and bath products, as well as fresh fruits and vegetables. The stores also have adjoining natural food restaurants.

HILO FRESH-FISH STORES

Milolii Fish Market, 660 Wainaku, has both fresh and frozen seafood.

HILO SPECIALTY SHOPS

Holsum Bakery Thrift Store, 290 Kamehameha Avenue, offers day-old baked goods at unbeatable prices.

KAILUA-KONA AREA GROCERY STORES

The best place to shop anywhere along the Kona Coast is in the town of Kailua. This commercial center features several supermarkets as well as a number of specialty shops. First choice among supermarkets is the **Foodland** at 75-5722 Hanama Place in the center of Kailua. It has everything you could possibly need.

If you'd prefer another supermarket with a similar selection, try **K.T.A. Superstore** in the Kona Coast Shopping Center. It's open every day from 7 a.m. to 11 p.m., and is another of the Kailua-Kona area's most convenient and accessible shopping facilities.

KAILUA-KONA AREA HEALTH FOOD STORES

Kona Healthways, in the Kona Coast Shopping Center, has an ample stock of vitamins, bathing supplies, grains, fruits, and vegetables. By the simple fact that it is the only store of its kind in the area, it wins my recommendation.

HILO TO KONA (NORTHERN ROUTE) GROCERY STORES

Sure Save Super Market, located in Waimea at the Parker Ranch Center, is the only large supermarket along this route. Open 7:30 a.m. to 9 p.m. daily except Sunday (7:30 a.m. to 8 p.m.).

Between Hilo and Waimea, your best chance is **Ishigo's General Store**. Located in Honomu on the road to Akaka Falls, Ishigo has a limited stock, but you may find what you need. If not, try **M. Ujiki Inc.** on Route 24 in Honokaa.

Past Waimea, on the western side of the island, there are several stores on the Kohala peninsula. **K. Takata Store,** on Route 27 in Hawi, is an old market with an ample stock of groceries. It's the best place to shop north of Kailua. **R. Arakaki Store,** on Route 27 in Halaula, is conveniently located for campers and picnickers headed out to Pololu Valley. **T. Doi and Sons** in Kawaihae has a small selection of groceries and dry goods. Between Kawaihae and Kailua there are no stores.

HILO TO KONA (NORTHERN ROUTE) HEALTH FOOD STORES

Rainbow Mountain Natural Foods (on Route 19, Waimea) has a fair supply of juices, vitamins, whole-food baked goods, spices, and so on.

HILO TO KONA (NORTHERN ROUTE) SPECIALTY SHOPS

If you're looking for meat products, definitely check out the **Kamuela Meat Market** in the Parker Ranch Center. The butchers sell delicious beef fresh from the ranch, and at good prices.

HILO TO KONA (SOUTHERN ROUTE) GROCERY STORES

Strung along Route 11 south of Kailua are a series of small towns which contain tiny markets. The only real supermarket en route is **Sure Save** at the Kealakekua Ranch Center in the town of Captain Cook. Past that, there's not another large store until Naalehu in the southeast corner of the island. Between Naalehu and Hilo, there are a few small markets including the **Wiki Wiki Mart** (in Keaau) and **Kalapana Store** (on Route 130, Kalapana).

HILO TO KONA (SOUTHERN ROUTE) HEALTH FOOD STORES

On the Kona side there are several places. **The Aloha Village Store** (on Route 11, Kainaliu) has an ample stock of vitamins, juices, fruits, and other health food items. Down the road in Kealakekua, **Ohana O Ka Aina General Store** has a similar inventory, plus an herb shop and juice bar.

On the Hilo side, there's **Pahoa Natural Groceries** (on Route 13, Pahoa) in the Puna district.

HILO TO KONA (SOUTHERN ROUTE) FRESH-FISH STORES

Stan's Fishery (on Route 11, Honaunau), about fifteen miles south of Kailua, has fresh seafood.

HILO TO KONA (SOUTHERN ROUTE) SPECIALTY SHOPS

In Pahoa, a rickety town in the Puna district, people often set up stands along the roadside. These freelance operations are great places to purchase fresh fish and home-grown fruits and vegetables.

The Great Outdoors
The Sporting Life

CAMPING

There are few activities on the Big Island more pleasurable than camping. Beautiful state and county parks dot the island, while enticing hiking trails lead to remote mountain and coastal areas.

No matter what you plan to do on the island, keep in mind that the Kona side is generally dry, while the Hilo side receives considerable rain. Also remember that the mountains can be quite cold and usually call for extra clothing and gear.

Camping at **county parks** requires a permit. These cost $1 per person per day (50¢ for children age thirteen through seventeen). Pick up permits from the County Department of Parks and Recreation, 25 Aupuni Street, Hilo, Hawaii, HI 96720 (961-8311) or at the Yano Center, Captain Cook, Hawaii, HI 96704 (323-3046). County permits are issued for both tent and trailer camping, and can be obtained for up to two weeks at each park (one week during the summer).

Free **state parks** permits can be obtained through the State Department of Land and Natural Resources, Division of State Parks, 75 Aupuni Street, Hilo, Hawaii, HI 96721-0936 (961-7200). Maximum stay at each park is five days. For information on cabin rentals and camping in Volcanoes National Park, see the individual listings in the "Beaches and Parks" section in this chapter.

Hilo Hawaii Sales and Surplus (284 Keawe Street, Hilo; 935-6398) and **Honsport** (111 East Puainako, Hilo; 959-5816) sell camping equipment. **Pacific United Rent-All** (1080 Kilauea Avenue, Hilo; 935-2974) rents tents, backpacks, sleeping bags, stoves, coolers, and other camping equipment.

Travel Camp (1266 Kamehameha Avenue, Hilo; 935-7406) rents campers by the week.

SKIN DIVING

Gold Coast Divers (King Kamehameha Hotel, Kailua; 329-1328) rents and sells equipment. For information on skin diving in Kona, see the section on "Skin Diving the Gold Coast" in this chapter.

SURFING AND WINDSURFING

Orchid Land Surfboards (832 Kilauea Avenue, Hilo; 935-1533) rents and sells surfboards. **West Hawaii Sailboards** (329-3669) rents both surfboards and sailboards. **Ocean Sports Hawaii** (Sheraton Royal Waikoloa Hotel; 885-5555) rents sailboards and offers lessons.

FISHING

The waters off the Kona Coast are some of the finest fishing grounds in the world, particularly for marlin. Many charter boats operate out of Kailua Bay; check the phone book for names or simply walk along the pier and inquire. **Kona Charter Skippers' Association** (329-3600) represents one of the larger outfits. Located on Alii Drive across the street from the King Kamehameha Hotel, they sponsor daily charters for marlin, yellowfin tuna, skipjack, and *mahimahi*. Using boats twenty-six to fifty feet in length, they charge $85 per person for a half day or $125 for a full day.

OTHER SPORTS

GOLF

Country Club (Hilo; 935-7388), **Hamakua Country Club** (Honokaa; 775-7244), **Hilo Municipal Golf Course** (Hilo; 959-7711), **Keauhou Kona Country Club** (Keauhou; 322-2595), **Mauna Kea Beach Golf Course** (Kawaihae; 882-7222), **Seamountain Golf Course** (Punaluu; 928-6222), **Volcano Golf and Country Club** (Volcanoes National Park; 967-7331), **Waikoloa Village Golf Course** (Waikoloa; 883-9621), **Waikoloa Sheraton Royal Golf Course** (Waikoloa; 885-6789), and **Mauna Lani Golf Course** (Kalahuipuaa; 885-6655) are the major golf centers.

SAILING AND PARA-SAILING

Sailing along the Kona Coast is a popular sport. Several companies offer sailing tours lasting from a few hours to several days. Another sport that's gaining increased notoriety is para-sailing, in which you're strapped to a parachute that's towed aloft by a motorboat. For information contact **Kona Water Sports, Inc.** (Kailua; 329-1593).

TENNIS

Call the **County Department of Parks and Recreation** (961-8311) for information on public courts; contact the **Hawaii Visitors Bureau** (961-5797 or 329-7787) for information concerning private courts.

WHALE-WATCHING

Between November and May, when about 400 humpback whales inhabit Hawaiian waters, a popular spectator sport is spotting whales in the channels around the islands.

SKIING

See the "Ski Hawaii" section in this chapter.

Beaches and Parks
(Plus Camping, Swimming, Snorkeling, Surfing, Fishing)

HILO BEACHES AND PARKS

Kalakaua Park—Located on the corner of busy Kinoole Street and Waianuenue Avenue, this pretty little park has a grand old banyan tree and a pleasant picnic area.

Reed's Bay Beach Park—Reed's Bay, a banyan-lined cove at the end of Banyan Drive, is a marvelous picnic spot. The bay is actually an arm of Hilo Bay, but unlike the larger body of water, Reed's Bay offers excellent swimming in smooth water.

Onekahakaha, Kealoha, and Leleiwi County Parks—None of these three parks have sand beaches, but all possess lava pools or other shallow places for swimming. They also have grassy plots and picnic areas, plus restrooms and showers. Both tent and trailer camping are allowed at Onekahakaha and Kealoha. (County permits are required.)

If you fish along these shores, chances are good you'll net *papio*, threadfin, mountain bass, mullet, big-eyed scad, mackerel scad, milkfish, bonefish, or goatfish.

All three parks are within five miles of Hilo, east along Kalanianaole Avenue.

Richardson's Beach (★)—This black-sand beach, on Hilo Bay's south shore, is without doubt the finest beach in the area. From here you can see the entire sweep of Hilo Bay, with Mauna Kea hulking in the background. Palm and ironwood trees fringe the beach, while a lava outcropping protects swimmers.

Facilities: **Richardson Ocean Center** (935-3830), an oceanographic museum, is located here. Free admission. Restaurants and markets lie about four miles away in Hilo.

Camping: Unofficial camping.

Swimming: Excellent. Good bodysurfing also.

Snorkeling: Good in protected areas.

Surfing: One of the best spots around Hilo. Winter break with right slides. Mornings and evenings are the prime times, but at all times beware of currents and riptides.

Fishing: Common catches include *papio*, threadfin, mountain bass, mullet, big-eyed scad, mackerel scad, milkfish, bonefish, and goatfish.

Getting there: Take Kalanianaole Avenue to within a quarter-mile of where the paved road ends; watch for the sign to Richardson Ocean Center. The beach is behind and to the right of the Center.

VOLCANOES NATIONAL PARK AND PUNA AREA BEACHES AND PARKS

Kipuka Nene—Easily accessible by paved road, this windswept campsite nevertheless offers considerable privacy. Tourists use the road less than most other thoroughfares in Volcanoes National Park, and the park remains relatively secluded. It's surrounded by a forest of dead trees and backdropped by Mauna Loa.

Facilities: Picnic area, water tank, and pit toilets. About ten miles back are a restaurant and information booth in the park center.

Camping: Tent and trailer camping. No permit is required, but there is a seven-day limit.

Getting there: Once in Volcanoes National Park, take Chain of Craters Road south from Crater Rim Road. Turn right onto Hilina Pali Road and follow it for five miles until Kipuka Nene appears on the left.

Namakani Paio—Situated in a lovely eucalyptus grove at the southern end of Volcanoes National Park, this campground offers both outdoor and cabin camping.

Facilities: Picnic area, restrooms. You're several miles from the restaurant and information booth in the park center.

Camping: Tent and trailer camping. No permit required, but, as always, campers should note that there is a seven-day limit. Cabins are rented from the Volcano House (967-7321). Each cabin has one double and two single beds, plus an outdoor grill. No firewood, bedding, or cooking utensils are provided. The units rent for $16 a day for up to four people. Sheets, blankets, and towels rent for $5 per day per person, and there is a $10 key deposit.

Getting there: Namakani Paio is located on Route 11 about two miles west of park headquarters and thirty-one miles south of Hilo.

Kamoamoa Campground—Located near an ancient Hawaiian village in the Puna section of Volcanoes National Park, this campground sits astride a rugged, wave-whipped coastline. There are ruins to explore and an ample seaside lawn for picnicking.

Facilities: Picnic area, outhouses, running water. It's several miles to the cafe and market in Kalapana.

Camping: An excellent campground with about a half-dozen private campsites, each equipped with a picnic table and grill. No permit is required.

Swimming, Snorkeling, Surfing: None. The coast is far too rugged.

Fishing: Only Hawaiians living in Kalapana are permitted to fish these waters.

Getting there: Located on Chain of Craters Road about thirty miles south of Hilo, in Volcanoes National Park.

Isaac Hale Beach Park—This small park on the Puna coast is pretty but run-down. There's a patch of black sand here and some hot springs nearby. A boat landing ramp makes this a popular park with local people.

Facilities: Picnic area, restrooms, showers. Several miles down the road are the cafe and market in Kalapana.

Camping: Tent and trailer camping. County permit required. I much prefer nearby MacKenzie State Park for overnighting.

Swimming: Okay when the sea remains calm.

Surfing: Summer and winter breaks.

Fishing: The most common catches here are *papio, moi,* mountain bass, *menpachi,* red bigeye, *ulua,* and goatfish.

Getting there: Located on Route 137 about two miles northeast of MacKenzie State Park.

MacKenzie State Park—This beautiful park lies in an ironwood grove along a rocky coastline. King's Highway, an ancient Hawaiian trail, bisects the area.

Facilities: Picnic area and restrooms. It's several miles to the cafe and market in Kalapana.

Camping: Tent camping; a state permit is required.

Swimming, Snorkeling, Surfing: None; a sea cliff borders the park.

Fishing: Good shore fishing.

Getting there: On Route 137 near the village of Opihikao.

Kaimu County Beach Park—This narrow swath of black sand is crowded with coconut trees. The palms run right to the water's edge, adding to the spectacular scenery along this crescent-shaped beach.

Facilities: Picnic area. There's a snack bar nearby.

Camping: None.

Swimming and Snorkeling: Extremely dangerous.

Surfing: Summer and winter breaks, right and left sides.

Fishing: For goatfish, *ulua,* red bigeye, *menpachi,* mountain bass, threadfin, and *papio.*

Getting there: Located on Route 13 about thirty miles south of Hilo.

Harry K. Brown Beach Park—Located along Kalapana black-sand beach, this county park is rich in history. The nearby *heiau* was reputedly built by a wizard. Even the boulders, some now arranged as picnic furniture, have legendary significance.

The park features a large grassy plot shaded (or rain-protected) by *hala* and palm trees.

Facilities: Picnic area, restrooms, showers, electricity, with a market and cafe nearby.

Camping: Tents and trailers allowed; county permit required.

Swimming: There's a rock pool near the beach; ocean swimming is okay when the sea is calm.

Surfing: Summer and winter breaks near a dangerous reef.

Fishing: Common catches include mountain bass, *papio,* threadfin, *menpachi,* red bigeye, *ulua,* and goatfish.

Getting there: Located on Route 13 about thirty miles south of Hilo.

KAU AREA BEACHES AND PARKS

Punaluu Beach Park—A black-sand beach fringed with palms and bordered by a breathtaking lagoon, this area, unfortunately, is regularly assaulted by tour buses. Still, it's a place of awesome beauty, one I would not recommend bypassing.

For more privacy, you can always check out **Ninole Cove,** a short walk from Punaluu. This attractive area has a tiny beach, grassy area, and lagoon.

Facilities: Picnic area, restrooms, showers, and electricity. There's a restaurant nearby, with a museum and tourist complex on the premises.

Camping: Tents and trailers are allowed; county permit required.

Swimming: With caution.

Snorkeling: Mediocre.

Surfing: Short ride over a shallow reef. Right slide.

Fishing: Principal catches are red bigeye, *menpachi, ulua,* and *papio.*

Getting there: Located about a mile off Route 11, eight miles north of Naalehu.

Whittington Beach Park—This pretty little park features a small patch of lawn dotted with coconut, *hala,* and ironwood trees. It's set on a lava-rimmed shoreline near the cement skeleton of a former sugar wharf. There are some marvelous tidepools here.

Facilities: Picnic area, restrooms, showers, and electricity. It's three miles to the markets and restaurants in Naalehu.

Camping: Both tent and trailer camping are allowed; county permit required.

Swimming: Access to the water over the sharp lava rocks is pretty rough on the feet. Once you're in, the water's fine.

Snorkeling: Very good.

Surfing: Summer break; left slide.

Fishing: Mullet, *menpachi*, red bigeye, *ulua*, and *papio* are the most frequent species caught.

Getting there: Across from the abandoned sugar mill on Route 11, three miles north of Naalehu.

HAMAKUA COAST AREA BEACHES AND PARKS

Kolekole Beach Park—Located at the mouth of a wide gulch lush with tropical vegetation, this comfortable park has a large and pleasant grassy area. A stream and waterfall tumble through the park down to the rocky, surf-torn shore.

Facilities: Picnic area, restrooms, showers, electricity. Five miles to both markets and restaurants in Honomu.

Camping: Tent and trailer. County permit required.

Swimming: Okay in the stream, but the ocean here is forbiddingly rough.

Fishing: Threadfin, *menpachi, papio, ulua,* and mountain bass are among the principal catches you can hope to reel in.

Getting there: Located just off Route 19 about fifteen miles north of Hilo.

Laupahoehoe Beach Park—Set on a low-lying peninsula which was inundated by the 1946 tidal wave, this hauntingly beautiful park is still lashed by heavy surf. A precipitous *pali* and a lava-strewn shoreline surround the area.

Facilities: Picnic area, restrooms, showers, and electricity. It's at least fifteen miles to any restaurants or markets in Honokaa, so bring a lunch.

Camping: Tent and trailer camping permitted. County permit required.

Swimming, Snorkeling, Surfing: Extremely dangerous, repeat, extremely dangerous.

Fishing: Common catches are mountain bass, *ulua, papio, menpachi,* and *moi.*

Getting there: One mile off Route 19 down a well-marked twisting road, about twenty-seven miles north of Hilo.

Kalopa State Park—A wooded retreat set in the mountains above the Hamakua Coast, this park has both untouched expanses ripe for exploring and several beautifully landscaped acres. It's a great place for hiking or just for escaping.

Facilities: Picnic area, restrooms, showers, cabins. About five miles to markets and restaurants in Honokaa.

Camping: Tent camping allowed with a state permit. Cabins are also available; call 961-7200 for reservations.

Getting there: Take Route 19 southeast from Honokaa for about three miles. A well-marked paved road leads from the highway another two miles to the park.

SADDLE ROAD AREA PARKS

Mauna Kea State Park— Situated on the tableland between Mauna Kea and Mauna Loa, this is an excellent base camp for climbing either mountain. The cabins here are also convenient for skiers headed up to Mauna Kea. With its stunning mountain views, sparse vegetation, and chilly weather, this rarefied playground hardly seems like Hawaii. For remoteness and seclusion, you can't choose a better spot. To be sure you fully enjoy it, dress warmly.

Facilities: Picnic area, restrooms, cabins. You'll need to go back thirty-five miles to the restaurants and markets of Hilo if you need any supplies, so plan ahead.

Camping: No tents or trailers allowed. The cabins can be rented from the Division of State Parks, 75 Aupuni Street, Hilo, Hawaii, HI 96720 (961-7200). The individual cabins, each accommodating up to six people, have two bedrooms, bath, kitchenette, and either a fireplace or electric heater. Personally, I think a fireplace is more romantic, but an electric heater is certainly less hassle. Cabins have loads of cooking utensils and sufficient bedding. Rates are on a sliding scale from $10 single, $14 double, to $30 for six. There are also four-plex cabinettes which rent for $8 single, $12 double, on up to $28 for eight people. (Kids under 12 are half-price.) These aren't nearly as nice as the individual cabins. They are one-bedroom units crowded with eight bunks; cooking is done in a community dining and recreation area next door.

Getting there: Located on the Saddle Road about thirty-five miles west of Hilo.

KAILUA-KONA AREA BEACHES AND PARKS

Hale Halawai—This small oceanfront park has an activities pavilion but no beach. Its central location in Kailua does make the park a perfect place to watch the sunset, though. Fringed with coconut trees, it's situated near the intersection of Alii Drive and Hualalai Road.

Old Airport Beach (★)—This white-sand beach parallels Kailua's former landing strip, extending for a half-mile along a lava-crusted shore. Very popular with Kailuans, this is a conveniently located spot for catching some rays.

Facilities: Picnic area, restrooms, showers. You can walk to the Kailua markets and restaurants less than a half-mile away.

Camping: Unofficial camping is common north of the runway.

Swimming: Poor. Shallow, wih rocky bottom.

Snorkeling: See the "Skin Diving the Gold Coast" section in this chapter.

Fishing: The principal catches are threadfin, big-eyed scad, bonefish, *papio*, and especially mullet.

Getting there: Located just a few hundred yards north of the King Kamehameha Hotel in Kailua. (Text continued on page 96.)

Skin Diving the Gold Coast

Hawaii's Kona Coast offers some of the world's most spectacular skin and scuba diving. All along this western shoreline lie magnificent submerged caves, lava flows, cliffs, and coral reefs.

Protected from prevailing trade winds by Mauna Kea and Mauna Loa, Kona enjoys the gentlest conditions. Usually the weather is sunny, the water clear, and the surf mild. It's small wonder, then, that adventurers travel from all over the world to explore Kona's underwater world.

This brief description of the best skin diving spots, with a list of shops that provide equipment and tours, will lead you to the water's edge. For more detailed information, just drop by one of the area's dive shops.

KAILUA-KONA AREA SKIN DIVING SPOTS

Kamakahonu Beach, the sand patch next to Kailua's King Kamehameha Hotel, is a crowded but conveniently located dive site. There are corals and many species of fish here, but watch out for heavy boat traffic along the nearby wharf. **Hale Halawai,** an oceanfront park in Kailua, has good snorkeling off its rocky beach. Nearby, off **Huggo's** restaurant, the underwater viewing is great, especially at night, when huge manta rays wing through here.

Old Airport Beach, just a stone's skip north of town, affords excellent diving all along its length. The entry is rocky, but once in, you'll find the waters spectacular. Many glass-bottom boats tour this area.

Honokohau Beach has some good spots south of the small-boat harbor. Stay away from the harbor itself, though; sharks are frequent.

Disappearing Sands Beach, several miles south of Kailua, offers some good spots around the rocks bordering the beach. But it's usually very crowded, so you might want to disappear yourself, to another beach.

Kahaluu Beach Park, a good place for beginners, abounds with tropical fish. There's also good diving off the **Kona Surf Hotel** at the south end of Alii Drive.

NORTH KONA AND KOHALA AREA SKIN DIVING SPOTS

Anaehoomalu Beach is good for beginners, but it lacks the scenic

diversity of other areas.
There's good diving at
the end of the road leading
to **Puako,** but it's a rocky entry.
"69" Beach (or **Waialea Bay**)
features excellent underwater op-
ortunities when the surf is mild.
Hapuna Beach State Park has an area
that abounds in coral and fish near the
rocks and cliffs at the end of the beach.
Spencer Beach Park is filled with coral and
suits beginners and experts alike.

Mahukona Beach Park is an old shipping area
littered with underwater refuse which makes for great exploring. **Kapaa
Beach Park** offers good diving, but it has a rocky entrance and tricky
currents. **Keokea Beach Park,** an excellent spearfishing area, is often
plagued by wind and high surf.

SOUTH KONA AREA SKIN DIVING SPOTS

Napoopoo Beach Park is an excellent diving spot—so good, in fact,
that it draws diving tours and glass-bottom boats. The best diving is
across Kealakekua Bay near the Captain Cook Monument.

Keei Beach features a lot of coral and, reportedly, a sea grotto. At
Puuhonua o Honaunau Park, next to the City of Refuge, there's a rocky
entry to some marvelous diving areas. **Hookena Beach Park** offers some
good dive spots near the cliffs south of the beach. **Milolii** has some
excellent diving areas as well as fascinating tidepools.

DIVING TOURS AND EQUIPMENT

The following shops rent and sell diving equipment or sponsor
diving tours: **Gold Coast Divers** (King Kamehameha Hotel, Kailua;
329-1328), **Jack's Diving Locker** (Kona Inn Shopping Center; 329-7585),
and **Fair Wind** (Keauhou Bay; 322-2788).

Honokohau Beach (★)— This is Kailua's nude beach. Folks come for miles to soak up the sun on this long narrow beach. Bordered by a lagoon, backdropped by distant mountains, protected by a shallow reef, and highly recommended for the adventurous.

Facilities: Zilch. It's three miles to the many markets and restaurants in Kailua.

Camping: A prime area for unofficial camping.

Swimming: Well-protected, but very shallow.

Snorkeling: See the "Skin Diving the Gold Coast" section in this chapter.

Fishing: Mullet, threadfin, big-eyed scad, bonefish, and *papio* are commonly caught. Good luck.

Getting there: Take Route 19 a couple miles north from Kailua. Turn onto the road to Honokohau Small Boat Harbor. From the north side of the harbor, walk about 600 yards farther north to the beach.

Disappearing Sands Beach—A small strand studded with volcanic rocks, this spot is also called **Magic Sands.** It seems that the white sand periodically washes away, exposing a lava shoreline. When still carpeted with sand, this is a very popular and crowded place.

Facilities: Restrooms and showers, with markets and restaurants nearby.

Camping: None.

Swimming: Good. Also a favorite area for bodysurfing.

Snorkeling: See the "Skin Diving the Gold Coast" section in this chapter.

Surfing: Principally bodysurfing here. The best surfing spot in Kona is just north of here at **Banyans,** with breaks year-round over a shallow reef. Right and left slides.

Fishing: Major catches include mullet, threadfin, big-eyed scad, bonefish, and *papio.*

Getting there: Located on Alii Drive four miles south of Kailua.

Kahaluu Beach Park—Set along the south shore of Kahaluu Bay, this county park is fringed with palm trees. The salt-and-pepper beach is small and often crowded.

Facilities: Picnic areas, showers, restrooms, plus a basketball court. A small market and restaurants are next door at the Keauhou Beach Hotel.

Camping: None.

Swimming: Excellent; the cove is partially protected by outlying rocks.

Snorkeling: See the "Skin Diving the Gold Coast" section in this chapter.

Fishing: For mullet, threadfin, big-eyed scad, bonefish, and *papio.*

Getting there: Located on Alii Drive five miles south of Kailua.

NORTH KONA AND KOHALA AREA BEACHES AND PARKS

Anaehoomalu Beach—An enchanting area, this is one of the island's most beautiful beaches. There are palm trees, a luxurious lagoon and a long crescent of white sand. Turn from the sea and take in the gorgeous mountain scenery. Very popular; often crowded; fronted by a major resort complex.

Facilities: Picnic tables, restrooms, showers. Restaurants available in the adjacent Sheraton Royal Waikoloa Hotel.

Camping: None.

Swimming: Excellent along this partially protected shore.

Snorkeling: See the "Skin Diving the Gold Coast" section in this chapter.

Fishing: Mullet, threadfin, big-eyed scad, bonefish, and *papio* are among the usual catches here.

Getting there: Located a half-mile off Route 19, about twenty-five miles north of Kailua.

"69" Beach or Waialea Bay (★)—No, it's not what you might think. This lovely beach is named for a nearby highway marker rather than for licentious beach parties. The white-sand shoreline extends several hundred yards along a rocky cove. Despite houses nearby, the spot is fairly secluded: fallen *kiawe* trees along the beachfront provide tiny hideaways.

Facilities: None. Three miles to market and restaurant in Kawaihae.

Camping: Unofficial camping.

Swimming: Very good, but exercise caution.

Snorkeling: See the "Skin Diving the Gold Coast" section in this chapter.

Surfing: Good breaks near the southwest end of the bay. Long paddle out.

Getting there: The name "69" derives from a highway mileage marker near the entrance to Hapuna Beach Park, three miles south of Kawaihae. From Route 19, turn into the park entrance. Then take the paved road which runs southwest from the park (between the beach and the A-frames). Go exactly six-tenths of a mile on this road and then turn right on a dirt road. When the road forks, after about one-tenth mile, go left. Follow this new road another tenth of a mile around to the beach.

Hapuna Beach State Park—Here's one of the state's prettiest parks. A well-tended lawn—studded with *hala,* coconut, and *kiawe* trees—

rolls down to a wide corridor of white sand. Maui's Haleakala crater looms across the water. This is a popular and generally very crowded place.

Facilities: Numerous picnic areas; restrooms, showers, electricity. Three miles to market and restaurant in Kawaihae.

Camping: Screened A-frame shelters, located on a rise above the beach, can be rented. These cottages are equipped with table, sleeping platforms, and electricity; they sleep up to four people. Bring your own bedding. Toilet and kitchen facilities are shared among all six A-frames. For reservations, contact the Division of State Parks, 75 Aupuni Street, Hilo, Hawaii, HI 96721-0936 (961-7200). No tent or trailer camping is allowed here.

Swimming: Currents prevalent; as always, exercise caution.

Snorkeling: See the "Skin Diving the Gold Coast" section in this chapter.

Fishing: You can hope to hook *papio*, red bigeye, mullet, threadfin, and *menpachi*.

Getting there: Located on Route 19, three miles south of Kawaihae.

Spencer Beach Park—Lacking the uncommon beauty of Anaehoomalu or Hapuna, this spacious park is still lovely. There's a wide swath of white sand, backed by a lawn and edged with *kiawe* and coconut trees. Very popular camping grounds.

Facilities: Picnic area, restrooms, showers, large pavilion, tennis courts, electricity. A market and restaurant are less than a mile away in Kawaihae.

Camping: Both tent and trailer camping are okay, but a county permit is required.

Swimming: Excellent.

Snorkeling: See the "Skin Diving the Gold Coast" section in this chapter.

Fishing: Common catches are *papio*, red bigeye, mullet, threadfin, and *menpachi*.

Getting there: Off Route 27 one mile south of Kawaihae.

Mahukona Beach Park—This now-abandoned harbor village and boat landing lies along a rocky windswept shore. The lawn is shaded with *kiawe* trees; there's no sandy beach here at all. Nicer areas lie to the south, but if you seek a site far from the frenzied crowd, this is a good retreat.

Facilities: Picnic area, restrooms, showers, electricity. About thirteen miles from restaurant and market in Kawaihae.

Camping: Tent and trailer. County permit required.

Swimming: Poor access from rocks.

Snorkeling: See the "Skin Diving the Gold Coast" section in this chapter.

Fishing: Frequent catches include threadfin, mullet, *menpachi, papio,* and red bigeye.

Getting there: Off Route 27 about thirteen miles north of Kawaihae.

Kapaa Beach Park—Besides a spectacular view of Maui, this rocky, wind-plagued park has little to offer. It does have a miniature cove bounded by *kiawe* trees, but lacks any sand, which is sometimes nice to have on a beach.

Facilities: Picnic area, restrooms. No drinking water. About fourteen miles to market and restaurant in Kawaihae.

Camping: Tents and trailers are allowed, but the terrain is very rocky for tent camping. County permit required.

Swimming: Poor access over rocks.

Snorkeling: See the "Skin Diving the Gold Coast" section in this chapter.

Fishing: At last, a sport benefiting from all those rocks! Stand out there and try for threadfin, mullet, red bigeye, *papio,* and *menpachi.*

Getting there: Off Route 27 about fourteen miles north of Kawaihae.

Keokea Beach Park—Seclusion is the password to this beautiful little park with its cliff-rimmed cove and tiered lawn fringed by *hala* and palm trees. Set way out on the Kohala peninsula, this retreat receives very heavy rainfall.

Facilities: Picnic area, restrooms, showers, electricity. Four miles to restaurants and markets in Hawi.

Camping: Tent and trailer. County permit required.

Swimming: Only with extreme caution.

Snorkeling: See the "Skin Diving the Gold Coast" section in this chapter.

Fishing: Mullet, *papio,* red bigeye, threadfin, and *menpachi* are the main catches here.

Getting there: Take Route 27 about six miles past Hawi. Turn at the sign and follow the winding road one mile.

SOUTH KONA AREA BEACHES AND PARKS

Napoopoo Beach Park—Many small boats moor at this black-rock beach on Kealakekua Bay. Set amidst cliffs which rim the harbor, it's a charming spot. Unfortunately it draws caravans of tour buses on their way to the nearby **Hikiau Heiau** and **Captain Cook Monument.**

Facilities: Picnic area, restrooms, showers. Try the soda stand just up from the beach. Two miles to the markets and restaurants in the town of Captain Cook.

Camping: None.

Swimming: Very good.

Snorkeling: See the "Skin Diving the Gold Coast" section in this chapter.

Surfing: There are several breaks here. In the bay there are good-sized summer breaks. Just north, at "Ins and Outs," the surf breaks year-round.

Fishing: A good locale for mullet, *moi,* bonefish, *papio,* and big-eyed scad.

Getting there: Take Route 11 south from Kailua twelve miles to the town of Captain Cook. Then turn onto the road leading two miles down to Kealakekua Bay.

Keei Beach (★) — This salt-and-pepper beach extends for a quarter mile along a lava-studded shoreline. Situated next to the creaky village of Keei, the beach offers marvelous views of Kealakekua Bay. It is far enough from the tourist area, however, that you'll probably encounter only local people along this hidden beach. What a pity — no white shoes and polyester here!

Facilities: None. Both markets and restaurants will be found several miles away in the town of Captain Cook.

Camping: You could pitch a tent, but only with difficulty along this narrow strand.

Swimming: The very shallow water makes swimming safe, but limited.

Snorkeling: See the "Skin Diving the Gold Coast" section in this chapter.

Fishing: Try here for mullet, threadfin, bonefish, *papio* and big-eyed scad.

Getting there: Take Route 11 to Captain Cook, then follow the road down to Kealakekua Bay. At the botton of the hill, go left toward the City of Refuge National Historical Park. Take this road a half-mile, then turn right onto a lava-bed road. Now follow this road another half-mile to the beach.

Puuhonua o Honaunau Park — This park, part of the City of Refuge National Historical Park, is an excellent picnic spot when you're sight-seeing. Besides the picnic tables and other facilities, enjoy the sandy sunbathing area. There's no beach, but the tidepools along the lava shoreline are fascinating. No camping, either.

Located just south of the City of Refuge Park.

Hookena Beach Park—Popular with adventurous travelers, this is a wide, black-sand beach, bordered by sheer rock walls. Coconut trees abound along this lovely strand, and there's a great view of the South Kona coast.

Facilities: Picnic area, restrooms, showers. Unpotable water. A small market is four miles away in Kealia.

Camping: None.

Swimming: Very good; bodysurfing also.

Snorkeling: See the "Skin Diving the Gold Coast" section in this chapter.

Fishing: Mullet, threadfin, bonefish, *papio,* and big-eyed scad are among the most common catches.

Getting there: Take Route 11 south from Kailua for about twenty-one miles to Hookena. Turn onto the paved road at the marker and follow it two miles to the park.

Milolii (★)—Even if you don't feel like a character from Somerset Maugham, you may think you're amid the setting for one of his tropical stories. This still-thriving fishing village is vintage South Seas, from tumbledown shacks to fishing nets drying in the sun. There are patches of beach near the village, but the most splendid resources are the tidepools, some of the most beautiful I've ever seen.

Facilities: Outhouse, picnic area, swings, and basketball court, but no running water. There's a small market up the street in town.

Camping: Permitted only in the seaside parking lot. Get there early and you can park a tent beneath the ironwood trees with the sea washing in just below. County permit required.

Swimming: This area is fringed with reefs which create safe, but shallow, areas. Exercise extreme caution if you go beyond the reefs.

Snorkeling: See the "Skin Diving the Gold Coast" section in this chapter.

Fishing: A prime area for mullet, bonefish, *papio,* threadfin, and big-eyed scad.

Getting there: Take Route 11 south from Kailua for about thirty-three miles. Turn off onto a well-marked macadam road leading five miles down to the village.

Manuka State Park—This lovely botanic park, almost 2,000 feet above sea level, has a beautiful ocean view. The rolling terrain is planted with both native and imported trees and carpeted with grass.

Facilities: Picnic area, restrooms.

Camping: No tent and trailers allowed, but you can park your sleeping bag in the pavilion. A state permit is required.

Getting there: Located on Route 11 about forty-one miles south of Kailua.

Hiking

Of all the islands in the chain, Hawaii has the finest hiking trails. The reason? Quite simply, it's the Big Island's size. Larger than all the other islands combined and boasting the highest peaks, Hawaii offers the greatest diversity to explorers. Mauna Loa and Mauna Kea, each rising over 13,000 feet, provide rugged mountain climbing. To the north, the Kohala Mountains feature trails through dense tropical terrain and along awesome cliffs. In Volcanoes National Park, hikers can experience the challenge of walking through a lava wasteland and into the belly of an active volcano.

Along Hawaii's shoreline lie the remains of the Makahiki trail, a series of paths which once circled the entire island. Also known as the William Ellis trail, this ancient Hawaiian track was named after the Makahiki gods and then renamed for Ellis, the bold missionary who explored it in 1823. Today sections of the trail can still be walked, though much of it is destroyed. Of the remaining portions, some cross private land and others are unmarked. But with a topographic map and a pair of sturdy boots you can still follow in the tracks of the gods, and for that matter, in the tracks of William Ellis.

Hawaii's official hiking trails run through four areas: Volcanoes National Park, Kau Desert, Mauna Kea, and the Kohala Mountains. These are popular and well-defined trails, many of which are described below.

VOLCANOES NATIONAL PARK TRAILS

The most interesting and easily accessible trails lead through the **Kilauea Crater** area. The crater, two-and-one-half miles long and 4,000 feet above sea level, can be explored either by hiking along one extended trail or over several shorter connecting trails.

Crater Rim Trail (11.6 miles long) begins near park headquarters and encircles Kilauea Crater. An excellent introduction to the volcanoes, this lengthy loop trail passes steam vents, the Kau Desert, the fractured Southwest Rift area, and a fascinating fern forest. The views from atop the crater are spectacular.

Sulphur Banks Trail (0.3 mile) begins at park headquarters and parallels Crater Rim Road past steam vents and sulphur deposits.

Halemaumau Trail (3.1 miles) starts near Volcano House, then descends into Kilauea Crater. The trail crosses the crater floor and affords astonishing views down into steaming Halemaumau crater, then climbs back up to join Crater Rim Trail. This has got to be one of the park's finest hikes.

Kilauea Iki Trail (4.0 miles) loops from the Thurston Lava Tube parking lot down into Kilauea Iki crater and returns via Crater Rim Trail. Crossing the crater floor, the trail passes over a lava crust beneath which lies a brewing pool of molten rock. Step lightly. (Text continued on page 107.)

The New Travel

Travel today is becoming a personal art form. A destination no longer serves as just a place to relax: it's also a point of encounter, where experience runs feverish and reality unravels. To many, this new wave in travel customs is labeled "adventure travel" and involves trekking glaciers or sweeping along in a hang glider; to others, it connotes nothing more daring than a restful spell in a secluded resort. Actually, it's a state of mind, a willingness not only to accept but seek out the uncommon and unique.

Few places in the world are more conducive to this imaginative new travel than Hawaii. Several organizations in the islands cater specifically to people who want to add local customs and unusual adventures to their vacation itineraries.

The Nature Conservancy of Hawaii (1116 Smith Street, #201, Honolulu, HI 96817; 537-4508), a non-profit conservation organization, conducts four-day and week-long natural history tours of Maui and Molokai. Led by expert guides, small groups explore untrammeled beaches, rainforests, and an ancient bog. The tours provide a singular insight into the plant and animal life of the islands.

For ocean-bound adventure, **Exploration Cruise Lines** (800-426-0600) sponsors tours around the islands aboard a motor-driven catamaran. This 49-passenger boat, with full amenities, provides an opportunity to comb the coasts and explore the interiors of all six islands.

Pacific Quest (P.O. Box 205, Haleiwa, HI 96712; 638-8338) features six-day sailing excursions to Maui, Molokai, and Lanai aboard a 35-foot sloop. They also offer camping trips which include hiking and snorkeling opportunities.

More in the Outward Bound tradition, **Wilderness Hawaii** (P.O. Box 61692, Honolulu, HI 96822; 737-4697) outfits four-day and 21-day expeditions on the Big Island. Challenging your self-reliance and wilderness skills, they explore from sea level to the 13,677-foot peak of Mauna Loa, rappel down a 60-foot drop, and leave you alone in the outback for two days.

Three smaller outfits conduct hiking tours of three separate islands. On Hawaii, **Paradise Safaris** (Box A-D, Kailua-Kona, HI 96745; 329-9282) probes the Big Island's backcountry from Waipio Valley to the peak of Mauna Kea. Their day-long tours visit several points of interest aboard a 4-wheel-drive wagon.

Hike Maui (P.O. Box 10506, Lahaina, HI 96761; 879-5270) leads backpacking trips all around the Valley Isle. Ranging from several hours to many days in duration, these treks can be custom designed to your interests. On Kauai, **Local Boy Tours** (P.O. Box 3324, Lihue, HI 96766; 822-7919) organizes half-day and full-day hikes as well as camping trips.

When you're ready to take up the challenge of this new style of free-wheeling travel, check with these outfits. Or plan your own trip. To traditional tourists, Hawaii means souvenir shops and fast-food restaurants. But for those with spirit and imagination, it's a land of untracked beaches and ancient volcanoes waiting to be explored.

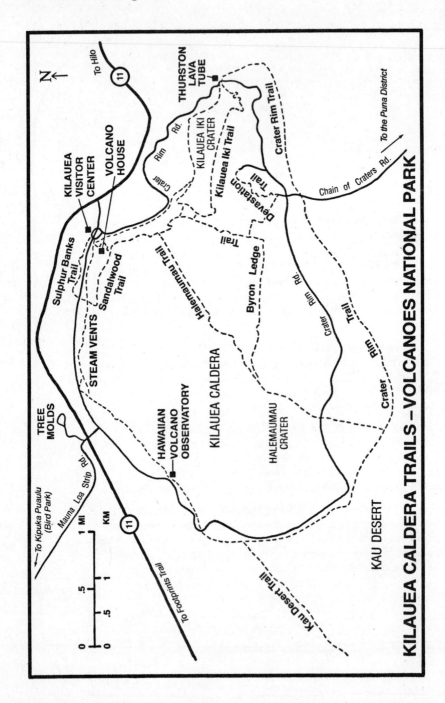

KILAUEA CALDERA TRAILS – VOLCANOES NATIONAL PARK

Sandalwood Trail (1.5 miles) loops from near the Volcano House past sandalwood and *ohia* trees and then along the side of Kilauea Crater.

Byron Ledge Trail (2.5 miles) branches off Halemaumau Trail, crosses the Kilauea caldera floor, and then climbs along Byron Ledge before rejoining Halemaumau. This makes an excellent connecting trail.

Ke Ala Kahiko (1.2 miles) begins near the Wahaula Visitor Center on the coast and passes sea cliffs, forest, and scattered remains of an ancient Hawaiian village.

Volcanoes National Park's premier hike is along **Mauna Loa Trail.** This tough eighteen-mile trek, requiring at least three days, leads to the top of the world's largest shield volcano. Cold-weather equipment and a sturdy constitution are absolute necessities for this challenging adventure.

Climbers usually hike seven miles the first day from the trailhead at the end of Mauna Loa Strip Road up to Red Hill. At this 10,035-foot way station there is a cabin with water, blankets, stove, lantern, and heater. A hearty eleven-mile trek the second day leads to another cabin inside Mokuaweoweo caldera, then to Mauna Loa's summit. The return trip takes one or two days, depending on how fast you want to come down.

Beware of altitude sickness and hypothermia (loss of body heat), and be sure to register at park headquarters before and after hiking. Purification tablets for the water and white gas for the stoves are also essential. Don't treat this as a casual jaunt; it's a real trek. Good planning will ensure your safety and enjoyment.

A dirt road, usually passable by passenger car, climbs from Saddle Road to an area near Mauna Loa summit. This alternative hiking route lacks the adventure but reduces the difficulty of a Mauna Loa ascent.

KAU DESERT TRAILS

From Volcanoes National Park's southern section several trails lead into the hot, arid Kau Desert. All are long, dusty trails offering solitude to the adventurous hiker.

Halape Trail (7.2 miles) begins at Kipuka Nene campground on Hilina Pali Road and rapidly drops 3,000 feet to a sand beach at Halape. There is also a shelter at Halape.

Kau Desert Trail (14.4 miles) branches off Crater Rim Trail and drops 2,000 feet en route to the lookout at the end of Hilina Pali Road. The shelter along the way, at Kipuka Pepeiau, provides a welcome resting place on this lengthy trek.

Mauna Iki Trail (8.8 miles) leads from Route 11 to Hilina Pali Road. The trail passes near Footprints Trail, where a sudden volcanic eruption in 1790 engulfed a Hawaiian army at war with Kamehameha.

MAUNA KEA TRAIL

This hike is not nearly as rigorous as the trek up Mauna Loa, but the scenery is just as stunning. A road leads off Saddle Road for nine miles to

(Text continued on page 110.)

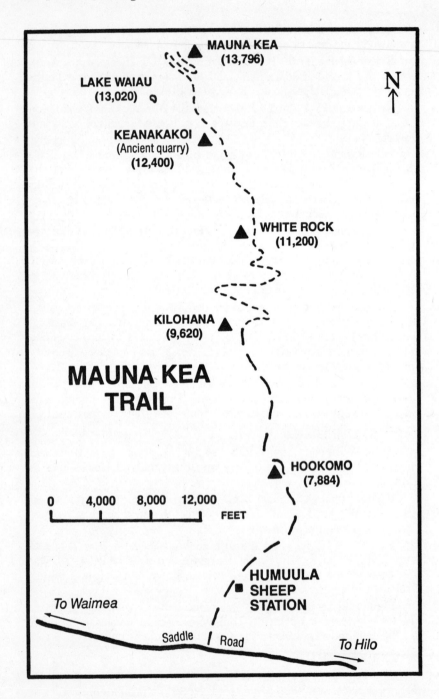

MAUNA KEA
(13,796)

LAKE WAIAU
(13,020)

KEANAKAKOI
(Ancient quarry)
(12,400)

WHITE ROCK
(11,200)

KILOHANA
(9,620)

**MAUNA KEA
TRAIL**

HOOKOMO
(7,884)

| 0 | 4,000 | 8,000 | 12,000 |
| | | | FEET |

HUMUULA
SHEEP
STATION

To Waimea

Saddle   Road   To Hilo

N

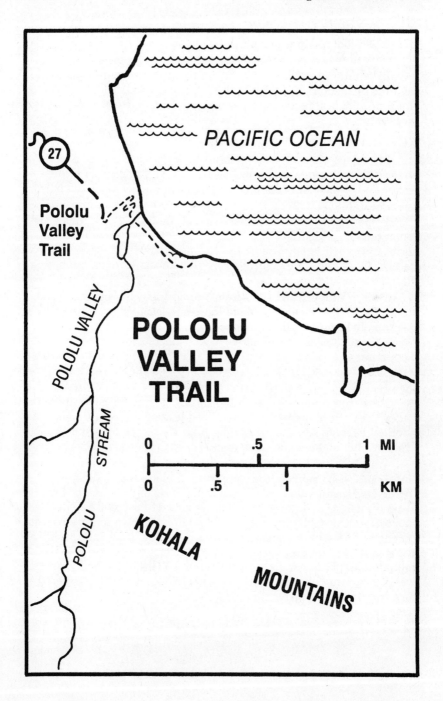

PACIFIC OCEAN

27

Pololu
Valley
Trail

POLOLU VALLEY

POLOLU STREAM

POLOLU

**POLOLU
VALLEY
TRAIL**

KOHALA

MOUNTAINS

| 0 | .5 | 1 MI |
| 0 | .5 | 1 | KM |

the trailhead at Kilohana. From this 9,620-foot elevation it is six miles to the 13,796-foot summit. Begin early and plan to make the hike in one day since no camping is permitted along the way.

In addition to vistas as breathtaking as the altitude, Mauna Kea features the nation's highest lake, Lake Waiau, at 13,020 feet. From atop the state's highest peak, you'll have a spectacular view of Maui's Haleakala crater.

KOHALA MOUNTAIN TRAILS

Stretching along Kohala peninsula's northeast coast are a series of sheer cliffs and wide valleys rivaling Kauai's Na Pali coast in beauty. At either end of this rainswept *pali* are lush, still valleys which can only be reached by hiking trails.

Pololu Valley Trail (0.5 mile) descends from the Pololu Valley lookout at the end of Route 27 to the valley floor 300 feet below. From here a series of trails leading through the Kohala Mountains begins. Unfortunately, these trails are controlled by the Kohala Corporation and are closed to hikers.

Waipio Valley Trail begins from Waipio Valley lookout at the end of Route 24. Waipio is comparable to Kauai's Kalalau Valley: a broad, lush, awesomely beautiful valley ribboned with waterfalls and rich in history. Here Kamehameha the Great received the blessing of his war god. Thousands of Hawaiians once populated this bountiful region, planting it with sugar cane and taro. But today only a few families brave the frequent floods and tidal waves which strike Waipio with devastating force.

From the trailhead, a jeep trail drops steeply for one mile to the valley floor. Here the trail joins one road leading up into the valley and another heading to the beach. The high road goes toward 1,000-foot Hiilawe Falls and to a now-abandoned Peace Corps training camp.

Waipio Valley is ripe for exploring, but if you want to leave civilization completely behind, continue instead along the **Waimanu Valley Trail.** This seven-mile track begins at the base of the cliff which marks Waipio's northwest border. It climbs sharply up the 1,200-foot rock face in a series of switchbacks, then continues up and down across numerous gulches, and finally descends into Waimanu Valley. This exotic place, half the size of Waipio Valley, is equally as lush. Here, in addition to wild pigs, mountain apple trees, and ancient ruins, you'll find naturally running water (requiring purification) and numerous beachfront campsites. You may never want to leave.

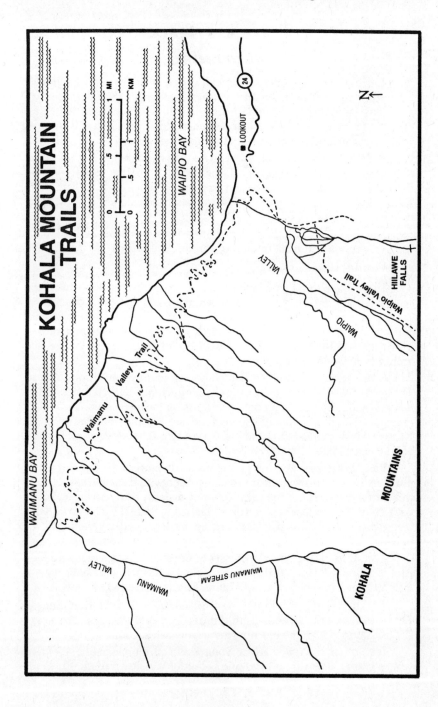

KOHALA MOUNTAIN TRAILS

WAIPIO BAY

WAIMANU BAY

LOOKOUT

24

N

HIILAWE FALLS

Waipio Valley Trail

WAIPIO VALLEY

Waimanu Valley Trail

WAIMANU VALLEY

WAIMANU STREAM

KOHALA MOUNTAINS

MI
1
.5
0

KM
1
.5
0

Travelers' Tracks
Sightseeing

Touring the Big Island could well prove to be the most fascinating adventure in all Hawaii. With its varied landscape, shimmering coast, and regal mountains, the island unveils countless scenes of matchless beauty. There is more country here than could be explored in a lifetime, so it seems absurd to reduce a sightseeing expedition to a matter of days.

But if your time is limited, you'll need to be more practical, so allow about five days to at least get the flavor of the island. This permits one day each touring Hilo, the Hamakua Coast and Waimea, Kohala and North Kona, South Kona and Kau, and Volcanoes National Park and the Puna district.

Starting with Hilo, then proceeding counterclockwise, I'll detail the major sights along the 300-mile route around the island.

HILO

There's one thing you'll rarely miss in this tropical city—rain. Hilo gets about 140 inches a year. The Chamber of Commerce will claim it rains mostly at night, but don't be deceived. It's almost as likely to be dark and wet at midday. There is a good side to all this bothersome moisture— it transforms Hilo into an exotic city crowded with tropical foliage, the orchid capital of America.

A visit to one of the city's many flower nurseries is an absolute must. These gardens—which grow orchids, anthuriums, and countless other flowers—usually charge a nominal admission for brief tours. Two that I recently visited and highly recommend are **Orchids of Hawaii** (2801 Kilauea Avenue; 959-3581) and **Nani Mau Gardens** (several miles south of Hilo near Route 11 at 421 Makalika; 959-9442).

Banyan Drive is another green thumb delight. Sweeping past Hilo's plushest hotels, this waterfront road is shaded with banyan trees. Next to this verdant arcade are the **Liliuokalani Gardens,** thirty acres exploding with color. These Japanese gardens, featuring both Hawaiian and Asian trees, are dotted with pagodas, arched bridges, and a ceremonial tea house.

A short footbridge nearby crosses to **Coconut Island,** a palm-studded islet in Hilo Bay. This old Hawaiian sanctuary presents a dramatic view of **Hilo Bay** and, on a clear day, of **Mauna Kea** and **Mauna Loa** as well.

A stone's skip across from the island, at **Suisan Fish Market** (Banyan Drive and Lihiwai Street), fishing boats land their catches. Try to get there around 7:30 in the morning for a lively fish auction.

It's not far to **Wailoa River State Park** (off Kamehameha Avenue), where grassy picnic areas surround beautiful **Waiakea Fishpond.** Across one of the pond's arching bridges, at **Wailoa Visitor Center** (961-7360), there are cultural exhibits and an information desk.

In downtown Hilo, the **Lyman Mission House** (276 Haili Street; 935-5021) is a fascinating example of a nineteenth-century missionary home. Built in 1839, the house is furnished with elegant period pieces which create a sense of this bygone era. A small admission fee buys a guided tour of the parsonage plus a look through the adjoining Hawaiian history museum.

Fronting the library on nearby Waianuenue Avenue are the **Naha** and **Pinao Stones.** According to legend, whoever moved the massive Naha Stone would rule all the islands. Kamehameha overturned the boulder while still a youth, then grew to become Hawaii's first king.

Continue up Waianuenue to **Rainbow Falls,** a foaming cascade in Wailuku River State Park. It's another two miles to **Boiling Pots,** where a series of falls pours turbulently into circular lava pools. The rushing water, spilling down from Mauna Kea, bubbles up through the lava and boils over into the next pool.

Kaumana Drive, branching off Waianuenue Avenue, leads five miles out of town to **Kaumana Caves.** A stone stairway leads from the roadside down to two fern-choked lava tubes, formed during Mauna Loa's devastating 1881 eruption. Explore the lower tube, but avoid the other—it's dangerous.

FROM HILO TO WAIMEA VIA THE HAMAKUA COAST

Route 19 leads north from Hilo along the rainy, windswept Hamakua Coast. Planted in sugar and teeming with exotic plant life, this elevated coastline is as lushly overgrown as Hilo. Several miles outside town, follow the signs to the **scenic drive.** This old coast road winds past cane fields and shantytowns before rejoining the main highway. Alexander palms line the road. Watch for Onomea Bay; there you'll see a sea arch that recently collapsed.

Back on the main road, you'll soon come to a turnoff heading inland to **Akaka Falls State Park.** Don't bypass it! A short nature trail leads past bamboo groves, ferns, *ti,* and orchids to Akaka Falls, which slide 420 feet down a sheer cliff face.

Countless gulches ribbon the landscape between Hilo and Honokaa. For a unique tour, take the road from Hakalau which winds down to **Hakalau Gulch** (★). Literally choked with vegetation, this gorge extends to a small beach. Towering above are an old sugar mill, a collapsing trestle, and the highway bridge.

Another side road several miles north corkscrews down to **Laupa-hoehoe Point,** a hauntingly beautiful peninsula from which twenty-four students and teachers were swept by the 1946 tidal wave.

The plantation town of **Paauilo** offers a glimpse of vintage Hawaii: decaying storefronts, tinroof cottages, a sea-rusted sugar mill. Then it's on to Honokaa, the world center of macadamia nut growing. The **Hawaiian Holiday Macadamia Nut Factory** (775-7743) is open, but don't anticipate a wildly informative visit. This establishment concentrates more on selling macadamia products to tourists. I'd bypass the place and head out Route 24 to **Waipio Valley**. One mile wide and six long, this luxurious valley, sparsely populated today, once supported thousands of Hawaiians. Agriculturally bountiful, Waipio is also rich in history. Here in 1780 Kamehameha the Great acknowledged the war god who would propel him to victory.

Taro patches and tumbledown cottages still dot the island's largest valley. From the lookout point at road's end, a jeep trail drops sharply into Waipio. Explorers can hike down or ride the **Waipio Valley Shuttle** (775-7121). This hour-and-a-half jeep tour visits the black-sand beach, then travels several miles up into the valley for eye-boggling views of 1,200-foot Hiilawe Falls. At $15, it's a helluva bargain.

After returning to Honokaa, get back on Route 19. It rises onto the Waimea plateau, passing tangled cane fields and majestic eucalyptus trees. Covered with rolling grassland and bounded by towering mountains, **Waimea** (also called **Kamuela**) is cowboy country. Here the *paniolos,* Hawaiian cowboys, ride the range on one of the world's largest independently owned cattle ranches. About 50,000 cattle roam Parker Ranch's sprawling 250,000-acre domain. Founded by John Palmer Parker, an adventurous sailor who jumped ship in 1809, the Parker preserve extends from sea level to over 9,000 feet. The museum at **Parker Ranch Visitor Center** (885-7655; admission) presents a glorified family history. I found the museum's incongruous Duke Kahanamoku Room, depicting Hawaii's famous swimmer and surfer, far more stimulating.

A much finer display can be found at the **Kamuela Museum** (at the junction of Routes 19 and 250; 885-4724; admission). Founded by J. P. Parker's great-granddaughter, this private collection of everything from Royal Hawaiian artifacts to moon-flight relics is fascinating, if poorly organized.

For a splendid example of *koa* woodworking, visit **Imiola Congregational Church** on the east side of town. Built in 1857, this clapboard church, which can be toured for free, has an interior fashioned entirely from the native timber.

FROM WAIMEA TO KAILUA-KONA VIA KOHALA

Near the Kamuela Museum, Route 25 heads north through the **Kohala Mountains.** Rising to 3,564 feet, the road rolls through cactus-studded range country and offers startling views down steep volcanic slopes to the sea.

The road descends near the northern tip of Kohala peninsula to intersect Route 27 in **Hawi.** This old plantation town contains both rustic buildings and freshly painted houses in a picturesque setting.

As Route 27 travels east into Kapaau, it passes the original **Kamehameha Statue.** The more famous Honolulu monument is actually only a replica of this gilt figure. Crafted in Florence around 1879 by an American sculptor, the original disappeared at sea on its way to Hawaii but was later recovered and installed here.

Along this lush, rainy side of the peninsula are taro patches and pandanus forests. Past the **Kamehameha Rock** (a large boulder which the mighty conqueror reputedly carried from the sea), the road ends at **Pololu Valley Lookout.** The view here overlooking Pololu Valley extends along the monumental cliffs which guard Hawaii's north coast.

From this cul-de-sac you must backtrack to Hawi, then continue south on Route 27 along the parched Kawaihae coast. If time permits, take the turnoff to Upolu Airport to reach **Mookini Heiau,** one of the island's most important temples. This thirteenth-century holy place is reached by taking a left at the airport, then following the dirt road for a mile and a half. The **Birthplace of Kamehameha I** lies one-third mile (and two gates) farther west along the same road.

The main road continues on to **Lapakahi State Historical Park** (889-5566), where a reconstructed village provides a unique glimpse into ancient Hawaiian ways. This is definitely worth a leisurely look-see.

Just past the harbor town of **Kawaihae** rest the remains of two *heiaus,* **Mailekini** and **Puukohola.** Kamehameha built the impressive tripletiered Puukohola in 1791 after a prophet related that doing so would ensure his victory over rival islands. At the temple dedication, the ambitious chief aided the prophecy by treacherously slaying his principal enemy.

From here, Route 19 moves south past the luxurious **Mauna Kea Beach Hotel,** built by Laurance Rockefeller. In nearby Puako are some of the finest **petroglyphs** in all the islands. Take the side road to Puako. A well-marked trail near the road's end leads a half-mile inland past three sets of rock carvings. The first is just two hundred yards from the road; the second set, the best, is a few hundred yards farther; and the third lies near trail's end.

Between Puako and Kailua-Kona lies a broad swath of lava-crusted country. There are views of **Maui** to the north, **Mauna Kea** to the east, and **Hualalai** to the south. Also along this desolate stretch of road is a type of **graffiti** unique to the Big Island. Setting white coral atop black lava, and vice versa, ingenious residents have spelled out their names and messages.

The resort town of **Kailua** features hotels, restaurants, and more shopping malls per square mile than I have ever seen. This old fishing village and former haunt of Hawaiian royalty still retains some of its charm, however. If you tour **Kailua wharf** around 4 p.m., the fishing boats may be hauling freshly caught marlin onto the docks.

Hulihee Palace (329-1877), a small but elegant estate built in 1838, sits on Alii Drive in the middle of town. Today it's a museum housing royal Hawaiian relics. There's a small entrance fee.

Mokuaikaua Church, directly across the street, is the oldest church in the islands. The first missionaries anchored offshore in 1820 after sailing over 18,000 miles around Cape Horn from Boston. They built the imposing lava-and-coral structure in 1836. By the way, that churchyard tree with the weird salami-shaped fruit is a sausage tree from West Africa.

Almost everything in Kailua sits astride **Alii Drive,** a waterfront street which extends south from town for about five miles. Several miles from Kailua, this road passes **Disappearing Sands** (or **Magic Sands**) **Beach.** The lovely white sand here washes away periodically, then mysteriously reappears.

Farther along, on the rocky shore of Kahaluu Bay, is **St. Peter's Catholic Church.** This blue-and-white clapboard chapel, precariously perched on a lava foundation, is reputedly the world's second smallest church.

Just across the bay, at the Keauhou Beach Hotel (322-3441), are several interesting historical sites. Ask in the hotel lobby for a free map detailing the location of two *heiaus* and the **King's Pool.** Continue on to Keauhou Bay and its heavily overgrown **Birthplace of Kamehameha III.**

FROM HILO TO KAILUA VIA SADDLE ROAD

This alternate route across the island climbs from Hilo to an elevation of over 6,500 feet. While the eastern section is heavily wooded, most of the roadway passes through the lava wasteland which divides **Mauna Kea** and **Mauna Loa.** Here you will have the finest view of these mountains anywhere on the island. Roads branch from the Saddle Road toward both peaks (see the "Hiking" section in this chapter).

Mauna Kea State Park, with cabins and recreation area, lies about midway along the Saddle Road. Take the dirt road which goes behind the park several hundred yards to a **bird sanctuary.** Among the species you'll see is the *nene,* an extremely rare goose native to Hawaii.

Saddle Road continues past a U.S. military base, then descends through stands of eucalyptus into Waimea cattle country. Here you can pick up Route 190 south to Kailua. Passing through sparsely populated range country over 2,000 feet high, this road has sensational views of the **Kona Coast** and **Maui.** Near the rustic village of **Puuanahulu** stands **Puuwaawaa,** the island's largest cinder cone.

It's only eighty-seven miles from Hilo to Kailua by way of this interior shortcut. Before setting out, check your gas gauge—there are no service stations or stores enroute. And consult the car rental agency: some do not permit driving on Saddle Road.

FROM KAILUA TO SOUTH KONA AND KAU DISTRICT

Rather than heading directly south from Kailua on Route 11, why not drive through **Kona coffee country?** Just take Route 190 uphill from Kailua, then turn right onto Route 18. This winding road cuts through old Kona in the heart of the growing region—watch for orchards of small trees with shiny green leaves. Before the coast road was built, this was the main route. Today it's somewhat off the beaten track, passing through funky old country towns before rejoining Route 11.

This main route continues south along the western slopes of **Hualalai.** Near the town of Captain Cook, a side road leads to Kealakekua Bay. First it passes a **coffee mill** (328-2411). I don't know about you, but I'm a confirmed "caffiend," happily addicted to java for years. So it was mighty interesting to watch the potent stuff go from berry to bean to bag, with a few stops between. If you haven't tried Kona coffee, the only brew grown anywhere in the United States, this is the time.

In Kealakekua Bay, check out the reconstructed temple, **Hikiau Heiau,** where Captain James Cook once performed a Christian burial service for one of his crewmen. Cook himself had little time left to live. Shortly after the ceremony he was killed and possibly eaten by natives who had originally welcomed him as a god. A white obelisk, the **Captain Cook Monument,** rises across the bay where the famous mariner fell in 1779. The cliffs rising behind this marker are honeycombed with **Hawaiian burial caves.**

City of Refuge National Historical Park (328-2288) sits four miles south of Kealakekua Bay. This ancient holy ground, known to Hawaiians as **Puuhonua-o-Honaunau,** was one of the few places to which *kapu* breakers and refugees could flee for sanctuary. Once inside the Great Wall, a lava barricade ten feet high and seventeen feet wide, they were safe from pursuers. Free booklets are available for self-guided tours to the palace, *heiaus,* and wooden idols which made this beachfront refuge one of Hawaii's most sacred spots.

St. Benedict's, my favorite church in all the islands, lies just up the hill. An imaginative Belgian priest, hoping to add color and imagery to the mass, transformed this rickety wooden chapel into a **Painted Church** by covering the interior walls with murals. He depicted several religious scenes and painted a vaulted nave behind the altar to give this tiny church the appearance of a great European cathedral. Stop by and take a look.

Route 11 continues its course through South Kona. Lifeless lava fingers cut across lush areas teeming with tropical colors. The contrast is overwhelming: rounding a bend, the road travels from an overgrown land of poinsettias and blossoming trees to a bleak area torn by upheaval, resembling the moon's surface.

About thirty miles south of Kailua, take the turnoff to the quaint Hawaiian fishing village at **Milolii** (see the "Beaches and Parks" section in this chapter). This is a vintage South Seas scene that should not be missed.

Continuing south, the highway passes **James Stewart's Hoomau Ranch,** then a sprawling **macadamia nut orchard,** and finally arrives at the **South Point** turnoff. South Point Road leads through eleven miles of rolling grassland to the nation's southernmost point. Fishermen have built **platforms** along the seacliff here to haul their catches up from the boats which troll these prime fishing grounds. There are also **ancient canoe moorings** in the rocks below, and the remains of a *heiau* near the light tower.

Several miles past the turnoff, in the somnolent village of Waiohinu, is the **Mark Twain Monkeypod Tree.** Planted by the young writer during his 1866 Hawaiian sojourn, the original tree fell to high winds several years back but was soon replaced when the present tree sprang from its roots.

Continue on to **Naalehu,** the nation's southernmost town, and then on to **Punaluu State Park.** With its palm trees and enchanting lagoon, Punaluu's black-sand beach is simply gorgeous. The tourist complex here detracts from the natural beauty, but to escape the madding mobs the explorer need wander only a couple of hundred yards east to the rocky remains of **Kaneeleele Heiau.** Or venture about one-third mile south to **Ninole Cove.** Though there's a condo complex nearby, this spot is a bit more secluded. Many of the stones along Ninole's pebbly beach are filled with holes containing "baby" stones that are said to multiply.

From Punaluu to Volcanoes National Park, the highway passes through largely uninhabited grassland and sugar cane areas. **Pahala,** the only town along this stretch, is a plantation colony. For an interesting side trip, go through Pahala to **Wood Valley Temple** (★), where a Tibetan Buddhist monk and his followers have taken over an old Japanese temple. To get there, go right onto Pikake Street at the first stop sign in Pahala. When it forks after a little more than four miles, go left and proceed two-tenths of a mile to the temple. The road continues up into luxuriant **Wood Valley** (★), the scene of a devastating 1868 earthquake and mudslide.

HAWAII VOLCANOES NATIONAL PARK
AND THE PUNA DISTRICT

The points of interest in this remarkable park begin soon after you enter it from the south on Route 11. Within a mile of the park boundary is the trailhead for **Footprints Trail.** This two-mile path leads to the area where Halemaumau's hellish eruption overwhelmed a Hawaiian army in 1790. The troops, off to battle Kamehameha for control of the island, left the impressions of their dying steps in molten lava. Many tracks have eroded, but some still remain imprinted on the ground.

Continuing along Route 11, turn up Mauna Loa Strip Road to the **Tree Molds.** Lava flowing through an *ohia* forest created these amazing fossils. The molten rock ignited the trees and then cooled, leaving deep pits in the shape of the incinerated tree trunks. It's a little farther to **Kipuku Puaulu** or **Bird Park,** a nature trail leading through a densely forested bird sanctuary. If the weather's clear, continue along this narrow, winding road for about ten miles to a **lookout** perched 6,000 feet high on the side of Mauna Loa.

Back on Route 11, continue a few miles to **Kilauea Visitor Center** (967-7311), containing a museum, souvenir shop, and information desk. Across the road at **Volcano House** there's a hotel and restaurant. The original Volcano House, built in 1877, currently houses the **Volcano Art Center,** right next to the visitor complex.

From here you can pick up Crater Rim Road, one of the islands' most spectacular scenic drives. This eleven-mile loop passes lava flows and steam vents in its circuit around **Kilauea Crater.**

Proceeding clockwise around the crater, the road leads near **Thurston Lava Tube,** a 450-foot tunnel set amid a fern forest. You can hike through the tunnel and along nearby **Devastation Trail,** a half-mile boardwalk which cuts through a skeletal forest of *ohia* trees devastated in a 1959 eruption.

Another short path leads to **Halemaumau Crater.** This firepit, which erupted most recently in 1982, is the home of Pele, the goddess of volcanoes. Even today steam and sulfurous gas blast from this hellhole, filling the air with a pungent odor and adding a sickly yellow-green luster to the cliffs. Halemaumau is actually a crater within a crater, its entire bulk contained in Kilauea's gaping maw.

Around the southern and western edges of the crater, the road passes part of the **Kau Desert** and the **Hawaiian Volcano Observatory,** a U.S. Geological Survey facility. Then it continues on to a series of **steam vents** from which hot mists rise continuously.

Route 11 zips into Hilo from the Kilauea Crater area, but for a far more interesting and leisurely drive take **Chain of Craters Road** down to the Puna district. You can pick it up from Crater Rim Road near the Devastation Trail turnoff. Chain of Craters Road recently reopened after being closed for several years by lava flows. Today it skirts several volcanic craters and dips toward the sea, arriving on the coast near **Puuloa,** where a short trail leads to an excellent collection of petroglyphs.

Here you'll be on the coast road, Route 130, which courses along the Puna shoreline past an ancient Hawaiian village at **Kamoamoa** and on to

Ski Hawaii

During your island tour you'll inevitably pull up behind some joker with a bumper sticker reading "Think Snow." Around you trade winds may be bending the palm trees, sunbronzed crowds will be heading to the beach, and the thermometer will be approaching 80°. Snow will be the farthest thing from your mind.

When I first came to Hawaii, I thought the only white powder on the islands was the precious stuff that drifts along mirrors and is plowed with a razor. But up on the 13,796-foot slopes of Mauna Kea, you're liable to see a bikini-clad skier schussing across a mantle of newly-fallen snow! Any time from December until May, there may be enough dry snow to create ski runs five miles long and fill bowls a half-mile wide and almost a mile long. The slopes range from beginner to expert; some have a vertical drop of over 5,000 feet.

Situated above the clouds about eighty percent of the time, this snow lover's oasis is baked by a tropical sun many times more powerful than at the beach. So it's easy to tan and easier yet to burn. Combined with the thin air and winds up to sixty miles per hour, Hawaii's ski slopes are not for the faint-hearted or fair-skinned.

But if you're seeking an incredible adventure and want a view of the Hawaiian islands from a 13,000-foot crow's nest, the heights of Mauna Kea await.

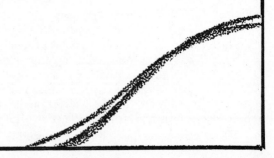

Wahaula Visitor Center. Behind this complex lies **Wahaula Heiau,** one of the islands' oldest temples. Built about 1250 A.D., this was the last *heiau* where priests practiced human sacrifice. There's also a **nature trail** here that loops along the coast and cuts through an earthquake fault.

For a startling confrontation with Hawaii's geology, turn left one mile beyond the information center and follow Royal Avenue uphill to the **Royal Gardens Subdivision.** The road ends at a twenty-foot wall of lava. Several side roads are also severed by lava flows which regularly threaten to devour this mountainside community.

Back on the main road, continue one-third mile to a gravel driveway on the right which leads to **Queen's Bath,** where you can swim in a rock pool once used by Hawaiian royalty. After drying off, travel on to **Kalapana,** a palm-studded black-sand beach. Beaches like this and others nearby form when molten lava reaches the sea and bursts into fragments. These bits of black glass are then ground sand-fine by the ocean's wave action.

The nearby **Star of the Sea Painted Church** is decorated with more of the fabulous folk art found in Kona's Painted Church. Behind the church is an **ancient canoe ramp** used by Polynesians to launch their outriggers.

There's another black-sand beach at **Kaimu,** where waves wash to the very foot of the palm trees. Continue along the coast via Route 137 through jungly undergrowth and past dazzling seascapes to the tiny villages of **Opihikao** and **Pohoiki.**

At the intersection of Route 137 with Route 132, take a right onto the dirt road and follow it seaward toward the site of a truly eerie occurrence. When the 1960 lava flow swept down to destroy this entire region, it spared the **Cape Kumukahi Lighthouse** on the state's easternmost point. Today you can see where the wall of lava parted, flowed around the beacon, then closed again as it continued to the sea. In the process, it added about 500 yards of land to the point — an awesome demonstration of how young this Big Island really is.

Now return to Route 132 and head west toward Pahoa. The road passes more of the **1960 lava flow,** which covered almost 2,000 acres and totally leveled the small village of Kapoho.

An earlier eruption, about 1790, caused the grotesque formations down the road at **Lava Tree State Park.** Here the molten rock swamped a grove of *ohia* trees, then hardened around the skeletons to create a fossil forest.

A few miles farther along is the tumbledown town of **Pahoa.** From here it's only about twenty miles back to Hilo and the completion of this all-too-brief sightseeing circuit of the Big Island.

On the way into Hilo stop at **Panaewa Rainforest Zoo** (Route 11 several miles outside town; 959-7224). Located in a lush region that receives over 125 inches of rain annually, this modest facility houses numerous rainforest animals as well as other species. There are water buffaloes and tigers, plus an array of exotic birds like pied hornbills, crowned cranes, macaws, parrots, Hawaiian stilts, and *nenes.*

Shopping

HILO SHOPPING

The most convenient way to shop in Hilo is at one of several shopping centers around the city. **Kaikoo Mall,** on Kilauea Avenue, is the main complex. Here you'll find jewelers, boutiques, curio and book stores, a photo shop, Penney's department store, and more. **Hilo Shopping Center** and **Kilauea Center,** both on Kilauea Avenue, also contain numerous shops.

The latest addition to the Hilo shopping scene is **Prince Kuhio Plaza** (Route 11 just outside town), a full-facility complex featuring everything from small crafts shops to swank boutiques to a sprawling department store. The Big Island's largest mall, it's a gathering place for local shoppers and a convenient spot for visitors.

But bargains and locally crafted products are probably what you're after. So it's a good idea to window-shop through the centers, checking out products and prices, then do your buying at smaller shops. For woodwork, just head across the street from Kaikoo Mall to **Hawaiian Handcrafts** (935-5587) at 760 Kilauea Avenue. The beautiful pieces are fashioned from banyan, sandalwood, *koa,* and *milo,* all priced reasonably. The Deluzs, the craftspeople who own the shop, do all their carving in a back-room workshop. If you'd like a description of how the *tikis* and bowls are made, they're happy to provide an informal tour.

The Most Irresistible Shop in Hilo (110 Keawe; 935-9644) doesn't quite live up to its bold name, but does create a strong attraction with jewelry, ceramics, books, toys, and T-shirts.

For Hawaiiana books, try **The Book Gallery** (Kaikoo Mall; 935-2447). This well-stocked shop also has many popular titles.

KAILUA-KONA SHOPPING

You might remember that song about how "L.A. is a great big freeway." Well, the Hawaiian version could easily be "Kailua is a great big mall." I've never seen so many shopping arcades squeezed into so small a space. Here are goldsmiths, boutiques, jewelers galore, travel agencies, sundries, knickknack shops, sandal-makers, T-shirt shops, and much much more, all crowded onto Alii Drive.

Personally I think most of the items sold along this strip are plastic or overpriced, and in some cases, both. You may find something worth buying, but you'll probably discover it's best to browse here and buy outside town. One place I do recommend is **Middle Earth Bookshoppe** (Kona Plaza Shopping Arcade; 329-2123). Here you'll find a good selection of Hawaiian books, as well as paperbacks and current bestsellers.

The **Kona Inn Shopping Village**, which parallels the waterfront along Alii Drive, features dozens of shops. Because of its convenient location and variety of stores it is the center of the visitor shopping scene.

SHOPPING ALONG THE NORTHERN ROUTE FROM HILO TO KAILUA-KONA

Several small shops between Hilo and Waimea are worth a visit. The **Honomu Plantation Store** (963-6203), on the road to Akaka Falls, is a modern emporium housed in a refurbished 1878 building. The historic photos decorating the place invite a stop. **Kamaaina Woods** (775-7722), in Honokaa, on the road to the macadamia nut factory, has a splendid assortment of handmade bowls and decorations. With items fashioned from *milo*, mango, monkeypod, and *koa*, this shop is practically a museum. And if you are interested in learning more about these woods, you can view the factory through the window. **The Waipio Woodworks** (775-0958), located on Route 24 near the Waipio Lookout, is also cluttered with woodcarvings. Made from several different woods, some of these creations are extremely beautiful. This shop also features paintings, ceramics, quilts, and other items crafted by local artists.

Parker Ranch Center is *the* shopping complex in Waimea's cattle country. This modern center features a sporting goods store, boutique, pharmacy, combination record-book-head shop, and more. If you're like me and enjoy browsing through stores in order to capture the flavor of a place, you'll find this mall in the center of Waimea.

For skillfully fashioned Japanese ceramics try **The Clay Body** (on Route 19 in the New Fukushima Store; 885-7474).

At nearby **Nikko Natural Fabrics and Gallery** (Route 19; 885-7661) there's an array of fine silk clothing including Japanese kimonos. This splendid shop also features beautiful batiks and a line of shell jewelry.

Way out on the Kohala peninsula, try not to miss **Vea Polynesian** (Route 27, Hawi; 889-6294). Owner Ika Vea, from Tonga, imports handiworks from his homeland as well as from Fiji, Samoa, and Tahiti. Ika also carves striking *tikis*; a friend of his decorates jewelry with designs from Hawaiian petroglyphs by inlaying silver with lava. The workmanship is of a very high quality, and the prices are often only twenty percent above wholesale.

Shopping in Kohala was once a matter of uncovering family-owned crafts shops in tiny towns. Now that it has become a major resort area, you can also browse at designer stores in several top-flight hotels. Simply drive along Route 19 between the Kohala Peninsula and Kailua; you'll encounter, from north to south, the **Mauna Kea Beach Hotel, Mauna Lani Bay Hotel,** and the **Sheraton Royal Waikoloa Hotel.** Each of these large resort complexes features an array of boutiques, knickknack shops, jewelers, and other outlets.

SHOPPING ALONG THE SOUTHERN ROUTE FROM KAILUA-KONA TO HILO

After escaping the tourist traps in Kailua, you can start seriously shopping in South Kona. Since numerous shops dot Route 11 as it travels south, I'll list the most interesting ones in the order they appear.

For hats and baskets woven from pandanus and bamboo and sold at phenomenally low prices, turn off Route 11 onto Route 18 and check out **Kimura Lauhala Shop** (324-0053) in Holualoa.

Holualoa is also a center for art galleries. Within the ambit of this one-street town you'll find the **Kona Arts Center,** housed in an old church, plus several privately-owned galleries nearby.

The old **Greenwell Store** (Route 11, Kealakekua; 323-3222), a stone building that dates to 1867, is a perfect place to combine shopping with museum browsing. The Kona Historical Society refurbished this old general store. Today it's filled with artifacts from Kona's early days plus contemporary postcards, calendars, and other items.

Blue Ginger Gallery (Route 11, Kainaliu; 322-3898) displays an impressive array of crafts items produced by local artisans. There are ceramics, custom glass pieces, woodwork, volcanic glass jewelry, and hand-painted silk scarves.

The Treasure Trunk (Route 11, Kealakekua; 322-2200) has an odd but intriguing assortment varying from *aloha* shirts to stained glass wall-hangings to used books.

My favorite shop is **Kealakekua's Grass Shack** (Route 11, Kealakekua; 323-2877). This place is crowded with Hawaiiana, not just from native Polynesians, but from the island's late arrivals as well—Americans, Chinese, Japanese, Portuguese. As owner John Jens explains, "We go all the way from *poi* to tofu." There are *milo* and *koa* wood pieces, black coral jewelry, handwoven baskets, and much more. Most interesting of all, to me at least, are the antique tools and handicrafts which Jens has gathered. This transplanted Dutchman is something of an authority on Hawaiian history and culture, combining a scholar's knowledge with a native's love for the islands. Ask him for a tour of his mini-museum and garden. It'll be an education in things Hawaiian.

Two other places I recommend are **Paradise Found** (322-2111) in Kainaliu for contemporary and Hawaiian-style clothes, and **Country Store Antiques** (323-3005) in Captain Cook for things old and aging.

Nightlife

Unless Kilauea is lighting the evening sky with molten lava during your visit, you'll find few hot scenes on the Big Island. There are clubs at the hotels in Hilo and Kona which feature live entertainment, plus a couple of good lounges. I found most to be pleasant places to spend an evening, but none brought me back a second night.

HILO NIGHTLIFE

The main scene here centers around the big hotels along Banyan Drive. By far the best place is the Naniloa Surf Hotel (935-0831). This luxury hotel has a nicely appointed nightclub, **The Crown Room.** The lounge usually books local groups, but every once in a while it imports a mainland band for special events. There's a cover charge and two-drink minimum. Then there is the hotel's **Hoomalimali Bar** which has a live band nightly from 9 o'clock on, but requires no cover or minimum.

Harrington's (135 Kalanianaole Avenue; 961-4966) hosts a jazz pianist during the week and a Hawaiian group on weekends. At **The Banyan Broiler** (111 Banyan Drive; 961-5802) there's entertainment nightly.

For a laid-back evening at a very hip bar frequented by local people, try **Rosey's Boathouse** (935-2112) at 760 Piilani. There's usually a small band, but happily no cover charge.

KAILUA NIGHTLIFE

The action here is near the shorefront on Alii Drive. **Huggo's** (329-1493) and the **Spindrifter Restaurant** (329-1344) feature live bands. The sound is a mix of rock and jazz; at the Spindrifter you'll also hear country and western. Both places have stunning ocean views and are usually packed.

For an evening of slow rhythms and dancing cheek-to-cheek, there's the **Windjammer Lounge** (329-3111) at the Kona Hilton. There's no cover tied to the evening entertainment at this lavish resort. When I went by recently the band was playing Hawaiian sounds.

Another good bet is the **Kona Surf Resort** (78-128 Ehukai Street; 322-3411), which sports several lounges. There's dancing nightly at the **Eclipse Restaurant** (75-5711 Kuakini Highway; 329-4686). And **Mitchell's at Keauhou** (Keauhou Shopping Village; 322-9966) features dancing to a live band Wednesday through Saturday; deejay music the other nights.

KOHALA NIGHTLIFE

Night owls along the Kohala Coast roost at one of three resort hotels. The Mauna Kea Beach Hotel (Route 19, Kawaihae; 882-7222) has a Hawaiian band at its **Cafe Terrace** and features dance music in the **Batik Room.** Nearby at the Mauna Lani Bay Hotel (Route 19, Kawaihae;

885-6622) there's a sleek rendezvous called "the bar" which hosts a jazz band nightly. At other places in this spacious resort, you can also dance, listen to Hawaiian music, or imbibe in a lovely, open-air setting. The night scene at the **Sheraton Royal Waikoloa Hotel** (Route 19, Waikoloa; 885-6789) centers around several watering holes which offer a variety of diversions ranging from ocean views to live bands to Polynesian revues.

Hawaii Addresses and Phone Numbers

HAWAII ISLAND

County Department of Parks and Recreation—25 Aupuni Street, Hilo (961-8311)
Hawaii Visitors Bureau—180 Kinoole, Hilo (961-5271); and Kona Plaza Shopping Arcade, Alii Drive, Kailua-Kona (329-7787)
State Department of Land and Natural Resources—75 Aupuni Street, Hilo (961-7200)
Volcanoes National Park Headquarters—(967-7311)
Weather Report—(935-8555 for Hilo; 961-5582 for entire island)

HILO

Ambulance—(961-6022)
Barber Shop—Faye's Barber Shop, 710 Kilauea Avenue (935-4990)
Books—Book Gallery 2, Kaikoo Mall (935-2447)
Fire Department—(961-6022)
Fishing Supplies—S. Tokunaga Store, 259 Keawe Street (935-6965)
Hardware—True Value Hardware Store, 300 Keawe Street (961-2875)
Hospital—Hilo Hospital, 1190 Waianuenue Avenue (969-4111)
Laundromat—Kaikoo Coin Laundry, 210 Hoku Street (961-6490)
Library—300 Waianuenue Avenue (935-5407)
Liquor—Kadota Liquor, 194 Hualalai Street (935-1802)
Pharmacy—Long's Drugs, 555 Kilauea Avenue (935-3357)
Photo Supply—Hawaii Photo Supply, 250 Keawe Street (935-6995)
Police Department—349 Kapiolani (935-3311)
Post Office—154 Waianuenue Avenue (935-6685)

KAILUA-KONA

Ambulance—(961-6022)
Barber Shop—Delilah's Barber, King Kamehameha Hotel (329-2577)
Books—Middle Earth Bookshoppe, Alii Drive (329-2123)
Fire Department—(961-6022)
Fishing Supplies—Yama's Specialty Shop, Alii Drive (329-1712)
Hardware—Trojan Lumber Company (329-3536)
Hospital—Kona Hospital, Kealakekua town (322-9311)

Laundromat—Hele Mai Laundromat, North Kona Shopping Center (329-3494)

Library—Hualalai Road (329-2196)

Liquor—Jug and Jigger, Alii Drive (329-2125)

Pharmacy—Pay 'n' Save Drug Store, Kona Coast Shopping Center (329-2729)

Photo Supply—Kona Photo Center, North Kona Shopping Center (329-3676)

Police Department—(323-2645)

Post Office—Palani Road (329-1927)

CHAPTER FIVE

Maui

Residents of Maui, Hawaii's second-largest island, proudly describe their Valley Isle by explaining that "Maui *no ka oi.*" Maui is the greatest. During the last decade, few of the island's visitors have disputed the claim. They return each year in increasing numbers, lured by the enchantment of a place possessing thirty-three miles of public beaches, one of the world's largest dormant volcanoes, beautiful people, a breeding ground for rare humpback whales, and a climate that varies from subtropic to subarctic.

Named after one of the most important gods in the Polynesian pantheon, Maui has retained its mythic aura. The island is famous as a chic retreat and jet-set landing ground. Its righteous homegrown, Maui Wowie, has attained legendary status as one of the world's most potent marijuana strains. To many people, Maui *is* Hawaii.

But to others who have watched the rapid changes during the past two decades, Maui is no longer the greatest. They point to the two million tourists (second only to Oahu) who visited during a recent year, to the condominiums mushrooming along the prettiest beaches, and to the increasing traffic over once rural roads. And they have a new slogan. "Maui is *pau.*" Maui is finished. Overtouristed. Overpopulated. Overdeveloped.

Today, among the island's 77,000 population, it seems like every other person is in the real estate business. On a land mass measuring 729 square miles, just half the size of Long Island, their goods are in short supply. Demand has driven land prices up faster than practically anywhere in the country. Maui is booming.

Yet over seventy-five percent of the island remains unpopulated. Despite wild-eyed speculation and a mondo-condo mentality, Maui still offers exotic, untouched expanses for the explorer. Most development is concentrated along the south and west coasts in Kihei and Kaanapali. The rest of the island, though more crowded than neighboring islands, is an adventurer's oasis. (Text continued on page 132.)

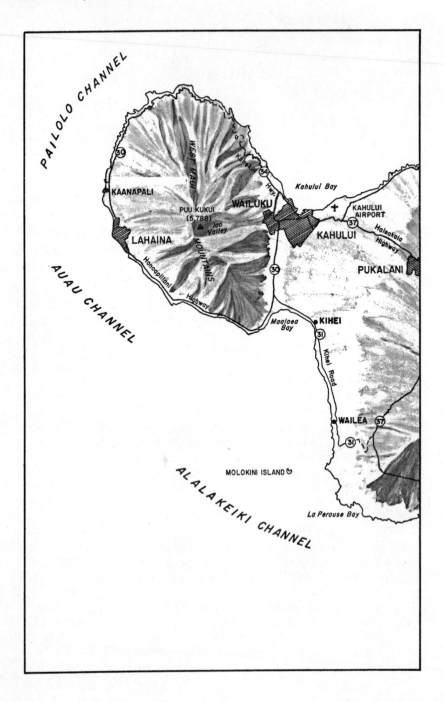

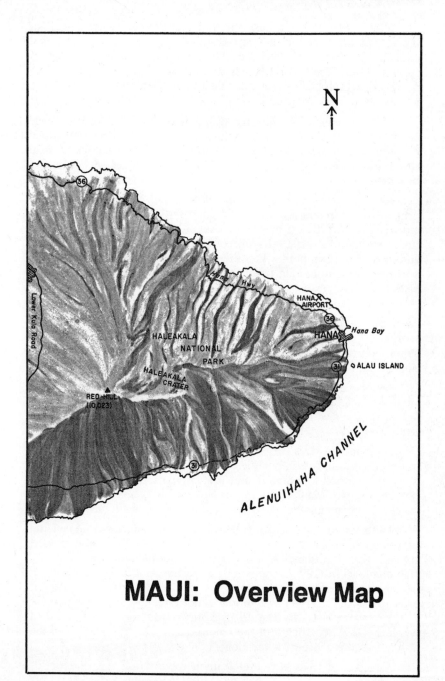

MAUI: Overview Map

The second youngest island in the chain, Maui was created about fifteen million years ago by two volcanoes. Haleakala, the larger, rises over 10,000 feet, and offers excellent hiking and camping within its gaping crater. The second firepit created the West Maui Mountains, 5,788 feet at their highest. Between the two lies Central Maui, an isthmus formed by volcanic erosion.

The twin cities of Kahului and Wailuku, Maui's commercial and civic centers, sit in this saddle. Most of the isthmus is planted in sugar, which became king in Maui after the decline of whaling in the 1860s. A road through the cane fields leads south to Kihei's sunsplashed resorts and beaches.

Another road loops around the West Maui Mountains. It passes prime whale-watching areas along the south coast and bisects Lahaina, an old whaling town that is now the jet set capital of Hawaii. Next to this timeworn harbor stretches the town of Kaanapali with its limitless beaches and endless condominiums. Past these plastic palisades, near the island's northwest tip, lie hidden beaches, overhanging cliffs, and spectacular vistas.

The road girdling Haleakala's lower slopes passes equally beautiful areas. Along the rainswept northeast coast are sheer rock faces ribboned with waterfalls and gorges choked with tropic vegetation. The lush, somnolent town of Hana gives way along the southeast shore to a dry unpopulated expanse ripe for exploration.

On the middle slopes of Haleakala, in Maui's Upcountry region, small farms dot the landscape. Here, in addition to guavas, avocados, and lichee nuts, grow the sweet Kula onions for which the Valley Isle is famous.

Back in the days of California's gold rush, Maui found its own underground nuggets in potatoes; countless bushels were grown in this area and shipped to a hungry San Francisco market. Today the crop is used to prepare Maui potato chips. Next to marijuana, these delicious snacks are becoming the island's most renowned agricultural product.

With its strategic location between Oahu and Hawaii, Maui has played a vital role in Hawaiian history. Kahekili, Maui's last king, gained control of all the islands except Hawaii before being overwhelmed by Kamehameha in 1790. Lahaina, long a vacation spot for Hawaii's rulers, became an important commercial center soon after Captain Cook sighted Maui in 1778. It served as a supply depot for ships, then as a port for sandalwood exports. By the 1840s Lahaina was the world capital of whaling. Now, together with the other equally beautiful sections of the Valley Isle, it is a mecca for vacationers.

Maui's magic has cast a spell upon travelers all over the world, making the island a vacation paradise. Like most modern paradises, it is being rapidly gilded in plastic and concrete. Yet much of the old charm remains. Some people even claim that the sun shines longer on the Valley Isle than any place on earth. They point to the legend of the demigod Maui who created his own daylight savings by weaving a rope from his sister's pubic hair and lassoing the sun by its genitals. And many hope he has one last trick to perform, one that will slow the course of development just as he slowed the track of the sun.

Easy Living

Transportation

ARRIVAL

Two airports serve Maui—**Kahului Airport** and **Hana Airport**.

The **Kahului Airport** is the main landing facility and should be your destination if you're staying in the Central Maui region or on the southeast coast in Kihei. **United Airlines** and **American Airlines** arrive non-stop from the mainland. Currently **Aloha Airlines, Hawaiian Airlines, Reeves Air,** and **Mid Pacific Air** fly here from other islands in the chain. The first two companies fly jets: the others use propeller-driven planes and often feature the lowest fares.

If you decide to land in Kahului, you'll arrive at a bustling airport which has been expanded. I never realized how popular Maui is until I first pushed through the mobs of new arrivals here. In addition to the masses, you'll find a coffee shop and lounge, snack bar, newsstand, gift shop, *lei* stand, and information booth (877-6431), but no lockers. The **Grayline** organization (877-5507) provides shuttle service both to and from the airport.

If you're staying on the west coast in Lahaina or Kaanapali, you can check the status of **Kaanapali Airfield.** The old airport is closed, but there are plans to construct a new one. **Hawaiian Airlines** is slated to service the airport. **Maui Shoreline Transportation** (661-3827) will probably be providing bus transportation to and from.

Hana Airport, really only a short landing strip and a one-room terminal, sits near the ocean in Maui's lush northeastern corner. Only **Princeville Airways** lands in this isolated community. And don't expect very much ground transportation waiting for you. There is no bus service, though there is a car rental agency.

CAR RENTALS

If, like most visitors to Maui, you arrive at the airport in Kahului, you certainly won't want for car rental agencies. There are quite a few with booths right at the airport: a number of others are located around town.

(Text continued on page 136.)

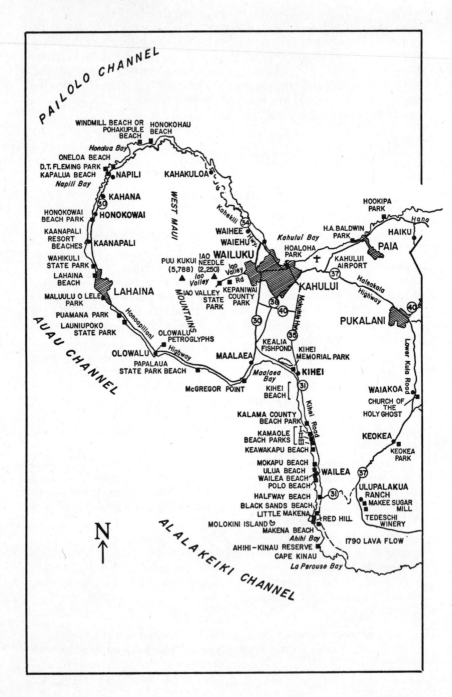

MAUI: Travel Map

HWY 36 TWIN FALLS

40

Haiku Rd

MAKAWAO

Piiholo Rd

Olinda Rd 39

377

PARK HEADQUARTERS

378

KULA BOTANICAL GARDENS

VISITOR CENTER

RED HILL (10,023)

POLI POLI STATE PARK

PUOHOKAMOA FALLS

KAUMAHINA STATE WAYSIDE

Honomanu Bay

KEANAE PENINSULA

KEANAE

KEANAE CHURCH

WAILUA

KEANAE ARBORETUM

Waikamoi Ridge

Honomanu Gulch

NAHIKU

PUAA KAA STATE PARK

Hana Hwy

HALEAKALA

NATIONAL

PARK

HALEAKALA CRATER

Kaupo Gap

Wailua Gulch Piilani Valley

KANAHUALII FALLS

KIPAHULU

WAIMOKO FALLS

SEVEN POOLS

WAILUA FALLS

WAIANAPANAPA STATE PARK

HANA AIRPORT

Ancient Shoreline Trail

36

HANA BEACH PARK

Hana Bay

HANA

BIRTHPLACE OF KAAHUMANU

KOKI PARK

31 ALAU ISLAND

HAMOA BEACH

KAUPO

31

Nuu Bay

HUIALOHA CHURCH

ALENUIHAHA CHANNEL

Naturally, the most convenient means of renting a car is through one of the outfits at the airport. The problem with these companies, however, is that you pay for the convenience.

The airport agencies are as follows: **Alamo Rent-A-Car** (877-3466), **Robert's Rent-A-Car** (871-6226), **Trans-Maui Rent-A-Car** (877-5222), **Andres Rent-A-Car** (877-5378), **Pacific Rent-A-Car** (877-3065), **American International Rent-A-Car** (877-7604), **Dollar Rent-A-Car** (877-6526), **Avis Rent-A-Car** (871-7575), **Budget Rent-A-Car** (871-8811), and **Hertz Rent-A-Car** (877-5167).

Then there are the agencies located away from the airport. Some of them will provide airport pick-up service when your plane arrives. I recommend that you check in advance and reserve a car from an outfit that extends this service. The others might be a little cheaper, but I've never considered the inconvenience worth the savings. Without a ride you'll be confronted with the Catch-22 situation of getting to your car. Do you rent a car in which to pick up your rental car? Take a bus? Or are you supposed to hitchhike?

Enough said. The car rental agencies outside the airport include two companies that rent older model cars at very competitive rates. These are **Word of Mouth Rent-A-Used-Car** (877-2436) and **Uptown Service** (244-0869).

The other companies, renting late model cars, are as follows: **El Cheapo Rent-A-Car** (877-5851), **Tropical Rent-A-Car** (877-0002), **Convertibles Hawaii** (661-3243), **VIP Car Rentals** (877-2054), **Sunshine Rent-A-Car** (871-6222), **Maui Car Rental & Leasing** (877-2081), **National Car Rental** (877-5347), and **Thrifty Rent-A-Car** (871-7596).

If you find yourself in the Lahaina-Kaanapali area wanting to rent a car try **Tropical Rent-A-Car** (661-0061), **Dollar Rent-A-Car** (661-3037), **Budget Rent-A-Car** (661-3546), **Avis Rent-A-Car** (661-4588), **Hertz Rent-A-Car** (661-3195), **Thrifty Rent-A-Car** (667-9541), **Rainbow Rent-A-Car** (661-8734), **National Car Rental** (667-9737), **Karat Kars,** (667-6289), or **United Car Rental** (667-2688). When the Kaanapali Airfield is completed, several rental car agencies will be servicing the facility.

In Hana there's one outfit that rents cars, **National Car Rental** (248-8237).

Kihei is served by **Holidaze Car Rentals** (879-1905) and **Kihei Rent-A-Car** (879-7257).

As elsewhere in the islands, there are a few points to remember when renting a car on Maui. First, the car rental agencies will charge several dollars a day extra for complete insurance coverage. Also, many of them will forbid you from driving the road around the West Maui Mountains and the road from Hana around the southeast side of the island.

(See Chapter 2 for a complete explanation of car rentals in Hawaii.)

JEEP RENTALS

There are several companies on the island of Maui which rent 4-wheel vehicles. Among the outfits offering jeeps are **Maui Rent-A-Jeep** (450 Dairy Road, Kahului; 877-6626), **Sunshine Rent-A-Car** (Dairy Road, Kahului; 871-6222), **Maui Sights and Treasures** (145 North Kihei Road, Kihei; 879-6260), and **United Car Rental** (905 West Mokuea Place, Kahului; 871-7328).

But for the most part, Maui roads, including cane roads, are accessible by car so you probably won't need a jeep. If you hit the rainy season, though, and want to explore the back roads, it can't hurt.

MOTOR SCOOTER AND MOTORCYCLE RENTALS

Go Go Bikes Hawaii (Kaanapali Transportation Center, Kaanapali; 661-3063), **A & B Moped Rental** (Honokowai General Store, Honokowai; 669-0027), and **Mopeds of Maui** (1975 South Kihei Road, Kihei; 879-3858) rent mopeds by the hour or day. These vehicles provide an exhilarating and economical way to explore the area. Though they are not intended for long trips or busy roadways, they're ideal for short jaunts to the beach.

PUBLIC TRANSPORTATION

There is only one major bus company on Maui—and its service is very limited. **Maui Shoreline Transportation** (661-3827) follows a route from Wailea to Kapalua, stopping in Maalaea, Lahaina, and Kaanapali. Fares range from $1.50 to $4 each way. The bus runs seven days a week. There's also a **Kaanapali Beach Resort jitney** traveling between the hotels and Whaler's Village (one-way fares are $1.25; all-day passes cost $2).

Outside the immediate Lahaina-Kaanapali area you'll have to rely on **Grayline** (877-5507). This well-known carrier operates shuttle services regularly from Kahului to Lahaina-Kaanapali for about $8.

BICYCLING

Maui presents bicyclists with their greatest challenge in all Hawaii—the ride to the top of Haleakala Crater. Considered by many to be the hardest bike ride in the world, the road rises over 10,000 feet in just forty miles. Like other bicycle routes on the Valley Isle, the scenic rewards are well worth the physical strain. The lazy way to "conquer the crater" is by cycling with gravity. **Cruiser Bob's Haleakala Downhill** (667-7717) drives cyclists to the top and then leads them on a bike tour down the mountainside.

Another spectacularly beautiful ride takes you over a narrow pockmarked highway to the rain-drenched town of Hana. This road, passing along Maui's lush northeastern side, winds around hundreds of curves and bobs up and down through countless gulches.

Maui also offers fairly level rides along its dry, sunny southwest shoreline. The roads from the Kihei-Wailea area to Lahaina and Kaanapali are ideal for combining swimming, sunbathing, and two-wheeling.

Except for the Hana Highway and unpaved stretches in the island's southeast and northwest corners, the roads are good. Most have narrow shoulders and are heavily traveled, so caution is advised.

RENTALS

Go Go Bikes Hawaii (Kaanapali Transportation Center, Kaanapali; 661-3063) rents bicycles. Call for rates.

REPAIRS

Cycle and Sports Shop has a facility in Kahului (111 Hana Highway; 877-5848) and another in Lahaina (West Maui Center; 661-4191). Both sell bicycles and accessories and do repair work.

HITCHHIKING

Officially, hitching is illegal on Maui, and the police have been known to arrest people. The local technique is not to extend your thumb. Just stand by the side of the road and face oncoming traffic as you would if you were hitching, but keep your hand down. Local people and some of the tourists will know you're hitching, and the police will leave you alone. If you do use your thumb, you'll be marking yourself as an outsider to the locals, and the police may feel the need to remind you of the law.

As everywhere else, luck hitching here varies. But the heavy traffic in most areas enhances your chances considerably.

TOURS AND DROPOFFS

Kenai Air Hawaii (Kahului Airport; 661-4426), **Maui Helicopters** (Hotel Intercontinental Maui; 879-1601), **Papillon Helicopters** (Pineapple Hill; 669-4884), and other outfits offer memorable helicopter tours of Maui.

Hotels

Staying in Maui means finding a place in Kahului, the Lahaina-Kaanapali area, Kihei, or Hana. Kahului, with several hotels, is conveniently located in the island's center, but lacks the sunshine anbeaches of Lahaina-Kaanapali and Kihei. Lahaina, an old wood-front whaling town, has several mid-priced hotels. Kaanapali and Kihei, with their endless white-sand beaches, are lined with condominiums. Hana, a world away on the other side of the island, has several hostelries tucked into its lush rain-spattered hills.

Personally speaking, I've always been partial to Lahaina and Hana. A lot of people complain that Lahaina has been overdeveloped and simply contains too many tourists, but it's such a pretty place, and so rich in Hawaiian history, that I have always considered it one of my favorite spots in all Hawaii. There's something about the falsefront stores and tumbledown houses along the waterfront that makes Lahaina positively enchanting. Of course Hana is everybody's favored destination, and I get very little argument in claiming it as another prime Maui place. For country living and outrageous colors, it's hard to surpass. Kihei, to my taste, is too developed (and lacks Lahaina's redeeming features). Kahului is simply a port town.

Wherever you decide upon, you'll find that budget hotels are limited, while condominiums are countless. Therefore I have included numerous condo listings; hotel space is greatly in demand on the Valley Isle, and you may find that a condo is your only resort.

KAHULUI-WAILUKU HOTELS

The hotel strip in this harbor town lies along the beach on Kahului Bay. Here, within a stone's skip of one another, are three moderately priced hostelries. Two of them, the **Maui Hukilau Hotel** and **Maui Seaside Hotel,** could almost be considered wings of the same complex. Operating under a single management, they sit beside each other along Route 32. Even the phone number (877-3311) is shared, as are the pool, restaurant, and lounge.

The **Hukilau** is the older and less attractive of the two. Rooms here are small but clean, carpeted, and highlighted with wall hangings. While the decor lacks flair, the surroundings are quite adequate. The hotel, like its counterpart, can be relied upon for steadfast service.

Just a few well-spent dollars more places you in a newer, larger, and far more attractive room at the **Seaside.** Those same wall decorations occur, but the appointments are more upscale and the place has the open, easy feeling of a more expensive hotel. Both facilities feature telephones and televisions and all the Maui Seaside Hotel rooms have air-conditioners.

The nearby **Maui Palms Resort** (877-0071) has comfortable and spacious rooms at moderate prices with wall-to-wall carpeting, telephone, and color television, but lacking decoration. This beach front facility has a pool tucked between the lobby and the rooms. There's also an Asian-American restaurant on the premises that provides a convenient dining facility for folks staying anywhere along Kahului's hotel row. The grounds are studded with palms; considering the price, the ambience is quite appealing.

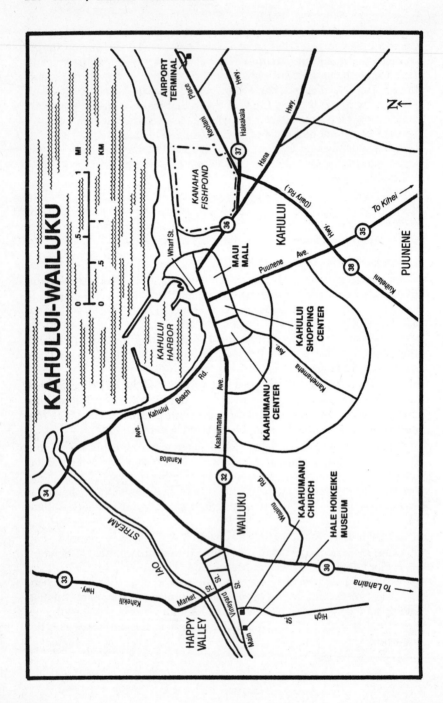

Along the Hana Highway out in Paia, about seven miles from Kahului, sits **Nalu Kai Lodge** (579-9035). Tucked behind "Larry's" restaurant near the town hub, this eight-unit resting place is a real sleeper. The last time I was by, only three rooms were available; the others were accommodating permanent residents. If you snag one of the vacant rooms, you'll check into a small, plain cubicle with no carpeting and little decoration. Sound unappealing? Well, even bare walls sometimes look good at low budget prices.

LAHAINA-KAANAPALI AREA HOTELS

To fully capture the spirit of Lahaina, there's only one place to stay—the **Pioneer Inn** (658 Wharf Street; 661-3636). Located smack on Lahaina's waterfront, this rickety wooden hostelry is the center of the area's action. On one side, sloops, ketches, and glass-bottom boats are berthed; on the other side lies bustling Front Street with its falsefront shops. The Inn is noisy, vibrant, and crowded with tenants and tourists. On the ground floor, you can hunker down over a glass of grog at the seaman's saloon, or stroll past the restaurants and shops lining the Inn's lushly planted courtyard.

Upstairs are the rooms. In the older section, over the bar, dark, noisy rooms with communal bathrooms price in the budget range. With private bath they're a little higher, though still in the budget category. You probably won't be able to sleep until the bar closes around 1 a.m., but you can sit on the lanai watching the moon reflect off the water. Or you can book a room in the newer, brighter, and quieter section overlooking the courtyard; moderate price. Like the older digs, these are small and plainly decorated, with telephones and overhead fans. But they trade stall showers for shower-tub combinations, swap a shared lanai for a private one, provide air-conditioning, and add a touch of sanity to the surroundings. If you seek adventure, try the old rooms; if you value your sleep, go for the new.

Lahaina's other budget accommodations are just off Front Street at the **Lahainaluna Hotel** (127 Lahainaluna Road; 661-0577). Set in the heart of town, this seventeen-unit establishment lacks the romance of the Pioneer Inn, but does offer attractive mountain and ocean views from the lanais of its rooms. These are tiny, undecorated, slightly weatherbeaten bedrooms with even tinier bathrooms plus carpeting, television, and air-conditioning. In some rooms you lose the lanai and part of the view. The Lahainaluna is far from a luxury resort, but its prices are pretty competitive.

LAHAINA-KAANAPALI AREA CONDOMINIUMS

Most condos in this area are along the beach near Kaanapali. They are ideally situated for swimming or sunbathing; the major drawback, ironically, is that there are so many other condos around. I have selected the most economical facilities, but I think you'll find they meet basic requirements for comfort and convenience. For a better idea of what to anticipate, check out the section on "Condominium Living" in Chapter 2.

Lahaina Shores Hotel (475 Front Street, Lahaina; 661-3309). Though it's more expensive than the others, this sprawling condominium has the advantage of a beachfront location in Lahaina. Studio apartments begin at $69 while one-bedroom units start at $94.

Maui Sands (on Lower Honoapiilani Highway, Kaanapali; 669-4811 or toll-free 800-367-5037). One-bedroom apartments begin at $61 single or double; two bedrooms run $85 for one to four people. Beachfront.

Paki Maui (on Lower Honopiilani Highway, Kaanapali; 669-8235 or toll-free 800-367-6098). One-bedroom apartments run from $95 to $120, sleeping one to four people; two-bedroom units start at $140, accommodating up to six people. Jacuzzi. Beachfront.

Honokowai Palms (3666 Lower Honoapiilani Highway, Honokowai; 669-6130). One-bedroom apartments without a lanai run $40 double; with lanai and ocean view they are $45. Two-bedroom units without lanai are $55 for one to four people. Located right across the street from the ocean.

Kaleialoha (on Lower Honoapiilani Highway, Honokowai; 669-8197). Studio apartments, $49 double; one-bedroom apartments, $59 double; $7.50 each additional person. Prices slightly higher from mid-December to mid-April. Oceanfront.

Polynesian Shores (on Lower Honoapiilani Highway, Honokowai; 669-6065). One-bedroom apartments, $65 double; two-bedroom apartments, $75 double. All units have ocean view.

Kahana Reef (on Lower Honoapiilani Highway, Kahana; 669-6491). Studio apartments, $70 single or double; one-bedroom apartments are $75 single or double; $20 less from Easter to December 18. All units are oceanfront and have daily maid service.

The Napili Bay (on Lower Honoapiilani Highway, Napili; 669-6044). Studio apartments are $80 double. Daily maid service. Non-oceanfront accommodations are $65.

KIHEI HOTELS

Like Kaanapali, this oceanfront strip features condominiums, but there are a couple of moderately priced hotels. The **Nona Lani Cottages** (455 South Kihei Road, Kihei; 879-2497) tops the list, with eight quaint wooden cottages situated across busy Kihei Road from a white-sand beach. Each is a one-bedroom unit with lanai, all-electric kitchen, and a living room capable of housing two extra sleepers. There's wall-to-wall carpeting and a shower-tub combination, plus television, but no phone or air-conditioner. Like most cottages in Hawaii, these are extremely popu-lar, so you'll need to reserve them far in advance.

Down the road at the **Surf and Sand Hotel** (2980 South Kihei Road, Kihei; 879-7744) you'll find a series of six buildings designed in mock-Hawaiian style and sandwiched between the highway and a white-sand beach. Here a moderate tab books a tiny, unimaginatively decorated room with carpeting, air-conditioning, and a clock radio.

KIHEI CONDOMINIUMS

Leilani Kai (1226 Uluniu Street, Kihei; 879-2606). This cozy nine-unit apartment hotel is right on the beach. Studio apartments are $42 double ($29 during the off-season, May 1 to December 5); one-bedroom units are $55 double ($37 off-season); two bedrooms will run you $68 for one to four people ($45 off-season).

Kihei Kai (61 North Kihei Road, Kihei; 879-2357). One-bedroom apartments are $55 to $60 double ($45 to $50 from mid-April to December 14).

Sunseeker Resort (551 South Kihei Road, Kihei; 879-1261). A small, personalized place where studios with kitchenettes go for $35 double, one-bedrooms $45 double, and two-bedrooms $60 for four people. Add $6 for each additional person.

Mana Kai–Maui Apartment Hotel (2960 South Kihei Road, Kihei; 879-1561). This high-rise condominium has "hotel units" which consist of the extra bedroom and bath from a two-bedroom apartment, renting for $57.50 ($65 from January 1 through April 15). The condo has a beachfront location, plus an adjoining restaurant and bar.

Lihi Kai (2121 Iliili Road, Kihei; 879-2335). This establishment has nine beach cottages in addition to its apartment units. All accommodations rent for $39 single or double. To be sure of getting a cottage, you'd best make reservations far in advance.

Kamaole Beach Royale (2385 South Kihei Road, Kihei; 879-3131). A six-story condo across the street from a beach park, this has one-bedroom apartments for $50 double; two-bedroom units, $60 double. From December to April the rates increase to $75 and $85 respectively.

Kapulanikai (73 Kapu Place, Kihei; 879-1607). A cozy place with only twelve apartments, all of which overlook the ocean. The two-story build-ings are constructed of wood and capped with tile roofs. One-bedroom apartments rent for $60 single or double ($45 from April to mid-Dec-ember).

HANA AREA HOTELS

A very convenient budget accommodation on the Hana Highway is the **Maui YMCA** hostel (248-8355) in Keanae. For $5 a night both men and women with hostel cards are welcome to roll out their sleeping bags on bunks in the dormitory. Set in a spacious wooden house overlooking the sea, this crash pad comes complete with a kitchen, hot showers, common room, and a gymnasium. Sorry, maximum stay is three nights.

Aloha Cottage (248-8420), perched on a hillside above Hana Bay, has two-bedroom units at moderate prices. Situated amid papaya and banana trees, these cozy cottages feature hardwood floors and walls fashioned from redwood. The decor is simple, the kitchens are all-electric, and many of the furnishings are rattan. Representing one of Hana's best bargains, the cottages have been recommended many times over the years by readers and friends. There are only four units at this small complex, so advance reservations are a good idea.

You can also consider heading down toward the water to the **Hana Kai Maui Resort** (248-8426). Located smack on a rocky beach, these two twin-story buildings sit amid lush surroundings. The swimming pool is a fresh-water affair fed by toe-dipping spring water. The location and exotic grounds rate a big plus. The bill? A studio apartment or a one-bedroom condominium will price in the deluxe category.

Speaking of scenery, **Heavenly Hana Inn** (248-8442) is blessed indeed. Located about two miles outside Hana, this hostelry is entered through a Japanese screen gate. On either side, stone lions guard a luxuriant garden. The interior mirrors this elegance. There's an Oriental touch to each two-bedroom apartment—Japanese screens, bamboo towel racks, Asian art objects. The walls are wood-paneled, the lanai's screened, the kitchenette is equipped with the usual accoutrements. They also have two cottages available, one near the beach at Hana Bay. Deluxe.

The finest resting place of all is the **Hotel Hana Maui** (248-8211), a luxurious retreat on a hillside above the bay. From ocean views to tropical landscape to rolling lawn, this friendly inn is a unique, world-class resort. Spread across the grounds are plush rooms, suites, and cottages, all elegantly designed, with prices in the ultra-deluxe range for two people on the American plan. The staff has been here for generations, lending a sense of home to an enchanting locale. Highly recommended.

And don't forget the cabins at **Waianapanapa State Park** (see the "Beaches and Parks" section in this chapter).

UPCOUNTRY HOTELS

Two mountain lodges on the road to Haleakala Crater offer cold-air retreats. Both of them are well-situated for anyone who wants to catch the sunrise over the crater at Haleakala. For years **Kula Lodge** (878-1535) has rented Swiss chalets complete with fireplaces, sleeping lofts, and sweeping views. The individual chalets are carpeted wall-to-wall and trimmed with stained-wood paneling. The central lodge features a cheery restaurant, bar, and stone fireplace. Prices are moderate, making it an ideal mountain hideaway.

The nearby **Silversword Inn** (878-1232) might be in the same neighborhood but certainly not the same class. Like Kula Lodge, it offers individual cottages and an adjacent restaurant, but the facilities here are rundown and poorly maintained. While the room tab is budget to moderate I'd recommend spending the extra money to stay in a place where the proprietors take pride in the premises. Both lodges are located along Route 377 at about the 3,000-foot elevation.

Restaurants

Kahului-Wailuku Area Budget Restaurants: The best place in Kahului for a quick, inexpensive meal is at one of several shopping arcades along Route 32. For Asian food I recommend **Ma-Chan's Okazuya** (877-7818) in Kaahumanu Center. It features a cafeteria as well as a full-fledged restaurant.

For more common fare, head over to the Maui Mall. Here you can drop in at **Restaurant Matsu** (871-0822), a short-order eatery that features such Japanese selections as tempura, yakitori, sushi, and *saimin*. Next door at **Siu's Chinese Kitchen** (871-0828) they serve a variety of Chinese fast foods; at breakfast there are American dishes. To round off the calorie count, you can try a cup of *guri guri* sherbet at **Tasaka Guri Guri Shop** (871-4513).

Up the road apiece in Wailuku there are a couple recommended ethnic restaurants guaranteed to please both the palate and the purse. The first, **Sam Sato's** (318 North Market Street; 244-7124), features Japanese and American cuisine. Open for breakfast and lunch, it specializes in *manju* (a bean cake pastry), dry *mein* (a noodle dish), and the ubiquitous *saimin*. The nearby **Fujiya** (133 Market Street; 244-0206) stirs up some similar moneybelt-tightening Asian meals. Either place is well worth a visit.

Kahului-Wailuku Area Moderately Priced Restaurants: A favorite dining spot of Kahului residents is **Aloha Restaurant** (127 Puunene Avenue; 877-6318). With meagerly decorated cinder-block walls, it's not much on looks, but the vivacious crowd that bursts in for lunch and dinner creates plenty of atmosphere. And the menu's enough to please any *kamaaina*. There's a sandwich menu for the wary, but culinary adventurers will probably go for one of several island plates, like the *kalua* pig, *lomi* salmon, and *poi* dinner, or the tripe stew with rice — both priced comfortably. If you really want to try something different, order a few a la carte dishes like squid with coconut milk, or *sashimi* (raw fish). I thought the chicken *hekka*, served in a bowl with bamboo shoots and vegetables, was *ono ono*. Four stars.

If you're staying at one of Kahului's bayfront hotels, you might try **Vi's Restaurant** (871-6494) in the Maui Hukilau Hotel. This open-air Polynesian-style establishment has seafood and other assorted dinners. The ambience here is quite pleasant, and the staff congenial, but in the past the service has sometimes been slow. Vi doesn't serve lunch, but at breakfast time she features a menu that includes banana and coconut hot cakes as well as an assortment of mainland-style dishes.

Just up the road in Kaahumanu Center, there's **Apple Annie's** (877-3107), a quaintly decorated coffee shop with rustic motif. In addition to several Mexican dishes which I thought lacked spice, Annie features numerous hamburgers, including a Windsor Burger topped with ham and a shrimp-and-avocado burger. Her breakfast specialty is omelettes; my favorite, a super vegetarian concoction, is made with tomato, sprouts, onion, green pepper, olives, mushrooms, and (what a mouthful!) cheddar cheese. Vegetarians might also try any of the several salads on the menu.

The **East-West Dining Room** (877-0071) lies just across Route 32 in the Maui Palms Resort Hotel. This spacious open-air restaurant looks past the hotel lawn out over Kahului Bay. True to its name, the East-West serves a Japanese buffet at dinner, and at lunch features American cuisine. Both the lunch and evening buffets are priced comfortably. The latter includes shrimp tempura, scallops, mixed vegetables, yakitori chicken, teriyaki steak, many different types of Japanese salad, as well as a host of other dishes. When I sampled the fare with several friends recently, we found the food delicious and the service adequate, but I'll still have to give the place a mixed review. It seems the table next to ours left in anger over what they considered poor service.

Up in Wailuku are two places I heartily recommend. **Wailuku Grill** (2010 Main Street; 244-7505) is a chic but moderate-priced restaurant with pastel walls, art deco fixtures, and track lighting. Open for every meal including weekend brunch, it serves three-course European dinners in the evening. These include a fresh fish, veal, or chicken entree as well as mousse or creme caramel for dessert. At lunch they serve pasta dishes, pizza with pesto and shrimp, plus grill entrees and sandwiches.

The other place is a species of a different color entirely. **Naokee's Steak House** (1792 Lower Main Street, below the overpass leading into town; 244-9444) is a local bar and grill with naugahyde booths and a down-home atmosphere. Dinner includes American, Korean, and French-style steak, fish platters, prawns, and pork chops. At lunch there are more steaks and other full-course meals. Prices are tabbed at the low end of the moderate range. Worth a visit, Naokee's is strong on local color.

Kahului-Wailuku Area Deluxe Restaurants: For elegant dining, there's nothing quite like **The Chart House** (500 North Puunene Avenue; 877-2476). Here you can lean back in a captain's chair and gaze past the woodwork and candlelight out over Kahului Bay. There's a lavish salad-bar-in-the-round centered in the main dining room, an open grill just to the side, and a cozy bar off in the wings. The menu offers a surf-and-turf selection featuring numerous dishes. I recently enjoyed a steak and lobster dinner here and would happily do so again.

Or, for masterfully prepared food without the sophisticated trappings, try **Mama's Fish House** (on Hana Highway; 579-9672) outside Paia. Unlike most well-heeled restaurants, this oceanfront nook is simply decorated: shell *leis*, an old Hawaiian photo here, a painting there, plus potted plants. Elegant simplicity. During lunch, there's a varied menu which includes California cuisine-style dishes and ever-changing specialties. Other than a few steak dishes, the dinner menu is entirely seafood. The evening entrees include scallops, bouillabaisse, crab legs, scampi, and Polynesian lobster. The last is Mama's specialty, cooked in butter and smothered with macadamia nuts and a specially prepared fruit glaze. Another of Mama's treats is fresh fish: there are always at least four varieties, prepared ten different ways.

Lahaina-Kaanapali Area Budget Restaurants: When I go to Lahaina, I usually get funky. There's something about the salty waterfront, the slapdash wooden shops, and the wild history of the place that makes me kick back and not give a damn. That's probably why one of my favorite light-food stops is a devil-may-care place called **Sunrise Cafe** (located around back at 693 Front Street; 661-3326). Set in a tiny clapboard house, it serves salads, sandwiches, special entrees like Cornish game hen, and espresso.

Other than this, you'll fare best at one of Lahaina's many shopping complexes, especially Lahaina Square on Wainee Street. Here **Amilio's Delicatessen** (661-8551) has sandwiches for vegetarians and carnivores alike. Amilio's manages to serve practically everything that you'd expect from a self-respecting deli, and the folks here do it with a special flair.

Across the street in the Lahaina Shopping Center, **Thai Chef Restaurant** (667-2814) has an inviting assortment of South East Asian dishes at lunch and dinner.

Unless you brown-bag it down to the beach, the only budget dining you'll do in Kaanapali is at **Ricco's Old World Delicatessen** (661-4433) in Whaler's Village. This European-style cafe has sidewalk tables shaded by umbrellas, plus a menu featuring sandwiches, burgers, pasta, salads, pizzas, and buffet platters. Priced fairly, the subs include meatballs, Italian sausage, and roast beef, as well as a vegetarian variation prepared with four types of cheese. And all of this within strolling distance of the beach!

Lahaina-Kaanapali Area Moderately Priced Restaurants: In keeping with the rickety old hostelry upstairs, **Pioneer Inn** (658 Wharf Street; 661-3636) has a patchwork of restaurants on its ground floor. **Snug Harbor**, the main dining room, is a cozy anchorage dotted with nautical fixtures. Outside, on the **South Seas Patio**, you can dine beneath umbrellas and palm trees. And across the lobby, on the **Harpooner's Lanai**, there's a view overlooking the Lahaina waterfront. The galley in Snug Harbor fixes steak and seafood dinners (nicely priced) plus a vegetarian special—eggplant and zucchini. Or you can save a few bucks broiling your own steak, *mahimahi*, or other dishes out on the South Seas Patio. Lunch, served in the ever friendly and commodious Harpooner's Lanai, features a soup-and-sandwich menu, with seafood chowder and Portuguese bean soup topping the bill. You can cast anchor at breakfast too.

Another of my special spots is the **Organ Grinder Restaurant** (811 Front Street; 661-4593). This is a rare catch indeed—an inexpensive restaurant smack on the Lahaina waterfront. At lunch this open-air eatery serves scallops, hamburgers with Maui onions, *mahimahi*, and so on. Then for dinner they prepare lobster, prawns in bacon, and other island delights.

Another outstanding choice is **Hamburger Mary's Organic Grill** (608 Front Street; 667-6989). This lovely garden restaurant offers hamburgers (with garnishings that range from bleu cheese to chili), an assortment of sandwiches, and several steak and seafood entrees.

For a taste of the Orient, I'd head to the Lahaina Shopping Center and the **Golden Palace Chinese Restaurant** (661-3126). Boldly decorated with Chinese reliefs, this dimly lighted establishment has an extensive Cantonese menu. There are beef, fowl, pork, and seafood dishes, as well as chop suey. In the afternoon, the Palace combines sweet-and-sour ribs, roast pork, chop suey, shrimp, and rice.

Over in Kaanapali, **La Familia** (667-7902) is located near the entrance to Kaanapali Beach Resort. A patio restaurant overlooking a golf course, it's a pretty place to dine on tostadas, enchiladas, and other Mexican favorites. Open for lunch and dinner, they expand the menu every evening to include steaks and fresh seafood.

The **Kaanapali Beach Hotel Coffee Shop** (in Kaanapali Beach Resort; 661-0011) serves cafeteria-style meals at prices which are surprisingly out of place for this exclusive hotel. But don't expect too much for so little. The menu is limited to a few egg dishes at breakfast, sandwiches and plate lunches, and dinners.

Lahaina-Kaanapali Area Deluxe Restaurants: At the top of the cognoscenti's list of gourmet establishments is an unlikely looking French restaurant in Olowalu called **Chez Paul** (661-3843). The place is located several miles outside Lahaina in a dilapidated building which also houses

Olowalu's funky general store. The interior promises little more. Minimalism seems to have been the designer's aesthetic: the furniture is understated, the decorations simple, and the kitchen is situated just a boardinghouse reach from the dining room. But for years this little hideaway has had a reputation far transcending its surroundings. You'll probably drive right past the place at first, but when you do find it, you'll discover a menu featuring such delicacies as *tournedos*, duck *a l'orange*, veal prepared with apples, scampi, and several other entrees. While the tab runs in the ethereal deluxe range, the rave reviews this prim dining room receives make it worth every franc.

Over in Lahaina, **Longhi's** (888 Front Street; 667-2288) specializes in Italian dishes. Informality is the password to this European-style cafe. The menu changes daily and is never written down; the waiter simply tells you the day's offerings. Usually there'll be several pasta dishes, sauteed vegetables, salads, a shellfish creation, steak, a wine-soaked chicken or veal dish, and perhaps eggplant parmigiana. Longhi's prepares most of its own bread and pasta, buys Maui-grown produce, and imports many cheeses from New York. The dinners, priced moderate to deluxe, reflect this diligence. Breakfasts and lunches are cooked with the same care. Definitely recommended, especially for vegetarians, who can choose from many of the dishes offered.

Kihei Budget Restaurants: Now that condominiums have mushroomed from its white sands, Kihei is no longer a poor person's paradise. Yet there are still several short-order griddles around. If you're coming from Lahaina or Kahului, the first chowhouse will be **Suda's Snack Shop** (61 South Kihei Road; 879-2668). There's another take-out window at **Azeka's Market Snack Shop** in nearby Azeka Place Shopping Center. For atmosphere there's a parking lot, but for food there's a fair choice, with hamburgers and plate lunches priced low.

For funkiness, I pick the **Dairy Queen** (1913 South Kihei Road; 879-3006), a slapdash structure with porch and picnic tables. I especially like the spicy burritos. They also fix burgers, dogs, tacos, and plate lunches. To top off a good junk food meal order a refreshing shave ice.

Surfside Spirits and Deli (1993 South Kihei Road; 879-1385) has a take-out delicatessen serving sandwiches, salads, and slaw.

Kihei Moderately Priced Restaurants: Pickings are even slimmer among sit-down restaurants. You can try **Halekope Coffee Shop** (575 South Kihei Road; 879-5881), a narrow pavilion adjoining the high-beamed (and even higher-priced) Longhouse Restaurant in the Maui Lu Resort. Their dinner menu features shrimp, *mahimahi*, catch of the day, and roast beef; you can also get hot sandwiches for lunch and a complete breakfast selection.

La Familia (2511 South Kihei Road; 879-8824) serves Mexican lunches and dinners. With an ocean-view lanai and tiled bar, it's quite an attractive place. As for the menu: there are *frijoles*, burritos, tacos, and (since this is Hawaii) they also feature crab enchiladas.

At **Gaspare's Place** (1993 South Kihei Road; 879-8881), on the other hand, the "old family recipes" relate to Italian food. In addition to spinning out pizzas, and preparing meatball, vegetarian, and submarine sandwiches, Gaspare's features a complete dinner menu.

Kihei Deluxe Restaurants: For a quiet, intimate meal, I like the **Sailmaker Saloon** (on South Kihei Road; 879-4446). Built on three levels and decorated in a nautical motif, it has a comfortable laid-back atmosphere. Dinner is primarily ribs, but there are seafood items as well. At lunch they serve up soup, salad, and sandwiches, plus several entrees. A gathering place for local residents, the Sailmaker also features a host of breakfast selections.

Island Fish House (1945 South Kihei Road; 879-7771) has the most complete seafood menu around. Not only is the selection broad (usually including about six fresh Hawaiian fish dishes), but the style of preparation varies as well. Snapper, yellowfin tuna, *ono, mahimahi,* and *paka* dishes come poached, sauteed, deep-fried, char-broiled, baked, and teriyaki-style. There are also a number of imported shellfish dishes, plus an extensive wine list. The casual decor at this cozy haunt is simple, but the dishes are elaborately prepared. Dinner only.

HANA AREA RESTAURANTS

If you plan to stay in Hana for any length of time, pack some groceries in with the raingear. You'll find only three restaurants along the entire eastern stretch of the island. Luckily, they cover the gamut from budget to ultra-deluxe. **Tutu's At Hana Bay** (248-8224), located within whistling distance of the water, whips up sandwiches and plate lunches. This take-out stand also serves a few egg dishes for breakfast.

Hana Ranch Restaurant (248-8255) is a small, spiffy establishment decorated with blond woods and offering great ocean views. There's a full bar here plus a flagstone lanai for outdoor dining. Open daily for breakfast and lunch, they serve dinner every Friday and Saturday. Lunch is buffet style; in the evening they offer fresh fish, chops, steak, and baby back ribs; moderate to deluxe. There's also a budget-priced **take-out stand** with picnic tables overlooking the ocean.

Hana's premier restaurant is the dining room of the **Hotel Hana Maui** (248-8211). This extraordinary resort, perched on a hillside overlooking the ocean, serves gourmet meals to its guests and the public alike.

At lunch there's an a la carte menu which includes tiger shrimp, New York steak, and *mahimahi*. The evening meal is a fixed-price affair with stir fry shrimp, veal chops, and three special entrees every night. Ultra-deluxe.

UPCOUNTRY RESTAURANTS

Dillons's (89 Hana Highway, Paia; 579-9113), on the way to Hana, is a down-home dining spot known to local folks for miles around. With its bamboo decor, potted plants, and Tiffany lamps the place perfectly fits the upcountry casual mood. Open for three meals, it serves an array of dinner entrees including homemade pasta dishes, *mahimahi*, and vegetarian lasagna. The lunch fare includes sandwiches, quiche, plus delectables like escargots and *sashimi*. Dine indoors or out on the patio at this enchanting nook. The prices are generally in the moderate range.

Just down the street you'll find **Larry's** (115 Hana Highway, Paia; 579-9035). This old-style restaurant, with bamboo partitions and a screen door that slams, is another favorite watering place for Paia residents. There's a glistening formica counter up front, and a cluster of tables in back. Dining in this local hangout is definitely casual. And the menu is somewhat limited: it generally includes ribs, roast beef, pork, *saimin*, and a selection of sandwiches. But the meals are comfortably priced and the local color is free.

There are several good places in Pukalani Terrace Center on the road to Haleakala. Among them is **Y's Okazu-Ya and Crack Seeds** (572-8258), a Japanese-Chinese-American cafeteria, open for breakfast and lunch only. Choose from such a la carte items as *chow fun*, tempura, Portuguese sausage, stew, or corned-beef hash. None are priced beyond the budget range, and several together comprise a hearty meal. At breakfast, try the eggs with Portuguese sausage.

Grocery Markets

Kahului, Kihei, and Lahaina are the best places to shop on Maui. Of these three towns, Kahului contains the greatest number of supermarkets, health food shops, and specialty stores. It's definitely the place to stock up for a lengthy sojourn away from civilization. Outside Kihei and Lahaina, you'll find the prices high and the inventory low at mom 'n' pop stores in the country.

KAHULUI-WAILUKU AREA GROCERY STORES

Kahului features two sprawling supermarkets: **Foodland** in

Kaahumanu Center and **Star Super Market** in the Maui Mall, both located on Route 32.

KAHULUI-WAILUKU AREA HEALTH FOOD STORES

Down to Earth Natural Foods (1910 Vineyard Street) in Wailuku has a complete line of health food items and fresh produce. Add to that a healthy stock of herbs and you have what amounts to a natural food supermarket. This gets my dollar for being the best place on Maui to shop for natural foods.

There are also stores in two of the shopping centers lining Route 32 in Kahului: **Jamar Health Foods** in Kahului Shopping Center and **Maui Natural Foods** in the Maui Mall.

KAHULUI-WAILUKU AREA FRESH-FISH STORES

Wakamatsu at 145 Market Street in Wailuku has fresh fish daily.

KAHULUI-WAILUKU AREA SPECIALTY SHOPS

Love's Bakery Thrift Shop (344 Ano Street) in Kahului and **Holsum Thrift Shop** (1380 Lower Main Street) in Wailuku sell day-old baked goods at old-fashioned prices.

For Japanese gourmet foods, try **Shirokiya** in the Kaahumanu Center.

LAHAINA-KAANAPALI AREA GROCERY STORES

Lahaina features two supermarkets, **Foodland** in Lahaina Square on Route 30 and **Nagasako Supermarket** in the nearby Lahaina Shopping Center. Foodland is open daily from 8:30 a.m. to 9 p.m. You can shop at Nagasako from 7 a.m. until 9 p.m. every day except Sunday (until 7 p.m.).

Out in the Kaanapali area, the best place to shop is **Honokowai Superette**, a small supermaket on Route 30 in Honokowai.

South of Lahaina, along Route 30 in Olowalu, the **Olowalu General Store** has a limited supply of grocery items.

KIHEI AREA GROCERY STORES

Foodland, a large supermarket in Kihei Town Center on South Kihei Road, has the biggest grocery selection in the area (open 24 hours daily). **Azeka's Market** up the road is often price-competitive, though.

If you're camping at Makena, you'll find **Wailea Pantry** very convenient, but I'm afraid you'll pay for the convenience. This small store, situated in the posh Wailea Shopping Village, is painfully overpriced.

KIHEI AREA SPECIALTY SHOPS

Paradise Fruit Maui, an outdoor stand near Kihei Town Center, has delicious fresh fruit at low-overhead prices.

HANA AREA GROCERY STORES

You'd better stock up before coming if you plan to spend very long in this remote region. There are few restaurants and even fewer stores. **Hana Store** and **Hasegawa General Store**, both in Hana, have limited stocks of grocery items.

UPCOUNTRY GROCERY STORES

Along the road to Haleakala Crater, Route 37, there's a **Foodland** supermarket in the Pukalani Terrace Center, open daily from 7 a.m. to 11 p.m.

Over on the Hana Highway in Paia, **Nagata Store** has a small supply of groceries. If you can't find what you need here, check the **Paia General Store** or **Bersamin's Market** down the street.

Clear across the island, along the back road to Hana, there's a sleeper called **Kaupo Store**. You'll find it tucked away in the southeast corner of the island. Whether it'll be open when you get there, or have what you want, isn't something I'd bet on, though.

UPCOUNTRY HEALTH FOOD STORES

Mountain Fresh Market (Baldwin Avenue, Makawao; 572-1488) and **Mana Foods** (49 Baldwin Avenue, Paia; 579-8078) have complete stocks of health foods and organic produce.

The Great Outdoors

The Sporting Life

CAMPING

Though extremely popular with adventurers, Maui has very few official campsites. The laws restricting camping here are more strictly enforced than on other islands. The emphasis on this boom island favors condominiums and resort hotels rather than outdoor living, but you can still escape the concrete congestion at several parks and unofficial campsites (including one of the most spectacular tenting areas in all Hawaii—Haleakala Crater).

Camping at **county parks** requires a permit. These are issued for a maximum of three nights at each campsite, and cost $3 per person per night, children 50¢. Permits can be obtained at War Memorial Gym adjacent to Baldwin High School, Route 32, Wailuku, or by writing the Department of Parks and Recreation, 1580 Kaahumanu Avenue, Wailuku, Maui, HI 96793 (244-9018).

State park permits are free and allow camping for five days. They can be obtained at the Division of State Parks in the State Building, High Street, Wailuku, or by writing the Division of State Parks, P.O. Box 1049, Wailuku, Maui, HI 96793 (244-4354). You can also rent cabins at Waianapanapa and Polipoli State Parks through this office.

If you plan on camping in Haleakala Crater, you must obtain a permit three months in advance at Haleakala National Park headquarters, located on the way to the crater. Or you can write them at P.O. Box 369, Makawao, Maui, HI 96768 (572-9306). These permits are allocated through a lottery system.

Remember, rainfall is heavy along the northeast shore around Hana, but infrequent on the south coast. Also, Haleakala crater gets quite cold; you'll need heavy clothing and sleeping gear.

For camping equipment, check **Makawao Mercantile.** Located at 3640 Baldwin Avenue in Makawao (572-4569), they sell and rent supplies. **Cycle and Sports Shop** (111 Hana Highway, Kahului; 877-5848) sells a limited amount of camping equipment.

SKIN DIVING

The following shops rent and sell equipment and offer tours for skin and scuba divers: **Central Pacific Divers** (780 Front Street, Lahaina; 661-8718), **Skindiving Maui** (2411 South Kihei Road, Kihei; 879-1502), **Kihei Sea Sports** (Kihei Town Center, South Kihei Road; 879-1919), and **Lahaina Divers Inc.** (710 Front Street, Lahaina; 661-4505).

SURFING AND WINDSURFING

These surf shops rent or sell equipment: **Lightning Bolt** (55 Kaahumanu Avenue, Kahului; 877-3484) and **Skootz Surf & Sailboards** (4310 Lower Honoapiilani Highway, Kahana; 669-0937).

FISHING

For deep-sea fishing contact **Maui Island Travel Connections** (661-8889), **Islander II** (661-3448), and **Lahaina Charter Boats** (667-6672), all located in Lahaina; also try **Luckey Strike Charters** (242-9277).

OTHER SPORTS

GOLF

To tee off, try **Waiehu Municipal Golf Course** (Waiehu; 244-5433), **Kapalua Golf Course** (Kapalua; 669-8044), **Royal Kaanapali Golf Course**

(Kaanapali; 661-3691), **Wailea Golf** (Kihei; 879-2966), and **Pukalani Country Club** (Pukalani; 572-1314).

HORSEBACK RIDING

Stables renting horses include **Rainbow Ranch Riding Stables** (Napili; 669-4991), **Pony Express Tours** (Makawao; 667-2202), and **Thompson Ranch Riding Stables** (Kula; 878-1910).

Beaches and Parks
(Plus Camping, Swimming, Snorkeling, Surfing, Fishing)

KAHULUI-WAILUKU AREA BEACHES AND PARKS

Hoaloha Park—This is Kahului's only beach, but unfortunately the nearby harbor facilities detract from the natural beauty of its white sands. There's heavy boat traffic on one side and several hotels on the other, so I don't recommend the place. It is a good spot, however, to beachcomb (particularly for Maui diamonds).

Facilities: Picnic tables.

Camping: Not permitted.

Swimming: Poor.

Snorkeling: Poor.

Surfing: Good breaks (two to six feet) off the jetty mouth near the north shore of Kahului Harbor. Left slide.

Fishing: Goatfish, *papio,* and triggerfish can be hooked from the pier; *ulua* and *papio* are often caught along the shore.

Getting there: Next to Kahului hotels on Route 32.

Kepaniwai County Park—Located in Wailuku on the road to Iao Valley, this beautiful park is surrounded by sheer cliffs. Here you'll discover paths over arched bridges and through gardens, pagodas, a thatch-roofed hut, a *taro* patch, and banana, papaya, and coconut trees. You'll also find picnic pavilions, restrooms, and a swimming pool. An ideal and romantic spot for picnicking.

H. A. Baldwin Park—This spacious county park, located several miles east of Kahului on the Hana Highway, is bordered by a playing field on one side and a crescent-shaped beach on the other. Palm and ironwood trees dot the half-mile long beach. There's good shell collecting and a great view of West Maui. This otherwise lovely park has at times been the scene of robberies and violence; if you camp here (which I do not recommend), exercise caution.

Facilities: Picnic area complete with large pavilion, showers, restrooms, and playground. Markets and restaurants are a short distance away in Paia.

Camping: Tent and trailer. County permit required.

Swimming: Good, but beware of currents. Good bodysurfing.

Snorkeling: Not recommended.

Surfing: Winter breaks. Right slide.

Fishing: Good for threadfin, mountain bass, goatfish, and *ulua.*

Getting there: Turn left off Route 36, about seven miles east of Kahului.

Hookipa Park—Situated several miles farther east on the Hana Highway, this is an unappealing strip of parkland on a hill about twenty feet above the ocean. There's a white-sand beach extending to the water's edge, where a protruding reef creates a rocky bottom. Nice view of West Maui.

Facilities: Picnic area, restrooms; markets and restaurants are down the road in Paia.

Camping: Not permitted.

Swimming: Not advisable due to strong currents.

Snorkeling: Good on extremely calm days, but generally not advisable.

Surfing: Long paddle out to huge walls. Summer and winter breaks. Wicked currents. This isn't kid stuff!

Fishing: Good.

Getting there: Follow Route 36 for about ten miles east of Kahului.

LAHAINA-KAANAPALI AREA BEACHES AND PARKS

Papalaua State Park—*Kiawe* trees and scrub vegetation spread right to the shoreline along Papalaua beach park. There are sandy patches between the trees large enough to spread a towel, but I prefer sunbathing at beaches closer to Lahaina.

Bounded on one side by Route 30, this narrow beach extends for a mile to join a nicer, lawn-fringed park, and then stretches on toward Olowalu for several more miles. If you want to be alone, just head down the shore.

Facilities: There's an outhouse and picnic area at the state wayside and picnic facilities at the grassy park. You'll find a small market several miles away in Olowalu.

Camping: Not allowed.

Swimming: Good.

Snorkeling: Okay out past the surf break.

Surfing: Not good here, but the south shore's best surfing can be found several miles east in Maalaea Bay.

Getting there: Located on Route 30 about ten miles south of Lahaina.

Olowalu Beaches—Both to the north and south of Olowalu General Store lie narrow corridors of white sand.

Facilities: None. Market nearby.

Camping: Not permitted.

Swimming: Very good.

Snorkeling: South of the general store, where road and water meet, you'll find an excellent coral reef.

Surfing: Good breaks about one-half mile north of the general store. Right and left slide.

Fishing: Often *ulua* are caught from Olowalu landing.

Getting there: Travel south from Lahaina on Route 30 for about six miles.

Launiupoko State Park—There's a seaside lawn shaded by palm trees, but no beach here. A rock sea wall slopes gently for entering swimmers, but offers little to sunbathers. Launiupoko is located near the West Maui Mountains, with great views of Kahoolawe and Lanai.

Facilities: Picnic area, restrooms, showers. Restaurants and markets are three miles away in Lahaina.

Camping: Not permitted.

Swimming: Mediocre.

Snorkeling: Mediocre.

Fishing: Good surf-casting from here south for three miles.

Getting there: Located three miles south of Lahaina on Route 30.

Puamana Park—A grass-covered strip and narrow beach wedged between Route 30 and the ocean, Puamana Park is dotted with ironwood trees. The excellent views make this a choice spot for a picnic. It's located on Route 30, about two miles south of Lahaina.

Maluulu o Lele Park—This park has one thing going for it—a convenient location in Lahaina. Otherwise, it's heavily littered, shadowed by Whaler's Market Place, and sometimes crowded. If you do stop by, try to forget all that and concentrate on the sandy beach, lawn, and truly startling view of Lanai directly across the Auau Channel.

Facilities: Restrooms and tennis courts are across the street near the playing field.

Swimming: Okay.

Snorkeling: Good past the reef.

Whale-Watching

Every year the humpback whales return to the Lahaina Roads after summering in the Bering Sea. Measuring forty-five feet and weighing over forty tons, these rare giants make the migration south in order to breed in Maui's warm waters.

Any time from November until May you can see them swimming in the tropic seas between Maui, Molokai, Lanai, and Kahoolawe. The best months for whale-watching are January to April; the most favorable times are from 8 until 11 a.m. and 1:30 to 5 p.m. Rough, windy days are best for watching them at their acrobatics — breaching, tailslapping, etc.

About 400 to 500 of the world's 7,000 humpbacks make the annual migration to Lahaina. Today they are an endangered species, protected by federal law from whalers. Several local organizations study these leviathans and serve as excellent information sources. The **Pacific Whale Foundation** can be contacted at 879-8811; **Maui Whale Watchers** and the local chapter of the **American Cetacean Society** have no central numbers but post public notices of their meetings. There is also a **Whale Report Center** (661-8527) for registering sightings.

A prime area for whale-watching lies along Route 30 between Maalaea Bay and Lahaina, particularly at McGregor Point. **Windjammer Cruises** (667-6834) and **Sea Bird Cruises** (661-3643) in Lahaina offer whale-spotting cruises.

So while you're visiting Maui always keep an eye peeled seaward for vaporous spume and a rolling hump. The place you're standing might suddenly become an ideal crow's nest.

Surfing: Summer breaks near the sea wall in Lahaina Harbor.

Fishing: Threadfin and *ulua* are common catches here.

Getting there: Easy to find, this park is right on Front Street next to Whaler's Market Place in Lahaina.

Lahaina Beach—This curving stretch of white sand is the best beach in Lahaina. It lacks privacy but certainly not beauty. From here you can look back to Lahaina town and the West Maui Mountains, or out over the ocean to Kahoolawe, Lanai, and Molokai. Or just close your eyes and soak up the sun.

Facilities: None. Restaurants and markets nearby in Lahaina.

Camping: Not permitted.

Swimming: Good, well-protected, shallow.

Snorkeling: Fair.

Surfing: Summer breaks nearby at Mala Wharf. Left slide.

Fishing: Threadfin and *ulua* are often caught.

Getting there: Take Front Street north from Lahaina for about a half-mile. Turn left on Puunoa Place and follow it to the beach.

Wahikuli State Park—This narrow stretch of beach and lawn, just off the road between Lahaina and Kaanapali, faces Lanai and Molokai. There are facilities aplenty, which might be why this pretty park is so popular and crowded.

Facilities: Picnic areas, restrooms; tennis courts across the street. Markets and restaurants nearby in Lahaina.

Camping: Not permitted.

Swimming: Very good.

Snorkeling: Fair. There's a better spot just north of here near the Lahaina Canoe Club.

Surfing: Poor.

Fishing: The most common catches are *ulua* and threadfin.

Getting there: Located on Route 30 between Lahaina and Kaanapali.

Hanakaoo Beach Park—Conveniently located beside Kaanapali Beach Resort, this long, narrow facility features a white-sand beach and grassy picnic ground. The road is nearby, but the views of Lanai are outstanding.

Facilities: Picnic areas, restrooms, showers. Restaurants and groceries nearby.

Camping: Not permitted.

Swimming: Good.

Snorkeling: Fair.

(Text continued on page 162.)

Shell Hunting

With over 1,500 varieties of shells washing up on its beaches, Hawaii has some of the world's finest shelling. The miles of sandy beach along Maui's south shore are a prime area for handpicking free souvenirs. Along the shores are countless shell specimens with names like horned helmet, Hebrew cone, Hawaiian olive, and Episcopal miter. Or you might find glass balls from Japan and sunbleached driftwood.

Beachcombing is the easiest method of shell gathering. Take along a small container and stroll through the backwash of the waves, watching for ripples from shells lying under the sand. You can also dive in shallow water where the ocean's surge will uncover shells.

It's tempting to walk along the top of coral reefs seeking shells and other marine souvenirs, but these living formations maintain a delicate ecological balance. Reefs in Hawaii and all over the planet are dying because of such plunder. In order to

protect this underwater world, try to collect only shells and souvenirs that are adrift on the beach and no longer necessary to the marine ecology.

The best shelling spots along Maui's south shore are Makena, Kihei beaches, Maalaea Bay, Olowalu, the sandy stretch from Kaanapali to Napili Bay, D.T. Fleming Park, and Honolua Bay. On the north coast, the stretch from Waiehu to Waihee (west of Kahului) and the black-sand beach at Hana are the choicest hunting grounds.

After heavy rainfall, watch near stream mouths for Hawaiian olivines and in stream beds for Maui diamonds. Olivines are small, semiprecious stones of an olive hue. Maui diamonds are quartz stones and make beautiful jewelry. The best places to find Maui diamonds are near the Kahului Bay hotel strip and in Olowalu stream.

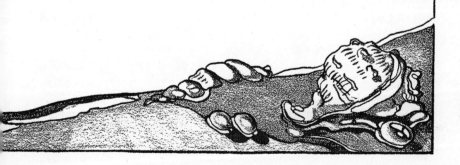

Surfing: Poor.

Fishing: Common catches include *ulua* and threadfin.

Getting there: Located on Route 30 between Lahaina and Kaanapali.

Kaanapali Resort Beaches—The sprawling complex of Kaanapali hotels along Route 30 sits astride a beautiful white-sand beach. Looking out on Lanai and Molokai, this is a classic palm-fringed strand. The entire area is heavily developed, and crowded by flaccid old ladies glistening in coconut oil. But it *is* an extraordinarily fine beach.

There's very good swimming plus excellent skin diving and body-surfing around Black Rock at the Sheraton Maui Hotel.

Take the public right-of-way to the beach at the former Kaanapali Airfield off Route 30, or you can enter between the resort hotels.

Honokowai Beach Park—Compared to the beaches fronting Kaanapali's nearby resorts, this is a bit disappointing. The large lawn is pleasant enough, but the beach itself is small, with a reef that projects right to the shoreline. The view of Molokai is awesome, though.

Facilities: Picnic tables, restrooms, showers. Directly across the street is a supermarket.

Camping: Not permitted.

Swimming: Good.

Snorkeling: Good.

Surfing: Not usually good.

Fishing: Threadfin and *ulua* are among the most frequent catches.

Getting there: On Lower Honoapiilani Road (which is the ocean-front section of Route 30) north of Kaanapali in Honokowai.

Napili Bay—You'll find wall-to-wall condominiums along this small cove. There's a crowded but beautiful white-sand beach studded with palm trees and looking out on Molokai.

Good swimming and snorkeling. Good surfing for beginners.

Located several miles north of Kaanapali, with rights-of-way to the beach from Route 30 via Napili Place or Hui Drive.

Kapalua Beach—This is the next cove over from Napili Bay. It's equally beautiful, but not as heavily developed.

Good swimming, fair snorkeling.

There's a right-of-way to the beach from Route 30 near the Napili Kai Beach Club.

D.T. Fleming Park—One of Maui's nicest beach parks, D.T. Fleming has a spacious white-sand beach plus a rolling lawn shaded with palm and ironwood trees. It's far enough from Kaanapali to escape the development blight, but close enough to make the beach easily accessible. Sometimes windy, the park is plagued by rough and dangerous surf in winter. There's a nice view of Molokai's rugged East End.

Facilities: Restrooms, picnic area, showers. Five miles to the market in Honokowai.

Camping: Not permitted.

Swimming: Good swimming and bodysurfing.

Snorkeling: Fair.

Surfing: Good breaks nearby at "Little Makaha," named after the famous Oahu beach.

Fishing: Prime catches here are *ulua* and *papio.*

Getting there: Just off Route 30 about seven miles north of Kaanapali.

Oneloa Beach or Slaughterhouse Beach (★)—This lovely patch of white sand is bounded by cliffs and looks out on Molokai. Set at the end of a shallow cove, the beach is partially protected.

Facilities: None. It's six miles south to the market in Honokowai.

Camping: Unofficial camping okay.

Swimming: Good.

Snorkeling: Good.

Surfing: Good breaks.

Fishing: Common catches include *papio,* leatherback, milkfish, *moano,* and big-eyed scad.

Getting there: Take Route 30 for exactly eight-tenths of a mile past D.T. Fleming Park. A steep path leads down about 100 yards from the parking area to the beach.

Honolua Bay (★)—A rocky beach makes this cliff-rimmed bay unappealing for sunbathers, but there are rich coral deposits offshore and beautiful trees growing near the water.

Facilities: None.

Camping: Unofficial camping.

Swimming: Good, but the bottom is rocky.

Snorkeling: Excellent, particularly on the right side of the bay.

Surfing: One of the finest breaks in all Hawaii. Perfect tubes up to fifteen feet.

Fishing: Milkfish, *papio,* leatherback, *moano,* and big-eyed scad are among the most frequent catches.

Getting there: Take Route 30 for about one-and-a-third miles north from D.T. Fleming Park. Turn left onto the dirt road and follow it several hundred yards to the bay. (Surfers should continue another eight-tenths of a mile on Route 30, then turn left onto the dirt road bordering the nearby pineapple field. A path from this road leads down a cliff to a small beach and the best breaks.)

Windmill Beach (or **Pohakupule Beach**) (★)—A white-sand beach studded with rocks, Windmill Beach is surrounded by cliffs and intriguing rock formations. Very secluded.

Facilities: None. Eight miles to the market in Honokowai.

Camping: Permit required from Maui Land and Pineapple Co., Honolua Division, Lahaina, Maui, HI 96761 (669-6201). No charge; three-day limit.

Swimming: Okay when calm.

Snorkeling: Excellent when calm. A fascinating reef extends along the coast all through this area.

Surfing: Fine peak in winter. Left and right slide.

Fishing: Leatherback, *papio,* milkfish, *moano,* and big-eyed scad are the primary catches.

Getting there: Go just three-and-a-half miles north from D.T. Fleming Park on Route 30, then turn left onto the dirt road. Follow it a short distance to the beach.

Honokohau Beach—A rocky beach surrounded by cliffs.

Facilities: None. Ten miles to markets in Honokowai.

Camping: Too rocky.

Swimming: Good when calm.

Snorkeling: Good when calm.

Surfing: Rugged two- to twelve-foot breaks.

Fishing: Milkfish, *papio,* leatherback, *moano,* and big-eyed scad are the principal species caught in these waters.

Getting there: Follow Route 30 about six miles north of D. T. Fleming Park.

KIHEI AREA BEACHES AND PARKS

Kihei Beach—This narrow, palm-fringed beach stretches from Maalaea Bay to Kihei. It can be seen from several points along Route 31 and is everywhere accessible from the highway. There are buildings and numerous condominiums along this strip but few large crowds on the beach. Beach joggers take note: you can run for miles along this unbroken strand, but watch for heavy winds in the afternoon.

Facilities: There are picnic tables and restrooms at **Kihei Memorial Park** (located midway along the beach). Markets and restaurants are nearby.

Camping: None.

Swimming: Well-protected by shoals, but very shallow.

Snorkeling: Fair (better at Kamaole beaches).

Surfing: Poor.

Fishing: Bonefish, *papio,* mullet, goatfish, *ulua, moano,* and mountain bass.

Getting there: Kihei Beach runs along Kihei Road between Maalaea and Kihei.

Kalama County Beach Park—This long, broad park has an ample lawn but very little beach. Rather than lapping along the sand, waves wash up against a stone sea wall. Backdropped by Haleakala, the park has stunning views of West Maui, Lanai, and Kahoolawe. Here's an excellent place for a picnic, but before you pack your lunch, remember Kalama, like all Kihei's beaches, is swept by afternoon winds.

Facilities: Picnic areas, restrooms, showers, tennis courts. Restaurants and markets nearby.

Camping: Not permitted.

Swimming: Shoals provide ample protection, but they also create shallows throughout this area.

Snorkeling: Fair.

Surfing: Summer breaks over a coral reef. Left and right slide.

Fishing: Poor.

Getting there: Located on South Kihei Road across from Kihei Town Center.

Kamaole Beach Parks, I, II, and III—Strung like beads along the Kihei shore are these three beautiful parks, their white sands fringed with grass and studded with trees. With Haleakala in the background, they all offer magnificent views of the West Maui Mountains, Lanai, and Kahoolawe. All are windswept in the afternoon, though.

Facilities: Each is equipped with picnic area, restrooms, and showers. Kamaole III also has a playground. Restaurants and markets are nearby.

Camping: Not permitted.

Swimming: Very good on all three beaches.

Snorkeling: Best near the rocks fringing Kamaole III.

Fishing: Common catches include bonefish, *papio,* mullet, goatfish, *ulua, moano,* and mountain bass.

Getting there: On South Kihei Road near Kihei Town Center.

Keawakapu Beach—Ho hum, another of Kihei's beautiful white-sand beaches. Like other nearby beach parks, Keawakapu has marvelous views of the West Maui Mountains and Lanai, but is plagued by afternoon winds.

Facilities: Showers. Short distance to the markets and restaurants of Kihei and Wailea.

Camping: Not permitted.

Swimming: Good, but not as well-protected as Kamaole beaches.

Snorkeling: Good around rocks.

Fishing: Excellent. Numerous species can be caught here.

Getting there: Located on South Kihei Road between Kihei and Wailea.

Mokapu and **Ulua Beaches**—Two crescent-shaped beaches fringed with palms and looking out toward Lanai and Kahoolawe, these have much of their natural beauty spoiled by the nearby hotel and condominium developments.

To get there, follow the signs near Stouffer's Wailea Beach Hotel in Wailea.

Wailea Beach—Another beach in the ultra-modern Wailea development, this lovely white-sand strip is fringed with *kiawes.* No facilities, but plenty of tourists. Oh well.

Located just half a mile south of Wailea Shopping Village.

Polo Beach—Though not quite so attractive as Wailea Beach, Polo is slightly more secluded. There's a bountiful stretch of white sand, plus great views of Kahoolawe and Molokini. No facilities.

Located about one mile south of Wailea Shopping Village.

Halfway Beach—This lovely white-sand beach derives its name from its location midway between Wailea and Makena. Next to Makena, Halfway is the prettiest beach in the area.

Facilities: None. Two miles from the market in Wailea.

Camping: Unofficial tenting is very common under the *kiawe* trees which front the beach.

Swimming: Good.

Snorkeling: Fair.

Fishing: Very good; many species are caught here.

Getting there: Continue on the coast road south past Wailea Shopping Village for about two miles. The road becomes bumpy as you leave Wailea. You'll see Halfway Beach from the road, off to your right, just before the Makena Surf development.

Black Sands Beach (★)—This is a long, narrow salt-and-pepper beach located just north of Red Hill, a shoreline cinder cone. Fringed with *kiawe* trees, this beach is less attractive but more secluded than Makena.

Facilities: Nonexistent; four miles to the market in Wailea.

Camping: Unofficial camping okay.

Swimming: Good.

Snorkeling: Fair.

Fishing: Very good; many species caught.

Getting there: Follow the coast road south from Wailea Shopping Village for exactly four-and-three-tenths miles. Turn right on the dirt road at the north end of Red Hill, then bear right.

Makena Beach (★) — Much more than a beach, Makena is an institution. For over a decade, it's been a countercultural gathering place. There are even stories about the Rolling Stones, Elton John, and other rock luminaries jamming here during Makena's heyday in the early 1970s. While once a hideaway for hippies, the beach today is increasingly popular with straight tourists and is slated for mondo-condo development. Hurry — so far this long, wide corridor of white sand curving south from Red Hill is still the most beautiful beach on Maui.

Little Makena, a pretty white-sand beach next to Makena Beach, is a nude beach. It's just across Red Hill from the main beach. But if you go nude here or at Makena, watch out for police; they regularly bust nudists.

Facilities: None. About four miles to the market in Wailea.

Camping: Unofficial camping is very popular here. Beware of ripoffs.

Swimming: Good. Good bodysurfing at Little Makena.

Snorkeling: Good near the rocks at the north end of the beach.

Fishing: Very good; many species caught.

Getting there: Follow the coast road south from Wailea Shopping Village for a little over four miles. The road turns from pavement to dirt. Watch for Red Hill, the large cinder cone on your right. Just past Red Hill, turn right onto any of several dirt roads and continue to the beach.

HANA AREA BEACHES AND PARKS

Honomanu Bay (★) — This tranquil black-sand-and-rock beach, surrounded by pandanus-covered hills and bisected by a stream, is a very beautiful and secluded spot. There are no facilities, and the water is often too rough for swimming, but it's a favorite with surfers.

Located off the Hana Highway (Route 36) about 30 miles east of Kahului. Turn off onto the dirt road east of Kaumahina State Park; follow it to the beach.

Waianapanapa State Park — Set in a heavenly seaside locale, this is one of Hawaii's prettiest parks. The entire area is lush with tropical foliage, especially palmy pandanus trees. There's a black-sand beach, sea arches, a blowhole, and two legendary caves. But pack your parkas; wind and rain are frequent. The cabins and campsites make this a very popular spot.

Facilities: Picnic area, restrooms, showers, cabins. About four miles to markets and restaurants in Hana.

Camping: State permit required. Campsites are on a grass-covered bluff overlooking the sea. The cabins are rented through the Division of State Parks (see "The Sporting Life" section in this chapter). These are plain but attractive accommodations renting on a sliding scale (starting at $10 single and $14 double up to $30 for six people). Each one contains a small bedroom with two bunk beds, plus a living room which can double as an extra bedroom. All cabins are equipped with bedding and complete kitchen facilities, and some have ocean views.

Swimming: Good when the water's calm.

Snorkeling: Good when the water's calm.

Fishing: Good.

Getting there: Just off the Hana Highway (Route 36) about four miles north of the town of Hana.

Hana Beach Park—Tucked into a well-protected corner of Hana Bay, this park features a large pavilion and a curving stretch of sandy beach.

Facilities: Picnic area, restrooms. Snack bars across the street.

Camping: Not permitted.

Swimming: Good.

Snorkeling: Good near the lighthouse.

Surfing: Summer and winter breaks on the north side of the bay. Left slide.

Fishing: There are bonefish, *ulua,* and *papio,* plus runs of *moi-lii* in June and July.

Getting there: Located on Hana Bay.

Koki Park—A pretty little white-sand beach backdropped by cliffs, this has no facilities. Treacherous currents preclude swimming, but on a sunny day Koki makes an ideal picnic spot.

To get there, head south from Hana on Route 36 for a couple of miles. Turn left onto the loop road that leads toward privately-owned Hamoa Beach. Koki will appear on the left before you reach Hamoa.

Oh'eo Gulch or **Seven Pools**—The stream which tumbles down Haleakala through the National Park's Kipahulu section forms seven large pools and numerous small ones. The main pools, known to many as the Seven Sacred Pools, descend from above the Hana Highway to the sea. This is a truly enchanting area—swept by frequent wind and rain, and shadowed by Haleakala. It overlooks Maui's rugged eastern shore.

You can swim in the pools' chilly waters and camp nearby on a bluff above the sea. There are picnic tables and outhouses. Three-day limit for campers; no permit required.

The pools are located on the Hana Highway about ten miles south of Hana.

UPCOUNTRY PARKS

Poli Poli State Park—Located at 6,200 feet on the slopes of Haleakala, this densely forested park is an ideal mountain retreat. Monterey and sugi pine, eucalyptus and Monterey cypress grow in stately profusion; not far from the campground there's a grove of redwoods. From Poli Poli's ethereal heights you can look out over Central and West Maui, as well as the islands of Lanai, Molokai, and Kahoolawe. Miles of trails, some leading up to Haleakala Crater, crisscross the park.

Facilities: Picnic area, restrooms, running water, cabin.

Camping: State permit required. The cabin houses up to ten people and rents on a sliding scale from $10 single and $14 double up to $50 for ten people. The spacious cabin (three-bedrooms) is sparsely furnished and lacks electricity. It does have a wood heating stove, gas cooking stove, gas lanterns, kitchen utensils, and bedding. It can be rented from the Division of State Parks (see "The Sporting Life" section in this chapter for the address).

Getting there: From Kahului, take Route 37 (Haleakala Highway) through Pukalani and past Waiakoa to Route 377. Turn left on 377 and follow it a short distance to the road marked for Poli Poli. This ten-mile road to the park is paved about halfway up. The second half of the track is extremely rough and often muddy. It is advisable to take a 4-wheel drive vehicle, especially if more than two people are in the car.

Keokea Park—A pleasant picnic spot on Route 37 in Keokea. There's a rolling lawn with picnic tables and restrooms.

Hiking

Many people complain that Maui is overdeveloped. The wall-to-wall condominiums lining the Kaanapali and Kihei beachfront can be pretty depressing to the outdoors lover. But happily there is a way to escape. Hike right out of it.

The Valley Isle has many fine trails which lead through Hana's rain forest, Haleakala's magnificent crater, up to West Maui's peaks, and across the south shore's arid lava flows. Any of them will carry you far from the madding crowd. It's quite simple on Maui to trade the mondo-condo tourist enclaves for virgin mountains, untrammeled beaches, and eerie volcanic terrain. If you're unfamiliar with the island, or uncomfortable about exploring solo, you might consider an organized tour. The National Park Service (Haleakala National Park, Box 369, Makawao, Maui, HI 96768; 572-9306) provides information to hikers interested in exploring Haleakala or other sections of the island.

If you'd rather head off alone, check the trail descriptions below for a basic guide to most of Maui's major trails.

KAHULUI-WAILUKU AREA TRAILS

The main trails in this Central Maui region lie in Iao Valley, Kahului, and along Route 34.

Two trails begin near the parking lot at Iao Valley State Park. **Table-land Trail** (2 miles long) climbs about 500 feet from the park lookout shelter to the tableland above Iao Valley. A detour along a short loop trail provides spectacular views of Iao Valley and Wailuku.

Iao Stream Trail (1 mile) leads from the park parking lot for half a mile along the stream. The second half of the trek involves wading through the stream or hopping across the shoreline rocks. But your efforts will be rewarded with some excellent swimming holes en route. You might want to plan your time so you can relax and swim.

Not far from the Kahului Airport on Route 36, bird watchers will be delighted to find a trail meandering through **Kanaha Pond Wildlife Sanctuary** (2 miles). This jaunt follows two loop roads, each one mile long, and passes the natural habitat of the rare Hawaiian stilt and the Hawaiian coot. Permits necessary from State Division of Forestry (244-4352).

Northwest of Kahului, along Route 34, are two trails well worth exploring, the Waihee Ridge and Kahakuloa Valley Trails.

Waihee Ridge Trail (2.5 miles) begins just below Maluhia Boy Scout Camp outside the town of Waihee. The trail passes through a guava thicket and scrub forest and climbs 1,500 feet en route to a peak overlooking West and Central Maui.

Kahakuloa Valley Trail (2 miles) requires driving over the rugged dirt road section of Route 34 to the picturesque town of Kahakuloa. This is one of the most beautiful, untouched spots on Maui. The trail begins across the road from a schoolhouse and passes burial caves, stands of guava and passion fruit, and old agricultural terraces.

KIHEI AREA TRAILS

King's Highway Coastal Trail (5.5 miles) follows an ancient Hawaiian route over the 1790 lava flow. The trail begins near La Perouse Bay at the end of the rugged road which connects La Perouse Bay with Makena Beach and Wailea. It heads inland through groves of *kiawe* trees, then skirts the coast and finally leads to Kanaloa Point. From this point the trail continues across private land.

HANA AREA TRAILS

Hana-Waianapanapa Coastal Trail (3 miles), part of the ancient King's Highway, skirts the coastline between Waianapanapa State Park and Hana Bay. The trail passes a *heiau*, sea arch, blowhole, and numerous caves while winding through lush stands of *hala* trees.

Waimoku Falls Trail (2 miles) leads from the bridge at Seven Pools up to Waimoku Falls. On the way it goes by four of the pools and traverses a bamboo forest. (Text continued on page 175.)

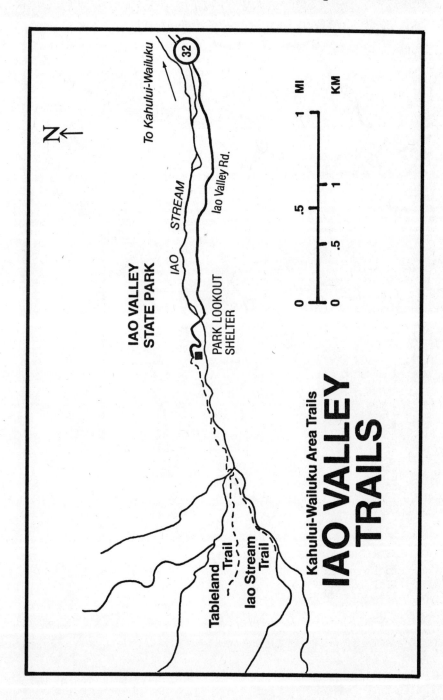

N

IAO VALLEY
STATE PARK

To Kahului-Wailuku

32

IAO   STREAM

Iao Valley Rd.

PARK LOOKOUT
SHELTER

Tableland
Trail

Iao Stream
Trail

Kahului-Wailuku Area Trails

IAO VALLEY
TRAILS

MI

KM

0   .5   .5   1

0   1

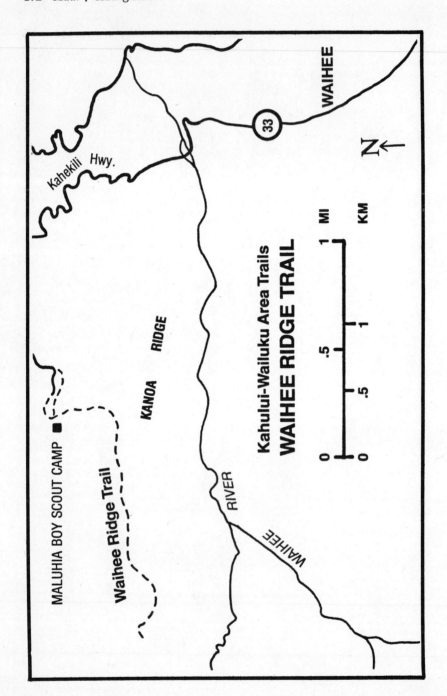

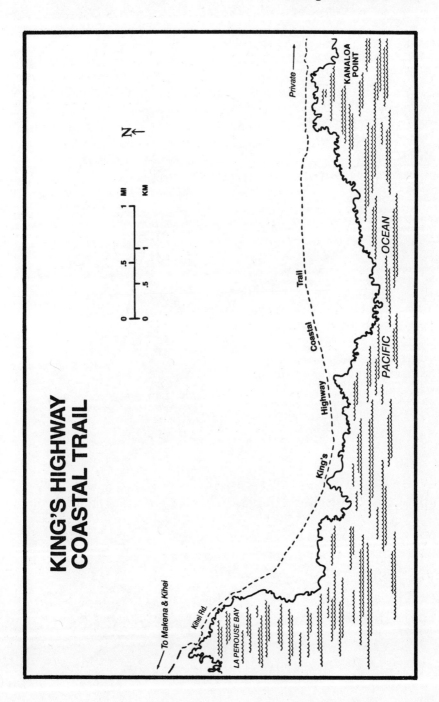

KING'S HIGHWAY
COASTAL TRAIL

N

MI

KM

0 .5 1

0 .5 1

To Makena & Kihei

Kihei Rd.

LA PEROUSE BAY

King's

Highway

Coastal

Trail

Private

KANALOA
POINT

PACIFIC

OCEAN

UPCOUNTRY TRAILS

The main trails in Maui's beautiful Upcountry lie on Haleakala's southern slopes. They branch out from Poli Poli State Park through the Kula and Kahikinui Forest Reserves.

Redwood Trail (1.7 miles) descends from Poli Poli's 6,200-foot elevation through impressive stands of redwoods to the ranger's cabin at 5,300 feet. There is a dilapidated public shelter in the old CCC camp at trail's end.

Plum Trail (2.3 miles) begins at the CCC camp and climbs gently south to Haleakala Ridge Trail. The route passes plum trees as well as stands of ash, redwood, and sugi pine. There are shelters at both ends of the trail.

Tie Trail (0.5 mile) descends 500 feet through cedar, ash, and sugi pine groves to link Redwood and Plum Trails. There is a shelter at the Redwood junction.

Poli Poli Trail (0.6 mile) cuts through cypress, cedars, and pines en route from Poli Poli Campground to Haleakala Ridge Trail.

Boundary Trail (4.4 miles) begins at the cattle guard marking the Kula Forest Reserve boundary along the road to Poli Poli. It crosses numerous gulches planted in cedar, eucalyptus, and pine; the trail terminates at the ranger's cabin.

Waiohuli Trail (1.4 miles) descends 800 feet from Poli Poli Road to join Boundary Trail. Along the way it passes young pine and grasslands, then drops down through groves of cedar, redwood, and ash. There is a shelter at the Boundary Trail junction.

Skyline Trail (6.5 miles) begins at 9,750 feet, near the top of Haleakala's southwest rift, and descends over 3,000 feet to the top of Haleakala Ridge Trail. The trail passes a rugged, treeless area resembling the moon's surface. Then it drops below timberline at 8,600 feet and eventually into dense scrub. The unobstructed views of Maui and the neighboring islands are awesome.

Haleakala Ridge Trail (1.6 miles) starts from Skyline Trail's terminus at 6,550 feet and descends along Haleakala's southwest rift to 5,600 feet. There are spectacular views in all directions and a shelter at trail's end.

(For **Haleakala Crater** trails see the "In the Belly of the Volcano" section in this chapter.)

(Text continued on page 179.)

In the Belly of the Volcano

While the views along the crater rim are awesome, the best way to see Haleakala is from the inside looking out. With thirty-two miles of hiking trails, two campsites, and three cabins, the crater provides a tremendous opportunity for explorers. Within the belly of this monstrous volcano, you'll see such geologic features as cinder cones, lava tubes, and spatter vents. The Hawaiians marked their passing with stone altars, shelters, and adze quarries. You may also spy the rare *nene* (a Hawaiian relative of the Canada goose), as well as chukar partridges,

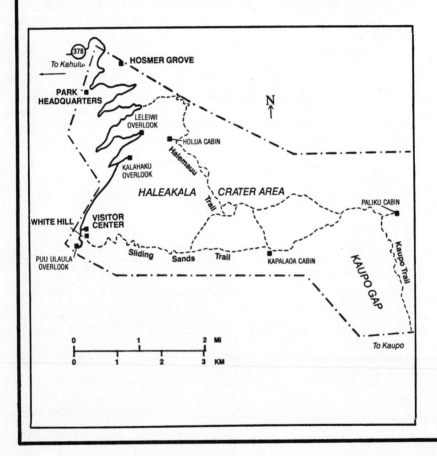

pheasants, mynahs, and white-tailed tropicbirds. Feral goats roam about, sometimes feeding on the endangered silversword plant.

The crater floor is a unique environment, one of constant change and unpredictable weather. Rainfall varies from twelve inches annually in the southwestern corner to two hundred inches at Paliku. Temperatures, usually hovering between 55° and 75° during daylight, may fall below freezing at night. Campers should come prepared with warm clothing and sleeping gear, a tent, poncho, and stove (no open fires are permitted). Don't forget the sunburn lotion, as the elevation on the crater bottom averages 6,700 feet and the ultraviolet radiation is intense.

(Text continued on page 178.)

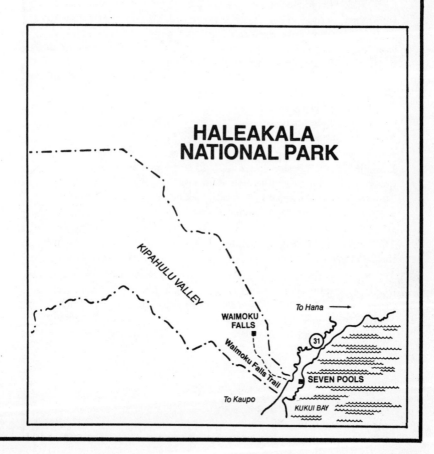

HALEAKALA
NATIONAL PARK

KIPAHULU VALLEY

To Hana →

WAIMOKU
FALLS

Waimoku Falls Trail

31

SEVEN POOLS

To Kaupo

KUKUI BAY

Within the crater you can explore three main trails. **Sliding Sands Trail,** a steep cinder and ash path, begins near the Visitor Center. It descends from the crater rim along the south wall to Kapalaoa cabin, then on to Paliku cabin. In the course of this ten-mile trek, the trail drops over 3,000 feet. From Paliku, the **Kaupo Trail** leaves the crater through Kaupo Gap and descends to the tiny town of Kaupo, eight miles away on Maui's southeast coast. **Halemauu Trail** (10 miles) begins from the road three-and-a-half miles beyond Park Headquarters and descends 1,400 feet to the crater floor. It passes Holua cabin and eventually joins Sliding Sands Trail near the Paliku cabin.

There are campgrounds at **Holua** and **Paliku** which require a permit from Park Headquarters. They have pit toilets and running water. Camping is limited to two days at one site and three days total at both. There is also a twelve-person cabin at each campsite and also at **Kapalaoa.** Equipped with wood stoves, pit toilets, cooking utensils, and mattresses, these primitive facilities are extremely popular. So popular, in fact, that guests are chosen by lottery and required to pay $15 a night for each adult, and $2.50 nightly minimum for children. If you can secure a cabin, your stay will be a memorable experience. It's definitely worth a try. For more information, write Haleakala National Park, P.O. Box 369, Makawao, Maui, HI 96768, or call 572-7749.

There is also a tent and trailer campground outside the crater at **Hosmer Grove.** Located in a heavily forested area below Park Headquarters, this site is easily accessible from the road leading to the crater. There's a picnic area, restroom, running water, and firewood. No permit is required, but camping is limited to three days.

Two private companies, **Pony Express Tours** (667-2202) and **Thompson Ranch Riding Stables** (878-1910), lead horseback trips through the crater. They sponsor half- and full-day excursions.

If time permits, don't bypass the opportunity to trek through this fragile and exotic wilderness area. At Park Headquarters you can obtain printed material on the different hikes, including some that can be done in a day. Here is a chance to explore an eerie and unsettling environment that comes as near as any place on earth to resembling the moon's surface.

Happy landing!

Travelers' Tracks

Sightseeing

There's a lot to see on Maui. Many sights are well-known and heavily touristed, but others will test your ingenuity as an adventurer. You may find some roads backed up with traffic and others rugged and wild.

To help you fully explore both the crowded and virgin regions of the Valley Isle, I'll divide the island into sections. We'll start with Central Maui in the Kahului-Wailuku area, then travel clockwise around the island's western half. This course heads through Lahaina and Kaanapali, then continues over a merciless dirt road along the knife-edge north shore.

Next is the southern route through Kihei and Wailea, past Makena Beach and out to La Perouse Bay.

Then another loop, this one encircling Maui's eastern sphere, will sweep the rain-spattered northeast coast and cut through Hana's heavenly village. Deteriorating as it progresses, the road will carry you past unpopulated stretches on the southeast coast, then into Maui's mountainous Upcountry.

From here a winding road leads to the climax of every Maui tour — Haleakala Crater.

CENTRAL AND WEST MAUI

KAHULUI, WAILUKU, AND IAO VALLEY

The island's commercial and civic centers are located in the adjoining cities of Kahului and Wailuku. **Kahului,** with its bustling harbor and busy shopping complexes, offers little to the sightseer. Coming from the airport along Route 32, you can wander through **Kanaha Pond Wildlife Sanctuary.** Once a royal fishpond, this is now an important bird refuge, especially for the rare Hawaiian stilt. The highway leads uphill to **Wailuku,** Maui's county seat. Older and far more interesting than Kahului, Wailuku sits astride the foothills of the West Maui Mountains. For a short tour of the aging woodfront quarter, take a right on Market Street and follow it several blocks to **Happy Valley.** This former red-light district still retains the charm, if not the action, of a bygone era.

The county government buildings rise along High Street. Just across the road sits picturesque **Kaahumanu Church.** Maui's oldest church, this grand stone and plaster structure was constructed in 1837, and has been kept in excellent condition for its many visitors.

There are several enticing sites up Iao Valley Road. First comes **Hale Hoikeike,** the Maui Historical Society museum. Housed in the Old Bailey

House (built in 1834), the displays include nineteenth-century Hawaiian artifacts, remnants from the early sugar cane industry, and period pieces from the missionary years (244-3326; admission).

Just up the road at **Kepaniwai Park** there's an outdoor cultural showcase to discover. Backdropped by Iao Valley's adze-like peaks, this adult playground features lovely Japanese and Chinese monuments, as well as a taro patch and thatch hut. There are arched bridges, a swimming pool, and an Oriental garden.

Uphill at the **John F. Kennedy Profile** you'll see Hawaii's answer to Mt. Rushmore, chiseled by nature. **Iao Valley State Park,** surrounded by those same moss-mantled cliffs, provides an excellent view of 2,250-foot **Iao Needle.** This awesome peak is, with the possible exception of Haleakala Crater, Maui's most famous landmark.

FROM KAHULUI-WAILUKU TO LAHAINA

Three highways cross the isthmus separating West Maui from the slopes of Haleakala. From Kahului, Route 35 tracks south to Kihei through this rich agricultural area. Route 38, running diagonally across sugar plantations, intersects Route 30's course from Wailuku along the **West Maui Mountains.**

Along Route 30, the road to Lahaina, lies **Maui Tropical Plantation** (244-7643; admission), a 120-acre enclave with orchards and groves displaying dozens of island fruit plants. There's a tropical nursery, museum, aquaculture display, and tram. Then as you pass the small boat harbor at **Maalaea Bay,** the highway hugs the southwest coast. There are excellent lookouts along this elevated roadway, especially near the lighthouse at **McGregor Point.** During whale season (see the "Whale-Watching" section in this chapter) you might spy a leviathan from this landlocked crow's nest. Just offshore there are prime whale breeding areas.

Down the road from McGregor Point, you'll see three islands anchored offshore. As you look seaward, the portside islet is **Molokini,** the crescent-shaped remains of a volcanic crater. **Kahoolawe,** a barren, desiccated island used for naval target practice, sits in the center. Hawaiian activists are demanding an end to the bombing of this sacred isle and have staged dramatic demonstrations by occupying its forbidden shores. The humpbacked island to starboard is **Lanai.** As you continue toward Kaanapali, **Molokai** comes into view.

The road drops back to sea level as it approaches the timeworn village of **Olowalu.** Here, in 1790, more than 100 Hawaiians were slaughtered by the crew of an American ship to avenge the death of a single sailor.

About a half-mile behind the Olowalu general store lie the **Olowalu Petroglyphs,** carved in a cliff two or three centuries ago. These may be closed to the public by the time you arrive, since recent vandalism is forcing local authorities to protect the precious rocks.

LAHAINA

It's just a few miles to Lahaina, one of Hawaii's most historic towns. A royal seat since the sixteenth century, this quaint port became a vital watering place for whaling ships in the 1820s. To the raffish sailors who favored it for its superb anchorage, grog shops, and uninhibited women, Lahaina was heaven itself. To the stiff-collared missionaries who arrived in 1823, the town was a hellhole—a place of sin, abomination, and vile degradation. Some of Lahaina's most colorful history was written when the Congregationalists prevented naked women from swimming out to meet the whalers. Their belligerent brethren anchored in the harbor replied by cannonballing mission homes and rioting along the waterfront.

Lahaina has a stately history too. Kamehameha the Great established a seat of power here after conquering Oahu in 1795. Kamehameha III had his capital here, and the town remained a royal center until the mid-nineteenth century.

Today Lahaina retains much of its old charm in the ramshackle storefronts which line the water. For a tour of the town's many historical sites, start at **Lahaina Harbor** and take a stroll along the docks. In addition to tour boats, pleasure craft from around the world put in here or cast anchor in the Lahaina Roads just offshore. During the heyday of the whaling industry, about 1840, the Auau Channel between Lahaina and Lanai was a forest of masts. **Carthaginian II**, the steel-hulled schooner at dock's end, preserves those days in a shipboard museum. There's a small admission charged.

Across Wharf Street sits the **Pioneer Inn,** a rambling hostelry built in 1901. Just north of here a Hawaii Visitors Bureau sign points out the chair-shaped **Hauola Stone,** a source of healing for ancient Hawaiians. To the south, a century-old **banyan tree,** among the oldest and largest in the islands, extends its rooting branches across almost an entire acre. This sprawling giant presses right to the **Old Courthouse** door. Intended as a palace for King Kamehameha III, the building was turned to more mundane uses and relocated in 1859. The **Old Jail** in the basement now incongruously houses an **Art Gallery.**

Those stone ruins on either side of the courthouse are restorations of the **Old Fort,** built during the 1830s to protect Lahaina from the sins and cannonballs of lawless sailors.

Across Front Street you'll find the **Baldwin Home,** Maui's oldest building (661-3262; admission). Constructed of coral and stone in the early 1830s, the place sheltered the family of Reverend Dwight Baldwin, a medical missionary. Today the house contains period pieces and family heirlooms, including some of the good doctor's rather fiendish-looking medical implements.

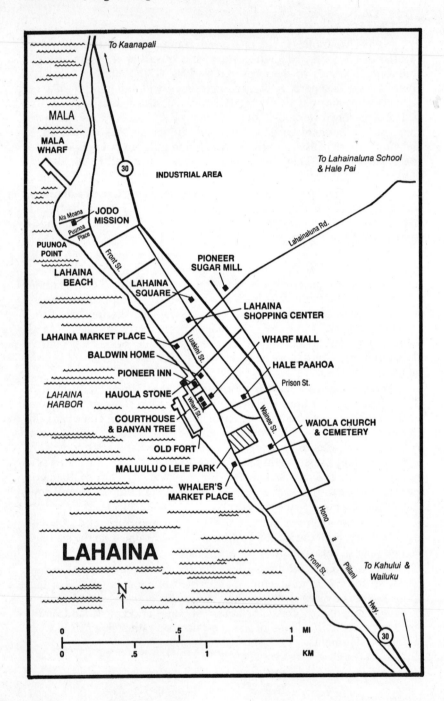

To Kaanapali

MALA

MALA WHARF

30

INDUSTRIAL AREA

To Lahainaluna School & Hale Pai

Ala Moana   JODO MISSION

Puunoa Place

Lahainaluna Rd.

PUUNOA POINT

Front St.

LAHAINA BEACH

LAHAINA SQUARE

PIONEER SUGAR MILL

LAHAINA SHOPPING CENTER

LAHAINA MARKET PLACE

WHARF MALL

Luakini St.

BALDWIN HOME

HALE PAAHOA

PIONEER INN

Prison St.

LAHAINA HARBOR

HAUOLA STONE

Wharf St.

Wainee St.

WAIOLA CHURCH & CEMETERY

COURTHOUSE & BANYAN TREE

OLD FORT

MALUULU O LELE PARK

WHALER'S MARKET PLACE

LAHAINA

N

Hono a Piilani Hwy

Front St.

To Kahului & Wailuku

30

0   .5   1   MI

0   .5   1   KM

Several other historic spots lie along Wainee Street, which parallels Front Street. **Waiola Cemetery,** with its overgrown lawn and eroded tombstones, contains graves dating to 1823. Maui's first Christian services were performed that same year on the grounds of **Waiola Church** next door. Down the street rise the menacing walls of old **Hale Paahao,** a prison built by convicts in 1854.

For a splendid view of Lahaina, head uphill along Lahainaluna Road to **Lahainaluna School.** Established by missionaries in 1831, it is one of the country's oldest high schools. **Hale Pai,** a printing house dating to 1836, is located nearby. On the way uphill you pass **Pioneer Mill,** a sugar company tracing back to 1860.

And don't miss **Lahaina Jodo Mission,** a Buddhist enclave one-half mile north of Lahaina on Ala Moana Street. There's a temple and pagoda here, as well as the largest ceremonial bell in Hawaii. The giant bronze Buddha, with the West Maui Mountains in the background, is a sight to behold.

FROM KAANAPALI AROUND THE WEST MAUI MOUNTAINS

Continuing north from Lahaina, Route 30 passes a heavily developed stretch between **Kaanapali** and **Napili.** The hotels and condominiums along this oceanfront strip mushroomed during the last decade.

Past Napili you'll journey from the ridiculous to the sublime, passing several hidden beaches along an exotic undeveloped shore (see the "Beaches and Parks" section in this chapter). Near the rocky beach at **Honokohau Bay,** Route 30 becomes Route 34. This macadam track snakes high above the ocean, hugging the coastline. From the highway rises a series of multihued **sandstone cliffs** which seems alien to this volcanic region.

After several miles, the road turns to dirt and soon deteriorates into a bone-jangling series of ruts punctuated with potholes. The scenery is some of the most magnificent on Maui. About a mile down the dirt road sits the rustic village of **Kahakuloa** (★). Nestled in an overgrown valley beside a deep blue bay, the community is protected by a solitary headland rising directly from the sea. Woodframe houses and churches, which appear ready to fall to the next gusting wind, are spotted throughout this enchanting area. Kahakuloa is cattle country, and you'll find that the villagers live and farm much as their forefathers did.

The road ascends again and improves somewhat outside Kahakuloa. Opening below you, one valley after another falls seaward in a series of spine-backed ridges. Above the road, the mountain range rises toward its 5,788-foot summit at **Puu Kukui.**

There are lush gulches farther along as the road returns to pavement and descends into the plantation town of Waihee. Here cane fields, dotted with small farm houses, slope from the roadside up to the foothills.

You're still on Route 34, but now it's a well-paved road, heading toward Kahului. Just north of town a side road leads to two sacred spots. The first, **Halekii Heiau,** overlooking Kahului Bay and Iao Stream, dates from the 1700s. Today this temple, once as large as a football field, is little more than a stone heap. **Pihana Kalani Heiau,** a short distance away, was once a sacrificial temple.

Before driving this route, as well as the back road from Hana to Ulupalakua, remember that the car rental agencies will not insure you over these rugged tracks. Many folks cover these roads anyway, and I highly recommend that you explore them both.

THE SOUTH COAST

KIHEI TO LA PEROUSE BAY

Across the Central Maui isthmus from Kahului-Wailuku, Kihei Road follows Maui's sunny, sandy south coast. Stretching from Maalaea Bay to Makena, miles of beautiful beach make this a favorite resort area. Placed strategically along this beachfront are cement **pillboxes,** reminders of World War II's threatened Japanese invasion.

After passing **Kealia fishpond,** the road continues beside rows of condominiums to **Kihei** and **Wailea.** You'll have to go well past Wailea, to where the coast road becomes a dirt track, to escape the condo complexes. I highly recommend visiting **Makena Beach,** several miles beyond the popular tourist enclave of Wailea. Although it's slated for development too, Makena is still one of Maui's finest strands. Past here the road gets even rougher as it presses south to **Ahihi-Kinau Reserve.** Encompassing over 2,000 acres of land and ocean bottom, this preserve harbors numerous fish and coral species. Plan to spend time exploring the lava flows, tidepools, and coral reefs which make this such a fascinating region.

The road continues on, bisecting the **1790 lava flow,** which resulted from Haleakala's last eruption. The flow created **Cape Kinau,** a thumb-shaped peninsula dividing Ahihi Bay and **La Perouse Bay.** When I drove this route recently in a compact rental car, I reached La Perouse Bay before being forced by poor road conditions to turn back. The bay is named for the ill-starred French navigator who anchored here in 1786. After a brief sojourn in this enchanting spot, he sailed off and was later lost at sea.

THE HANA LOOP

NORTHEAST COAST FROM KAHULUI TO HANA

The Hana Highway (Route 36), a bumpy, tortuous road between Kahului and Hana, is one of the most beautiful drives in all Hawaii. There are over 600 twists and turns along this adequately maintained paved road. It will take you at least three hours to drive the fifty-one miles to Hana. To make the entire circuit around the south coast, plan either to sleep near Hana or to leave early and drive all day. If you can, take your time—there's a lot to see.

About seven miles east of Kahului, you'll pass the quaint, weather-beaten town of **Paia.** Within the next ten miles the roadway is transformed as your slow, winding adventure begins. You'll drive past sugar cane fields, across verdant gorges, through valleys dotted with tumbledown cottages, and along fern-cloaked hillsides.

About twenty miles out, a short trail marked near the roadside leads to an idyllic swimming hole at **Twin Falls.** Farther along, on **Waikamoi Ridge,** you'll see picnic areas and a nature trail. Another picnic area nearby at **Puohokamoa Falls** nestles beside a waterfall and a large pool. If you packed a lunch, this is a perfect place to enjoy it.

A few zigzags further, at **Kaumahina State Wayside,** a tree-studded park overlooks Honomanu Gulch and Keanae Peninsula. From here the road descends the gulch, where a side road leads left to the **black-sand beach** at Honomanu Bay.

Above Keanae Peninsula, you'll pass **Keanae Arboretum.** You can stroll freely through these splendid tropical gardens. Just past here, turn left onto the road to the peninsula. This rocky, windswept point offers stunning views of Haleakala. You'll pass rustic houses, a patchwork of garden plots, and a **coral-and-stone church** built around 1860. The church isn't open to visitors, but stop and take a look anyway.

Another side road descends to **Wailua,** a lush agricultural and fishing village. Back on the main road, there's yet another picnic area and waterfall at **Puaa Kaa State Park.** Past here another detour, down a side road, bumps three miles through picturesque **Nahiku** village to a bluff overlooking the sea. The view spreads across three bays all the way back to Wailua. Directly below, the ocean pounds against rock outcroppings, spraying salt mist across a stunning vista.

Several miles before Hana, be sure to stop at **Waianapanapa State Park.** There's a **black-sand beach** here with a **lava tube** through which you can walk to the water's edge. Offshore are several **sea arches,** and nearby a **blowhole** spouts periodically.

To reach **Hana,** you can take the old Hawaiian shoreline trail (see the "Hiking" section in this chapter) or continue on the highway. This Eden-like town, carpeted with pandanus, taro, and banana trees, sits above an inviting bay. Known as "heavenly Hana," it's a ranch town inhabited primarily by part-Hawaiians. The rain which continually buffets Hana makes it a prime agricultural area and adds to the luxuriant, unsettling beauty of the place. Head down to **Hana Bay.** Here you can stroll the beach, explore the wharf, and take a short path along the water to a plaque which marks the **Birthplace of Kaahumanu,** King Kamehameha I's favorite wife. The grand lady was a key player in the 1819 overthrow of the ancestral Hawaiian religious system.

Near the Hotel Hana-Maui, you can drive or hike up a short road to **Mount Lyons** (that camel-humped hill with the cross on top). From this aerie there's a fine view of Hana Bay and the surrounding coastline.

Also be sure to take in the **Hana Cultural Center** (248-8622). This enticing little gallery displays such artifacts from Hana's past as primitive stone tools, rare shells, and Hawaiian games. There are also antique photographs and elaborately stitched quilts.

FROM HANA TO ULUPALAKUA

Past Hana the road, now designated Route 31, worsens. A side road several miles outside town leads along the coast past privately owned **Hamoa Beach.** The uninhabited islet just offshore is **Alau Island.** The main road winds on to **Wailua Gulch,** where two massive cascades—**Kanahualii** and **Wailua Falls**—pour down sharp cliff faces. At nearby **Oh'eo Gulch,** better known as **Seven Pools,** a series of falls tumbles into seven large pools before reaching the sea. The pools are rock-bound, some are bordered by cliffs, and several provide excellent swimming holes. This is an eerie and beautiful place from which you can see up and down the rugged coastline.

Another special spot, **Charles Lindbergh's grave** (★), rests on a promontory overlooking the ocean. The great aviator spent his last days here and lies buried beside Palapala Hoomau church. The whitewashed chapel and surrounding shade trees create a place of serenity and remarkable beauty. (To find the grave, continue 1.2 miles past Seven Pools. Watch for the green-and-white church through the trees on the left. Turn left onto an unpaved road and drive several hundred yards, paralleling a stone fence. Turn left into the churchyard.)

Not far from Seven Pools, in **Kipahulu,** the paved road gives way to dirt. It's seven miles to the nearest pavement, so your rental car should have good shock absorbers. The road rises along seaside cliffs, some of which are so steep they jut out to overhang the road. This is wild, uninhabited country, ripe for exploration.

Huialoha Church, built in 1859, rests below the road on a wind-wracked peninsula. The last time I visited this aging worship hall, horses were grazing in the churchyard. Nearby you'll encounter the tinroof town of **Kaupo** with its funky general store. Directly above the town is **Kaupo Gap,** through which billowing clouds pour into Haleakala Crater.

The road bumps inland, then returns seaward to **Nuu Bay's** rocky beach. From here the rustic route climbs into a desolate area scarred by lava and inhabited with scrub vegetation. The sea views are magnificent as the road bisects the **1790 lava flow.** This was the last volcanic eruption

on Maui; it left its mark in a torn and terrible landscape which slopes for miles to the sea.

It's several miles farther to **Ulupalakua Ranch,** a lush counterpoint to the lava wasteland behind. Here you can view the ruins of **Makee Sugar Mill** (1878) and take a taster's tour of **Tedeschi Winery** (878-6058). Producing a pineapple wine called Maui Blanc, the winery rests in an old jailhouse built of lava and plaster in 1857.

UPCOUNTRY

You're in Maui's **Upcountry** now, a verdant mountainous belt that encircles Haleakala along its middle slopes. Situated between coastline and crater rim, it's a region of ample rainfall and sparse population. This is an ideal area for camping, hiking, or just wandering (see "The Great Outdoors" section in this chapter).

Around Ulupalakua, the main road becomes Route 37 as it heads north to Kula. (Route 31 becomes a dirt road which descends to Makena, providing a convenient, though bumpy, shortcut to the Kihei area.) You can follow Route 37 to the **Church of the Holy Ghost,** an octagonal structure built in 1897, or turn up Route 377 to **Kula Botanical Gardens** (878-1715; admission). An excellent place for picnicking, the landscaped slopes contain an aviary, pond, "Taboo Garden" with poisonous plants, and forty varieties of protea, a rare flowering shrub. Either route will take you through cattle-grazing country and past garden patchworks to **Pukalani.**

Since this town has little to offer besides a modern shopping center, turn onto Route 40 for an offbeat tour of northside Upcountry. The road leads to **Makawao.** Battered buildings, falsefront stores, and a guns-and-ammo shop create an Old West atmosphere in this tiny town. This is Maui's cowboy country, similar to Waimea plateau on the Big Island, with a rodeo every Fourth of July.

From Makawao the possibilities for exploring the Upcountry area are many. There are two loop tours (★) I particularly recommend. The first climbs from town along Olinda Road (Route 39) past **Pookela Church,** a coral sanctuary built in the 1850s. It continues through a frequently rain-drenched region to the **Tree Growth Research Area,** jointly sponsored by state and federal forestry services. You can circle back down toward Makawao on Piiholo Road past **Olinda Nursery** and the **University of Hawaii Agricultural Station.**

The second loop leads down Route 40 to the Hana Highway; turn left on the highway for several miles to Haiku Road, then head left along this country lane to Route 40. You'll drive into overgrown areas, across one-lane bridges, past banana patches, and through the tinroof town of **Haiku.**

HALEAKALA NATIONAL PARK

It seems only fitting that the approach to Haleakala Crater is along one of the world's fastest-climbing roads. From Kahului to the crater rim—a distance of forty miles along Routes 37, 377, and 378—the macadam road rises from sea level to over 10,000 feet, and the silence is broken only by the sound of ears popping from the ascent.

At the crater lip you look out over an awesome expanse—seven miles long, over two miles wide, twenty-one miles around. The crater floor, 3,000 feet below the rim, is a multihued wasteland filled with cinder cones, lava flows, and mini-craters. It's a legendary place, with a mythic tradition that's as vital as its geologic history. It was from Haleakala that the demigod Maui lassoed the sun and slowed its track across the sky to give his mother more daylight to dry her *tapa* cloth.

In the afternoon, the volcano's colors are most vivid, but during the morning the crater is more likely to be free of clouds. Before going up Haleakala, call 572-7749 or 877-5124 for a weather report. Then you can decide what time of day will be best for your explorations. Many people arrive at dawn to see the sun rise over the edge of the crater.

On the way up, past the campground at **Hosmer Grove,** you'll come first to **National Park Headquarters.** With its information desk and maps, this is a good starting point. The first crater view comes at **Leleiwi Overlook,** an 8,800-foot perch from which you'll be able to see all the way from Hana across the island to Kihei. Here at sunset, under correct meteorological conditions, you can see your shadow projected on the clouds and haloed by a rainbow. To experience this "Specter of the Brocken," stand atop the crater rim looking toward the cloud-filled crater with the setting sun at your back.

Up the hill a side road leads to **Kalahaku Overlook,** a 9,325-foot aerie that offers a unique view of several cinder cones within the crater. Just below the parking lot are numerous **silverswords.** Related to sunflowers, these spike-leaved plants grow only on Maui and the Big Island. They remain low bristling plants for up to twenty years before blooming into a flowering stalk. Each plant blossoms once, sometime between May and November, and then dies.

The best view of the crater is farther up the road at the **Visitor Center,** where you'll find an information desk and mini-museum as well as a short trail up **White Hill.** Composed of andesite lava and named for its characteristic light color, this mound is spotted with stone windbreaks once used as sleeping places by Hawaiians who lived on the lower slopes but periodically visited the summit of Haleakala.

It's a short drive to the crater summit at **Puu Ulaula Overlook.** From the plate-glass lookout you can view the Big Island, Molokai, Lanai, West Maui, and the crater itself.

Shopping

KAHULUI-WAILUKU SHOPPING

For everyday shopping needs you should find the Kahului malls very convenient. Three sprawling centers are strung along Route 32.

Kaahumanu Center is the best and most modern, with **Liberty House** (877-3361) and **Sears** (877-3321) department stores, a photo studio, **Waldenbooks** (871-6112), boutiques, shoe stores, candy stores, a sundries shop, and a jeweler.

Nearby **Maui Mall** has a similar inventory of shops. **Sir Wilfred's Tobacconist** (877-3711) stocks a connoisseur's selection of tobaccos and coffees; there's also a coffee bar here.

You might also try **Kahului Shopping Center**, though I prefer the other, more convenient malls.

The Coral Factory (877-7631), out near Kahului Airport, features a wide variety of black and pink coral jewelry at low prices. The folks here will show you where they fashion all their own products; and if you're interested, they have a film about making black coral jewelry.

Up in Wailuku, a tumbledown town with a friendly face, you'll find the little shops and solicitous merchants that we have come to associate with small-town America.

LAHAINA-KAANAPALI SHOPPING

Lahaina's a great place to combine shopping with sightseeing. Most shops are right on Front Street in the dilapidated wooden buildings facing the water. For a walking tour of the stores and waterfront, start from Pioneer Inn at the south end of the strip and walk north on the *makai* or ocean side. Then come back along the *mauka* or mountain side of the street.

One of the first shops you will encounter on this consumer's tour of Lahaina will be **Apparels of Pauline** (697 Front Street; 661-4774). In addition to an attractive line of Hawaiian fashions, Pauline features many mainland designs.

At **The Kite Store** (703 Front Street; 661-3159) you'll find butterflies and skybirds, even flying dragons. **Vagabond** (709 Front Street; 661-8616) has everything from knapsacks to aloha shirts. **Haimoff and Haimoff Creations in Gold** (661-3920) nearby spotlights original jewelry by local craftsman Harry Haimoff, who is well known for his elegant work.

Past the sea wall in an overgrown cottage set back from the street, lay several shops including **Pacific Vision** (819 Front Street; 661-0188) with its hand-etched glass and crystal pieces. And just down the street at **South Seas Trading Post** (851 Front Street; 661-3168) you can barter greenbacks for Nepali wedding necklaces, Chinese porcelain opium pillows, or New Guinea masks.

There are just a few more street numbers before this shopper's promenade ends. Then if you cross the road and walk back in the opposite direction, with the sea to your right, you'll pass **The Necklace Gallery** (858 Front Street; 661-8885). Here you should be able to find a wide variety of coral jewelry.

Alexia Natural Fashions (712 Front Street; 661-8122) has stylish women's clothing from the island of Cyprus.

Nearby at **The Wharf** mall (658 Front Street) there's a maze of stores. One, **Lobster and Roses** (661-3062), features floral patterns in its line of women's fashions. For headgear, head over to the **Maui Mad Hatter** (661-8125), just a corridor away.

Then it's upstairs to **Upstart Crow & Co.** (667-9544). This nifty shop features an unbeatable combination—good books and fine coffee. One of the best book stores around, it doubles as a coffeehouse where you can sit back, read, and sip a cappuccino.

Village Gallery has two locations (120 Dickenson Street, 661-4402; and Lahaina Cannery, Front and Kapunakea streets; 661-3280), both featuring paintings by modern Hawaiian artists. Amid the tourist schlock is some brilliant artwork.

Lahaina Cannery (Front and Kapunakea streets), a massive complex designed in the style of an old canning factory, is the area's most ambitious project. Dozens of shops are housed in this multitiered facility.

Dickenson Square (Dickenson and Wainee streets) represents another theme mall, fashioned after an early-20th century plantation manor.

Also worthy of mention is **Whaler's Village** in the Kaanapali Beach Resort on Route 30. This sprawling complex combines a shopping mall with an outdoor museum. Numbered among the stores you'll find gift emporia featuring coral and shells, a shirt store with wild island designs, other stores offering fine men's and women's fashions, a bookstore, and the local branch of Hawaii's own **Liberty House** (661-4451) department store.

And then, to help make shopping the grand adventure it should be, are the displays. Within this mazework mall you'll discover blunderbusses, intricate scrimshaw pieces, the skeletal remains of leviathans, and whaling boats with iron harpoons splayed from the bow. Practically everything, in fact, that a whaler (or a cruising shopper) could desire.

For serious shoppers, ready to spend money or be damned, there is nothing to compare with the neighboring hotels in Kaanapali Beach Resort. Set like gems within this tourist cluster are several world-class hotels, each hosting numerous elegant shops.

Foremost is the **Hyatt Regency Maui**, along whose wood-paneled lobby are stores that might well be deemed mini-museums. One shop contains exquisite pieces of hand-chiseled crystal. Another, called **Elephant Walk** (667-2848), displays *koa* wood furniture, baskets, and Niihau shell jewelry. There are art galleries, fabric shops, candy stores, a luggage shop, and more—set in an open-air lobby that is filled with rare statuary and exotic birds.

PAIA SHOPPING

This rustic falsefront town seven miles outside Kahului is my favorite place to shop on Maui. Many fine artisans live in the Upcountry area and come down to sell their wares at the small shops lining the Hana Highway. The town itself is a work of art, with old wooden buildings that provide a welcome respite from the mondo-condo shores of Kaanapali and Kihei.

I'll mention just the shops I like most. Browse through town to see for yourself. If you discover places I missed, please let me know.

On display at the **Maui Crafts Guild** (579-9697) are paintings and drawings by local artists. There are also numerous gift items, including a line of ceramics that ranges from functional to fanciful. You'll also discover craftspeople here working with wood, leather, and textiles.

Paia Trading Company (579-9472) has a few interesting antiques and a lot of junk. Among the more noteworthy items: turquoise and silver jewelry, wooden washboards, apothecary jars, and cribbage boards carved from fossilized whale bone.

Summerhouse Boutique (579-9201) might be called a chic sundries shop. They sell everything from sunglasses, jewelry, postcards, and porcelain masks to swimwear and natural fiber garments.

Around the corner on Baldwin Avenue lies another shop worth browsing. **The Clothes Addict** (579-9266) features a fine selection of women's fashions, including antique clothes, manufactured designs, and locally made styles. They also have '30s and '40s *aloha* shirts for men, plus handmade silk kimono clothing.

The rustic town of Makawao attracts talented artists and now features several imaginative shops. Among the foremost are **Goodies** (3633 Baldwin Avenue; 572-0288) with jewelry and women's fashions produced by local designers; and **Gecko Trading Company** (3625 Baldwin Avenue; 572-0249), a small shop which also features contemporary fashions at reasonable prices. Both are enchanting spots in a town well worth exploring.

Nightlife

Stepping out on Maui means stepping over to Lahaina and Kaanapali. Lahaina has the nightclubs; Kaanapali features rock. Together, the duo cooks up Hawaii's hottest scene outside Honolulu.

On the rest of the island, you'll probably be asleep by midnight. Kahului-Wailuku and Kihei offer a few places; most other night spots are numbingly low-key.

KAHULUI-WAILUKU NIGHTLIFE

If Kahului can be said to have an entertainment strip, Kaahumanu Avenue (Route 32) is the place. Apple Annie's has a small lounge, **Guacamoles** (877-3107), in her Kaahumanu Center restaurant. With overstuffed furniture to sink into and an outsize television that dominates the room, this is no wild swinger's saloon. But it is a cozy place to share a drink until the 9 p.m. closing time. Or you can mellow out to the piano music and dancing at **Maui Palms Hotel** (877-0071) on the weekends.

The **Red Dragon Room** fires up on weekends at the Maui Beach Hotel (877-0051). Wednesday, Friday, and Saturday night, the Dragon rolls back the banquet tables and wheels in the **Red Dragon Disco**. There's a cover and two-drink minimum.

Up in Wailuku, **Yori's** (309 North Market; 244-3121) entertains a local crowd almost every night around its bar. Located in Wailuku's "happy valley" section, it's a good place to meet people, or just to sit back and enjoy a tall, cool drink. Another neighborhood hangout just up the street and around the corner is the **Vineyard Tavern** (2171 Vineyard; 244-9597). With a falsefront exterior and swinging doors, this establishment is reminiscent of a Wild West saloon. But the music is contemporary and the ambience is definitely Mauian.

LAHAINA-KAANAPALI NIGHTLIFE

Front Street's the strip in Lahaina—a dilapidated, decaying row of buildings from which stream some of the freshest sounds around.

The place of places along this surging waterfront is **Longhi's** (888 Front Street; 667-2288). The upper story of this fabled restaurant is painted brilliant white and decorated in a startling black-and-white motif; the dance floor is native koa wood. The result is a club that draws a jet set crowd. George Benson, Al DiMeola, and a host of others have all landed here unannounced to jam. There's no cover or minimum to see the stars; they're usually just friends of the club who happen to be in town. If no one wildly famous turns up, you'll hear a local jazz or rock group working out onstage every Friday and Saturday from 10:30 to 1:30. I'm sure you're familiar with the Maui mythology—luscious *wahines*, well-heeled swingers, rose-colored sunsets. This is it, in nightclub form.

A jaunt down to The Wharf mall, then a short jog upstairs, will put you in **Fisherman's Wharf** (658 Front Street; 667-9535). Overlooking Lahaina harbor, it's a splendid lounge. The entire place is done in dark wood and decorated with pendent lamps and table candles. Though they often feature rock-and-roll bands, the last time I happened along the place was alive with the rhythms of a country-and-western group. Attesting to the quality of the sound, the crowd had packed the place right to the rails.

Over at the **Old Whaler's Grog Shop** (661-3636) the standard fare is N'Orleans jazz Tuesday through Saturday; bluegrass and more on other nights. Tucked into a corner of the Pioneer Inn, this spot features a nautical motif complete with harpoons, figureheads, and paintings of naked ladies. Usually packed to the bulkheads with a lively crew, it's a great place to hunker down over a glass of rum.

Moose McGillycuddy's (667-7758), a hot club fronting Front Street, has a large dance floor and video-disco format. The house is congenial and the drinks imaginatively mixed; for contemporary melodies and late night meals, it's a good bet.

Lahaina's gay scene centers around a place called **Hamburger Mary's** (608 Front Street; 667-6989) that bills itself as "an open bar for open-minded people." There's a friendly ambience and a pleasant palm-and-bamboo setting in this garden lounge.

If you want to just sit back, with one arm slung over a balcony rail and the other reaching for a *mai tai*, try the piano bar at **Whale's Tale** (666 Front Street; 661-3676).

Over in Kaanapali, it's rock city. Along the row of seafront hotels at Kaanapali Beach Resort, the strobe dancehalls are packed as tight as swingers on a crowded floor. One of the hot spots is the **Banana Moon** at the Maui Marriott (667-1200), a spacious split-level club with two dance floors. The place is ablaze with color. And sound—the music's non-stop. There's a deejay spinning a full menu of platters, a video screen, and an array of oversized speakers. Popular with local folks and visitors alike.

One of Maui's premiere night spots, tucked into the basement of the island's finest hotel, is a disco called **Spats II** (Hyatt Regency Maui, Kaanapali Beach Resort; 667-7474). Named after a hot Waikiki club, this opulent lounge doubles as an elegant Italian restaurant. That's why you see marble tabletops, antique armchairs, and brass chandeliers surrounding the wood-inlay dance floor. The music is strictly soundtrack, though it draws the crowds. No cover or minimum, but there is a strict dress code that bars sandals while requiring slacks and collar shirts. (While you're nightowling here, take a stroll through the Hyatt Regency's atrium-style lobby. The hotel is lavishly decorated with rare artworks and inhabited by exotic birds.)

Possibly the prettiest place in these parts to enjoy a late night drink 'neath the tropic moon is **El Crab Catcher** (661-4423). Located in the Whaler's Village mall, this club features contemporary Hawaiian music nightly. The place is located right on the water, so you can listen to a slow set, then stroll the beach.

For soft entertainment in a relaxed setting, try the **Bay Club** (669-8008) at the Kapalua Bay Hotel. This open-air piano bar is set in a lovely restaurant overlooking the water. The melodies are as serene and relaxing as the views of neighboring Molokai.

KIHEI NIGHTLIFE

Wednesdays through Saturdays, the **Sailmaker Saloon** (South Kihei Road; 879-4446) remakes the third tier of its multideck restaurant into a disco. Despite the deejay spinning platters, the place still looks like a converted restaurant, but it's the hottest spot in Kihei's lukewarm night scene.

The Wailea Beach Hotel (879-4900) draws a mixture of youngbloods and geritolized swingers to its **Lost Horizon** nightclub (South Kihei Road) down in Wailea.

For low-key entertainment, one Kihei night spot you might consider is **La Familia Restaurant** (2511 South Kihei Road; 879-8824). It's an informal place where you can lean back and enjoy sounds or watch videos.

Several other clubs, also located on South Kihei Road, feature live music. The Maui Lu Resort's **Longhouse** (879-5881) features a luau each and every Saturday night. Down in Wailea, the **Inu Inu Lounge** at the Hotel Inter-Continental (879-1922) mixes smoky dance music with a little jazz and rock 'n' roll.

Maui Addresses and Phone Numbers

MAUI ISLAND

County Department of Parks and Recreation—Wailuku (244-9018 and 244-7750)
Division of State Parks—Wailuku (244-4354)
Haleakala National Park Headquarters—(527-7749 and 572-9306)
State Division of Game—(244-4352)
Weather Report—(877-5111 for entire island; 877-5124 for recreational areas; 572-7749 for Haleakala National Park)
Whale Report Center—(661-8527)

KAHULUI-WAILUKU

Ambulance—911
Barber Shop—Kahului Barber Shop, Kahului Shopping Center, Route 32 (871-4221)
Books—Waldenbooks, Maui Mall Shopping Center (877-0181)
Fire Department—911
Fishing Supplies—Maui Fishing Supply, 51 Market Street, Wailukua (244-3449)

Hardware—A and B Hardware, Maui Mall, Route 32 (877-0011)
Hospital—Maui Memorial Hospital, Route 32, Wailuku (244-9056)
Laundromat—The Washhouse, 74 Lono Avenue, Kahului; 877-6435.
Library—251 High Street, Wailuku (244-3945)
Liquor—Party Pantry, 1900 Main Street, Wailuku (244-9227)
Pharmacy—Long's Drugs, Maui Mall, Route 32 (877-0041)
Photo Supply—Roy's Photo Center, Maui Mall, Route 32 (871-4311)
Police Department—911
Post Office—70 South High Street, Wailuku (244-4815)

LAHAINA

Ambulance—911
Barber Shop—For Shear, 724 Luakini Street (667-2866)
Books—Upstart Crow and Co., The Wharf mall, Front Street (667-9544)
Fire Department—911
Fishing Supplies—Lahaina Fishing Supply, Lahaina Shopping Center,
Wainee Street (661-8348)
Hardware—A and B Hardware, 1087 Limahana (661-4025)
Laundromat—Donna's Laundry Service, 747 Luakini Street (667-9892)
Library—Wharf Street (661-0566)
Liquor—Party Pantry, 1217 Front Street (661-3577)
Pharmacy—Craft's Drug, Lahaina Shopping Center, Wainee Street
(661-3119)
Photo Supply—Lahaina Camera Center, Lahaina Shopping Center,
Wainee Street (661-3306)
Police Department—911
Post Office—1760 Honoapiilani Highway (667-6611)

KIHEI

Ambulance—911
Fire Department—911
Police Department—911

HANA

Ambulance—911
Fire Department—911
Police Department—911

CHAPTER SIX

Lanai

Eight miles from Maui, across the famous whaling anchorage at Lahaina Roads, lies the pear-shaped island of Lanai. The word *lanai,* usually meaning "porch," is more appropriately translated as "swelling" on this humpbacked isle. In profile this island resembles the humpback whales which frequent its waters. It rises in a curved ridge from the south, then gradually tapers to the north. The east side is cut by deep gulches, while the west is bounded by spectacular sea cliffs rising 1,500 to 2,000 feet.

First discovered by Captain Cook's men in 1779, Lanai was long avoided by mariners, who feared its reef-shrouded shores and saw little future in the dry, barren landscape. You can still see testaments to their fear in the rotting hulks which lie off Shipwreck Beach. Ancient Hawaiians believed Lanai was inhabited only by evil spirits until Kaululaau, son of the great Maui chief Kakaalaneo, killed the spirits. Kaululaau, a Hawaiian-style juvenile delinquent who chopped down fruit trees with the gay abandon of young George Washington, had been exiled for such destructive behavior to Lanai by his father. After the wild youth redeemed himself by making the island safe from malevolent spirits, Lanai was settled by Hawaiians and controlled by powerful Maui chiefs.

Even today Lanai retains something of a bad reputation. Hawaii's smallest island is also the least visited. Most tourists, hearing that Lanai is nothing but pineapples and possesses only twenty miles of paved roads, leave the place to the antelopes and wild goats. Herein lies the charm of this lovely little isle. Actually only a fraction of Lanai's 140 square miles is planted in pineapples. The rest of Lanai is covered with a network of jeep and hiking trails guaranteed to keep the heartiest adventurer happy.

Here is an entire island which fits the description "hidden Hawaii." Almost all of Lanai's 2,100 citizens live in rustic Lanai City at the island's center. Around this company town lie mountains, tablelands, and remote beaches — untouched realms ripe for exploration. With a tourist trade hosted by a single ten-unit hotel, Lanai is the ideal hideaway for visitors seeking solitude and serenity.

A threat to this idyllic retreat is a tourism master plan which calls for over 1,000 hotel rooms and an eventual population of 15,000. But to date Castle and Cooke, the huge conglomerate which bought out Dole and which now owns ninety-eight percent of the island, has taken no steps to implement the scheme. They are content to profit from the 16,000-acre pineapple plantation (one of the world's largest) which comprises Lanai's sole industry. The Pineapple Island has always been too dry for sugar cultivation. Lying in Maui's windshadow, the highland areas receive only thirty-five inches of rainfall annually while the lower levels get a piddling twelve inches.

During the nineteenth century, Lanai was a ranchers' island with large sections of flat range land given over to grazing. Missionaries became active saving souls and securing property in 1835; by the 1860s one of their number had gained control of Lanai's better acreage. This was Walter Murray Gibson, a Mormon maverick whose life story reads like a sleazy novel. Despite being excommunicated by the Mormon church, Gibson went on to become a formidable figure in Hawaiian politics. His land changed hands several times until Jim Dole bought the entire island in 1922 for a mere $1.1 million. Dole, descended from missionaries, was possessed of a more earthly vision than his forebears. Pineapples. He converted the island to pineapple cultivation, built Lanai City, and changed the face of Lanai forever.

Filipinos, now about fifty percent of the island's population, were imported to work the fields. Today they are bent to the same labor, wearing goggles and gloves to protect against the sharp spines bristling from the low plants. Pineapples are cultivated through plastic sheets to conserve precious water; you'll see the plastic stretched across the fields as you drive along. Harvesting is by hand. Downtown Lanai may roll up the streets at 9 p.m., but the lights burn bright in the pineapple fields as crews work through the night loading the hefty fruits onto conveyor belts.

But Dole was not the only man with a dream for Lanai. George Munro, a New Zealand naturalist, came to the island in 1911. While Dole later cultivated the arable tablelands, Munro worked in the rugged highlands. He extended the native forest, planting countless trees to capture moisture and protect eroded hillsides. He restored areas ravaged by feral goats and imported the stately Norfolk pines which brought a mountain ambience to Lanai City. And most important, Munro introduced an ecological awareness which still pervades this enchanting, virgin island.

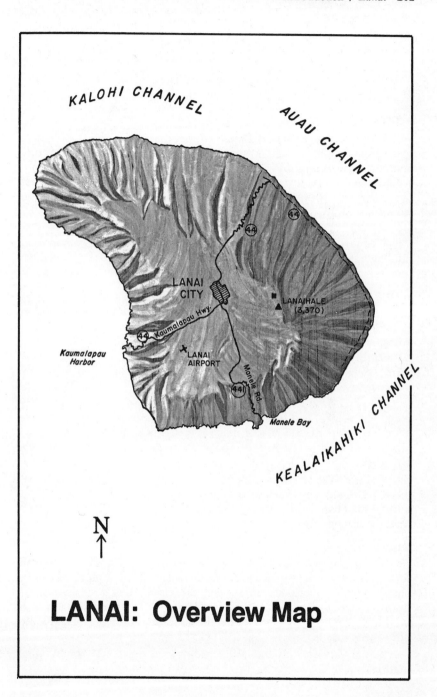

LANAI: Overview Map

Easy Living

Transportation

ARRIVAL

Planes to Lanai land at **Lanai Airport** (565-6757) amid an endless maze of pineapple fields four miles from downtown Lanai City. This tiny landing strip has no shops, lockers, car rentals, or public transportation. A few rooms house airline offices. The largest line, **Hawaiian Airlines**, offers the most frequent service, via jet, to other islands. **Princeville Airways** and **Reeves Air** fly propeller-driven planes and feature the lowest rates.

If you're staying at Hotel Lanai, the hotel will provide transportation into town, as will either of the island's garages if you're renting a vehicle from them.

CAR AND JEEP RENTALS

Lanai City Service Inc. (565-6780) and **Oshiro's Service Station** (565-6952) rent cars. Both outlets have automatic compacts with free mileage. But renting a car on Lanai is like carrying water wings to the desert: there's simply nowhere to go. Rental cars are restricted to pavement, while most of Lanai's roads are jeep trails: 4-wheel drive is the only way to fly.

The first time I visited the island of Lanai, I rented a vintage 1942 jeep. The vehicle had bad brakes, no emergency brake, malfunctioning windshield wipers, and no seat belts. It was, however, equipped with an efficient shock absorber—me. Today, Oshiro's rents new and reliable CJ5 jeeps.

Oshiro's also offers guided tours, custom-designed to your personal interests. Generally ranging from two to four hours and requiring a minimum of two people, these tours can cover places of major interest or obscure corners of the island.

BICYCLING

Given the lack of paved roads, bicycle use is somewhat restricted on Lanai. There are a few nice rides from Lanai City, but all are steep in places and pass over pockmarked sections of road. One goes south eight miles to Manele Bay and the beach at Hulopoe, another diverts west to busy little Kaumalapau Harbor, and the last heads north fourteen miles to Shipwreck Beach.

Lanai City Service Inc. (565-6780) is a good place to obtain information concerning Lanai roads.

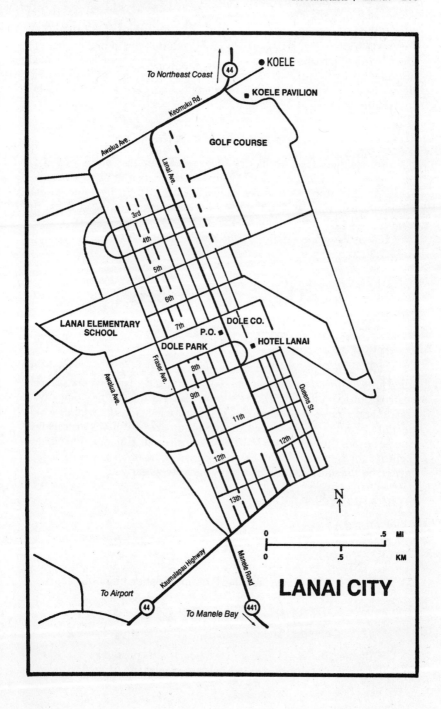

If the lodge restaurant is closed, there are only two alternatives. **S.T. Property** (565-6537), a Lanai City luncheonette, sits in one corner of a store lined with flashing pinball machines, and serves breakfast and lunch at budget prices. Similarly, **Dahang's Pastry Shop** (565-6363) serves egg dishes in the morning, plus sandwiches, hamburgers, and plate lunches in the afternoon, all at budget prices.

Grocery Markets

For standard food needs, try **Richard's Shopping Center** (565-6047) on Eighth Street in Lanai City. This "shopping center" is really only a small grocery store with a dry goods department. If, by some strange circumstance, you can't find what you're seeking here, head down the street to **Pine Isle Market** (565-6488).

Richard's is open daily except Sunday from 8:30 a.m. to noon and from 1:30 to 5:30 p.m.

The Great Outdoors

The Sporting Life

CAMPING

With so few people and so much virgin territory, Lanai should be ideal for camping. But here, as on the other islands, landowners severely restrict outdoors lovers. The villain on Lanai is the Koele Company, a Castle and Cooke subsidiary charged with managing the island. Koele permits island residents to camp where they like, but herds visitors into one area on the south coast. This campsite, at Hulopoe Beach, has facilities for six tents. Once filled to capacity, no other camping is permitted on the entire island! So make reservations early.

OTHER SPORTS

GOLF
Cavendish Golf Course (Lanai City) is *the* place to go.

TENNIS
Call the Lanai schools (565-6464) for information on public courts.

Beaches and Parks
(Plus Camping, Swimming, Snorkeling, Surfing, Fishing)

Hulopoe Beach—Lanai's finest beach also possesses the island's only fully developed park. Set in a half-moon inlet and fringed with *kiawe* trees, this white-sand beach is an excellent spot for all sorts of recreation. As a result, it's quite popular and, by Lanai standards, sometimes crowded.

Facilities: Picnic area, restrooms, showers. Eight miles from the markets and restaurants of Lanai City.

Camping: This is it! There are six campsites at the far end of the beach. Permits are issued by the Koele Company (565-6661), P.O. Box L, Lanai City, Lanai, HI 96763. Expect to pay a $5 registration fee plus a charge of $5 per camper per day.

Swimming: Excellent. The beach is partially protected, and there's a small lava pool for children.

Snorkeling: Very good around the lava pool and near the rocks at either end of the beach. Nearby Manele Bay, a few hundred yards away, is another excellent spot.

Surfing: Good for both surfboards and bodysurfing.

Fishing: A prime area for threadfin, *ulua,* and bonefish, this is also the most accessible surf-casting beach on the island.

Getting there: Take Route 441 south from Lanai City for eight miles.

Manele Bay—Primarily a small-boat harbor, this cliff-fringed inlet is populated by sailboats from across the Pacific. You can carouse with the crews, walk along the jetty, or scramble up the rocks for a knockout view of Maui's Haleakala crater. There's a park for picnicking, and just around the corner at Hulopoe Beach are facilities for camping, swimming, and other sports.

To get there, take Route 441 south from Lanai City.

Koele Pavilion—This small tree-lined park overlooks Cavendish Golf Course and the surrounding countryside. It's an excellent place for a picnic, with tables, restrooms, and a pavilion. Located on the northern outskirts of Lanai City just off Route 44.

Polihua Beach (★)— A wide white-sand beach situated along Lanai's northwest shore, this isolated strand, with a stunning view of Molokai, rivals Kauai's trackless beaches. Often very windy.

Facilities: None.

Swimming: Good, but exercise caution.

Snorkeling: Water here is sometimes muddy. When it's clear, you can dive for lobsters.

Fishing: According to local fishermen, this is the best spot on the island. Common catches include *papio, ulua,* bonefish, threadfin, and red snapper.

Getting there: It's about eleven miles from Lanai City through pineapple fields and the Garden of the Gods. The last half of the drive is over a rugged jeep trail. For specific directions and road conditions, check with the jeep rental garages.

Shipwreck Beach (★)—This strand is actually a string of small sandy patches along the north coast. The glass fishing balls on the beach and the remains of misguided ships on the reef make this a beachcomber's paradise. Sometimes windy.

Facilities: None. Ten miles to Lanai City restaurants and markets.

Swimming: Shallow, with a sandy bottom. Protecting reef 200 yards offshore.

Snorkeling: Very good along the reef. Diving for lobsters.

Fishing: There's good fishing for threadfin, bonefish, and *ulua* in the area between the squatters' houses and the petroglyphs.

Getting there: Head north on Route 44. See the "Sightseeing" section in this chapter for details.

Naha Beaches (★)—A string of salt-and-pepper-colored sand beaches lies along the twelve-mile dirt road to Naha. While none are very pretty and most are crowded with shoals, they do offer great views of Molokai, Maui, and Kahoolawe. The Naha road winds in and out along the seafront, with numerous access roads leading to the shore.

Facilities: Several beaches, including Naha, have small picnic areas and makeshift facilities on grassy plots.

Swimming: Most beaches are well-protected by shoals, but the waters are shallow.

Snorkeling: Good.

Fishing: The reefs are too far away to make this a prime angling area.

Getting there: Take Route 44 north from Lanai City and continue on after it turns southward and becomes a dirt road. The road ends at Naha.

Hiking

Hikers on Lanai are granted much greater freedom than campers. Jeep trails and access roads are open to the public; the only restriction is that hikers cannot camp along the trails.

Since all Lanai's trails lead either to beaches or points of interest, they are described in the accompanying "Beaches and Parks" and "Sightseeing" sections.

Travelers' Tracks

Sightseeing

In this little corner of the world, all roads lead to Lanai City. For the sightseer they lead *from* Lanai City, radiating like spokes from this tiny urban hub to the mountains and sea.

Situated at 1,620 feet, **Lanai City** is a trim community of corrugated-roofed houses and small garden plots. Tourist brochures present the place as a quaint New England village, but I found it rather drab and depressing. Most of the houses were built around the 1920s and look alike. Norfolk pines break the monotony, but otherwise things seem regimented throughout this plantation center. Advertising claims to the contrary, it's just another company town.

The really interesting places lie outside town, and most require driving or hiking over jeep trails. It's advisable to get specific directions wherever you go, since the maze of pineapple roads can confuse even the most intrepid pathfinder. Where possible, I've included directions; otherwise, check with the jeep rental shops in Lanai City.

To be extra safe, ask about road conditions too. The slightest rain can turn a dusty jeep road into a tricky slick surface, and a downpour can transmogrify it into an impassable quagmire. I once dumped a jeep into a three-foot ditch when the trail to Polihua Beach collapsed. It had been raining steadily for three days and the soft shoulder couldn't support the weight of a vehicle. I was eleven miles from Lanai City with the wheels hopelessly embedded and an hour left until dark. The way back led past pretty menacing country, heavily eroded and difficult to track through. Rain clouds brought the night on in a rush. I gathered up my poncho and canteen, convinced myself that the worst to come would be a cold and wet night outdoors, and began trekking back to civilization. Fortunately, after five miserable hours I made it. But the entire incident could have been avoided if I had first checked road conditions and had allowed at least several hours of daylight for my return.

This shouldn't discourage you, though. With the proper precautions, exploring Lanai can be a unique experience, challenging but safe. To make things easy, I'll start with a journey to the island's northeastern shore, part of which is over a paved road. Then I'll continue clockwise around the island.

NORTHEAST—SHIPWRECK BEACH AND NAHA

From Lanai City, Route 44 winds north through hot, arid country. The scrub growth and red soil in this barren area resemble a bleak southwestern landscape, but the sweeping views of Maui and Molokai could be found only in Hawaii.

By the way, those stones piled atop one another along the road are neither an expression of ancient Hawaiian culture nor proof of the latest UFO landing. They were placed there by imaginative hikers.

Just before the macadam road ends, turn left onto a dirt road. This track leads past colonies of inhabited squatters' shacks, many built from the hulks of vessels grounded on nearby **Shipwreck Beach**. The coral reef paralleling the beach has been a nemesis to sailors since whaling days. That rusting hulk down the beach is a World War II Liberty Ship which lost its battle far from Japanese guns.

At the end of the dirt road, a path marked with white paint leads to clusters of ancient **petroglyphs** depicting simple island scenes. Those interested in extensively exploring the coast can hike all the way from Shipwreck west to Polihua Beach along jeep trails and shoreline.

Back on the main road, continuing straight ahead as the macadam gives way to a dirt road, you can travel along the northeast shore for twelve teeth-clicking miles. The ghost town of **Keomuku**, marked by a ramshackle church seemingly forsaken by God, lies six miles down the road. It's another mile and a half to **Kahea Heiau**, a holy place which many claim is the reason Keomuku was deserted. It seems that stones from this temple were used to build the nearby Maunalei Sugar Company plantation despite warnings against disturbing the sacred rocks. So when the plantation failed in 1901 after its sweet water mysteriously turned brackish, the Hawaiians had a heavenly explanation.

Several miles further, past numerous salt-and-pepper-colored beaches, the road ends at the old Hawaiian village of **Naha**. Today nothing remains of this once prosperous colony.

THE MUNRO TRAIL

Named for New Zealand naturalist George Munro, this seven-mile jeep trail climbs through rain forest and stands of Norfolk pine en route to **Lanaihale**, the highest point on Lanai. From this 3,370-foot perch you can see every Hawaiian island except Kauai.

On the way to Lanaihale, about two miles up the trail, you'll pass **Hookio Gulch**. The ridge beyond is carved with a defense work of protective notches made by warriors who tried futilely to defend Lanai against invaders from Hawaii in 1778. A nearby footpath leads to an overlook above 2,000-foot deep **Hauola Gulch**, Lanai's deepest canyon.

From Lanaihale you can either turn around or descend through pineapple fields to Hoike Road, which will connect with Route 441.

The Munro Trail begins in Koele off Route 44 about a mile north of Lanai City. While it's rough going at times, the trail affords such magnificent views from its windswept heights that it simply must not be ignored by the adventurous sightseer.

SOUTHEAST—LUAHIWA PETROGLYPHS AND MANELE BAY

Heading south from Lanai City on Route 441, the explorer can detour to the **Luahiwa Petroglyphs**, off the main highway about a mile from town. Finding them requires obtaining explicit directions, then driving through a pineapple field, and finally climbing a short distance up a steep bluff. But the Luahiwa petroglyphs are among the finest rock carvings in Hawaii and are definitely worth the search. As you approach each cluster of boulders, you'll see pictographic stories begin to unfold. One in particular depicts a large outrigger canoe, sails unfurled, being loaded Noah-style with livestock. Preparing, perhaps, for the ancient migration north to the Hawaiian Islands?

Return to the main road, which leads through pineapple fields, and then winds down to the twin inlets at **Manele Bay** and **Hulopoe Bay**. The small-boat harbor at Manele, rimmed by lava cliffs along the far shore, contains ruins of old Hawaiian houses. Hulopoe offers the island's nicest beach and park, a perfect place to take a rest after searching out the petroglyphs.

SOUTHWEST—KAUMALAPAU HARBOR AND KAUNOLU VILLAGE

Another southerly route, along Route 44, descends six miles to **Kaumalapau Harbor**. This busy little harbor was built by pineapple interests and is used primarily to ship the fruit on barges to Honolulu. On either side of Kaumalapau, you can see the *pali* which rises straight up as high as 1,000 feet, protecting Lanai's southwestern flank.

The most interesting point along this route involves a detour near the airport and a journey down a rugged jeep trail to **Kaunolu Village**. A favored playground of Kamehameha the Great and now a national landmark, this ancient fishing community still contains the ruins of over eighty houses as well as stone shelters and graves. Pick your way through it carefully, lest you step on a ghost. Kamehameha's house, once perched on the eastern ridge, looked across to **Halulu Heiau** on the west side of Kaunolu Bay. From nearby **Kahekili's Leap**, warriors proved their courage by plunging over sixty feet into the water below. If they cleared a fifteen-foot outcropping and survived the free fall into twelve feet of water, they were deemed noble soldiers worthy of their great king.

NORTHWEST—GARDEN OF THE GODS

From Lanai City, a graded pineapple road which disintegrates into an ungraded dirt track leads about seven miles to the **Garden of the Gods**. This heavily eroded area resembles the Dakota Badlands and features multihued boulders which change color dramatically during sunrise and sunset.

Shopping

You're in the wrong place, I'm afraid.

Nightlife

Visitors find this a great spot to get the sleep they missed in Lahaina or Honolulu. If rest isn't a problem, Lanai may be a good place to catch up on your reading or letter-writing. One thing is certain—once the sun goes down, there'll be little to distract you. You can have a drink while listening to local gossip at the **Hotel Lanai** (565-6605), but on an average evening even this night owl's nest will be closed by 10 o'clock.

Lanai Addresses and Phone Numbers

LANAI ISLAND

Camping Permits—Koele Company, P.O. Box L, Lanai City (565-6661)
Weather—(565-6033)

LANAI CITY

Ambulance—(565-6411)
Fire Department—(565-6766)
Hospital—Lanai Community Hospital, 628 7th Street (565-6411)
Laundromat—On 7th Street next to Elmura Jewelry
Library—Fraser Avenue (565-6996)
Police Department—312 8th Street (565-6525)
Post Office—731 Lanai Avenue (565-6517)

CHAPTER SEVEN
Molokai

Between the bustling islands of Oahu and Maui lies an isle which in size and shape resembles Manhattan, but which in spirit and rhythm is far more than an ocean away from the smog-shrouded shores of the Big Apple. Molokai, Hawaii's fifth-largest island, is thirty-seven miles long and ten miles wide. The slender isle was created by three volcanoes which mark its present geographic regions: one at West End where the arid Mauna Loa tableland rises to 1,381 feet, another at East End where a rugged mountain range along the north coast is topped by 4,970-foot Mount Kamakou, and the third, a geologic afterthought, which created the low, flat Kalaupapa Peninsula.

Kaunakakai, a sleepy port town on the south shore, is the island's hub. From here a road runs to the eastern and western coasts. Kalaupapa and the north *pali* are accessible overland only by mule and hiking trails.

Even in a region of islands, Molokai has always been something of a backwater. In pre-Western days it was subservient to Maui. When Kamehameha the Great took it in 1795, he was actually en route to the much grander prize of Oahu. Leprosy struck the islands during the next century, and wind-plagued Kalaupapa Peninsula became the living hell to which the disease's victims were exiled. Beginning in 1866, lepers were torn from their families and literally cast to their fates along this stark shore. Here Father Damien de Veuster, the Martyr of Molokai, came to live, work, and eventually die among the afflicted.

For years Molokai was labeled The Lonely Isle or The Forgotten Isle. By 1910 a population which once totaled 10,000 had decreased to one-tenth that size. Then, in 1921, Polynesians began settling homesteads under the Hawaiian Homes Act. The advent of pineapple agriculture in 1923 added to the population influx. Molokai soon became The Friendly Isle, with the largest proportion of native Hawaiians anywhere in the world. With them they brought a legacy from old Hawaii, the spirit of *aloha*, which still lives on this marvelous island. Young Hawaiians, sometimes hostile on the more crowded islands, are often outgoing and

215

generous here. And of all the islands, Molokai offers you the best opportunity to "go native" by staying with a Hawaiian family.

Today the island's population numbers about 6,500. The pineapple industry is waning, and, tragically, tourism is being slated to boost the ailing economy. Change is coming, but like everything on Molokai, it is arriving slowly. Time still remains to see Hawaii as it once was.

Easy Living

Transportation

ARRIVAL

When your plane touches down at Molokai Airport, you'll realize what a one-canoe island you're visiting. There's a snack bar and adjoining lounge which seem to open and close all day, plus a few car rental and airline offices. It's seven miles to the main town of Kaunakakai. There is no public transportation available.

The airport is served by numerous airlines: some large, some small, others nosediving out of business. The jets of **Hawaiian Airlines** offer the most frequent service to all the islands. **Princeville Airways** and **Panorama Air** fly small prop planes and are the most exciting way to reach Molokai. To fly direct from Honolulu to Kalaupapa, try Princeville Airways, which can always be relied upon for friendly service.

CAR RENTALS

Molokai being a small island, there's not much in the way of car rentals. At last count, only three firms were supplying visitors with infernal combustion machines. But considering that Molokai is off the flight path of tourists, there should be enough cars for visiting adventurers.

The existing companies, in no particular order, are as follows: **Molokai Island U-Drive** (567-6156), **Tropical Rent-A-Car** (567-6118), and **Avis Rent-A-Car** (567-6814). Any of them should prove quite adequate.

JEEP RENTALS

The lone company renting jeeps has closed, so at present there are no 4-wheel-drive vehicles available on the island.

BICYCLING

Traffic is light and slow-moving, making Molokai an ideal place for two-wheeling adventurers. The roads are generally good, with some potholes out East End near Halawa Valley. The terrain is mostly flat or

MOLOKAI: Overview Map

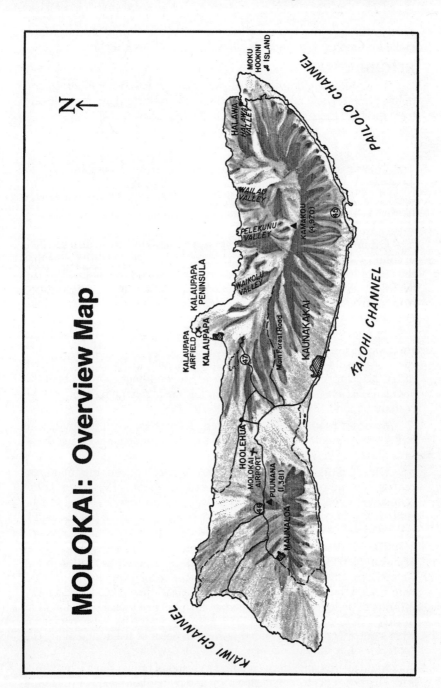

N

KAIWI CHANNEL

PAILOLO CHANNEL

KALOHI CHANNEL

MOKU HOOKINI ISLAND

HALAWA
HALAWA VALLEY

WAILAU VALLEY

PELEKUNU VALLEY

KAMAKOU (4,970)

WAIKOLU VALLEY

KALAUPAPA PENINSULA

KALAUPAPA AIRFIELD

KALAUPAPA

Maui Forest Road

KAUNAKAKAI

HOOLEHUA

MOLOKAI AIRPORT

PUUNANA (1,381)

MAUNALOA

gently rolling, with a few steep ascents. Winds are strong and sometimes make for tough going. Sorry, no bicycle shops of any kind here.

HITCHHIKING

Thumbing is officially illegal. Actually the law is not enforced and police are rarely even seen on the roads. The traffic is light, but rides are frequent (and there's never very far to go). So happy trucking.

Hotels

There's slim pickings in these parts. You can choose from a few accommodations: three hotels and several condos. With the tourist influx there'll be more, but so far Molokai has largely escaped the development blight. As a matter of fact, the island doesn't yet have a building over three stories high.

Oftentimes in opting for seclusion, you have to anticipate a sacrifice in comfort. On Molokai that's not necessarily the case. While it is true that the island has only a few amenities to offer visitors, you will find that the facilities here rate highly by mainland standards and are often priced competitively. So you should be able to combine the best of hidden Hawaii with a few creature comforts.

The choicest spot on the entire island to do so is at the cozy **Pau Hana Inn** (553-5342), Molokai's oldest hotel. The beachfront is lackluster, but there's a lovely view across the Kalohi Channel to Lanai. You'll find a quiet, lazy ambience here with cottages and buildings spotted about the lawns. Relax and enjoy the lush vegetation, small swimming pool, and the restaurant and bar down near the waterfront.

Standard rooms are budget priced. They're small yet pleasant, with twin beds, simulated wood paneling, and a quaint decor featuring drawings of ancient Polynesia.

Deluxe units are larger and newer. Add a fan, lanai, tub, and extra double bed and you'll pay something in the moderate price range. These rooms are a good choice if you're traveling with friends—they can be rented with tiny kitchenettes. (To make reservations from the mainland, call 800-536-7545, toll-free.)

There's Polynesian architecture but less island spirit at **Hotel Molokai** (553-5347). Set on a small unappealing beach two miles east of Kaunakakai, this hotel charges a moderate price for a very tiny room with twin beds. I found spotty mirrors, bumpy rugs, shared lanai, and a tacky interior of shingled (yes, shingled) walls. All that's okay in a low-rent hostelry, but why pay more for less? Actually, you're probably paying for what's outside: a shrub-rimmed lawn with coconut trees, and along the shore a pool, restaurant-lounge, and thatch pavilions.

Amid all this splendor you'll find a cluster of brown shingle buildings with elegantly curved Polynesian roofs and plate-glass windows reflecting

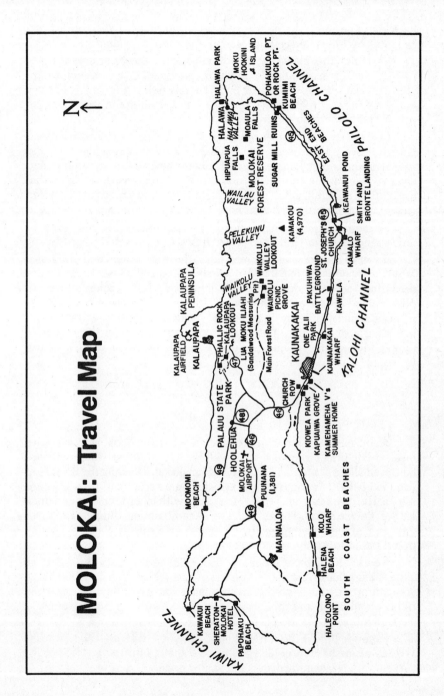

MOLOKAI: Travel Map

the view. These are the deluxe rooms (priced deluxe); they have wood paneling, high-beamed ceilings, and a much more appealing atmosphere.

Far from the madding crowd, you'll find the **Sheraton-Molokai** (552-2555). This sprawling 292-room complex is set near a luscious three-mile beach on the island's west end. There's nothing for miles but dry range country. It's Molokai's premier hotel, combining seclusion and comfort with Sheraton service.

Here you'll find the essence of plush living: wasp-waisted pool, tennis courts, golf course, a view of Diamond Head out past the reef, and an oceanfront lounge and restaurant. Rooms have all the necessities and most luxuries: lanai, color television, tile bathroom, overhead fan, rattan furniture. For an ultra-deluxe price tag you can buy a piece of that ocean view in a standard room. Rooms with garden views are tabbed deluxe.

Ke Nani Kai (552-2761), a nearby condominium, has one-bedroom units at moderate rates (deluxe priced from December 15 to April 15).

If you're traveling with several folks, there are other condominiums: **Molokai Shores** (553-5954) and **Wavecrest Resort** (558-8101). Both offer oceanfront accommodations with kitchenette, lanai, color television, pool, putting green, and picnic area. Of the two, Wavecrest, twelve miles east of Kaunakakai, is the best bargain. In addition to a few extra features including a dishwasher, the rates are slightly lower (in the moderate range). Molokai Shores, just one mile east of Kaunakakai, charges deluxe prices.

Restaurants

A gourmet will starve on Molokai, but someone looking for a square meal at fair prices should depart well-fed. The budget restaurants are clustered along Ala Malama Street in Kaunakakai. Heading the list is **Hop Inn** (553-5465), a nondescript cafe featuring a varied and tasty Chinese menu. Here you can challenge your palate with an order of almond duck or egg flower soup. There are several combination dinners for small groups, and the house specialty is a nine-course spread. Open every day from 11 a.m. to 9 p.m., it is budget priced.

Nearby **Kanemitsu's Bakery** (553-5855) serves tasty breakfasts at appetizing prices. Just across the street at the **Mid-Nite Inn** (553-5302) you can order from a predominantly meat-and-fish menu. The price is right. Small lunch and dinner platters, served with rice and vegetables, are budget priced, as are the breakfasts.

If you're into Filipino food, try either of two tiny cafes nearby. **Oviedo's Lunch Counter** (553-5014) and **Rabang's Restaurant** (553-5878) serve up spicy steaming dishes at low, low prices.

The **Pau Hana Inn** (553-5342) charges more, but throws in an ocean view. Here you can dine seaside near a century-old banyan tree or in a spacious dining room indoors. The lunch and dinner menus offer standard fare and come with a salad bar; prices are moderate; breakfast also served.

Most people on Molokai consider the Sheraton the island's bid for world-class resort status. If that's true, then the Pau Hana Inn must be Molokai's classic Hawaiian retreat. The lingua franca at this local hangout is pidgin English and the password is *laid-back*. While enjoying a meal here you'll find all the accoutrements to furnish a tropical dream, from overhead fans to Hawaiian altos plucking slack-key guitars. Charm is the Pau Hana's middle name, which is why it's such a popular spot among savvy travelers.

The **Hotel Molokai** (553-5347), two miles east of Kaunakakai, hosts hungry travelers in its attractive **Holoholo Dining Room.** Just a stone's skip from shore you can order from a surf-and-turf menu featuring such delectables as escargot, shrimp tempura, teriyaki steak, *mahimahi*, and Hawaiian-style stew. Prices are on the deluxe side.

Out in the one-street town of Maunaloa there's a neighborhood gathering spot called **Jojo's Cafe** (552-2803). Priced along the border between budget and moderate, it serves a variety of ethnic and all-American dishes.

The aforementioned **Sheraton-Molokai** (552-2555), on the island's far west end, has a pennysaver snack bar with sandwiches.

That's just light artillery to back up Sheraton's big gun, the **Ohia Lodge,** Molokai's finest restaurant. This multilevel, handsomely appointed establishment (high-beamed ceiling, rattan furnishings, strolling Hawaiian minstrels) looks out on the distant lights of Honolulu. The menu features several steak dishes and roast pork, plus such delicacies as stuffed prawns and duck *a l'orange*. Seeking a place to splurge? Well, this is it. Open for three meals and priced deluxe.

Grocery Markets

The nearest Molokai approaches to a supermarket is **Misaki's** (553-5505), a medium-sized grocery store on Kaunakakai's main drag, Ala Malama Street. The prices are higher and the selection smaller here than at the chain markets, so it's wise to bring a few provisions from the larger islands. Open 8:30 a.m. to 8:30 p.m., Sunday 9 a.m. to noon.

Molokai Buyer's Food Cooperative (553-3377), down the street and around the corner from Misaki's, offers a friendly atmosphere as well as juices, herbs, dried fruit, fresh fruit, and other health food items.

Try **Kanemitsu's Bakery** (553-5855) for delicious bread and pastries.

If you're heading out West End way, stock up—there's no grocery store until you beach at Oahu. On the East End, **Wavecrest Resort,** twelve miles out, has a "general store" with a very limited supply of groceries (primarily canned goods) and a hearty stock of liquor. About fifteen miles from Kaunakakai, a small outlet called the **Neighborhood Store 'n' Snack Bar** sells fresh fruit and groceries.

The Great Outdoors

The Sporting Life

CAMPING

With so little development and such an expanse of untouched land, Molokai would seem a haven for campers. Unfortunately, large segments of the island are owned by Molokai Ranch and other private interests: with the exception of a few beaches on Molokai Ranch property, these tracts are closed off behind locked gates.

There *are* a few parks for camping. A county permit is required for O'ne Alii Park. Permits cost $3 per person a day and are obtained at the County Parks and Recreation (553-3221) office in Kaunakakai. Permits for Kiowea Park and Moomomi Beach are issued by the Hawaiian Homelands Department (567-6104) in Hoolehua. The fee is $5 per night for a group of any size. Camping at Palaau State Park and Waikolu Picnic Grove is free (seven-day limit) but requires a permit from the Department of Land and Natural Resources (567-6083) situated amid the easily located state offices in Kaunakakai. A permit and $50 deposit are required for campgrounds on Molokai Ranch property. For information contact Molokai Ranch, P.O. Box 8, Kaunakakai, HI 96748 (553-5115).

Molokai Fish and Dive Corporation (553-5926) in Kaunakakai sells and rents a limited supply of camping gear.

SKIN DIVING AND FISHING

Molokai Fish and Dive Corporation (553-5926) sells equipment. For deep-sea fishing contact **George Peabody** (553-8253) in Kaunakakai.

OTHER SPORTS

GOLF

Ironwood Hills Golf Course (Kalae; 567-6121) and **Kalua Koi Golf Course** (Sheraton-Molokai; 552-2739) are all that Molokai has to offer to the golfing set.

HORSEBACK RIDING

Halawa Valley Horse Rides (553-3214) sponsors saddle tours of the East End valley and also rents horses.

Beaches and Parks
(Plus Camping, Swimming, Snorkeling, Surfing, Fishing)

EAST END BEACHES AND PARKS

O'ne Alii Park—This spacious park features a large grass-covered field and coconut grove plus a narrow beach with an excellent view of Lanai.

Facilities: Picnic area, restrooms, showers, electricity. Markets and restaurants are four miles away in Kaunakakai.

Camping: Very popular and therefore sometimes crowded and noisy. County permit required. Tent and trailer camping.

Swimming: A reef far offshore makes this area very shallow and affords ample protection. Excellent for children.

Snorkeling: Mediocre.

Surfing: All the action is far out on the reef and that's rarely any good.

Fishing: Surf-casting isn't bad here but it's even better farther to the east. Most common catches are *manini*, red and white goatfish, parrotfish, *papio, ulua,* milkfish, and mullet.

Getting there: Located four miles east of Kaunakakai on Route 45.

Kakahaia Picnic Ground—This is a long, narrow park wedged tightly between the road and the ocean. Picnicking, swimming, snorkeling, surfing, and fishing are much the same as at O'ne Alii Park. Day use only. Head east on Route 45 from Kaunakakai for six miles.

Kumimi Beach, Pohakuloa Point, and Other East End Beaches— Beginning near the eighteen-mile marker and extending for about four miles lies this string of small sandy beaches. These are among the island's loveliest, featuring white sands and spectacular views of Maui and Lanai.

Facilities: There is a small market near the fifteen-mile marker. **Kumimi Beach,** at the twenty-mile marker, has picnic facilities.

Camping: None.

Swimming: Very good, but beware of heavy currents and high surf.

Snorkeling: Very good. There's a lot of coral in this area. The diving for lobsters is pretty good.

Surfing: Numerous breaks throughout this area. **Pohakuloa Point** (or **Rock Point**), located eight-tenths of a mile past the twenty-mile marker, is one of Molokai's top surfing spots.

Fishing: Particularly good. Barracuda are sometimes caught in the deeper regions. Also bonefish, mountain bass, threadfin, *manini,* red and white goatfish, *ulua, papio,* parrotfish, milkfish, and mullet.

Halawa Park—Set in lush Halawa Valley, one of Molokai's most splendid areas, the park is tucked neatly between mountains and sea on a grassy plot dotted with coconut palms and ironwood trees. Cliffs, waterfalls, black-sand beach—altogether a heavenly spot, though sometimes rainy and almost always windy.

Facilities: The park is a bit weatherbeaten and overgrown. Picnic area; restrooms; running water which must be boiled or treated chemically.

Camping: Not permitted in park.

Swimming: Very good. Partially protected by the bay, but exercise caution anyway.

Snorkeling: Also good.

Surfing: One of the very best spots on the island.

Fishing: Reefs studding this area make it a prime locale for many of the species caught along the East End Beaches.

Getting there: Located at the far end of Route 45, twenty-eight miles east of Kaunakakai.

WEST END BEACHES AND PARKS

Kiowea Park—Watch for falling coconuts in this beautiful grove. Towering palms extend almost to the water, leaving little space for a beach. A nice place to visit, but I wouldn't want to camp here.

Facilities: Picnic area; restrooms. One mile to Kaunakakai's restaurants and markets.

Camping: Permit required from Hawaiian Homelands Department, which is located in the town of Hoolehua. Camping permits are $5 per night. For information contact 567-6104.

Swimming: Beach well-protected by a distant reef. Shallow.

Snorkeling: Mediocre.

Surfing: Forget it.

Fishing: Common catches include mullet, *manini,* parrotfish, milkfish, and *papio,* plus red, white, and striped goatfish.

Getting there: Travel one mile west of Kaunakakai on Route 46.

Palaau State Park—Set in a densely forested area, this thirty-four-acre park is ideal for a mountain sojourn. Several short trails lead to petroglyphs, a startling phallic rock, and the awesome Kalaupapa Lookout. The trail down to Kalaupapa Peninsula is also nearby.

Facilities: Picnic area; restrooms; showers; electricity. Eight miles to markets and restaurants in Kaunakakai.

Camping: State permit required. Tent camping only.

Getting there: Take Route 46 four miles west from Kaunakakai, then follow Route 47 about four more miles.

Moomomi Beach (★)—A small, remote beach studded with rocks and frequented only by local people . . . what more could you ask?

Facilities: Picnic area; restrooms; showers.

Camping: On a grassy plot elevated from the beach. No permit required, but a pass from Hawaiian Homelands Department (567-6104) is needed.

Swimming: Good; partially protected. Rocky bottom.

Snorkeling: Very good along reefs and rocks.

Surfing: Fair breaks at the mouth of the inlet.

Fishing: Good surf-casting off the rocks which border the inlet.

Getting there: Take Route 46 west from Kaunakakai to Hoolehua. Go right on Route 481 (Puupeelua Avenue), then left on Farrington Avenue. Farrington starts as a paved road, then turns to dirt. After two-and-two-tenths miles of dirt track, the road forks. Take the right fork and follow it a half-mile to the beach.

Halena and Other South Coast Beaches (★)—Don't tell anyone, but there's a dirt road running several miles along a string of trackless beaches on the south shore. The first one, **Halena,** is a very funky ghost camp complete with a dozen weatherbeaten shacks and a few primitive facilities. To the west lies **Haleolono Point,** with its pleasant bay and lagoon. To the east is **Kolo Wharf** (an abandoned pier collapsing into the sea), plus numerous fishponds, coconut groves, and small sand beaches. This is an excellent area to explore, camp, hike, fish, and commune with hidden Hawaii.

Facilities: The shacks, picnic facilities, and running water are open to visitors at Halena. After that you're on your own. Better boil or chemically treat the water.

Camping: Molokai Ranch permits camping along all the beaches in this region.

Swimming: The water is muddy, but otherwise swimming is good.

Snorkeling: Muddy water.

Fishing: You might reel in mountain bass, threadfin, *inenui,* or even red goatfish. This is also a prime area for limpets.

Getting there: Take Route 46 to Maunaloa. As you first enter town (before the road curves into the main section), you'll see houses on the left and a dirt road extending perpendicularly to the right. Take this road two-and-eight-tenths miles to the Molokai Ranch gate and continue along the rugged road that extends beyond the gate. Take this road one-and-eight-tenths miles to where it forks.

Now, to get to Halena, take a right at the fork, then a quick left, then drive a short way, just a few hundred yards, to the end. The shore is nearby; simply walk west along the beach several hundred yards to the shacks.

To get to Haleolono, walk about a mile west along the beach from Halena.

To get to Kolo Wharf and the other beaches, go straight where the road forks. Kolo is two miles east over an equally rugged road. Sand beaches, coconut groves, and fishponds extend for another six miles past Kolo. Then the road turns inland, improving considerably, and continues for seven miles more until it meets the main road two miles west of Kaunakakai.

(Note: The road to these beaches is locked, making access impossible to all but hikers.)

Kawakui Beach (★)—This idyllic spot is my favorite Molokai campground. Here a small inlet, tucked away in Molokai's northwest corner, is edged by a beautiful beach with a sandy bottom. Nearby is a shady grove, fringed by the rocky coastline. On a clear night you can see the lights of Honolulu across Kaiwi Channel.

Facilities: Forget it. Try Kaunakakai, nineteen miles behind you.

Camping: That shady grove is a perfect site to pitch a tent. Camping permitted by Molokai Ranch on Friday, Saturday, Sunday, and holidays only.

Swimming: Very good. The inlet offers some protection, but exercise caution.

Snorkeling: Good near the rocks when the surf is low.

Surfing: Good, but variable. Shore wind plagues this area.

Fishing: Mountain bass, threadfin, *inenui,* and red goatfish are commonly caught here.

Getting there: Take Route 46 west from Kaunakakai for about twelve miles. Then take a right onto the dirt road that leads downhill. Follow this bumpy dirt road about seven miles to the beach. The road forks a few hundred yards before the ocean. Take the right fork to Kawakui; the left fork leads to a series of white-sand beaches, offering excellent possibilities for exploring and swimming. (A key to open the gates en route must be obtained from Molokai Ranch at their office in Kaunakakai; 553-5115.)

Papohaku Beach —This splendid beach extends for three miles along Molokai's west coast; it's an excellent place to explore, collect *puka* shells, or just lay back and enjoy the view of Oahu.

Facilities: Picnic areas, restrooms, showers; the Sheraton-Molokai, with snack bar and restaurant, is about a half-mile away.

Camping: Tent only.

Swimming: Excellent, but use caution.

Snorkeling: Mediocre; there's not much rock or coral here.

Surfing: Good breaks when the wind isn't blowing from the shore.

Fishing: Mountain bass, threadfin, *inenui,* and red goatfish are the most common catches.

Getting there: Take Route 46 for about fourteen miles from Kaunakakai. Turn right onto the road to the Sheraton-Molokai Hotel. Continue past the hotel (don't turn onto the hotel road) and down the hill. Follow this macadam track, Kalua Koi Road, as it parallels the beach. Sideroads from Kalua Koi Road and Pohakuloa Road (an adjoining thoroughfare) lead to Papohaku and other beaches.

Hiking

Molokai features some splendid country and numerous areas that seem prime for hiking, but few trails have been built or maintained and most private land is off-limits to visitors. Some excellent hiking possibilities, but no official trails, are offered along the beaches described above. Palaau State Park also has several short jaunts to points of interest.

The only lengthy treks lead to the island's rugged north coast. Four valleys—Halawa, Wailau, Pelekunu, and Waikolu—cut through the sheer cliffs guarding this windswept shore.

The **Pelekunu Trail** begins several hundred yards beyond the Waikolu Valley Lookout (see the section on "Molokai's Outback"). I had trouble gathering information on this trail: some sources insisted it didn't even exist. I did learn that it is unmaintained and *extremely* difficult. The trail leads to a lookout point and then drops into the valley.

The **Wailau Trail** is maintained by the Sierra Club. This is another very difficult trail which takes six to eight hours and passes through some muddy rain-forest regions. The trailhead is off Route 45 about fifteen miles east of Kaunakakai. To reach it, you must obtain permission from Pearl Petro (558-8113) to cross private land. The trail extends across nearly the entire island from south to north.

The **Kalaupapa Trail** is the easiest and best-maintained trail descending the north *pali.* A trail description is given in the "Sightseeing" section in this chapter. To hike here you must obtain permission and pay $17.50 for a mandatory tour of the leper colony. Call Damien Tours (567-6171) or Molokai Mule Ride (567-6708) for permission and information.

The only valley accessible by car is Halawa. The **Halawa Valley Trail,** one of Molokai's prettiest hikes, extends for two miles from the mouth of the valley to the base of Moaula Falls. This 250-foot cascade tumbles down a sheer cliff to a cold mountain pool perfect for swimming. Hipua-

Molokai's Outback

For a splendid tour of Molokai's mountainous interior, take a drive or hike on the Main Forest Road. This bumpy dirt road is studded with "4-Wheel Drive Only" signs along its ten-mile length, but it's passable by car in dry weather.

Deer, quail, pheasant, doves, and chukkar partridge populate the route. Numerous secondary roads and trails lead to the very edge of the mammoth Molokai Forest Reserve through which the main road passes. These side roads offer excellent possibilities for adventurous hikers.

After nine miles, the main road passes **Lua Moku Iliahi,** known to the English-speaking world as the **Sandalwood Measuring Pit.** This depression, cut to the hull size of an old sailing vessel, was used by nineteenth-century Hawaiians to gauge the amount of sandalwood needed to fill a ship. It's another mile to **Waikolu Picnic Grove,** a heavily wooded retreat ideal for lunching or camping. Here you'll find picnic facilities, an outhouse, and running water. (State permit required to camp.) Across the road, **Waikolu Valley Lookout** perches above Waikolu Valley, which descends precipitously over 3,000 feet to the sea.

To reach the Main Forest Road, take Route 46 west from Kaunakakai. There is a white bridge a little more than three-and-a-half miles from town, just before the four-mile marker. Take a right on the dirt road right before the bridge and you're on the Main Forest Road.

pua Falls, a sister cascade just a third of a mile north, shoots 500 feet down the *pali*. This can be reached by taking a trail near Moaula Falls, then climbing along the rocks.

The Moaula trail is well-marked and relatively easy to hike. It takes about ninety minutes each way and climbs 250 feet. The path passes several homes as well as the remains of houses wiped out when the 1946 tidal wave swept the valley. Numerous fruit trees line the way and wildlife abounds. If you decide to swim in the pool, you might heed the warning of ancient Hawaiians. They would tie a stone to a *ti* leaf and set it adrift here. If the leaf floated, they plunged in; if it sank, they recognized that the legendary lizard *moo* would drown anyone disturbing his lair.

To get to the trail, take Route 45 to Halawa Valley. The trail is marked near the end of the road a short distance from the beach.

Travelers' Tracks

Sightseeing

Across its brief expanse, Molokai offers many rewards to the curious. The greatest, of course, is the pilgrimage to the Kalaupapa leper colony. Second only to this is a tour of the East End.

KAUNAKAKAI TO HALAWA VALLEY

From Kaunakakai to Halawa Valley a narrow macadam road leads past almost thirty miles of seascapes and historic sites. Route 45 runs straight along the south shore for about twenty miles, presenting views across Kalohi and Pailolo Channels to **Lanai** and **Maui**. Then the road snakes upward and curves inland before descending again into Halawa Valley.

Prior to departing for points east, tour the rustic town of **Kaunakakai.** This somnolent village, with its falsefront buildings and tiny civic center, is the hub of Molokai. Nearby is the **wharf**, extending seaward almost a half-mile and offering gorgeous views. Close to the pier landing rest the rocky remains of **Kamehameha V's Summer Home,** where Hawaii's king luxuriated in the late nineteenth century.

Several miles from town, the Hawaii Visitors Bureau marker points to the ancient battleground at **Kawela.** Two battles were fought at nearby **Pakuhiwa Battleground.** In his drive to become Hawaii's first monarch, Kamehameha the Great launched a canoe flotilla which reportedly extended four miles along this shore.

Just past the ten-mile marker, a dirt road leads to **Kamalo Wharf,** an old pineapple shipping point. It's a half-mile further to **St. Joseph's Catholic Church,** a tiny chapel built by Father Damien in 1876.

A monument marks the **Smith and Bronte Landing,** an inhospitable spot where two aviators crash-landed after completing the first civilian transpacific flight in 1927. An opening in the trees nearby reveals **Keawanui Pond.** Of Molokai's many fishponds built for Hawaiian chiefs, this is one of the largest.

The ruins of the island's first **sugar mill** stand near the highway's twenty-mile marker. Just beyond the marker is **Kumimi Beach,** which presents your first view of **Moku Hookini Island.** The road now begins a sinuous course along a string of pearl-white beaches, then climbs above a rocky coastline. You'll pass the sacred **Whispering Stone** of which fishermen asked good luck. Now the scenery begins to change dramatically to rolling pastureland fringed with tropical vegetation.

The route winds on to **Halawa Valley.** A river bisects this luxuriant region. At the far end, surrounded by sheer walls, two waterfalls— Hipuapua and Moaula—spill down the mountainside. Obviously East End has withheld its most spectacular scenery until the last.

KAUNAKAKAI TO MAUNALOA

Just a mile west of town on Route 46 are the magnificent coconut groves at **Kiowea Park** and **Kapuaiwa Grove,** planted in the 1860s by Kamehameha V. Strung like rosary beads opposite the grove are seven tiny churches. This **Church Row** includes Protestant, Mormon, Jehovah's Witness, and several other denominations. Stop by and inquire about services; visitors are always welcome.

A side trip along Route 47 leads to the **Kalaupapa Lookout** for an unsurpassed view of the steep northern coast, the leper colony, and Kalaupapa Peninsula. A short hike away, **Phallic Rock** protrudes obscenely from the ground amid an ironwood stand as thick as pubic hair. Legend says that a woman offering gifts and spending the night here will return home pregnant.

Route 46 continues over dry rolling plains to **Maunaloa.** With the departure of Dole's operations, this company town is fading into a ghost town. Today it has the dusty, falsefront feel of the Wild West after the mines petered out and the saloons shut down.

Perhaps the island's most unexpected and exotic feature is the **Molokai Ranch Wildlife Safari.** Part of Molokai Ranch's sprawling 60,000-acre spread is a game preserve roamed by over 400 animals. Barbary sheep, eland, sable, antelope, ibex, ostrich, axis deer, giraffe, greater kudu, and oryx are among the species that have transformed Molokai's West End into a kind of "Little Africa." Camera safaris of this unusual refuge are led by Grayline Molokai (P.O. Box 253, Hoolehua, Molokai, HI 96729; 567-6177 for information and 552-2622 for reservations).

KALAUPAPA

The most awesome experience on Molokai is a visit to the **Kalaupapa leper colony.** Here about 100 victims of Hansen's Disease live in solitude. Doctors have controlled the affliction since 1946 with sulfone drugs, and all the patients are free to leave. But many are sixty to eighty-five years old, and have lived on this windswept peninsula most of their lives.

Their story goes back to 1866 when the Hawaiian government began exiling lepers to this lonely spot on Molokai's rain-plagued north coast. In those days Kalaupapa was a Hawaiian fishing village, and lepers were segregated in the **old settlement** at Kalawao on the windy eastern side of the peninsula. The place was treeless and barren—a wasteland haunted by slow death. Lepers were shipped along the coast and pushed overboard. Abandoned with insufficient provisions and no shelter, they struggled against both the elements and disease.

To this lawless, hopeless realm came Joseph Damien de Veuster, Father Damien. The Catholic priest, arriving in 1873, brought a spirit and energy which gave the colony new life. He built a church, attended to the afflicted, and died of leprosy sixteen years later. Perhaps it is his spirit which even today marks the indescribable quality of Kalaupapa. There is something unique and inspiring about the place, something you'll have to discover yourself.

To visit Kalaupapa you can fly, hike, or ride muleback; there are no auto access roads. Once there you must take a guided tour; no independent exploring is permitted. And no children under sixteen are allowed. Flights and hiking tours are organized by **Damien Tours** (567-6171) and **Molokai Mule Ride** (567-6088). For flights, check **Princeville Airways** (567-6115).

As far as I'm concerned, the mule ride is the only way to go. The Molokai Mule Ride conducts four-legged tours daily, weather permitting. You saddle up near the Kalaupapa Lookout and descend a 1,664-foot precipice. Kalaupapa unfolds below as you switchback through lush vegetation on this three-mile-long trail. The ride? Exhilarating, a bit frightening, but safe. And the views are otherworldly.

Definitely visit Kalaupapa. Fly in and you'll undergo quite an experience; hike or ride a mule and it will become a pilgrimage.

Shopping

Across the Kaiwi Channel in Honolulu.

Nightlife

Confirmed party-goers will find Molokai a pretty dead scene. Probably the best place around is at the venerable **Pau Hana Inn** (553-5342) in Kaunakakai. It's certainly popular among the local folks. The Pau Hana Inn blazes with local color weeknights and cranks up the band on weekends. The ocean view stars nightly. At Hotel Molokai's **Holoholo Dining Room** (553-5347) you'll find Hawaiian music Thursday through Saturday. It's a nice place to kick back and relax.

To step out in style, head west to Sheraton-Molokai's **Ohia Lounge** (552-2555). The rattan furnishings, knee-deep carpets, overhead fans, and marvelous view of Honolulu, not to mention the band, make it *the* place.

Molokai Addresses and Phone Numbers

MOLOKAI ISLAND

County Parks and Recreation — Kaunakakai (553-5141)
Department of Land and Natural Resources — Kaunakakai (567-6083 and 553-5019)
Hawaiian Homelands Department — Hoolehua (567-6104)
Weather — (552-2477)

KAUNAKAKAI

Ambulance — (553-5911)
Fire Department — (553-5401)
Laundromat — Molokai Launderette (567-6703)
Library — Ala Malama Street (553-5483)
Liquor — Molokai Wines and Spirits, Ala Malama Street (553-5009)
Pharmacy and Photo Supply — Molokai Drugs, Ala Malama Street (553-5790)
Police Department — (553-5355)
Post Office — Ala Malama Street (553-5845)

CHAPTER EIGHT

Oahu

Honolulu, Somerset Maugham once remarked, is the meetingplace of East and West. Today, with its high-rise cityscape and crowded commercial center, Hawaii's capital is more the place where Hong Kong meets Los Angeles. It's the hub of Hawaii, a city which dominates the political, cultural, and economic life of the islands.

And it's the focus of Oahu as well. Honolulu has given Oahu more than its nickname, The Capital Island. The city has drawn four-fifths of Hawaii's population to this third-largest island, making Oahu both a military stronghold and a popular tourist spot.

With military installations at Pearl Harbor and outposts seemingly everywhere, the armed forces control about one-quarter of the island. Most bases are off-limits to civilians; and tourists congregate in Honolulu's famed resort area—Waikiki. Both defense and tourism are big business on Oahu, and it's an ironic fact of island life that the staid, uniformly-dressed military peacefully coexists here with crowds of sun-loving, scantily-clad visitors.

The tourists are attracted by one of the world's most famous beaches, an endless white-sand ribbon that has drawn sun worshippers and water lovers since the days of Hawaiian royalty. In ancient times Waikiki was a swamp; now it's a spectacular region of world-class resorts.

Indeed, Waikiki is at the center of Pacific tourism, just as Honolulu is the capital of the Pacific. Nowhere else in the world will you find a population more varied or an ambience more vital. There are times when Waikiki's Parisian-size boulevards seem ready to explode from the sheer force of the crowds. People in bikinis and wild-colored *aloha* shirts stroll the streets, while others flash past on mopeds or in rickshaws.

And just beyond Honolulu's bustling thoroughfares stretches a beautiful island, featuring countless beaches and two incredible mountain ranges. Since most of the crowds congregate in the southern regions around Honolulu, the north is rural. You can experience the color and velocity of the city, then head for the slow and enchanting country.

(Text continued on page 238.)

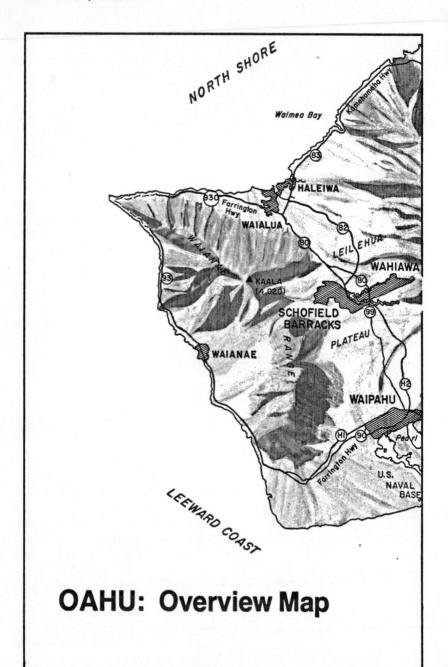

OAHU: Overview Map

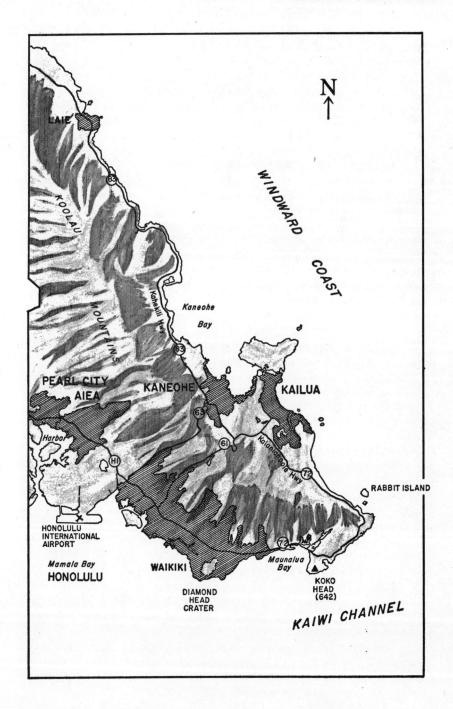

Naturally, this is just my opinion, but as you begin to explore for yourself, you'll find Oahu does have something special to offer: history. *Oahu* means "gathering place" in Hawaiian, and for centuries it has been an important commercial area and cultural center. Warring chiefs long battled for control of the island until Kamehameha I seized power in 1795 by sweeping an opposing army over the cliffs of Nuuanu Pali north of Honolulu. Several years earlier the British had "discovered" Honolulu Harbor, a natural anchorage destined to be one of the Pacific's key seaports.

In 1850 the city which had grown up around the shipping port, and become the focus of Hawaii, became the archipelago's capital as well. Here in 1893 a band of white businessmen illegally overthrew the native monarchy. Almost a half-century later, in an ill-advised but brilliantly executed military maneuver, the Japanese drew America into World War II with a devastating air strike against the huge naval base at Pearl Harbor.

There are some fascinating historical monuments to tour throughout Honolulu, but I recommend you also venture outside the city to Oahu's less congested regions. Major highways lead from the capital along the east and west coasts, and several roads bisect the central plateau en route to the north shore. Except for a five-mile strip in Oahu's northwest corner, you can drive completely around the island.

Closest to Honolulu is the east coast, where a spectacular seascape is paralleled by the Koolaus, a jagged and awesomely steep mountain range. This is Oahu's rainswept windward shore. Here, traveling up the coast past the bedroom-communities of Kailua and Kaneohe, you'll discover beautiful and relatively untouched white-sand beaches. On the north shore are some of the world's most famous surfing spots—Waimea Bay, Sunset, the Banzai Pipeline—where winter waves twenty and thirty feet high roll in with crushing force.

The Waianae Range, rising to 4,040 feet, shadows Oahu's western coast. The sands are as white here, the beaches as uncrowded, but I've always felt uncomfortable on the Waianae coast. A lot of racial hostility is aimed at visitors on Oahu, as evidenced by theft, vandalism, and beatings. It is particularly bad along this shore. I've been robbed and had a car window smashed in separate incidents here. Wherever you go on Oahu you have to be careful not to leave valuables unattended, but be particularly watchful around Waianae.

Between the Koolau and Waianae Ranges, remnants of the two volcanoes that created Oahu, spreads the Leilehua Plateau. This fertile region is occupied by sugar and pineapple plantations as well as several large military bases.

Hosting millions and millions of tourists over the years, Oahu has become a favorite location among travel agents and tour-book writers. Many people can't even conceive of visiting Hawaii without going to "the gathering place," and some never venture out to any of the other islands. Oahu does have its virtues. But if, like me, you think of a vacation in terms of experiencing the crowds, then leaving them behind—plan on fully exploring Oahu and then continuing on to the Neighbor Islands.

Easy Living

Transportation

ARRIVAL

There's one airport on Oahu and it's a behemoth. **Honolulu International Airport** is a Pacific crossroads, an essential link between North America and Asia. Most visitors arriving from the mainland land here first, and find it a convenient jumping-off point for venturing farther to the various Neighbor Islands. **Aloha Airlines, Hawaiian Airlines,** and **Mid-Pacific Air** provide regular jet service to the outer islands, while smaller outfits like **Reeves Air** and **Princeville Airways** fly prop planes.

Honolulu International includes all the comforts of a major airport. Here you can check your bags or rent a locker; fuel up at a restaurant, coffee shop, or cocktail lounge; shop at any of several stores; or shower.

To cover the eight or so miles into town, it's possible to hire a cab for $13, plus a small charge for each bag. **Grayline** (922-4011) runs a shuttle service to Waikiki hotels for $5. For $4 **Airport Motorcoach** (926-4747) will take you to your hotel or condominium. And city bus #19 or #20 travels through downtown Honolulu and Waikiki. This is the cheapest transportation, but you're only allowed to carry on baggage that fits on your lap. So, unless you're traveling very light, you'll have to use another conveyance.

CAR RENTALS

Of all the islands, Oahu offers the most rental agencies and the worst service. Elsewhere you'll usually receive a spotless car, recently tuned, ready to roll; here you're liable to get an unwashed auto, spotted with litter, and sometimes running poorly. I once rented a car which sputtered to a halt after several days. When I tucked my head under the hood looking for trouble, I discovered the engine lacked an air filter. The carburetor had been breathing dirt, sand, and moisture all across the island! So check the car carefully before you leave the lot, as some of these rental agencies are worse than used car dealers.

At the airport, **Dollar Rent-A-Car** (926-4251), **Hertz** (836-2511), **Avis** (836-5511), and **Budget Rent-A-Car** (922-3600) all have booths. Although conveniently located, these agencies usually charge a little more for their cars. (Text continued on page 242.)

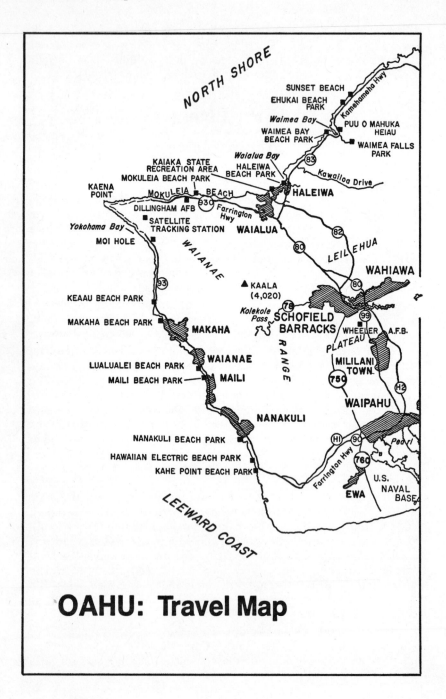

OAHU: Travel Map

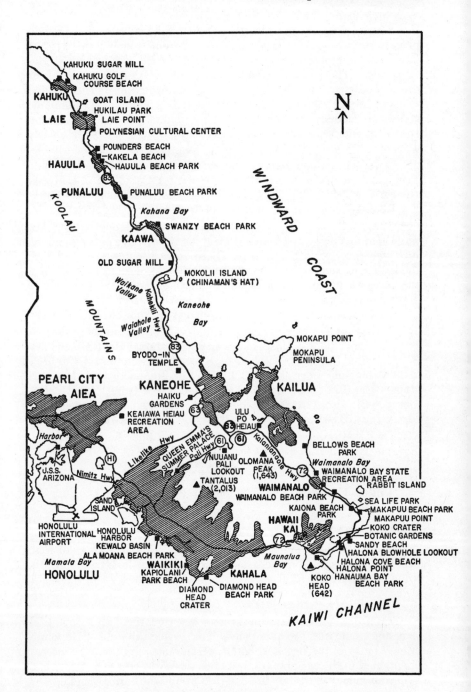

Several agencies outside the airport offer low rates and provide pick-up service when your plane arrives. Foremost among these is **National Car Rental** (836-2655; or from the mainland, 800-227-7368). National serves Hawaii, Maui, and Kauai, as well as Oahu. I have used their cars for years and highly recommend the company for its friendly and efficient service. While they provide a number of different automobile styles and models, the best bargains are generally found by renting a stick-shift compact. These economical cars are quite adequate for any driving you might do on Oahu.

Several other outfits provide airport pick-up service. These include **Tropical Rent-A-Car** (836-1041), **Thrifty Rent-A-Car** (836-2388), **Five-O Rent-A-Car** (836-1028), **Travelers Rent-A-Car** (833-3355), **Ugly Duckling Rent-A-Car** (538-3825), and **World Rent-A-Car** (833-1866).

There are many other Honolulu-based companies offering very low rates but providing no pick-up service at the airport. I've never found the inconvenience worth the savings. There you are—newly-arrived from the mainland, uncertain about your environment, anxious to check in at the hotel—and you're immediately confronted with the Catch-22 of getting to your car. Do you rent a vehicle in which to pick up your rental car? Take a bus? Hitchhike? What do you do with your bags meanwhile?

If your budget is important, consider one of the following cheaper but less convenient outfits: **American International Rent-A-Car** (833-3355), **United Car Rental** (922-4605), **Robert's Hawaii Rent-A-Car** (947-3939), **Honolulu Ford** (531-0491), **VIP Car Rental** (946-1671), **Sears Rent-A-Car** (922-3805), **Compact Rent-A-Car** (833-0059), **Gem Rent-A-Car** (538-3143), or **Greyhound Rent-A-Car** (923-3022). If you really want to risk it, try **BJ's Used Car Rentals** (235-5569) or **Rent-A-Junk** (926-7209).

Or if you prefer to go in high style, rent a Rolls Royce, Mercedes Benz, or Porsche from **Silver Cloud** (524-7999).

JEEP RENTALS

United Car Rental (2352 Kalakaua Avenue; 922-4605) provides jeeps.

MOTOR SCOOTER AND MOTORCYCLE RENTALS

Aloha Funway Rentals (1982 Kalakaua Avenue; 942-9696) rents scooters, motorcycles, mopeds, and roller skates; **Apollo Car Rentals** (133 Uluniu Avenue; 926-8336) rents mopeds. Call for rates.

PUBLIC TRANSPORTATION

Oahu has an excellent bus system that runs regularly to points all over the island and provides convenient service throughout Honolulu. Many, many of the beaches, hotels, restaurants, and points of interest mentioned in this chapter are just a bus ride away. It's even possible to pop your money in the fare box and ride around the entire island.

TheBus carries almost 200,000 people daily, loading them into any of 300 yellow-and-orange vehicles that rumble along city streets and country roads from 5 a.m. until midnight.

If you stay in Waikiki you'll inevitably be sardined into a #19 or #20 bus for the ride through Honolulu's tourist mecca. Many bus drivers are Hawaiian; I saw some hysterical scenes on this line when tourists waited anxiously for their stop to be called, only to realize they couldn't understand the driver's pidgin. Hysterical, that is, after those early days when *I* was the visitor with the furrowed brow.

But you're surely more interested in meeting local people than tourists, and you can easily do it on any of the buses outside Waikiki. They're less crowded and a lot more fun for people-watching.

For information on bus routes call **TheBus** at 531-1611. And remember, the only carry-on luggage permitted is baggage small enough to fit on your lap.

In Waikiki you might want to check out the **pedicabs.** These three-wheeled rickshaws, pedaled by young and often street-savvy drivers, are expensive but entertaining conveyances. Several dollars will carry you from one place in Waikiki to another. Even if you decide not to ride around in this grand colonial style, you'll find the drivers are good sources of information. Many know the local scene intimately. If you're looking for a hot night spot or a good restaurant, check them out.

BICYCLING

Oahu is blessed with excellent roads, well-paved, and usually flat, and cursed with heavy traffic. About four-fifths of Hawaii's population lives here, and it sometimes seems that every person owns a car.

Honolulu can be a cycler's nightmare, but outside the city the traffic is somewhat lighter. And Oahu drivers, accustomed to tourists driving mopeds, are relatively conscious of bicyclists.

Keep in mind that the east coast is the wet side, the north shore's slightly drier, and the south and west coasts are driest of all. And remember, ripoffs are a frequent fact of life on Oahu. Leaving your bike unlocked is asking for a long walk back.

If you'd like a little two-wheeled company, check out the **Hawaii Bicycling League** (Box 4403, Honolulu, Oahu, HI 96813), which regularly sponsors bike rides.

RENTALS

Aloha Funway Rentals (1984 Kalakaua Avenue; 942-9696) in Waikiki rents bicycles.

REPAIRS

The following shops do repair work, plus sell bikes and accessories: **Eki Cyclery** (Ala Moana Center, Honolulu; 946-5444), **The Bike Shop**

(1149 South King Street, Honolulu; 531-7071), **Kailua Bike Shop** (354 Hahani Street, Kailua; 261-9213), and **Waipahu Bicycle** (94-320 Waipahu Depot Street, Waipahu; 671-4091).

HITCHHIKING

Thumbing is not as popular on Oahu as one might think, so the competition for rides is not too great. The heavy traffic also increases your chances considerably. Officially, you're supposed to hitch from bus stops only. While I've seen people hitching in many different spots, I'd still recommend standing at a bus stop. Not only will you be within the law, but you'll also be able to catch a bus if you can't hitch a ride.

Hotels

The hotel scene on Oahu can be described in one word—Waikiki. This little section of Honolulu, favored by travelers, is crowded with facilities. Venturing out from this enclave, you'll find only a few accommodations. For your convenience when hotel-hunting, I'll divide Honolulu into "Waikiki" and "Greater Honolulu," then list the few rural hotels on the island according to their locations on the Windward (East) Coast, the North Shore, or the Leeward (West) Coast.

WAIKIKI HOTELS

Waikiki Budget Hotels: While it may no longer be the simple country retreat it was at the century's turn, Waikiki does have one advantage; believe it or not, it's a great place to find low-rent hotels. A lot of the cozy old hostelries have been torn down and replaced with high-rises, but a few have escaped the urban assault. Some of those skyscrapers, too, are cheaper than you might think. So let's take a look at some of the better bargains Waikiki has to offer.

The **Malihini Hotel** (217 Saratoga Road; 923-9644) will give you a feel for Honolulu's earlier low-rise era. An attractive complex which spreads out instead of up, this twenty-eight-unit hotel is just a short stroll from the beach. Though pretty on the outside, its sparse furnishings, scant decoration, and cinder-block walls give a vacant feel to the place. But the studios are spacious and come equipped with kitchenettes. The one-bedroom apartments will sleep up to five people.

If you're willing to sacrifice intimacy, you may find that the **Coral Seas Hotel** (250 Lewers Street; 923-3881) is the best deal in Waikiki. This seven-story hostelry, located just a hundred yards from the beach, has rooms at very modest prices. They are appealing accommodations with air-conditioning, telephones, wall-to-wall carpeting, and small lanais. In some units you can add a mini-kitchenette to the list of extras. If you want, just for the hell of it, to intimately experience the Waikiki tourist scene, this is the place. The Coral Seas Hotel is at the heart of the action, and has a pool.

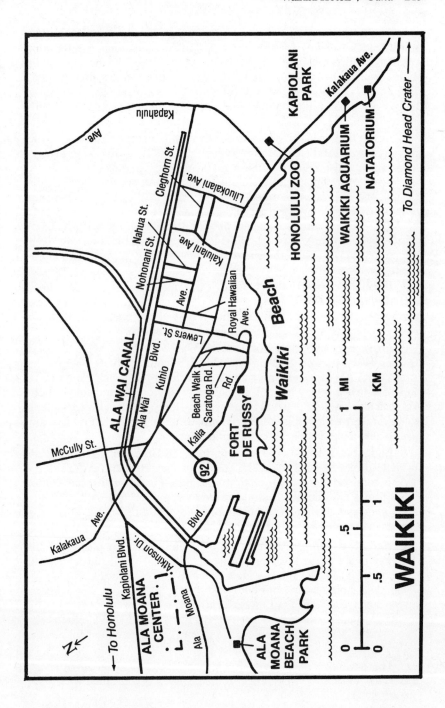

Also in the center of Waikiki is the nearby **Edgewater Hotel** (2168 Kalia Road; 922-6424). Located a stone's skip from the beach, this 180-unit colossus offers excellent accommodations at low prices. Each room comes with telephone, carpeting, television, cable movies, and a shared lanai. The decor is bland but the furniture comfy. Downstairs is an open-air lobby with adjoining restaurant and pool. The deluxe rooms come with kitchenettes.

Rising higher from the ground, while still keeping costs low, is the **Royal Grove Hotel** (151 Uluniu Avenue; 923-7691), a six-story, eighty-five-unit establishment. If you can get past the garish pink exterior here, you'll find the rooms more tastefully designed. All are comfortably furnished, and some are decorated in simple but appealing styles. There are televisions, telephones, and carpeting in many of the higher-priced rooms upstairs, plus an almond-shaped pool and spacious lobby downstairs. Rents vary according to which wing of this sprawling building your bags are parked in. But even the standard rooms come equipped with kitchenettes, so it's hard to go wrong here.

If you'd like to stay directly across the street from the beach, check into the **Waikiki Circle Hotel** (2464 Kalakaua Avenue; 923-1571). This fourteen-story hotel-in-the-round has rooms at reasonable rates. Most have an ocean view, which is the main advantage here.

An inexpensive place for men in Waikiki is the **YMCA Central Branch** (401 Atkinson Drive; 941-3344). It's handily situated across the street from Ala Moana Center and a block from the beach. And you're welcome to use the gym, pool, saunas, television room, and coffee shop. You can also expect the usual Y ambience—long sterile hallways leading to an endless series of identical, cramped, uncarpeted rooms. But low prices help make up for the lack of amenities.

Budget travelers should also consider the **Hale Aloha Hostel** (2417 Prince Edward Street; 946-0591). This helpful facility features dormitory-style accommodations and private studio units. The latter are plain cinder block rooms with hotplate, mini-refrigerator, and private bath. Open to both men and women, the hostel provides bedding, requires a daily chore, and creates a family-style atmosphere.

Waikiki Moderately Priced Hotels: There are two places in this category that I particularly recommend. Both are small, intimate, and close to the beach. First is the **Hale Pua Nui** (228 Beachwalk; 923-9693), a congenial home away from home. There are twenty-two studio apartments here, each spacious, well-furnished, and cross-ventilated. The rooms are quaintly decorated, carpeted, and equipped with kitchenettes. The personalized service you receive from the management makes the Hale Pua Nui an ideal vacation spot.

The second is **Kai Aloha Apartment Hotel** (235 Saratoga Road; 923-6723) just around the corner. Here intimacy is combined with modern convenience; each room has air-conditioning, an all-electric kitchen, radio, telephone, and carpeting. Studio apartments have lovely rattan furniture and are attractively decorated with old drawings and paintings. The one-bedroom apartments will comfortably sleep four people. Daily maid service.

The **Honolulu Prince Hotel** (415 Nahua Street; 922-1616) was once a college dormitory. Today it's a ten-story hotel with a comfortable lobby. The standard rooms are small and blandly decorated; some are equipped with mini-kitchenettes (stove and refrigerator, but no sink or oven). Located near the beach, this hotel also has one- and two-bedroom apartments available.

Venture Isle Hotel Apartments (2467 Cleghorn Street; 923-6363) is another small, personalized place. Set on a quiet street and surrounded by potted plants, it's weatherbeaten but quaint. There are spacious studio apartments, featuring a curtained-off area perfect for a third sleeper, as well as larger one-bedroom apartments. All are decorated in a funky but imaginative style with paintings and drawings; all have separate kitchenettes. Be forewarned: this place is extremely popular, so make your reservations far in advance.

White Sands Garden Hotel (431 Nohonani Street; 923-7336) is more expensive but also more fashionable. This is a modern, attractive complex of three low-slung buildings surrounding a garden and swimming pool. The rooms come with all-electric kitchenette, telephone, color television, and air-conditioning. Quite posh for the price.

Waikiki Holiday Apartment Hotel (450 Lewers Street; 923-0245), a ten-story high-rise, has moderately priced accommodations, some with kitchenettes. They're postage-stamp-sized rooms with the tiniest beds I've ever seen. Each room has a small lanai, telephone, and wall-to-wall carpeting; all are air-conditioned. Pool, cocktail lounge, free parking.

If the **Waikiki Surf Hotel** (2200 Kuhio Avenue; 923-7671) has no space in its central facility, they can probably fit you into one of their two other buildings. All are located in central Waikiki. The rooms are adequately, if unimaginatively, decorated and come with television, air-conditioning, telephone, and lanai.

Hawaii Dynasty Hotel (1830 Ala Moana Boulevard; 955-1111), another good bargain, is easy walking distance from both Ala Moana Center and the beach. For the price, accommodations at this seventeen-story caravansary are relatively plush. Each room has air-conditioning, television, telephone, decorations, carpeting, a shower-tub combination, and comfortable furnishings. The room I saw was quite spacious and contained a king-size bed.

Lastly (but not leastly) is the **Waikiki Grand Hotel** (134 Kapahulu Avenue; 923-1511), across the street from lush Kapiolani Park. The standard rooms are comfortable, pleasant places to park your bags. Downstairs there's a windswept lobby.

If you'd prefer to go native and stay in a private home, contact one of the bed and breakfast referral numbers. These include **Bed and Breakfast Honolulu** (595-6170), **Pacific Hawaii Bed and Breakfast** (262-6026), or **Bed and Breakfast Hawaii** (536-8421). They offer accommodations on all islands, priced in the moderate range.

For condominium rentals, contact **Hawaiiana Resorts** (523-7785), **Island Colony** (923-2345), or one of the many condo operators listed in the yellow pages.

Waikiki Deluxe and Ultra-Deluxe Hotels: There are two hotels right on the beach at Waikiki that capture the sense of old Hawaii. Waikiki was little more than a thatch-hut village when its first deluxe hotel went up in 1901. Today the **Moana Hotel** (2365 Kalakaua Avenue; 922-3111) retains the aura of those early days in its colonial architecture and Victorian decor. Insist on a room in the main building with its cherry wood writing desks, brass beds, and marble tables. Downstairs you'll find restaurants, bars, a lobby filled with wicker furniture, and an ancient banyan tree beneath which Robert Louis Stevenson once wrote. Deluxe.

Two doors down resides the *grande dame* of Hawaiian hotels. Built in 1927 and affectionately known as "The Pink Palace," the **Royal Hawaiian** (2259 Kalakaua Avenue; 923-7311) is an elegant, Spanish Moorish-style building complete with colonnaded walkways and manicured grounds. This castle away from home is decorated in French provincial fashion and features a fabulous lobby bedecked with chandeliers. Worth visiting even if you never check in, it's my favorite Hawaiian hotel. Ultra-deluxe.

There are also two very attractive facilities on the edge of Waikiki which I particularly recommend. The **New Otani Kaimana Beach Hotel** (2863 Kalakaua Avenue; 923-1555) rests beside beautiful Sans Souci Beach in the shadow of Diamond Head. Its two restaurants and oceanside bar lend the feel of a big hotel, but the friendly staff and comfortable rooms create a family atmosphere.

Another hotel, equally secluded, has been nicely refurbished. Located even closer to the fabled crater, the **Diamond Head Beach Hotel** (2947 Kalakaua Avenue; 922-1928) is an ultra-contemporary establishment. The rooms are done in soft pastel tones and adorned with quilted beds and potted plants. Located on the ocean, this 13-story facility is one of the most chic resting places around. Continental breakfast is served to the guests and some rooms come with a kitchen.

GREATER HONOLULU HOTELS

The **Honolulu International Youth Hostel** (2323 Sea View Avenue; 946-0591) is a dormitory-style crash pad with separate living quarters for men and women. Kitchen facilities are available. Budget.

There are also two YMCAs in downtown Honolulu. **Armed Services YMCA** (250 South Hotel Street; 524-5600) has ample athletic facilities and will house men, women, and children at extremely reasonable cost. The **Nuuanu YMCA** (1441 Pali Highway; 536-3556) also has complete recreational facilities, but permits men only. Both are budget priced.

Centrally located between Waikiki and downtown Honolulu is the **Nakamura Hotel** (1140 South King Street; 537-1951). It's a pleasant place, but the only reason I can conceive for staying here is the locale. The hotel itself is adequate; the rooms are neatly furnished, carpeted, and equipped with private telephones for guests. I'd ask for accommodations on the *mauka* side, since the other side fronts noisy King Street. Budget.

Farther downtown, on the outskirts of Chinatown, is the **Town Inn** (250 North Beretania Street; 536-2377). This is an excellent spot to capture the local color of Honolulu's Chinese section, though the hotel itself is rather nondescript. The rooms are clean and carpeted, sparsely furnished, and practically devoid of decoration. Budget.

Hawaii's foremost bed and breakfast inn rests in a magnificent old mansion near the University of Hawaii campus. Set in the lush Manoa Valley, the **John Guild Inn** (2001 Vancouver Drive; 947-6019) is a 1915 brown-shingle house featuring seven guest rooms and an adjacent cottage. Decorated with patterned wallpaper and old-style artworks, the rooms are furnished in plump antique armchairs. Guests enjoy a sun room and parlor, as well as the mansion's spacious porch and lawn. For luxury and privacy, this historic jewel is one of the island's finest spots. Deluxe.

WINDWARD COAST HOTELS

Out in the suburban town of Kailua, where trim houses front a beautiful white sand beach, you'll discover **Kailua Beachside Cottages** (204 South Kalaheo Avenue; 261-1653). Overlooking Kailua Beach Park and about 100 yards from the beach sits a cluster of woodframe cottages. Each is equipped with a full kitchen and cable television. Don't expect the Hilton—there are no phones and the furniture is nicked, but these duplex units are clean and cozy. They sit in a yard shaded with *hala* and breadfruit trees and provide an excellent bargain at the low end of the deluxe range. Ask for a cottage fronting the beach.

If you don't mind funky living, check out the **Countryside Cabins** (53-224 Kamehameha Highway; 237-8169) in Punaluu. These old clapboard structures, complete with fading paint and linoleum floors, are set in beautiful garden surroundings across the street from the ocean. Depending on your taste, you'll find the one-room cottages either claustrophobic or quaint. But no one will find fault with the budget prices on these units and the two-bedroom cottages, or with Margaret Naai, the charming Asian woman who runs this unique establishment.

Just down the road, but a world away, you'll find **Pat's At Punaluu** (53-567 Kamehameha Highway; 293-8111), a 136-unit high-rise condo on the Punaluu beach. The one-bedroom "lodge" units come complete with lanai, kitchen, washer-dryer, and shower-tub combinations. Brick walls and carpeting create a pleasant atmosphere. Even cozier, however, are the four-plex cottages next to the beach, which house up to four people. "Lodge" accommodations are less. All rooms have an ocean view; the condo also contains a pool, sauna, and exercise room. Its excellent location and friendly staff make Pat's an outstanding choice. Moderate to deluxe.

For a resort experience at a reasonable rate, consider the **Turtle Bay Hilton** (293-8811) on Kamehameha Highway in Kahuku. This rural retreat sprawls across 880 acres on a dramatic peninsula. With a broad beach at the doorstep and mountains out back, it's an overwhelming spot. Add to that riding paths, a golf course, tennis courts, and a pair of swimming pools. Every room features a sea view and is priced in the deluxe range.

NORTH SHORE HOTELS

The **Mokuleia Beach Colony** (68-615 Farrington Highway, Waialua; 637-9311) claims to be "Hawaii's best-kept secret." It's an ideal hideaway, located along a sandy beach on Oahu's rustic north shore. The living is condo style in a colony of duplex cottages scattered across palm-studded grounds. Each unit is a spacious one-bedroom apartment with an enclosed lanai and all-electric kitchen. The cottages are quite modern—they were built in the '60s—and combine shingle roofs with attractive wood trim. There's a pool and courts (tennis, paddle-tennis, and basketball) on the property, plus a polo field next door. Minimum stay is one week. Moderate to deluxe.

LEEWARD COAST HOTELS

There are several oceanfront condominiums along Oahu's western shore in Makaha. I was not impressed with any of them. Also, I feel the local hostility toward visitors and the frequent ripoffs make this area undesirable. But I'll list the condos and let you decide for yourself.

Makaha Beach Cabanas (84-965 Farrington Highway; 696-2166) has very small, attractive one-bedroom apartments at moderate prices. There is a three-night minimum. This high-rise condo fronts a pretty white-sand beach.

Makaha Surfside (85-175 Farrington Highway; 696-6325) offers one-bedroom units at moderate prices. This sprawling facility fronts a rocky beach and has two swimming pools, a sauna, and a jogging path.

Set back from the sea, bounded by the Waianae Mountains, is the **Sheraton Makaha Resort** (84-626 Makaha Valley Road, Waianae; 695-9511). Since this sprawling complex is removed from everything, it provides a host of guest facilities. There are two restaurants, tennis courts, swimming pool, golf course, stables, playground, jogging track, croquet lawn, and exercise equipment. The rooms, priced in the deluxe range, are set in multi-unit "cottages." It's a beautiful resort in a luxurious setting at a relatively reasonable cost.

Restaurants

WAIKIKI RESTAURANTS

This tourist mecca is crowded with restaurants. Since the competition is so stiff, the cafes here are cheaper than anywhere on the islands. There are numerous American restaurants serving moderately good food at modest prices, so diners looking for standard fare will have no problem. But as you're probably seeking something more exotic, I'll list some interesting Oriental, Hawaiian, health food, and other offbeat restaurants.

Waikiki Budget Restaurants: For a culinary adventure Hawaiian style, you'll have to cross the Ala Wai Canal to **Ono Hawaiian Food** (726 Kapahulu Avenue; 737-2275). This informal cafe (the walls are covered with autographed photos of local performers) serves delicious Hawaiian food at *kanaka* prices. There are several specialties including a *lau lau* plate with *lomi* salmon and *poi*, plus a la carte dishes like *opihi* (limpets), *kalua* pig, squid, dried *aku* (a local fish), and many more. I lunched here once and found myself the only *haole* in one very crowded cafe. Highly recommended.

For just a tad more you can dine overlooking the water at **Waikiki Circle Restaurant** (2464 Kalakaua Avenue; 923-1571). There's a varied dinner menu that includes teriyaki steak, shrimp tempura, and *mahimahi* as well as such standard fare as chops, chicken, and steak.

Over on Kuhio Avenue, just a block in from the beach strip, there's a cluster of good, inexpensive restaurants. **Bobby's Cafe** (2139 Kuhio Avenue; 924-9699) is a patio restaurant serving Mediterranean barbeque dishes. In addition to falafels and kabobs they offer seafood and chicken dishes. Budget.

Caffe Guccini (2139 Kuhio Avenue; 922-5287), with indoor and al fresco dining, features spaghetti carbonara, lasagna, veal scallopine, and other Italian favorites. This informal espresso bar also offers a complete lunch menu. It's a great place for bistro-style dining. Budget to moderate.

Of course there's always **Hamburger Mary's Organic Grill** (2109 Kuhio Avenue; 922-6722), a sidewalk cafe fringed with potted plants. The adjoining bar is gay, but Mary's organic-panic sandwiches attract gays and straights alike. You can pull up a producer's chair, kick back in the sunshine, and order a plain Hamburger Mary, a salsa-smothered Hamburger Maria, or any of several vegetarian sandwiches. All are tagged at competitive rates and served on wheat grain bread. There's also a concoct-your-own omelette: just add avocado, shrimp, sprouts, pineapple, cheese, or several other goodies.

If you're willing to go Mediterranean, try **It's Greek To Me** (2201 Kalakaua Avenue; 922-2733). Located in the Royal Hawaiian Center, it features falafels, spanakopita, and hummos, plus some delicious Greek desserts. Open for breakfast, lunch, and dinner, it's a great place to snack.

Waikiki Moderately Priced Restaurants: **Perry's Smorgasbord,** with its two locations—at the Outrigger Hotel (2335 Kalakaua Avenue; 926-9872) and the Coral Seas Hotel (250 Lewers; 923-3881)—has an inexpensive buffet at dinner, lunch, and breakfast. With an extensive salad bar, plus a host of meat and fish dishes, this all-you-can-eat emporium is hard to beat. I'd suggest the Outrigger branch; it's right on the waterfront.

At the International Market Place's **Colonial House Cafeteria** (2330 Kalakaua Avenue; 923-0441) you can dine out on the lanai and watch the crowds passing under the banyan tree. With wooden shutters, brick partitions, and white pillars, this bustling restaurant has a vague aura of Hawaii's bygone colonial days. The price tag on most hot meals is a welcome anachronism too.

Upstairs at the **Cock's Roost** (923-3229) there's a wrought-iron patio overlooking the marketplace. Dinners at this spiffy establishment are quite good and include barbequed baby back ribs, chicken, and teriyaki steak. There's also an inexpensive sandwich menu in the afternoon.

The young crowd gathering at the **Shore Bird Beach Broiler** (Reef Hotel, 2169 Kalia Road; 922-2887) is attracted by the disco. But this beachfront dining room is also a great place to enjoy a moderate-priced dinner and an ocean view. This is a cook-your-own-food facility which offers filet-mignon kabob, fresh fish, teriyaki chicken, and barbequed ribs. One of the best bargains on Waikiki Beach, the Shore Bird is inevitably crowded, so try to dine early.

For oceanfront dining at a moderate price, **The Beachside Cafe** (Sheraton Surfrider Hotel, 2353 Kalakaua Avenue; 922-3111) is true to its name. With indoor and patio dining, it's a standard-fare American restaurant lacking in imagination but filled with beautiful views. Open for breakfast, lunch, and dinner, the cafe serves steak, seafood, hamburgers, and egg dishes. Ask for a table outside.

The Noodle Shop (2375 Ala Wai Boulevard; 922-4744), a unique restaurant in the Waikiki Sand Villa Hotel, features a wide variety of meals, all prepared with a common ingredient—noodles. There's spaghetti, beef stroganoff, fettuccine, sukiyaki, *udon* (Oriental noodles cooked in sukiyaki sauce), *pansit* (the same noodles prepared with ham, bamboo shoots, onions, and other vegetables), and of course *saimin*. All these meals are set comfortably at a reasonable price and include a visit to the salad bar. There's an additional menu for the anti-noodle contingent, plus soups, salads, and plate lunches.

Honolulu's wackiest restaurant has to be **Bobby McGee's Conglomeration** (2885 Kalakaua Avenue; 922-1282). First there's the interior, a high-gauche design with gilded mirrors, woodstoves, and a salad bar served in an old bathtub. Then there are the waiters and waitresses, each dressed in a different costume and simulating caballeros, magicians, dancehall girls, referees, etc. The menu is more predictable, consisting of steak, seafood, fowl, and combinations thereof. A culinary adventure.

Waikiki Deluxe and Ultra-Deluxe Restaurants: Apart from the bustle of Waikiki but still right on the beach is the **Hau Tree Lanai** (2863 Kalakaua Avenue; 923-1555). Here beneath the interwoven branches of twin *hau* trees you can enjoy patio dining with a view that extends across Waikiki to the distant mountains of Waianae. I particularly favor the place for breakfast (the French toast is delicious), but they also have a lunch and dinner menu that ranges from steamed vegetables to beef kabob to fresh island fish. In the evening the place is illuminated by torches, and soft breezes wisp off the water, adding to the enchantment. Deluxe.

Tropical atmosphere is rare in busy Waikiki but **Banyan Gardens Restaurant** (2380 Kuhio Avenue; 923-2366) captures it. The setting is a Polynesian garden complete with waterfalls, bamboo, ferns, and arching shade trees. The menu carries the theme through with flame-broiled *ono*, fresh lobster, and Polynesian shrimp; at lunch and dinner there are also beef and chicken dishes. Good food, lovely surroundings, deluxe price.

Canlis Restaurant (2100 Kalakaua Avenue; 923-2324), in the islands since 1947, comes well-recommended by several gourmet friends. With its high-beamed ceiling and smoky ambience, Canlis is a prime place for a relaxed meal. A la carte selections include Canlis' specialties such as avocado with crab, lobster, and shrimp, or veal and French peppercorn steak prepared over a keawe charcoal fire. The service is excellent, the food delicious, and the desserts downright sinful. Deluxe.

For high dining I like **Michel's** (Colony Surf Hotel, 2895 Kalakaua Avenue; 923-6552), a white-tablecloth French restaurant replete with chandeliers, statuettes, and oil paintings. The lovely ocean view highlights an haute cuisine atmosphere. The a la carte menu features a host of gourmet delights. Michel serves a few beef dishes and a wealth of seafood selections, including lobster, a surf platter with shrimp, lobster, and crab, and a similar dish, baked avocado with crabmeat, prepared in Michel's unique style. Then of course there are tournedos, veal *medaillons*, filet mignon, chateaubriand, and on. For the ultimate in elegance try Michel's, but remember your dinner jackets, please. Ultra-deluxe.

GREATER HONOLULU RESTAURANTS

Rather than list the city's restaurants according to price, I'll group them by area. As you get away from Waikiki you'll be dining with a more local crowd and tasting foods more representative of island cuisine. So I would certainly advise checking out some of Honolulu's eating places.

Right next to Waikiki, in Ala Moana Center (1450 Ala Moana), there are several good restaurants. Best of all is **Patti's Chinese Kitchen** (946-5002), a crowded and noisy cafeteria. At Patti's you can choose two or more main dishes plus a side order of fried rice, chop suey, or *chow fun*. The courses include almond duck, lemon sauce chicken, tofu, beef tomato, sweet-and-sour pork, barbecued ribs, pig's feet, and shrimp with vegetables. It's quite simply the best place near Waikiki for a low-cost meal. Budget.

There's also the **Poi Bowl**, with both a take-out stand and sit-down restaurant serving Hawaiian dishes, and **Lyn's Delicatessen** (941-3388), featuring a full line of deli sandwiches as well as chicken baskets and plate lunches. Budget.

For health foods, try **The Haven** (947-8040), a largely vegetarian cafe. The many varieties of natural sandwiches are served on wheat grain bread with lettuce, tomato, and sprouts. They include cucumber, pineapple, and cream cheese concoctions, plus several more creative sandwiches fashioned from traditional fixings like ham, Italian-style salami, and cheese. There are also salads, juices, and smoothies. All moderately priced.

Ward Centre, located at 1200 Ala Moana Boulevard, midway between Waikiki and downtown Honolulu, is a focus for gourmet dining. A warren of wood-paneled restaurants, it features several outstanding eateries. Particularly recommended is **Il Fresco** (523-5191), a California-style dining room decorated in brass and tile and featuring a wood-burning oven. In addition to pasta dishes and calzone, this moderate-priced nook offers grilled fresh fish, chicken entrees, and outrageous desserts.

Also consider **Compadres** (523-1307), upstairs in the same complex. This attractive Mexican restaurant, with oak bar and patio dining area, prepares a host of dishes from south of the border. Priced moderately, it specializes in tropical ambience, good food, and fishbowl-size margaritas.

Honolulu has several fine seafood restaurants. Some of them, fittingly enough, are located right on the water. But for an authentic sea-front feel, it's nice to be where the fishing boats actually come in. **Fisherman's Wharf** (1009 Ala Moana Boulevard; 538-3808) provides just such an atmosphere. Boasting "two decks of superb dining," this sprawling facility is festooned with nautical gear. The "Captain's Bridge" topside has a shoalful of seafood selections ranging from broiled salmon to Alaska king crab, priced from moderate to deluxe.

One of the ethnic restaurants most popular with local folks is **Keo's Thai Cuisine** (625 Kapahulu Avenue; 737-8240). Fulfilling to all the senses, this intimate place is decorated with fresh flowers and tropical plants. The cuisine includes such Southeast Asian dishes as the "evil jungle prince," a sliced beef, pork, and chicken entree in hot sauce. At lunch and dinner you can choose from dozens of fish, shellfish, fowl, and meat dishes. The food is moderately priced, very, very spicy, and highly recommended.

For Japanese dining, my favorite moderate-priced restaurant is **Irifune** (563 Kapahulu Avenue; 737-1141), a charming place with a warm and friendly ambience. There are tasty sukiyaki, curry, teriyaki, and tempura dishes here, plus several other Asian delectables.

To combine fine dining with a unique Polynesian experience, book a reservation at **The Willows** (901 Hausten Street; 946-4808). The flowering trees and thatch-topped roofs are reminiscent of ancient Hawaii. There's a carp pond adding to the atmosphere, and a menu which features excellent Hawaiian and seafood dishes. Dedicated to "the very best that nature and Hawaii provide," the restaurant serves sauteed scallops, scampi, and a traditional Hawaiian dinner (with island favorites like *laulau*, *poi*, and *lomi* salmon). Deluxe in quality and price.

Near the University of Hawaii campus, there's pizza, hero sandwiches, spaghetti, or salad bar at **Mama Mia** (in Puck's Alley, 1015 University Avenue; 947-5233). Open for lunch and dinner, it's a great place to snack or stop for a cold beer. Moderate.

Or you can check out **Anna Banana's** (2440 South Beretania Street; 946-5190), a combination bar and Mexican restaurant that draws a swinging crowd. Located a half-mile from campus, this dim eatery serves burritos, enchiladas, and other south-o'-the-border favorites. Decorated in slapdash fashion with propellers, antlers, boxing gloves, and trophies, Anna's is the local center for slumming. Moderate.

For health foods, **Healthy's** (2525 South King Street; 955-2479) is a full-scale restaurant; **Vim and Vigor** (in Puck's Alley, 1015 University Avenue; 947-5700) has a snack bar in its store.

Waialae Avenue, a neighborhood strip several miles outside Waikiki, is fast becoming a gourmet ghetto. **The Pottery Steak and Seafood Restaurant** (3574 Waialae Avenue; 735-5594) has been around for years, featuring a dining room which sits adjacent to a potters' studio. The restaurant's ceramics are fashioned on the premises and one dish, Cornish game hen, is fired in a pot which is presented to you after the meal. The deluxe-priced restaurant offers excellent meals in a craft's gallery atmosphere.

Other dining spots have located right across the street. **Azteca Mexican Restaurant** (3569 Waialae Avenue; 735-2492) is a vinyl-booth-and-plastic-panel eatery that serves a delicious array of Mexican food at budget prices.

Che Pasta (3571 Waialae Avenue; 735-1777), several doors away, is a fashionable new restaurant, strongly influenced by California cuisine, that makes its own pasta and serves a variety of Italian dishes. In addition to fettuccine al pesto and lasagna, this moderne establishment features specials like saffron ravioli, veal shank, and canneloni stuffed with a variety of cheeses. Prices are moderate, the wine list extensive, and both lunch and dinner are served.

There are several dining spots located midway between Waikiki and downtown Honolulu which I particularly like. For Italian-style seafood, **Philip Paolo's** (2312 South Beretania Street; 946-1163) is highly recommended by local residents. Set in a trim woodframe house and serving dinner only, it features shrimp scampi, *frutti di mare* (seafood combination), and a host of pasta dishes. By moderate-price restaurant standards, the interior is very fashionably done.

In the same part of town sits one of Honolulu's best budget-priced Chinese restaurants. The decor at **King Tsin Restaurant** (1486 South King Street; 946-3273) is rather bland, but the Mandarin cuisine adds plenty of spice. You can order Szechuan dishes like shredded pork or a Mongolian beef dish. These are plenty hot; you might want to try the milder seafood, pork, vegetable, fowl, and beef dishes. Budget.

For Southeast Asian cuisine, try the **Thai House** (1254 South King Street; 521-1606). At this modest cafe you can savor *kang som* (hot-and-sour fish soup), fried pork with garlic and pepper, or mustard green cabbage.

In downtown Honolulu, near the city's financial center, are two modest cafes which I particularly like. One, **People's Cafe** (1310 Pali Highway; 536-5789), has been serving Hawaiian food for over forty years. The place is owned by a Japanese family, which helps explain the teriyaki dishes on the menu. But primarily the food is Polynesian: this is a splendid spot to order *poi, lomi* salmon, *kalua* pig, and other island favorites. *Ono, ono!* Moderate.

The **Tasty Broiler** (corner of Nimitz Highway and Smith Street; 533-3329) is my other haunt. It ain't much on atmosphere—just a couple of counters with swivel seats, some tables, and chairs. But it's the only place I've been where you can get a lobster tail dinner for a moderate cost, plus other, more pedestrian plates at plebeian prices.

For Chinese food, try **Yong Sing Restaurant** (1055 Alakea Street; 531-1367). This high-ceilinged establishment, catering to local business-people, has some delicious dishes. I thought the oyster sauce chicken particularly tasty. With its daily lunch specials, Yong Sing is a perfect stopoff when you're shopping or sightseeing downtown. Moderate.

But for the true flavor of China, head over to Chinatown, just a few blocks from downtown Honolulu. Amid the tumbledown buildings and jumble of shops, there's one restaurant you must not miss—**Wo Fat** (115 North Hotel Street; 533-6393). Operating for over 100 years, this is the area's oldest eating place, an institution in itself. If you don't eat here, at least tour the place. This cavernous establishment contains three floors and a knockout decor. The second story, where I'd recommend dining, is painted from pillar to ceiling with dragons and ornate Oriental designs. Add Chinese lanterns, brush paintings, and a mural, and you have an extravagant display of Chinese art. The cuisine, too, is varied: you'll have to go to Hong Kong for a wider choice of delicious Cantonese dishes. There are hundreds of pork, beef, duck, seafood and chicken dishes, plus old standbys like won ton, chop suey, and chow mein. All are generally priced in the budget to moderate range.

Fat Siu Lau (100 North Beretania Street; 538-7081), another imposing establishment, in the Cultural Plaza, is highly recommended by local gourmet Malcolm Tyau. This gilt-edged eatery also offers a Cantonese cuisine with dishes tabbed moderately. Dim sum is served at lunch.

WINDWARD COAST RESTAURANTS

Spotted along Oahu's eastern shore are a number of moderately priced restaurants which may prove handy if you're beachcombing or camping. Most are located on or near Routes 72 (Kalanianaole Highway) and 83 (Kamehameha Highway), the adjoining roads leading from Honolulu along the coast. For the sake of convenience I'll list the restaurants as they will appear when you travel north.

The first, **Stromboli's Ristorante** (7192 Kalanianaole Highway; 396-6388), in the Koko Marina Shopping Center, is convenient when you're at a beach in Oahu's beautiful southeast corner. Open for lunch and dinner, this spot offers deli food as well as full-course Italian dinners and makes its own pasta. Moderate.

Farther north, **Denny B's** (41-857 Kalanianaole Highway; 259-5950) has breakfasts, plate lunches, and sandwiches at greasy-spoon prices. No gourmet's delight, this tiny eatery is well-placed for people enjoying Waimanalo's beaches.

Kailua is a bedroom community with little to offer the adventurer. But since you might find yourself nearby at lunchtime or when returning from the beach, I'll briefly describe a few restaurants. For a tasty Italian meal, try **Cella's Cafe** (324 Kuulei Road; 261-7116). **Vim and Vigor** (301-B Hahani Street; 262-9911) has a snack bar in its health food store.

In Kaneohe, another suburban town next to Kailua, you might like **Koa Omelette House** (46-126 Kahuhipa Street; 235-5772). Moderate in price, it's a tastefully appointed restaurant with a bill of fare that includes pancakes, waffles, crepes suzettes, eggs, and things. Or, if you want to take a snack to the beach, check out **Fuji Delicatessen and Restaurant** (46-138 Kahuhipa Street; 235-5633) with its inexpensive sandwiches and Japanese plates.

The **Crouching Lion Inn** (51-666 Kamehameha Highway, Kaaawa; 237-8511), set in a vintage 1927 wood-shingle house, serves sandwiches and hamburgers, *mahimahi,* and quiche lorraine for lunch. At dinner there's a surf-and-turf menu priced from moderate to deluxe. Enjoying a beautiful ocean view, this attractive complex is popular with tour buses; so try to arrive at an off hour.

There's one restaurant on the windward coast which I recommend for those special occasions when elegance and price are both important. That's **Pat's at Punaluu** (53-567 Kamehameha Highway; 293-8502). Wicker chairs, lauhala wallhangings, and a windswept patio create an inviting atmosphere; the view at this beachfront establishment adds to the tropic ambience. At dinner there's a surf-and-turf menu, priced from moderate to deluxe, which includes rack of lamb, steak, barbequed ribs, Hawaiian seafood curry, shrimp tempura, and the catch of the day. The seafood is exceptionally good. Pat's lunch menu offers several salad and sandwich selections, plus hamburgers. Also serving breakfast, this favored dining spot features a full-course brunch on Sunday.

The Turtle Bay Hilton (293-8811), several miles north, features two good restaurants. At the **Palm Terrace,** overlooking the hotel's lovely grounds, you'll encounter moderate-priced dining in an attractive environment. The restaurant, serving three meals, offers everything from hamburgers to *saimin* and teriyaki to beef stroganoff. Or, for a splurge meal, try **The Cove.** This gourmet establishment, priced deluxe, serves lobster, lamb chops, filet mignon, a seafood gumbo dish, and a host of other delights. Reservations are required, but dress is casual.

NORTH SHORE RESTAURANTS

When you're around Sunset Beach, **Eat to the Max** (59-176 Kamehameha Highway; 638-8200) is quite convenient. It's a roadside take-out stand preparing various foods. Here you can order soups, salads, sandwiches, smoothies, or Mexican dishes at low prices.

Otherwise the best place to chow down is in Haleiwa, the main town on the north shore. My prime recommendation is **Sea View Haleiwa** (corner of Kamehameha Highway and Haleiwa Road; 637-4165). This L-shaped cafe, with an adjoining lounge, has a mixed menu. There are seafood dishes, steaks, and other entrees, all moderately priced; at lunch there are platters, sandwiches, and hamburgers.

Celestial Natural Foods (66-145 Kamehameha Highway; 637-6729) has a juice bar and snack shop.

How to Beat the Heat with a Sweet Treat

Since the early days of Hawaiian royalty, people have complained about Honolulu's shirt-sticking weather. Come summer, temperatures rise and the trade winds stop blowing. Visitors seeking a golden tan discover they're baking without browning. And residents begin to think that their city, renowned as a cultural melting pot, is actually a pressure cooker.

With the ocean all around, relief is never far away. But a lot of folks, when not heading for the beaches, have found another way to cool off. Shave ice. Known as ice frappes among the Japanese originators and snow cones back on the mainland, these frozen treats are Hawaii's answer to the Good Humor man.

They're made with ice that's been shaved from a block into thin slivers, packed into a cone-shaped cup, and covered with sweet syrup. Health-minded people eat the ice plain, and some folks ask for a scoop of ice cream or sweet black beans underneath the shavings. Most people just order it with their favorite syrup flavors—grape, root beer, cola, cherry, orange, lemon-lime, vanilla, fruit punch, banana, strawberry, or whatever.

Whichever you choose, you'll find it only costs about half a buck at the many stands sprinkled around town. Near Waikiki, you might try **Goodie Goodie Drive Inn** (946 Coolidge) and on the Windward Coast there's **Island Snow Hawaii** (130 Kailua Road, Kailua). Watch for stands up on the North Shore, too. No doubt you'll see a long line outside Oahu's most famous shave ice store, **Matsumoto's** (66-087 Kam Highway in Haleiwa).

As a matter of fact, anyplace where the sun blazes overhead you're liable to find someone trying to beat the heat by slurping up a "snow cone" before it melts into mush.

And **Banzai Bowl** (66-200 Kamehameha Highway; 637-9122), a small Japanese restaurant, has a selection of Korean plates as well as Japanese dishes, omelettes, and hamburgers. Budget.

For a fashionable spot overlooking the ocean, try **Jameson's By The Sea** (62-540 Kamehameha Highway; 637-4336). This split-level establishment features a patio downstairs and a formal dining room upstairs. For lunch there are sandwiches, chowders, and fresh fish dishes; at dinner they specialize in seafood. Moderate to deluxe in price.

LEEWARD COAST RESTAURANTS

This sparsely populated strip of shoreline has several dining spots. All are located on Farrington Highway, the main road, and most are in the town of Waianae. Within a short distance of one another are **Cathay Inn Chop Suey** (86-088 Farrington Highway; 696-9477), a good choice for Chinese cuisine, and **Masago's Restaurant** (85-888 Farrington Highway; 696-6137) for Japanese and Hawaiian food.

Nearby **E. J.'s Pizza** (85-773 Farrington Highway; 696-9676) operates from a tiny roadside stand, but the owners boast that they'll "make you a pizza you can't refuse." They might just be right; not only is the food delicious, it's cheap too. In addition to pizzas, E. J.'s also serves Mexican snacks and sandwiches at budget prices.

If you'd like something with more class, there's the **Rusty Harpoon** (87-064 Farrington Highway; 696-6345) in Maili. It's an attractive open-air restaurant with a balcony overlooking the ocean. Ceiling fans, captains' chairs, and nautical lamps lend charm to this restaurant. The lunch menu features inexpensive salads and sandwiches, and specialty platters (*mahimahi*, chopped steak, barbecued ribs, etc.) for slightly more. At dinnertime the menu rises sharply into the moderate to deluxe range with prime rib, chicken teriyaki, *mahimahi*, shrimp tempura, and other seafood dishes.

Out at the luxurious Sheraton Makaha Resort (84-626 Makaha Valley Road, Waianae; 695-9511) are two restaurants. The **Pikake Cafe**, overlooking the pool and golf course, serves breakfast, lunch, and dinner at moderate prices. In the evening guests also adjourn to the **Kaala Dining Room**, a vault-ceilinged structure surrounded by plate glass. The cuisine at this deluxe-priced gathering place includes salmon, *mahimahi*, lobster, teriyaki steak, Cornish game hen, and curry chicken.

Grocery Markets

Not surprisingly, the best place to shop on Oahu is in the Greater Honolulu area, where you'll find stores to fit all needs. Try not to shop in Waikiki, where the stores are overpriced and understocked.

Once outside Honolulu, there are grocery markets concentrated on the windward coast in suburban Kailua and Kaneohe, on the north shore in the town of Haleiwa, and along the leeward coast in Waianae.

WAIKIKI GROCERY STORES

There are two moderate-sized supermarkets in Waikiki. Both the **Fastop** food market (Discovery Bay Shopping Center, 1178 Ala Moana Boulevard) and **The Food Pantry** (2370 Kuhio Avenue) are inflated in price, but conveniently located.

ABC Discount Stores, a chain of sundry shops with branches all around Waikiki, are also convenient, but have a very limited stock and even higher prices.

If you are willing and able to shop outside Waikiki, you'll generally fare much better price-wise. Try the **Foodland** supermarket in the Ala Moana Center (1450 Ala Moana Boulevard) just outside Waikiki. Cheaper than Waikiki groceries, it's still more expensive than greater Honolulu stores.

WAIKIKI HEALTH FOOD STORES

Vim and Vigor has a standard stock of natural food items in its store in Ala Moana Center (1450 Ala Moana Boulevard).

GREATER HONOLULU GROCERY STORES

The best place to shop near the University of Hawaii's Manoa campus is at **Star Market,** 2470 South King Street.

Midway between Waikiki and downtown Honolulu there's a **Times Supermarket** at 1290 South Beretania, and a **Safeway** at 1121 South Beretania. There's another **Safeway** in downtown Honolulu at 1360 Pali Highway.

You might want to browse around the mom 'n' pop grocery stores spotted throughout Chinatown. They're marvelous places to pick up Chinese foodstuffs and to capture the local color.

GREATER HONOLULU HEALTH FOOD STORES

The best place in Honolulu to buy health foods is at **Down To Earth Natural Foods** (2525 South King Street) near the University of Hawaii's Manoa campus. **Kokua Country Foods,** a cooperative market nearby at 2357 South Beretania, is another excellent choice.

In downtown Honolulu look for **The Carrot Patch** (700 Bishop Street) with its health and diet products.

GREATER HONOLULU SPECIALTY SHOPS

Don't miss the **Open Market** (along North King Street between River and Kekaulike streets) in Chinatown. It's a great place to shop for fresh foods. There are numerous stands selling fish, produce, poultry, meat, baked goods, and island fruits, all at low-overhead prices.

WINDWARD COAST GROCERY STORES

A convenient place to shop in Oahu's southeast corner is at the Koko Marina Shopping Center's **Foodland** in Hawaii Kai (7192 Kalanianaole Highway). Open 24 hours a day.

Proceeding north along the coast, there's **Mel's Market** (41-1029 Kalanianaole Highway), a small store in Waimanalo.

Then, in the suburban towns of Kailua and Kaneohe, you'll encounter large supermarkets. **Times Supermarket** (in Kailua Shopping Center on Kailua Road) and **Foodland** (Windward City Shopping Center at Kamehameha Highway and Kaneohe Bay Drive in Kaneohe) are the most convenient.

These are good places to stock up, since the next large supermarket is the **IGA** in Hauula (Hauula Kai Center on Kamehameha Highway).

Between these major shopping complexes there are smaller facilities at the **7-11** (51-484 Kamehameha Highway, Kaaawa). North of Hauula, on Kamehameha Highway in Kahuku, there's **Lindy's Food**.

WINDWARD COAST HEALTH FOOD STORES

In Kailua you might try the **Vim and Vigor** store (301-B Hahani Street). Up near Oahu's northern tip, there's **Country Health Foods** (Laie Shopping Center; 55-510 Kamehameha Highway) in Laie.

Then, all along the Kamehameha Highway in Waiahole and Waikane valleys, there are small stands selling **fresh fruit**. The produce is grown right in this lush area and is sold pretty cheaply along the roadside.

WINDWARD COAST FRESH-FISH STORES

You can get fresh fish at **Masa and Joyce Fish Market** in the Temple Valley Shopping Center on the Kahekili Highway (Route 83), just north of Kaneohe.

NORTH SHORE GROCERY STORES

Haleiwa Supermarket (66-197 Kamehameha Highway, Haleiwa), the only large market on the entire north coast, is the best place to shop. There's also **Sunset Beach Store** (59-026 Kamehameha Highway), which has a small stock but is conveniently located near Sunset Beach.

NORTH SHORE HEALTH FOOD STORES

Celestial Natural Foods (Haleiwa Shopping Plaza, 66-145 Kamehameha Highway, Haleiwa) has an ample supply of health foods and fresh produce.

LEEWARD COAST GROCERY STORES

Big Way Supermarket (Waianae Mall Shopping Center, 86-120 Farrington Highway) in Waianae, is the prime spot in this area for shopping.

The Great Outdoors

The Sporting Life

CAMPING

Along with its traffic and crowds, Oahu has numerous parks. Unfortunately these disparate elements overlap, and you may sometimes find you've escaped from Honolulu's urban jungle and landed in a swamp of weekend beachgoers. So it's best to plan outdoor adventures far in advance and to schedule them for weekdays if possible.

Camping at **county parks** requires a permit. Tent camping is permitted every night except Wednesday and Thursday; there are no trailer hook-ups. Permits can be obtained from the Department of Parks and Recreation, Honolulu Municipal Building, 650 South King Street, Honolulu, Oahu, HI 96813 (523-4525) or at any of the "satellite city halls" around the island.

State park permits are free. They allow camping for five days and work on a first come, first served basis. They are issued by the Division of State Parks, 1151 Punchbowl Street, Room 310, Honolulu, Oahu, HI 96813 (548-7455).

Remember when planning your trip, rainfall is heaviest on the windward or east coast, a little lighter on the north shore, and lightest of all on the west coast.

For camping equipment, check with **Omar The Tent Man.** Located at 650 Kakoi Street (836-8785) in Honolulu, Omar rents and sells supplies. The following Honolulu sporting goods stores also sell gear: **The Bike Shop** (1149 South King Street; 531-7071), **Honsport** (Ala Moana Center, 1450 Ala Moana Boulevard; 949-5591), and **Big 88** (330 Sand Island Access Road; 845-1688). Honsport also has a store out in Kailua (Kailua Shopping Center, Kailua Road).

Renting a camper is another excellent way for the adventurer to explore Oahu's countryside; in this way you can travel turtle-like, with your shelter on your back. **Beach Boy Campers** (1720 Ala Moana Boulevard, Honolulu; 955-6381) has models starting at $50 a day, 6¢ a mile.

SKIN DIVING

The **Haleiwa Surf Center** (Haleiwa-Alii Beach Park, Haleiwa; 637-5051) teaches such sports as snorkeling, surfing, swimming, life-saving, windsurfing, and sailing. This county agency is also an excellent source of information on island water sports and facilities.

The following shops rent and sell skin-diving equipment and offer underwater tours: **South Seas Aquatics** (1050 Ala Moana Boulevard,

Honolulu; 538-3854), **Aloha Dive Shop** (Koko Marina Shopping Center, 7192 Kalanianaole Highway, Hawaii Kai; 395-5922), and **Aaron's Dive Shop** (602 Kailua Road, Kailua; 261-1211). Up in the north shore town of Haleiwa, be sure to check out **Surf 'n Sea** (62-595 Kamehameha Highway; 637-9887).

SURFING AND WINDSURFING

Oahu boasts some of the finest surfing and windsurfing anywhere. There are international contests here every year. For more information on both the participatory and spectator aspects of these sports, contact the **Haleiwa Surf Center** (Haleiwa-Alii Beach Park, Haleiwa; 637-5051), or check out the island's many surf shops. Several stores, located in different parts of the island, rent boards and sails: **Local Motion** (1714 Kapiolani Boulevard, Honolulu; 944-8515), **Downing Hawaii** (3021 Waialae Avenue, Honolulu; 737-9696), and **Windsurfing Hawaii** (156-C Hamakua Drive, Kailua; 261-3539). If you'd like to surf Waikiki, you can rent a board from **DeRussy Beach Service** (949-3469) on Fort DeRussy Beach, **Waikiki Beach Services** (in front of the Cinerama Reef Hotel), the **Outrigger Beachboy Service** (in front of the Outrigger Hotel), and the **Aloha Beach Service** located near the Surfrider and Sheraton-Waikiki.

FISHING

For deep-sea fishing, contact **Coreene-C Sport Fishing Charters** (536-7472) or **Island Charters** (536-1555) in Honolulu's Kewalo Basin. In Haleiwa try **Surf 'n Sea** (62-595 Kamehameha Highway; 637-9887).

OTHER SPORTS

GOLF

For a round of golf, try the **Ala Wai Golf Course** (Honolulu; 296-4653), **Hawaii Kai Championship** (Honolulu; 395-2358), **Mililani Golf Club** (Mililani; 623-2254), **Olomana Golf Links** (Waimanalo; 259-7926), **Bay View Golf Center** (Kaneohe; 247-0451), **Pali Golf Course** (Kaneohe; 261-9784), **Kahuku Golf Course** (Kahuku; 293-5842), **Turtle Bay Hilton** (Kahuku; 293-8811), **Hawaii Country Club** (Aiea; 622-1744), **Ted Makalena Golf Course** (Waipahu; 671-0021), or **Sheraton Makaha West Golf Course** (Waianae; 695-9544).

SAILING

Honolulu Sailing Company (45-995 Wailele Road; 235-8264) and the beach stands in front of Hilton Hawaiian Village in Waikiki sponsor cruises.

TENNIS

Call the **County Department of Parks and Recreation** (923-7927) for information on public courts, or the **Hawaii Visitors Bureau** (923-1811) for private courts.

Beaches and Parks
(Plus Camping, Swimming, Snorkeling, Surfing, Fishing)

WAIKIKI BEACHES AND PARKS

Waikiki Beach—This two-mile stretch of sand is one of the most famous beaches in the world. It's also among the most popular. There are times when it's so crowded it seems like the Pacific's answer to Coney Island. Most of the beach is lined with high-rise hotels and dotted with concession stands. The view of Diamond Head crater is legendary.

I try to avoid Waikiki Beach entirely. When I do go here, it's usually to the parks at either end of the beach—**Ala Moana Beach Park** or **Kapiolani Beach Park**. You might want to stroll the rest of the strand to people-watch and check out hotel row. But if you'd like to sunbathe and swim without hordes of tourists around, head for the parks.

Ala Moana Beach Park—Located directly across from Ala Moana Center, this seventy-six-acre park is a favorite with Hawaii residents. On weekends every type of outdoor enthusiast imaginable turns out to swim, fish, jog, fly model airplanes, sail model boats, and so on. There's a curving length of beach, a grassy park area, recreation facilities galore, and a helluva lot of local color.

Facilities: Picnic area, restrooms, showers, concession stands, tennis courts, recreation building, bowling green, and lifeguards. Markets and restaurants are nearby.

Camping: Not permitted.

Swimming: Good.

Snorkeling: Fair.

Surfing: There are three separate breaks here. "Concessions," "Tennis Courts," and "Baby Haleiwa" all have summer waves.

Fishing: The most common catches are *papio*, bonefish, goatfish, and *moano*.

Getting there: Located on Ala Moana Boulevard at the west end of Waikiki, across from Ala Moana Center.

Kapiolani Beach Park—This is the shoreline section of beautiful Kapiolani Park. It's also one of the liveliest beaches in Hawaii, complete with a gay section and weekend conga drummers. The beach attracts a young, racially-mixed crowd. In addition to the unique culture, there's a white-sand beach, spacious lawn, an aquarium, and the Natatorium, the world's largest saltwater swimming pool.

Facilities: Picnic areas, restrooms, shower rooms, and concession stand. Markets and restaurants are nearby.

Camping: Sorry, not permitted.

Swimming: Good.

Snorkeling: Fair.

Surfing: There are several summer breaks along this shore.

Fishing: The principal catches are *ulua, papio,* and *mamao.*

Getting there: Located at 2475 Kalakaua Avenue near the east end of Waikiki.

GREATER HONOLULU BEACHES AND PARKS

Sand Island State Park—This 140-acre park wraps around the south and east shores of Sand Island, with sections fronting both Honolulu Harbor and the open sea. Despite the name, there's no sandy beach here, and jet traffic from nearby Honolulu International might disturb your snoozing. But there is a great view of Honolulu. Open 7 a.m. to 8 p.m. in the summer; 7 a.m. to 6:45 p.m. from September through May.

Facilities: Restrooms and picnic area. Markets and restaurants nearby.

Camping: State permit required for tent camping in the grassy area facing the ocean.

Swimming: Poor.

Snorkeling:: Poor.

Surfing: Summer breaks.

Fishing: Bonefish, goatfish, *papio,* and *moano* are the prime catches.

Getting there: From Waikiki, take Ala Moana Boulevard and Nimitz Highway several miles west to Sand Island Access Road.

Diamond Head Beach Park—This twisting ribbon of white sand sits directly below the crater. It's close enough to Waikiki for convenient access but far enough to shake most of the crowds. The Kuilei cliffs, covered with scrub growth, loom behind the beach.

Facilities: Shower. It's about two miles to markets and restaurants in Waikiki.

Camping: None.

Swimming: Mediocre.

Snorkeling: Good. Coral reef extends offshore throughout this area.

Surfing: Year-round juice at "Lighthouse" breaks.

Fishing: Your chances are good to reel in *ulua, papio,* or *mamao.*

WINDWARD COAST BEACHES AND PARKS

Hanauma Bay Beach Park—One of Oahu's prettiest and most popular beaches, this curving swath of white sand extends for almost a half-mile. The bottom of the bay is a maze of coral reef, and the entire area has been designated a marine preserve. As a result, the skin diving is unmatched and the fish are tame enough to eat from your hand.

You can also hike along rock ledges fringing the bay and explore some mind-boggling tidepools. Crowded though it is, this is one strand that should not be bypassed.

Facilities: Picnic area, restrooms, showers, snack bar, volleyball court, snorkeling equipment rentals, and lifeguards. One mile to restaurants and markets at Koko Marina Shopping Center.

Camping: None.

Swimming: Very good.

Snorkeling: Superb. But beware of "Witches Brew," a turbulent area on the bay's right side, and the "Molokai Express," a wicked current sweeping across the mouth of the bay. No fish spearing.

Surfing: None.

Fishing: Strictly prohibited.

Getting there: Located about nine miles east of Waikiki. Take Route 72 to Koko Head, then turn onto the side road near the top of the promontory. This leads to a parking lot; leave your vehicle and walk the several hundred yards down the path to the beach.

Halona Cove Beach—This is the closest you'll find to a hidden beach near Honolulu. It's a patch of white sand wedged between Halona Point and the Halona Blowhole lookout. Located directly below the Kalanianaole Highway (Route 72), this is not exactly a wilderness area. But you can still escape the crowds massed on the nearby beaches.

Facilities: None. It's two miles to the markets and restaurants in Koko Marina Shopping Center.

Camping: Not permitted.

Swimming: Good when the sea is gentle, but extremely dangerous if it's rough.

Snorkeling: Good.

Surfing: None.

Fishing: Prime catches are *ulua, papio,* and *mamao*.

Getting there: Stop at the Halona Blowhole parking lot on Route 72, about ten miles east of Waikiki. Follow the path from the right side of the lot down to the beach.

Sandy Beach—This long, wide beach is a favorite among Oahu's youth. The shorebreak makes it one of the finest, and most dangerous, bodysurfing beaches in the islands. It's a pleasant place to sunbathe, but if you go swimming, plan to negotiate a pounding shoreline. Should you want to avoid the crowds, head over to **Wamamalu Beach** next door to the east.

Facilities: Picnic area, restrooms, showers. Three miles to the restaurants and markets in Koko Marina Shopping Center.

Camping: Not permitted.

Swimming: Mediocre.

Snorkeling: Poor.

Surfing: Good, and very popular. Beware of rip currents.

Fishing: Among the principal catches are *ulua, papio,* and *mamao.*

Getting there: Head out on Route 72 (Kalanianaole Highway) about twelve miles east of Waikiki.

Makapuu Beach Park—It's set in a very pretty spot with lava cliffs in the background and Rabbit Island just offshore. This is a short, wide rectangle of white sand favored by Hawaii's bodysurfers. With no protecting reef and a precipitous shoreline, Makapuu is inundated by awesome swells that send wave riders crashing onto shore. Necks and backs are broken with frightening regularity here, so if the waves are large and you're inexperienced—play the spectator. If you take the plunge, prepare for a battering!

Facilities: Picnic area, restrooms, lifeguard. There's a restaurant across the road in **Sea Life Park.**

Camping: County permit required.

Swimming: Though okay in summer, at other times the ocean is too rough. This is Hawaii's most famous bodysurfing beach.

Snorkeling: Usually poor.

Surfing: Not permitted.

Fishing: Looks good for *ulua, papio,* and *mamao.*

Getting there: Located on Route 72 (Kalanianaole Highway) about thirteen miles east of Waikiki.

Waimanalo Beach Park—Located at the southeast end of Waimanalo's three-and-a-half-mile-long beach, this is a spacious 38-acre park. It's studded with ironwood trees and equipped with numerous recreation facilities.

Both this county park and **Waimanalo Bay State Recreation Area,** a mile farther north, are excellent spots for picnicking, swimming, and sunbathing. The state park is farther removed from the highway in a grove of ironwood trees known to local residents as "Sherwood Forest," but camping is permitted only at the county facility.

Facilities: Picnic area, restrooms, showers, playground, basketball court, baseball field at Waimanalo Beach Park. Restaurants and markets nearby.

Camping: Tent and trailer. County permit required.

Swimming: Good; well-protected. State park has good body-surfing.

Snorkeling: Good.

Surfing: Poor.

Fishing: The most frequently caught fish here is *papio*; bonefish, milkfish, and goatfish are also common.

Getting there: Located at 41-471 Kalanianaole Highway (Route 72) about fifteen miles east of Waikiki.

Bellows Beach Park—This is one of Oahu's prettiest parks. There's a broad white-sand beach bordered by ironwood trees, with a marvelous view of the Koolau mountains. Sounds great, huh? The catch is that Bellows Park is situated on a military base and is open to visitors only from Friday noon until 8 a.m. Monday.

Facilities: Picnic area, showers, restroom, lifeguard. Restaurants and markets are about a mile away in Waimanalo.

Camping: County permit required.

Swimming: Very good.

Snorkeling: Good.

Surfing: Good for beginners.

Fishing: The most abundant species at Bellows is *papio*, followed by bonefish, milkfish, and goatfish.

Getting there: Turn off Kalanianaole Highway (Route 72) toward Bellows Air Force Station. The park is located near Waimanalo, about seventeen miles east of Waikiki.

Swanzy Beach Park, Punaluu Beach Park, and **Hauula Beach Park**—These three county facilities lie along Kamehameha Highway (Route 83) within seven miles of one another. Camping is permitted at all three, but none compare aesthetically with other beaches to the north and south. Swanzy is located directly on the highway and lacks a sandy beach; Punaluu, though possessing a pretty palm-fringed beach, is cramped; and Hauula, a spacious park with beach, is visited periodically by tour buses. So put these parks near the bottom of your list, and bring them up only if the other beaches are too crowded.

Facilities: All three have picnic areas and restrooms; all are within a few miles of markets and restaurants.

Camping: Tents and trailers allowed at Swanzy Beach Park and Hauula Beach Park. County permit required.

Swimming: Generally good.

Snorkeling: Best diving is at Swanzy.

Surfing: Swanzy has surfing for experts only at nearby "Crouching Lion" breaks. Hauula's winter breaks are for beginners.

Fishing: Along this coast the most abundant fish is *papio*, followed by bonefish, milkfish, and goatfish.

Getting there: These parks are all located along Kamehameha Highway (Route 83). Swanzy lies about twelve miles north of Kaneohe, Punaluu is four miles farther north, and Hauula is about three miles beyond that.

Kahana Valley State Park—This 5,260-acre paradise, set on a white-sand beach, offers something for every adventurer. You can pick fruit in a lush forest, picnic in a coconut grove, and sightsee the ancient Huilua Fishpond. A 5.3-mile trail (hiking permit required) leads past old Hawaiian farms deep into the florid Kahana Valley.

Facilities: Picnic areas, restrooms. Markets and restaurants nearby.

Camping: Across the street. County permit required.

Swimming: Generally good.

Snorkeling: Mediocre.

Surfing: Mediocre.

Fishing: Good spot for *papio*, bonefish, milkfish, and goatfish.

Getting there: Located along Kamehameha Highway (Route 83) about fourteen miles north of Kaneohe.

Kakela Beach—Here's one of the prettiest beaches on the windward shore. There's a privately owned park here, with trees and a lawn that extend toward the white-sand beach. I highly recommend this spot for camping and day-tripping alike. You should check in at the caretaker's house in the park before entering the beach area. The park is closed Sundays.

Facilities: Picnic area, restrooms. Restaurants and markets nearby.

Camping: Tent and trailer. Permits issued by Zions Securities Corp., 55-510 Kamehameha Highway, Laie, Oahu, HI 96762 (293-9201). The charge is 50¢ per person per night.

Swimming: Good. Bodysurfing is also good both here and at **Pounders Beach**, the next beach to the north.

Snorkeling: Mediocre.

Surfing: Winter breaks up to six feet, with right and left slide.

Fishing: The most frequent catch? *Papio,* then bonefish, goatfish, and milkfish.

Getting there: Located at 55-051 Kamehameha Highway (Route 83) in Laie about twenty miles north of Kaneohe.

Hukilau Park—This privately owned facility (open to the public) fronts a beautiful white-sand beach which winds for over a mile. Part of the beach is lined with homes, but much of it is undeveloped. Several small islands lie anchored offshore, and the park contains a lovely stand of ironwood trees. All in all this enchanting beach is one of the finest on the windward coast.

Facilities: There are no facilities here, but you'll find both markets and restaurants located nearby.

Camping: Tent and trailer. Permits, obtained from Zions Securities Corp., 55-510 Kamehameha Highway, Laie, Oahu, HI 96762 (293-9201), are free.

Swimming: Good. The bodysurfing is also recommended.

Snorkeling: Fair.

Surfing: Small waves with left and right slides.

Fishing: Principal catch is *papio*; milkfish, bonefish, and goatfish are also frequently caught.

Getting there: Located on Kamehameha Highway (Route 83) in Laie about twenty-two miles north of Kaneohe.

Malaekahana State Recreation Area and **Goat Island**—This is a rare combination. The Malaekahana facility is one of the island's prettiest parks. It's a tropical wonderland filled with palm, *hala*, and ironwood trees, and graced with a curving white-sand beach. And then there's Goat Island, just off shore. Simply put, if you visit Oahu and don't explore it, you'll be missing an extraordinary experience. I hope you'll make an extra effort to get here. It's a small, low-lying island covered with scrub growth and scattered ironwood trees. On the windward side is a coral beach; to leeward lies a crescent-shaped white-sand beach that seems drawn from a South Seas dream. Goat Island (which no longer contains goats) is now a state bird refuge, so you might see wedge-tailed shearwaters nesting. You can camp, picnic, swim, do anything here, as long as you don't disturb the birds. Goat Island will return the favor—there'll be nothing here to disturb you either.

Facilities: Showers, bathrooms, barbeque pits.

Camping: State permit required. There are also very rustic cabins available here. These beachfront units rent for $25 nightly. Bring your own bedding and cooking gear and be prepared for funky accommodations. For information call 293-1736.

Swimming: Good; the leeward beach is shallow and well-protected.

Snorkeling: Good.

Surfing: Long paddle out to winter breaks with left slide.

Fishing: You may well reel in *papio*, the most abundant fish along here; goatfish, milkfish, and bonefish are also caught.

Getting there: Located on Kamehameha Highway (Route 83) in Laie about twenty-three miles north of Kaneohe.

Kahuku Golf Course Park—Other than Goat Island, this is about the closest you'll come to a hidden beach on the windward coast. Granted, there's a golf course paralleling the strand, but sand dunes hide you from the duffers. The beach is long, wide, and sandy white.

Facilities: Restrooms and showers. A restaurant and market are nearby.

Camping: Unofficial camping perhaps.

Swimming: Fair, but exercise caution.

Snorkeling: Poor.

Surfing: "Seventh Hole" breaks has winter surf up to eight feet. Right and left slide.

Fishing: Most likely you'll catch some *papio*, but bonefish, goatfish, and milkfish may turn up too.

Getting there: In Kahuku, about twenty-five miles north of Kaneohe, turn off Kamehameha Highway (Route 83) toward the ocean. Then walk across the golf course to the beach.

NORTH SHORE BEACHES AND PARKS

Sunset Beach—If you've ever owned a surfboard, or even a Beach Boys album, you know this beach. Sunset is synonymous with surfing: it's one of the most famous, challenging, and dangerous surf spots in the world. During winter months, fifteen- and twenty-foot waves are common.

The beach, two miles long and about two hundred feet wide, is one of Oahu's largest. I think the best way to do Sunset is by starting from **Ehukai Beach Park**. From here you can go left to the "Banzai Pipeline," where crushing waves build along a shallow coral reef to create tube-like formations. To the right lies "Sunset," with equally spectacular surfing waves.

Facilities: Ehukai Beach Park has picnic areas, restrooms, and showers. Nearby there are also markets and restaurants.

Camping: Not permitted.

Swimming: Fair in summer; extremely dangerous in winter. From September to April, high waves and strong currents prevail. Be careful!

Snorkeling: Poor; but some of the island's best snorkeling is at **Pupukea Beach Park**, a marine reserve on Kamehameha Highway six miles northeast of Haleiwa.

Surfing: See above.

Fishing: *Papio, menpachi,* and *ulua* are common.

Getting there: Ehukai Beach Park is off Kamehameha Highway (Route 83) about seven miles northeast of Haleiwa.

Waimea Bay Beach Park—If Sunset is *one* of the most famous surfing spots in the world, Waimea is *the* most famous. The biggest surfable waves in the world roll into this pretty blue bay.

There's a wide white-sand beach and a pleasant park with a tree-studded lawn. It's a marvelous place for picnicking and sunbathing. In summer you can swim, and in winter you can sunbathe and watch the surfers.

Facilities: Picnic area, restrooms, showers, lifeguard. Restaurant and market about a mile away near Sunset Beach.

Camping: Not permitted.

Swimming: Good in summer; extremely dangerous in winter. Good bodysurfing in shorebreak.

Snorkeling: Good when the bay is calm.

Surfing: See above.

Fishing: *Papio, menpachi,* and *ulua* are common.

Getting there: On Kamehameha Highway (Route 83) about five miles northeast of Haleiwa.

Haleiwa Beach Park—This is an excellent refuge from the north shore's pounding surf. Set in Waialua Bay, the beach is safe for swimming almost all year.

Facilities: Picnic area, restrooms, showers, snack bar, ballfield, basketball court, volleyball courts, and playground.

Camping: Both tent and trailer camping are allowed. You'll need a county permit.

Swimming: Good.

Snorkeling: Fair.

Surfing: None.

Fishing: The primary catches are *papio, menpachi,* and *ulua*.

Getting there: Located on Kamehameha Highway (Route 83) in Haleiwa.

Kaiaka State Recreation Area—The setting at this park is beautiful. There is a secluded area with a tree-shaded lawn and a short strip of sandy beach. A rocky shoreline borders most of this peninsular park, so I'd recommend it more for picnics than water sports.

Facilities: Picnic area, restrooms. Restaurants and markets are nearby in Haleiwa.

Camping: Not permitted.

Swimming: Mediocre; rocky bottom.

Snorkeling: Good.

Surfing: Poor.

Fishing: Good area for *papio, menpachi,* and *ulua*.

Getting there: Located on Haleiwa Road just outside Haleiwa.

Mokuleia Beach Park and **Mokuleia Beach** (★)—The twelve-acre park contains a sandy beach and large unshaded lawn. An exposed coral reef detracts from the swimming, but on either side of the park lie beaches with sandy ocean bottoms. You'll have to contend with noise from nearby Dillingham Airfield, but the park is an excellent starting point for exploring the unpopulated sections of Mokuleia Beach.

To the west of the park, this beach stretches several miles along a secluded coast. You can hike down the beach or reach its hidden realms by driving farther west along Farrington Highway (Route 930), then turning off onto any of the numerous dirt side roads.

Facilities: Picnic area, restrooms, and showers at the park. Markets and restaurants are several miles away in Haleiwa.

Camping: Tent and trailer camping are allowed in the park, with a county permit. Unofficial camping along the undeveloped beachfront is common.

Swimming: Good, but exercise caution, especially during winter months.

Snorkeling: Good.

Surfing: Winter breaks up to ten feet near Dillingham Airfield. Right and left slide.

Fishing: Common catches include *papio, menpachi,* and *ulua*.

Getting there: The beach park is on Farrington Highway (Route 930) about seven miles west of Haleiwa.

LEEWARD COAST BEACHES AND PARKS

Keaiwa Heiau State Recreation Area—Amazing as it sounds, this is a wooded retreat within easy driving distance of Honolulu. Situated in the Koolau foothills overlooking Pearl Harbor, it contains a *heiau* once used by Hawaiian healers. There's an arboretum of medicinal plants, a forest extending to the far reaches of the mountains, and a network of hiking trails.

Facilities: Picnic area and restrooms. Markets and restaurants several miles away.

Camping: Tents only. State permit required.

Getting there: Located in Aiea Heights. To get there from Honolulu, take Route 90 west to Aiea, then follow Aiea Heights Drive to the park.

Hawaiian Electric Beach Park—This privately owned park, across the highway from a monstrous power plant, is open to the public. There's a rolling lawn with palm and *kiawe* trees, plus a white-sand beach and coral reef. The drawbacks are the lack of facilities and the park's proximity to the electric company.

Facilities: Picnic area.

Camping: Not allowed here; but tent and trailer camping are okay at nearby **Kahe Point Beach Park,** with a county permit.

Swimming: Good.

Snorkeling: Good.

Surfing: Small breaks year-round with right slide.

Fishing: Common catches include *papio, ulua, moano,* and *menpachi.*

Getting there: Located on Farrington Highway (Route 93) about seven miles south of Waianae.

Nanakuli Beach Park—This park is so large that a housing tract divides it into two parts. The main section features a white-sand beach, *kiawe*-studded camping area, and a recreation complex. It's simply a park with everything, unfortunately including weekend crowds.

Facilities: Picnic areas, restrooms, showers, ballfield, basketball court, and playground.

Camping: Tent and trailer camping allowed, but a county permit is required.

Swimming: Good.

Snorkeling: Good.

Surfing: Winter breaks; right and left slide.

Fishing: Frequently seen are *papio, ulua, moano,* and *menpachi.*

Getting there: On Farrington Highway (Route 93) about five miles south of Waianae.

Maili Beach Park—A long winding stretch of white sand is the high point of this otherwise unimpressive facility. The park contains shade trees and a spotty lawn.

Facilities: Restrooms and showers. Market and restaurant are nearby.

Camping: Not permitted here, but tent camping, with a county permit, is allowed at nearby **Lualualei Beach Park.**

Swimming: Good.

Snorkeling: Fair.

Surfing: Winter breaks; right slide.

Fishing: Principal game fish are *papio, ulua, menpachi,* and *moano.*

Getting there: Located on Farrington Highway (Route 93) in Maili a few miles south of Waianae.

Makaha Beach Park—Some of the finest surfing in the world takes place right offshore here. This is the home of the Makaha International Surfing Championship, which attracts expert surfers every year.

For more relaxed sports, there's a white-sand beach to sunbathe on and some good places to skin dive. The precipitous Waianae Mountains loom behind the park.

Facilities: Picnic tables, restrooms, showers. A market and restaurant are nearby.

Camping: Not permitted.

Swimming and Snorkeling: Both are good when the sea is calm; otherwise, exercise extreme caution.

Surfing: Terrific; see above.

Fishing: Primary game fish caught here are *papio, ulua, moano,* and *menpachi.*

Getting there: Located on Farrington Highway (Route 93) in Makaha, two miles north of Waianae.

Keauu Beach Park—Except for the absence of a sandy beach, this is the prettiest park on the west coast. It's a long, narrow grassy plot spotted with trees and backdropped by the Waianaes. Sunsets are spectacular here, and on a clear day you can see all the way to Kauai. There's a sandy beach just west of the park. Unfortunately, a coral reef rises right to the water's edge, hindering water sports other than snorkeling.

Facilities: Picnic area, restrooms, showers. Markets and restaurants are several miles away in Waianae.

Camping: Tent and trailer. County permit required.

Swimming: Good, but entry into the water is difficult. Bodysurfing is also good.

Snorkeling: Very good.

Surfing: Good summer breaks; left slide.

Fishing: Principal catches are *papio, ulua, moano,* and *menpachi.*

Getting there: Located on Farrington Highway (Route 93) about five miles north of Waianae.

Yokohama Bay—This curving stretch of white sand is the last beach along Oahu's northwest coast. With the Waianae Range in the background and coral reefs offshore, it's a particularly lovely spot. Though officially a state park, the area is largely undeveloped. You can walk from Yokohama past miles of tidepools to Oahu's northwest corner at Kaena Point. Yokohama Bay is a prime region for beach lovers and explorers both.

Facilities: Restrooms, showers.

Camping: Not permitted.

Swimming: Good when the sea is calm, but exercise extreme caution if the surf is up.

Snorkeling: Excellent if the sea is calm.

Surfing: Summer breaks up to fifteen feet over a shallow reef; left slide.

Fishing: Principal game fish caught in this area are *papio, ulua, moano,* and *menpachi.*

Getting there: Located at the end of the paved section of Farrington Highway (Route 93), about nine miles north of Waianae.

Hiking

There are numerous hiking trails within easy driving distance of Honolulu. I have listed these as well as trails in the windward and north shore areas. Unfortunately, many Oahu treks require special permission from the state, from the armed services, or from private owners. But you should find that the hikes suggested here, none of which require official sanction, will provide ample adventure.

To hike with a group or to obtain further information on hiking Oahu, contact the **Sierra Club** (P.O. Box 11070, Honolulu, Oahu, HI 96826; 946-8494) or the **Hawaii Trail and Mountain Club** (P.O. Box 2238, Honolulu, Oahu, HI 96804). Both agencies sponsor hikes regularly.

GREATER HONOLULU TRAILS

If you're staying in Waikiki, the most easily accessible hike is the short jaunt up **Diamond Head** crater. There's a sweeping view of Honolulu from atop this famous landmark. The trail begins inside the crater, so take Diamond Head Road around to the inland side of Diamond Head, then follow the tunnel leading into the crater.

In the Koolau Mountains above Diamond Head there are two parallel trails which climb almost 2,000 feet and afford excellent views of the Windward Coast. The head of **Wiliwilinui Trail** (3 miles long) can be reached by taking the Kalanianaole Highway (Routes H-1 and 72) east past the Kahala Mall Shopping Center. Then turn left on Laukahi Street and follow it a couple of miles to the top of the road. To get to **Lanipo Trail** (3 miles), located to the west of Wiliwilinui, take Waialae Avenue off Route H-1. Then turn up Wilhelmina Road and follow it to Maunalani Circle and the trailhead.

For spectacular views of the lush Palolo and Manoa Valleys, you can hike **Waahila Ridge Trail** (2 miles). To get there take St. Louis Heights Drive (near the University of Hawaii campus) and then follow connecting roads up to Waahila Ridge State Recreation Area.

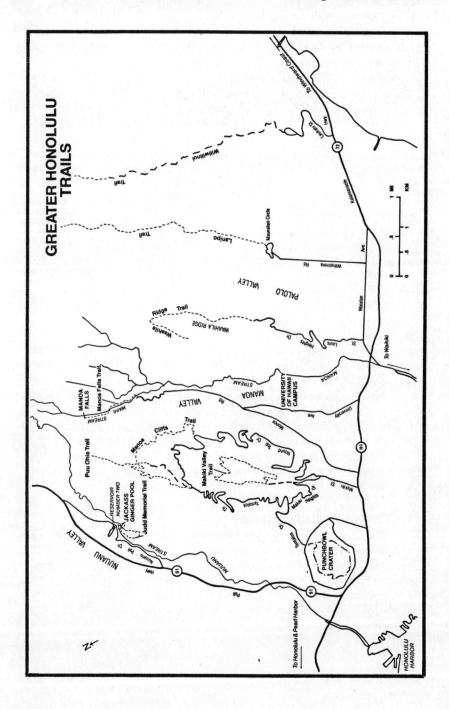

Another hike, along **Manoa Falls Trail** (0.8 mile), leads right through the valley. This is a pleasant jaunt which follows Waihi Stream through a densely vegetated area to a charming waterfall.

Manoa Cliffs Trail (3 miles), a pleasant family hike, follows a precipice along the west side of Manoa Valley. And **Puu Ohia Trail** (2 miles), which crosses Manoa Cliffs Trail, provides splendid views of Manoa and Nuuanu Valleys. Both trails begin from Tantalus Drive in the hills above Honolulu.

Makiki Valley Trail (2 miles) begins near Tantalus Drive. Composed of three interlinking trails, this loop passes stands of eucalyptus and bamboo trees and offers some sweeping views of Honolulu.

Another loop trail, **Judd Memorial** (1.3 mile), crosses Nuuanu Stream and traverses bamboo, eucalyptus, and Norfolk pine groves en route to the Jackass Ginger Pool. This is a marvelous place to swim and, if you've tried some of the nearby mud-sliding chutes, to wash off as well. To get there, take the Pali Highway (Route 61) several miles north from Honolulu. Turn onto Nuuanu Pali Drive and follow it about a mile to Reservoir Number Two spillway.

In the mountains above Pearl Harbor, at Keaiwa Heiau State Park, you'll find the **Aiea Loop Trail** (4.8 miles). Set in a heavily forested area, this hike passes the wreckage of a World War II cargo plane. It provides an excellent chance to see some of the native trees—*lehua, ohia,* and *koa*—used by local woodworkers. (For directions to the state park, see the "Beaches and Parks" section in this chapter.)

Another hike in this general area, along **Waimano Trail** (7 miles), climbs 1,600 feet to an astonishing vista point above Oahu's Windward Coast. There are swimming holes en route. To get there take Kamehameha Highway (Route 90) west to Waimano Home Road (Route 730). Turn right and go two-and-a-half miles to a point along the road where you'll see a building on the right and an irrigation ditch on the left. The trail follows the ditch.

WINDWARD COAST TRAILS

There are several excellent hikes along this raindrenched shore. The first few are within ten miles of Waikiki, near **Hanauma Bay**. From the beach at Hanauma you can hike two miles along the coast and cliffs to the Halona Blowhole. This trek passes the Toilet Bowl, a unique tidepool with a hole in the bottom which causes it to fill and then flush with the wave action. Waves sometimes wash the rocks along this path, so be prepared to get wet.

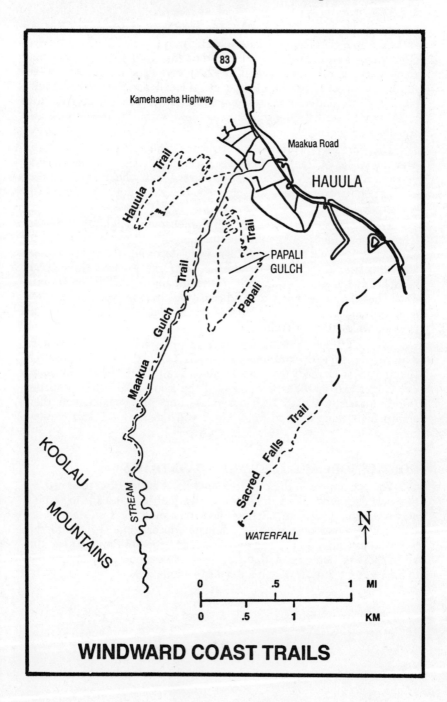

WINDWARD COAST TRAILS

At the intersection where the short road leading down toward Hanauma Bay branches from Kalanianaole Highway (Route 72), there are two other trails. **Koko Head Trail,** a one-mile hike to the top of a volcanic cone, starts on the ocean side of the highway. This trek features some startling views of Hanauma Bay, Diamond Head, and the Koolau Mountains. Another one-mile hike, along **Koko Crater Trail,** leads from the highway up to a 1,208-foot peak. The views from this crow's nest are equally spectacular.

There are several other particularly pretty hikes much farther north, near the village of Hauula. **Sacred Falls Trail** (2.2 miles) gently ascends into a canyon and arrives at a waterfall and swimming hole. The trailhead for this popular trek is near Kamehameha Highway (Route 83) just south of Hauula.

Then, in Hauula, if you turn off Kamehameha Highway and head inland about a quarter-mile up Hauula Homestead Road, you'll come to Maakua Road. Walk up Maakua Road, which leads into the woods. About 300 yards after entering the woods, the road forks. **Maakua Gulch Trail** branches to the left. If you continue straight ahead you'll be on **Hauula Trail,** but if you veer left onto Maakua Gulch Trail, you'll encounter another trail branching to the left in about 150 yards. This is **Papali Trail** (also known as Maakua Trail).

Maakua Gulch Trail (3 miles), en route to a small waterfall, traverses a rugged canyon with extremely steep walls. Part of the trail lies along the stream bed, so be ready to get wet. **Hauula Trail** (2.5 miles) ascends along two ridges and provides fine vistas of the Koolau Mountains and the Windward Coast. **Papali Trail** (2.5 miles) drops into Papali Gulch, then climbs high along a ridge from which you can view the surrounding countryside.

NORTH SHORE AND LEEWARD COAST TRAILS

You can approach the trail to **Kaena Point** either from the north or the west shoreline. It's a dry, rock-strewn path which leads to Oahu's northwest tip. There are tidepools and swimming spots en route, plus spectacular views of a rugged, uninhabited coastline. To get to the trailhead just drive to the end of the paved portion of Route 930 on the north shore or Route 93 on the west coast. Then follow the jeep trail out to Kaena Point. Either way, it's about a two-mile trek.

Travelers' Tracks

Sightseeing

Sightseeing on Oahu is spelled Honolulu. Steeped in history, this capital city offers countless relics and monuments as well as places of remarkable natural beauty. If you want to thoroughly tour the city, plan to take several days. Or, if time is limited, you might glance through this section to find just a few places that look particularly interesting. I especially recommend Diamond Head, Mission Houses Museum, Iolani Palace, Chinatown, and the Bishop Museum.

After touring Honolulu in the pages that follow, we'll travel around the island counter-clockwise up the Windward Coast, along the North Shore, and back down through the Leilehua Plateau in the island's interior. Then we'll head west along the Leeward Coast.

GREATER HONOLULU

DIAMOND HEAD AND WAIKIKI

There could be no more appropriate point to begin a Honolulu tour than the place which has become symbolic of all Hawaii. **Diamond Head,** a 760-foot-tall crater, is the state's most famous landmark. The Hawaiians called it *Leahi,* seeing in its sloping face the brow of an *ahi,* or yellowfin tuna. Nineteenth-century sailors, mistaking its volcanic glass for priceless gems, gave the promontory its present name. If you follow Diamond Head Road around the crater to its inland side, then through the tunnel, you can drive into the crater itself. A foot-path three-quarters of a mile long leads to the crater rim for marvelous views of Honolulu.

Diamond Head marks the east end of **Waikiki.** To sightsee this tourist quarter, head west to **Kapiolani Park.** This 140-acre spread contains a **Rose Garden** (Monsarrat and Paki avenues) as well as jogging tracks, tennis courts, picnic areas, and so on. It also includes the **Waikiki Aquarium** (2777 Kalakaua Avenue; 923-9741; admission) with a fascinating tropical fish collection, and the **Honolulu Zoo** (923-7723; admission).

Along busy Kalakaua Avenue, a favorite nesting place for construction cranes, are two old hotels. The **Moana Hotel** (2365 Kalakaua Avenue), built in 1901, was one of Waikiki's earliest high-rises. Its woodframe structure, vaulted ceilings, and large rooms represent the days when Hawaii was strictly a rich man's retreat. The nearby **Royal Hawaiian Hotel** (2259 Kalakaua Avenue) is Hawaii's "pink palace," a Spanish baroque-style caravansary constructed in 1927. With its intricate gardens, arcades, and balconies, this is Waikiki's most interesting edifice.

Of course a tour of Waikiki is not complete without a stroll through the **shopping malls** (see the "Shopping" section in this chapter) and a walk along the **beach** (see the "Beaches and Parks" section in this chapter).

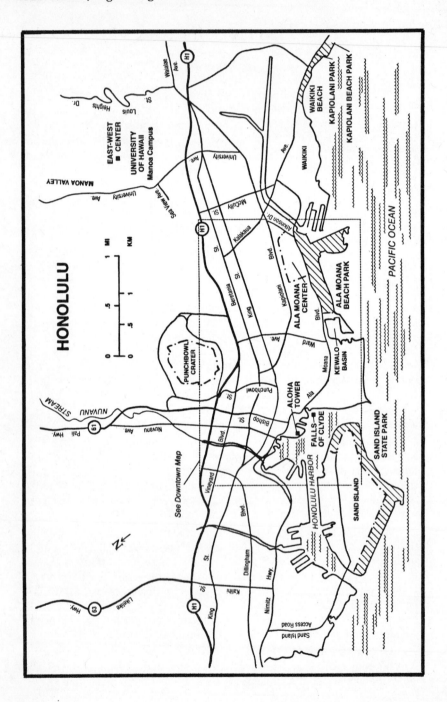

DOWNTOWN HONOLULU

From this tourist enclave it's a short drive, but a long walk, to the center of Honolulu. On the way downtown there are several points of interest. **Kewalo Basin** (Ala Moana and Ward avenues) or **Fisherman's Wharf** is home port for sport fishing boats. The **Honolulu Academy of Arts** (900 South Beretania Street; 538-3693) often displays the James Michener collection of woodblocks from Japan, plus works by old masters and young locals. And, if you'd like to see a Sunday church service delivered in Hawaiian, attend **Ke Alaula O Ka Malamalama Church** (910 Cooke Street).

Your tour of historic downtown Honolulu can begin with the oldest wooden house in the islands. **Mission Houses Museum** (553 South King Street; 531-0481; admission), dating to the first missionaries, contains a **Frame House** pre-fabricated in New England and erected here in 1821. This Yankee-style structure sheltered newly arrived missionary families. The nearby **Chamberlain Depository** was constructed of local coral in 1831 and used primarily as a storehouse. Another coral building, the **Printing House,** rose in 1841 and today contains a replica of the first press to print the Hawaiian language. The **Mission Cemetery,** across the road from these houses, dates to 1823. Together this complex represents a seminal center for the missionaries who made Hawaiian a written language and then rewrote the entire history of Hawaii.

Towering above the cemetery is Honolulu's oldest church, **Kawaiahao Church** (South King and Punchbowl streets). Built of coral and timber in 1842, this imposing cathedral became Hawaii's mother church, where kings were christened, inaugurated, and mourned. Services are still performed here in Hawaiian and English every Sunday at 10:30 a.m.

Across South King Street, that brick structure with the stately white pillars is the **Mission Memorial Building,** constructed in 1916 to honor the early church leaders. The nearby Renaissance-style building with the tile roof is **Honolulu Hale,** the City Hall. You might want to venture into the central courtyard, an open-air plaza surrounded by stone columns.

As South King Street leads toward downtown Honolulu, **Iolani Palace** (538-1471) will be on your right. Built for King Kalakaua in 1882, this beautiful Renaissance-style mansion served as the royal residence until Queen Liliuokalani was overthrown in 1893. Following the abortive 1895 restoration, the ill-starred monarch was imprisoned here. It later became the capitol building for the Territory of Hawaii, and today is the only royal palace in the United States. Also on the palace grounds are the **Iolani Barracks,** built in 1871 to station the Royal Household Guards, and the **Bandstand,** constructed for King Kalakaua's 1883 coronation. You can wander the royal grounds for free; there's an admission fee to tour the palace, open Wednesday to Saturday. Children under five not admitted.

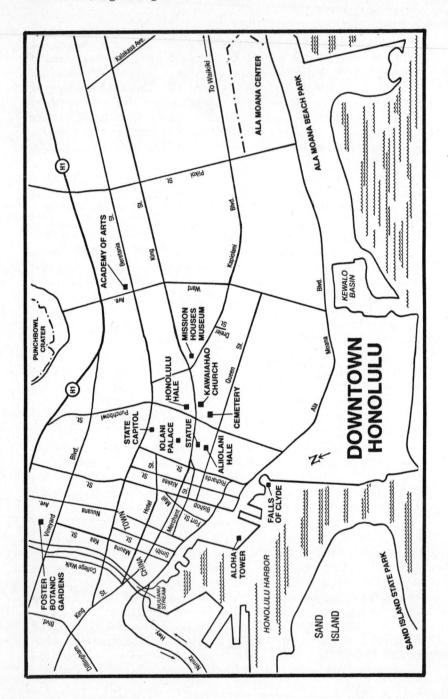

Behind the palace rises the **State Capitol Building** (South Beretania and Punchbowl streets). Surrounded by flared pillars resembling palm trees, this structure represents a variety of Hawaiian themes. A statue of Father Damien, the leper martyr of Molokai, stands at the entrance. The House and Senate chambers are cone-shaped to resemble volcanoes. The open-air courtyard reflects the state's balmy weather.

Back on South King Street, across from Iolani Palace, stands the **King Kamehameha Statue**, a huge gilt-and-bronze figure cast in Italy. Unveiled for Kalakaua's inauguration, this statue is actually a replica of the original, which rests in Kapaau on the Big Island. Behind Kamehameha is **Aliiolani Hale**, the **Judiciary Building**, which was completed in 1874 and originally housed the Hawaiian Parliament.

For a tour of Honolulu's waterfront, go left on Richards Street toward Pier 7 where the **Falls of Clyde** (536-6373) is berthed. This century-old ship plied the Pacific carrying sugar and oil. Built in Scotland, it is reputedly the only fully-rigged four-masted ship in the world. For a nominal admission you can tour this marvelous floating museum.

From here, follow the water to **Aloha Tower** (Pier 9; 537-9260). Anytime from 8 a.m. until 9 p.m. you can elevator up to the tenth-floor observation deck for a crow's-nest view of Honolulu harbor and city.

Back at ground zero, head *mauka* across the highway and up **Fort Street Mall** to Merchant Street. The late-nineteenth- and early-twentieth-century buildings along Merchant Street mark the **old downtown** section of Honolulu's business district.

At the end of Merchant Street take a right on Nuuanu, then a left on Hotel Street for a tour of **Chinatown**. From Hotel Street you can explore side streets and check out the Chinese groceries, medicinal herb shops, import stores, and noodle factories. Or sign up for one of the walking tours conducted every Tuesday by the Chinese Chamber of Commerce (533-3181). The Chinese guide will lead you past old temples and other points of interest, then stop for lunch at a local restaurant.

This weatherbeaten ghetto, a vital part of Honolulu's history, has long been a center of controversy. When bubonic plague savaged the Chinese community in 1900, the white-led government tried to contain the pestilence by burning down afflicted homes. The bumbling white fathers managed to raze most of Chinatown, destroying businesses as well as houses.

Today Hotel Street, a favorite haunt among servicemen, is Honolulu's red-light district. This street and other sections of the Chinese ghetto are presently the subject of a bitter controversy. The fight centers around an urban renewal plan which calls for the condemning of many buildings. The local Chinese and Filipino communities have already demonstrated several times against the plan.

Continuing along Hotel Street across Nuuanu Stream, go right on College Walk. You'll pass the tile-roofed **Tokyo Theatre** (1230 College Walk), dating to 1938, and **Izumo Taishakyo Mission**, a Shinto shrine. Next you can walk through **Foster Botanic Garden** (50 North Vineyard Boulevard; 533-3406; admission), planted with palms, orchids, coffee trees, poisonous plants, and countless exotic species. Then, returning down the other side of Nuuanu Stream, stop and tour the **Cultural Plaza** (Beretania and Maunakea streets) with its many Oriental shops and displays.

NUUANU AVENUE

If you have a car, or want to do some urban hiking, go from downtown Honolulu up Nuuanu Avenue. Along this busy thoroughfare and its quieter side streets are some strikingly beautiful temples. First is the **Soto Mission of Hawaii** (1708 Nuuanu), home of a meditative Zen sect. Then, set in from the road beside a small stream, sits **Honolulu Myohoji Temple** (2003 Nuuanu), capped with a peace tower. Uphill from this Buddhist shrine lies **Honolulu Memorial Park**, a Japanese cemetery (22 Craigside Place). Here you'll find **Kyoto-Kinkakaku-ji**, an ancestral monument bounded on three sides by a carp pond, and the enchanting **Sanju Pagoda**.

Nearby **Tenrikyo Mission** (2236 Nuuanu) is a woodframe temple which was moved here from Japan. Sections of this delicate structure were built without nails. The **Royal Mausoleum**, across the street, is the resting place for many members of the Kamehameha and Kalakaua families, who ruled nineteenth-century Hawaii.

The climax of this side tour is a visit to the most stately temple of all—the home of the **Chinese Buddhist Association of Hawaii** (42 Kawananakoa Place). This grand, multihued edifice contains an elaborate worship place displaying statues of Buddha and other luminaries.

PUNCHBOWL AND TANTALUS

At the end of Ward Avenue, off Prospect Drive, lies **Punchbowl**, the circular crater of a dead volcano. Together with Diamond Head, this is Honolulu's best example of the volcanic action which created Hawaii. Today Punchbowl is a national cemetery, with the graves of over 20,000 war dead spread across the bottom of the bowl. You can pass through this memorial park up along the crater rim for some breathtaking views of Honolulu.

Then you can explore yet higher by taking Tantalus Drive as it climbs up the side of 2,013-foot **Tantalus**. After winding through a rain forest, this country road becomes Round Top Drive and leads to **Puu Ualakaa Park**, a hilltop retreat with even more exotic Honolulu vistas. Round Top then drops back into the city, completing a scenic loop into Honolulu's hill country.

MANOA VALLEY

Located in Manoa Valley about a mile from Waikiki, the **University of Hawaii** is a cultural center. With over 20,000 students and 2,000 faculty members, it's an excellent place to meet people. You should certainly visit the **East-West Center** (1777 East-West Road; 944-7111), where there's always an opportunity to encounter foreign students. The Center, designed by world-renowned architect I. M. Pei, is devoted to the study of Asian and American cultures.

Nearby **Paradise Park** (3737 Manoa Road; 988-6686; admission) is a tropical theme park landscaped with ponds, lagoons, waterfalls, flower gardens, and sinuous pathways. This imaginative facility also features an aviary complete with performing birds and a history gallery.

PEARL HARBOR

From 8 a.m. to 3 p.m. daily the Navy has free boat tours out to the **U.S.S. Arizona** (422-0561). This is an excellent opportunity to view Pearl Harbor, a once-beautiful anchorage which today is surrounded by military installations. The boat ride out to the sunken hulk and accompanying museum will take you through an area heavily bombed by the Japanese in the December 7, 1941, sneak attack. The United States lost eighteen ships and over 3,000 men in what became the nation's greatest military disaster. Over 1,100 men were entombed alive in the Arizona.

THE CROSS-ISLAND EXPRESS

After you've finished touring the Honolulu area and are ready for the Windward Coast, you might be interested in taking one of the two highways which shortcut from Honolulu across the Koolau Range. Likelike Highway (Route 63) travels to Kaneohe, a bedroom community which also houses a large military base. Before venturing across the mountains, stop at the **Bishop Museum** (847-1443) near the intersection of Routes H-1 and 63. Built around the turn of the century, the museum contains an excellent collection of Hawaiian and Pacific artifacts. There are cultural and historical displays aplenty, plus a planetarium right next door. Admission charged.

The other, more scenic, cross-mountain route is the Pali Highway (Route 61), which passes several points of interest. The first is **Queen Emma's Summer Palace** (595-3167). Built in 1843 and used by King Kamehameha IV and his wife, this white-pillared house is now a museum. For a small admission fee you can see the Queen's personal artifacts as well as other period pieces. Tree-shaded **Nuuanu Valley Park** adjoins the estate. Then, for a tour through this exotically forested valley, turn onto **Nuuanu Pali Drive** and follow it until it rejoins the highway.

Farther up, there's a turnoff to **Nuuanu Pali Lookout,** a vista point that should not be missed! Without doubt, this is Oahu's finest view. You can scan the rugged face of the Koolau cliffs as they knife-edge 3,000 feet down to a gently rolling coastal shelf. The view extends from Makapuu Point to the last reaches of Kaneohe Bay, and from the cliff rim far out to sea. It was over this precipice that Kamehameha I drove his enemies when he conquered Oahu in 1795.

WINDWARD COAST

DIAMOND HEAD TO MAKAPUU

If, rather than taking one of these shortcuts, you'd prefer to travel the long route to the Windward Coast, then start near the base of Diamond Head crater. From here you can explore east along Diamond Head Road and Kahala Avenue. This route passes **Diamond Head Lighthouse** and offers picturesque views of the south coast. It also travels past the posh **Kahala District,** featuring some of Honolulu's loveliest homes.

In Kahala, turn left on Kealaolu Avenue and follow it to Kalanianaole Highway (Route 72). This thoroughfare cuts through other residential areas, then climbs the slopes of 642-foot **Koko Head,** an extinct volcano. **Koko Crater,** the second hump on the horizon, rises to over 1,200 feet. This firepit, according to Hawaiian legend, is the vagina of Pele's sister. It seems that Pele, goddess of volcanoes, was being pursued by a handsome demigod. Her sister, trying to distract the hot suitor from Pele, spread her legs across the landscape.

From the top of Koko Head a side road and path lead down to **Hanauma Bay.** This breathtakingly beautiful bay is also an extinct volcano, one wall of which was breached by the sea. Today it's a marine preserve, filled with multicolored coral and teeming with underwater life.

The main road corkscrews along the coast, offering views of Lanai and Molokai, to an overlook at **Halona Blowhole.** Geysers of seawater blast through this lava tube, reaching dramatic heights when the ocean is turbulent.

Sandy Beach, one of Hawaii's finest bodysurfing spots, is just down the hill. Across from the beach a side road leads up to **Koko Crater Botanic Gardens** (next to Koko Head Stables at 408 Kealahou Street), a 200-acre collection of cacti, plumeria, and other flowering plants.

The main road rounds Oahu's southeast corner and climbs to a scenic point above the windward shore. You can scan this stunning seascape for miles. That slope-faced islet just offshore is **Rabbit Island** and the distant headland is **Mokapu Peninsula.** The strand below the vista spot is **Makapuu Beach.** That complex of buildings is **Sea Life Park** (923-1531; admission), a "marine world" attraction featuring 2,000 sea creatures in a giant oceanarium, trained dolphins, and a 70-foot whaling ship replica.

MAKAPUU TO THE NORTH SHORE

The road descends along the shoreline and cuts between white-sand beaches and the **Koolau Range.** If wind and weather permit, you'll see

hang gliders dusting the cliffs as they sail from the mountains down to the beach. That dagger-point spire beyond Waimanalo is **Olomana Peak**, a favorite among equally daring rock climbers.

The highway continues to the suburban town of Kailua, where it intersects Route 61 (Kailua Road). If you go right a short distance you'll reach **Ulu Po Heiau**. (It's behind the YMCA at 1200 Kailua Road.) The temple, according to legend, was constructed by Hobbit-like Menehunes who passed the building stones along a six-mile-long bucket brigade in a one-night construction project.

Back on Route 61 in the opposite direction you can pick up Route 83, which will carry you to **Kaneohe**. Past this bedroom community Route 83 is known as the Kamehameha Highway. Just outside town you can visit the graceful **Haiku Gardens** (46-316 Haiku Road) with an enchanting lily pond and acres of exotic plant life. Farther along Kamehameha Highway, don't bypass the **Valley of the Temples**. A truly inspiring sight here is the Buddhist **Byodo-In Temple** (47-200 Kahekili Highway; admission), shadowed by the sharply rising peaks of the Koolau Range.

The road runs along **Kaneohe Bay** and passes **Waiahole** and **Waikane Valleys**. This verdant area—which produces papayas, bananas, and sweet potatoes—has been a political battleground since the local government began evicting Hawaiian farmers. At one time roadside signs here protested the bureaucracy's attempt to develop a prime agricultural region. Developers have already helped pollute Kaneohe Bay by destroying vegetation that protected against erosion. Today the bay, which has the only barrier reef in Hawaii, is clouded with silt.

Anchored just outside the bay is Mokolii Island, better known by its shape, **Chinaman's Hat**. Route 83 passes an **old sugar mill** and continues past a rock formation resembling a **Crouching Lion**. It rims coral-studded **Kahana Bay**, then, still crowding the coastline, traverses the tiny towns of **Punaluu** and **Hauula**. The aging **Hauula Door of Faith Church**, a tiny clapboard chapel, is surrounded by palms. Not far from here there's another old woodframe church, **Hauula Congregational Christian Church**, a wood-and-coral sanctuary dating to 1862.

In the nearby town of Laie you'll enter Mormon country. There's a temple here and a branch of Brigham Young University. Nearby lies the **Polynesian Cultural Center** (293-3333), Hawaii's answer to Disneyland. For a bullet-biting admission you'll receive a guided tour through simulated Hawaiian, Samoan, Tahitian, Fijian, Marquesan, New Zealand, and Tongan villages. The center is owned and operated by the Mormons, who in the 1800s helped destroy some of the cultures they're now recreating. It is closed on Sunday.

For a marvelous view of seascape and mountains, try the short side road which travels to Laie Point. There are two islets offshore, one of which has partially collapsed to create a natural arch. Then the main road goes past **Kahuku Sugar Mill.** In years past you could tour this old cane processing plant by trolley; it was a great way to learn what these factories were like in the days when sugar was king. Despite repeated reports that the mill would reopen, it remains closed at present.

NORTH SHORE

Broad beaches extend for miles along Oahu's turbulent north coast. **Sunset Beach** and **Waimea Bay,** two of the most famous surfing spots in the world, lie along this strip. Sunset is the site of the "Banzai Pipeline," where thunderous waves form into tube-shaped curls as they pass over a shallow reef. Waimea Bay sports the world's highest (up to thirty feet) surfable waves. Even if you're not a surfer, you might stop by to watch the incredible surfing performances here.

Between these two beaches, side roads lead to **Puu o Mahuka Heiau** and **Waimea Falls Park** (638-8511; admission). The *heiau* is a split-level structure once used for human sacrifices. There's a fantastic view of the north shore from this ethereal sanctuary. Waimea Falls Park, a 1,800-acre tropic preserve, contains archaeological ruins, botanical gardens, and a bird sanctuary. A tram leads to the falls, where you can swim and picnic.

Farther along Kamehameha Highway another side road, Kawailoa Drive, turns up through an **old plantation village,** where you'll see tin-roofed houses and a lovely old church. If you continue on the main road you'll arrive in **Haleiwa,** a former plantation town with a new facelift. Fortunately the contemporary architects who performed the operation had an eye to antiquity and designed modern shopping centers that blend comfortably into the village landscape. Most modern of all is the community: with its young surfer crowd Haleiwa has become a center of contemporary culture.

From here, head west and pick up Farrington Highway (Route 930). This country road parallels miles of unpopulated beachfront, and arrives at Dillingham Airfield, where you can take a **glider ride** along the Waianae Mountains (call 677-3404 for information). Beyond this landing strip, the road continues for several miles between ocean and mountains before turning into a very rugged dirt track. Though this unpaved portion might be passable in dry weather, the driving is generally so tortuous that I'd recommend hiking to **Kaena Point** on Oahu's northwest corner (see the "Hiking" section in this chapter).

ACROSS OAHU VIA THE LEILEHUA PLATEAU

Several highways lead from Haleiwa back to the Honolulu area. These cross the 1,000-foot **Leilehua** or **Schofield Plateau,** a rich agricultural area planted in pineapple and sugar. Stretching between the Koolau and Waianae Ranges, this tableland has become an important military headquarters. Schofield Barracks, Wheeler Air Force Base, and several other installations occupy huge stretches of land here. Wahiawa, a small, grimy city, is the region's commercial hub.

Somehow, between the agriculture and armed forces, I've never found much in this part of Oahu. I usually pass quickly through this area on my way north or south. But there are a few places you might find worth touring.

For example, from Haleiwa south to Wahiawa you can take Route 80, a pretty road with excellent views of the Waianaes, or follow Route 82, which passes through verdant pineapple fields. If you take this latter highway, watch for a Hawaii Visitors Bureau sign pointing the way over a dirt road to **Kukaniloko,** a cluster of sacred birth stones marking the spot where Hawaiian royalty gave birth.

Route 82 connects with Route 99, which passes Schofield Barracks. If you have time for a scenic detour, pull up to the sentry gate at Schofield and ask directions to **Kolekole Pass.** It was through this notch that Japanese planes streaked toward Pearl Harbor. You'll be directed through Schofield up into the Waianaes. When you reach Kolekole Pass, there's another sentry gate. Ask the guard to let you continue a short distance farther to the observation point. From here the Waianaes fall away precipitously to a plain which rolls gently to the sea. There's an astonishing view of Oahu's west coast. If you're denied permission to pass the sentry point, then take the footpath which begins just before the gate, leading up the hill. From near the cross at the top, you'll have a partial view of both the Waianaes' western face and the central plateau region.

From the Wahiawa-Schofield area south toward Honolulu, you can barrel down either the H-2 superhighway or Route 99, or take the slower, more scenic Route 750. This last road, which parallels the Waianaes and offers marvelous views, is my favorite.

LEEWARD COAST

From Honolulu you can visit Oahu's dry, sunny western shore by traveling west on Route H-1 or Route 90. If you want to tour a prime sugar-growing area, take Route 90 past Pearl Harbor, then turn left on Fort Weaver Road (Route 76). This country lane leads to the plantation town of **Ewa.** With its busy sugar mill and trim houses, Ewa is an enchanting throwback to the days when sugar was king. It's a terrific town to just wander around in.

Near Oahu's southwest corner, Routes H-1 and 90 converge to become the Farrington Highway (Route 93). This road heads up the west coast through the tableland which separates the **Waianae Range** and the ocean. It's a region of stark beauty, resembling the Southwest, with rocky crags and cactus-studded hills.

Hawaiian and Samoan farmers populate the Waianae coast. Since most of the other parts of Oahu have been developed, this region is one of the last strongholds for local culture. Residents here jealously guard the customs and traditions which they see slipping away in the rest of Hawaii. If you turn up Mailiilii Street in Waianae, you'll pass placid Hawaiian homesteads and farmlands. This side road also provides sweeping views of the mountains.

The highway continues along the coast past several beaches and parks. Across from Kaena Point State Park you'll come upon **Moi Hole,** a lava cavern large enough for exploring. And beyond that, where the road turns to dirt, lies **Yokohama Bay,** with its curving sand beach. **Kaena Point Satellite Tracking Station** sits atop the nearby mountains. The road past Yokohama is partially passable by auto, but it's very rough. If you want to explore **Kaena Point** from this side of the island, I recommend hiking. It's about two miles to the northwest corner of Oahu, past tidepools teeming with marine life.

Shopping

GREATER HONOLULU SHOPPING

Honolulu is *the* place to shop in all Hawaii. This city by the sea not only supports over half Hawaii's populace, but most of its stores and businesses as well. Honolulu is the only large metropolitan area within a 2,000-mile radius, so whatever merchandise you seek can most likely be found here.

WAIKIKI

This tourist mecca is a great place to look but not to buy. Browsing the busy shops is like studying a catalog of Hawaiian handicrafts. It's all here. You'll find everything but bargains. With a few noteworthy exceptions, the prices include the unofficial tourist surcharges that merchants worldwide levy against visitors. Windowshop Waikiki, but plan on spending your shopping dollars elsewhere.

One Waikiki shopping area I do recommend is **Duke's Lane.** This alleyway, running from Kalakaua to Kuhio near the International Market Place, may be the best place in all Hawaii to buy coral and jade jewelry. Either side of the Lane is flanked by mobile stands selling rings, necklaces, earrings, stick pins, bracelets, etc. It's a prime place to barter for tiger eyes, opals, and mother-of-pearl pieces.

The main shopping scene is in the malls. **Waikiki Shopping Plaza** (2270 Kalakaua Avenue) has six floors of stores and restaurants. Here are jewelers, sundries, and boutiques, plus specialty shops like **Waldenbooks** (922-4154), with an excellent line of paperbacks as well as bestsellers, and **Asia Arts and Furniture** (922-2655).

Then there's **King's Village** (on Kaiulani Avenue between Kalakaua Avenue and Kuhio Avenue), a mock Victorian town which represents how Britain might have looked had the nineteenth-century English invented polyethylene. The motif may be trying to appear antiquated, but the prices are unfortunately quite contemporary.

International Market Place (2330 Kalakaua Avenue) is my favorite browsing place. With tiny shops and vending stands spotted around the sprawling grounds, it's a relief from the claustrophobic shopping complexes. There's an old banyan spreading across the market, plus thatched treehouses, a carp pond, brick sidewalks, and woodfront stores. You won't find many bargains, but the sightseeing is priceless.

The large hotels usually contain shopping plazas too. Best among these are **Hemmeter Center** in the Hyatt Regency Hotel (2424 Kalakaua Avenue) and the **Rainbow Bazaar** at the Hilton Hawaiian Village (2005 Kalia Road). Here you'll find that the quality is as fine and the fashions are as elegant as the prices are high.

DOWNTOWN HONOLULU

Ala Moana Center, on the outskirts of Waikiki (1450 Ala Moana Boulevard), is reputedly the world's largest shopping center. This multi-tiered complex has practically everything. Where most self-respecting malls have one department store, Ala Moana has four: **Sears** (947-0211), **Penney's** (946-8068), Hawaii's own **Liberty House** (941-2345), and a Japanese emporium called **Shirokiya** (941-9111). There's also a **Woolworth's** (941-3005) and **Long's Drug Store** (941-4433), both good places to buy inexpensive Hawaiian curios. For imported goods you might try **India Imports International** (949-5777); and for contemporary fashion there is **Benetton** (943-0629). You'll also find an assortment of stores selling liquor, antiques, tennis and golf supplies, stationery, leather goods, cameras, shoes, art, tobacco, etc., etc., etc.

And, in a paragraph by itself, there's **Honolulu Book Shop** (941-2274). Together with its sister store downtown at 1001 Bishop Street, this is Hawaii's finest bookstore. Both branches contain excellent selections of Hawaiian books, bestsellers, paperbacks, magazines, and out-of-town newspapers.

Honolulu's newest and most chic shopping mall is **Ward Centre** (1200 Ala Moana Boulevard), an ultra-modern facility. Streamlined and stylized, it's an elite enclave filled with designer shops and sleek restaurants. In addition to boutiques and children's shops, there's a bookstore, a contemporary art gallery called **Images International of Hawaii** (538-6755), and a gourmet grocery, **R. Field Wine Co.** (521-4043). Adorned with blond-wood facades, brick walkways, and brass-rail restaurants, the shopping complex provides a touch of Beverly Hills.

Ala Moana may be the biggest, but **Ward Warehouse** is another very interesting shopping center. Located on Ala Moana Boulevard between

Waikiki and downtown Honolulu, it's worth visiting if only for one store—
Rare Discovery (524-4811). Filled with ingenious decorations and unique
art, this is the most fascinating shop I've ever entered. You've probably
seen glass menageries and wood jigsaw puzzles, but how about ceramic
penguins or fiber artworks? There are ceramic aquariums, beautifully
carved wood boxes, Oriental jewelry, and other creations.

Scattered around town are several other shops that I recommend you
check out. **Cost Less Imports**, at 2525 South King Street near the University of Hawaii's Manoa campus, has a warehouse full of bargains from all
over the world. It's a great place to pick up wickerware, ceramics, and
handcrafted items.

At **Lanakila Crafts** (1809 Bachelot Street; 531-0555) most of the
goods are made by the disabled, and the craftsmanship is superb. There
are shell necklaces, woven handbags, monkeypod bowls, and homemade
dolls. You'll probably see these items in other stores around the islands,
with much higher price tags than here at the "factory."

The **Foundry Arts Center** (899 Waimanu; 538-7288) consists of a
network of artisans producing ceramics, metal sculptures, jewelry,
stained glass, photographs, paintings, and leather goods. It's a very
informal affair: you can tour the workshops and sometimes bargain with
craftspeople for their wares.

If you're seeking Oriental items, then Chinatown is the place. Spotted throughout this tumbledown sector are small shops selling statuettes,
pottery, woodcrafts, and other curios. It's also worthwhile wandering
through the **Cultural Plaza,** on the corner of Beretania and Maunakea
streets. This mall is filled with Oriental jewelers, bookstores, and
knickknack shops.

For secondhand items you might try the flea market at the **Kam
Drive-In Theatre** (98-850 Moanalua Road; 488-5822). It's a great place to
barter for bargains, meet local folks, and find items you'll never see in
stores. It's open Monday, Wednesday, Saturday, Sunday, and most
holidays.

WINDWARD COAST

Pine Grove Village, on Kalanianaole Highway (Route 72) in
Waimanalo, features small outdoor stalls selling jewelry and other locally-
made products.

Then, north of Kaneohe on Route 83, you'll pass **Oriental Antiques
and Objets d'Art** (47-659 Kamehameha Highway; 923-2240). It's by ap-
pointment only, thank you, to view the collection of Asian art pieces here.

Up in Punaluu, the **Punaluu Art Center** (53-352 Kamehameha Highway; 237-8049) has some very fine sculptures, paintings, weavings,
ceramics, and silkscreens created by local artists.

Of course the trendy shoppers head for the burgeoning town of Haleiwa. During the past several years boutiques and galleries have mushroomed throughout this once somnolent town. Now there's a modern shopping center and an array of shops. Since Haleiwa is a center for surfers, it's a good place to buy sportswear and aquatic equipment.

Nightlife

Honolulu is definitely the nightlife capital of Hawaii. You'll find most every brand of entertainment here, from unique Hawaiian slack-key guitar music to the latest rock sounds. There are waterfront watering holes where you can relax and quietly watch the moon over Diamond Head, and Honolulu also sports swinging clubs that are ablaze with lights and activity until four in the morning.

Hawaii has a strong musical tradition, kept alive by a number of excellent groups performing their own compositions as well as old Polynesian songs. I'm not talking about the "Blue Hawaii"–"Tiny Bubbles"–"Beyond the Reef" medleys that draw tourists in droves, but *real* Hawaiian music as performed by the Brothers Cazimero, Keola and Kapono Beamer, Marlene Sai, Melveen Leed, and others.

If you spend any time in Honolulu, don't neglect to check out such authentic sounds. One or more of these musicians will probably be playing at a local club. Consult the daily newspapers, or, if you want to hear these groups before paying to see them, listen to KCCN at 1420 on the radio dial. This all-Hawaiian station is the home of island soul.

One place that frequently headlines talented Hawaiian performers is the **Garden Lanai** at the Ala Moana Hotel (410 Atkinson Drive; 955-4811). Cover.

Over at **Nick's Fishmarket** (2070 Kalakaua Avenue; 955-6333) the hot sounds of a contemporary band draw flocks of local folks and visitors alike.

For a quiet drink in an intimate atmosphere, I recommend **The Library** (2552 Kalakaua; 922-6611). This relaxing piano bar is located in the Hawaiian Regent Hotel, next door to the renowned Third Floor Restaurant. It's a choice spot to sit back and recollect at the end of an enervating day. Good drinks, good service—who could ask for more?

Trappers, nestled in a corner of the plush Hyatt Regency Hotel (2424 Kalakaua Avenue; 922-9292), is another intimate bar. It's a split-level affair, beautifully appointed, with private booths. The music is low-key, the mood mellow, and the staff friendly.

The **Oahu Bar** (Sheraton Waikiki Hotel, 2255 Kalakaua Avenue; 922-5566) is a congenial spot. Situated right on Waikiki Beach, this cozy club features live entertainment and spectacular ocean views every night of the week.

Waikiki is definitely rock and roll central. Every big hotel seems to have converted a dusty ballroom or sluggish restaurant into a throbbing strobe-lit dance hall. Out-of-town folks and locals alike pack these electric night spots. **Spat's,** the Hyatt Regency's (2424 Kalakaua Avenue; 922-9292) contribution to the latest dance craze, is the poshest. With stuffed chairs, oil paintings, and stained glass, it looks more the part of a fashionable restaurant. And until the deejay cranks up his victrola nightly at 10, that's exactly what it is. But after the witching hour, anything goes. Cover; no minimum; dress slacks and closed-toe shoes required.

The Point After (Hawaiian Regent Hotel, 2552 Kalakaua Avenue; 922-6611) is another hot young club. As you might guess from the name, the design motif is football, with more flashing lights than an exploding scoreboard. There is a cover charge.

After the Point After you can ride 30 stories in a tubular glass elevator to **Annabelle's,** a luxurious club located atop the Ilikai Hotel (1777 Ala Moana Boulevard; 949-3811). Starting early in the evening with big band sounds, the place segues into pop music and rocks 'til 4 a.m. Cover.

The Jazz Cellar (205 Lewers Street; 923-9952) specializes in loud rock, serious drinking, and lively crowds rather than jazz. It's a top spot for a hot night. Cover charge.

Then there's **The Noodle Shop** at the Waikiki Sand Villa Hotel (2375 Ala Moana Boulevard; 922-4744). The big draw at this tiny club is Frank DeLima, one of the island's top comedians. Cover charge plus two drink minimum.

Over by the University of Hawaii's Manoa campus, there's **Anna Banana's** (2440 South Beretania Street; 946-5190). A popular hangout for years, this wildly decorated spot has live entertainment several nights a week. There's likely to be a local band cranking it up and a local crowd headed for the dance floor. Cover charge.

The gay scene centers at several clubs around Waikiki's Kuhio Avenue. **Hamburger Mary's** (2109 Kuhio Avenue; 922-6722) is the most dynamic. There's no dancing, just drinking and carousing. It's simply a U-shaped bar with a side patio, but the place draws huge crowds.

Together with **Hula's Bar and Lei Stand** (923-0669) next door, it forms an unbeatable duo. Hula's, a disco complete with strobe-lit dance floor, rocks nightly until 2 a.m. No cover.

The Honolulu red-light scene centers around Hotel Street in Chinatown. This sleazy, run-down strip is lined with hostess bars and adult book stores. Prostitutes, straight and gay, are on the street regularly.

Well-heeled prostitutes work Waikiki around Kalakaua Avenue and near the big hotels. The trade here is much more tourist-oriented. Along Hotel Street it's aimed primarily at sailors.

Oahu Addresses and Phone Numbers

OAHU ISLAND

County Department of Parks and Recreation—Honolulu Municipal Building, 650 South King Street, Honolulu (523-4525)

Division of State Parks—1151 Punchbowl Street, Room 310, Honolulu (548-7455)

Hawaii Visitors Bureau—2270 Kalakaua Avenue, Honolulu (923-1811)

Weather Report—(836-0234 for Honolulu; 836-0121 for entire island; 836-1952 for surfing weather)

HONOLULU

Ambulance—911

Barber Shop—Waikiki Barber Shop, 2863 Kalakaua Avenue (923-0374)

Books—Honolulu Book Shops, Ala Moana Center or 1001 Bishop Street (941-2274 or 537-6224)

Fire Department—911

Fishing Supplies—K. Kaya Fishing Supplies, 901 Kekaulike (538-1578)

Hardware—McCully Hardware, 1111 McCully Street (941-5990)

Hospital—Queen's Medical Center, 1301 Punchbowl (538-9011)

Laundromat—Outrigger Laundromat, 2335 Kalakaua Avenue (923-0711)

Library—478 South King Street (548-4775)

Pharmacy—Long's Drugs, Ala Moana Center, 1450 Ala Moana Boulevard (941-4433)

Photo Supply—Francis Camera Shop, Ala Moana Center, 1450 Ala Moana Boulevard (946-2879)

Police Department—1455 South Beretania Street (911)

Post Office—330 Saratoga Road (941-1062)

WINDWARD COAST

Ambulance—911

Fire Department—911

Laundromat—Kailua Laundromat, Aulike Street, Kailua (261-9201)

Police Department—1455 South Beretania Street (911)

NORTH SHORE

Ambulance—911

Fire Department—911

Police Department—911

LEEWARD COAST

Ambulance—911

Fire Department—911

Laundromat—Waianae Speed Wash, 85-802 Farrington Highway (696-9115)

Police Department—911

CHAPTER NINE

Kauai

Seventy miles northwest of Oahu, across a storm-wracked channel which long protected against invaders, lies Kauai. If ever an island deserved to be called a jewel of the sea, this Garden Isle is the one.

Across Kauai's brief thirty-three-mile expanse lies a spectacular and wildly varied landscape. Along the north shore is the Hanalei Valley, a lush patchwork of tropical agriculture, and the rugged Na Pali Coast with cliffs rising 2,700 feet above the boiling surf. Here, among razor-edged spires and flower-choked gorges, the producers of the movie *South Pacific* found their Bali Ha'i. To the east flows the fabled Wailua River, a sacred area to Hawaiians.

Along the south coast stretch the matchless beaches of Poipu, with white sands and an emerald sea that seem drawn from a South Seas vision. These give way to rustic Hanapepe, an agricultural town asleep at the turn of the century, and Waimea, where in 1778 Captain James Cook became the first Westerner to tread Hawaiian soil.

In the island's center, Mount Waialeale rises over 5,000 feet to trap a continuous stream of dark-bellied clouds which spill 500 inches of rain annually, making this gloomy peak the wettest spot on earth. Yet to the west, just a thunderstorm away, lies a barren landscape seemingly borrowed from Arizona and featuring the 3,600-foot deep Waimea Canyon, the Grand Canyon of the Pacific.

From Lihue, Kauai's largest and most important city, Route 50 travels to the south while Route 56 heads along the north shore. Another highway climbs past Waimea Canyon into the mountainous interior.

Papayas, taro, and bananas grow in lush profusion along these roads, but sugar is still Kauai's major crop, extending for miles from the foothills to the sea's edge. Kauai Buds, marijuana vying with Maui Wowie in potency, is another important, though unofficial, cash crop. Tourism is also becoming increasingly vital to the island's 43,000 population. The tourist industry has multiplied in the past two decades, and the ominous

(Text continued on page 304.)

301

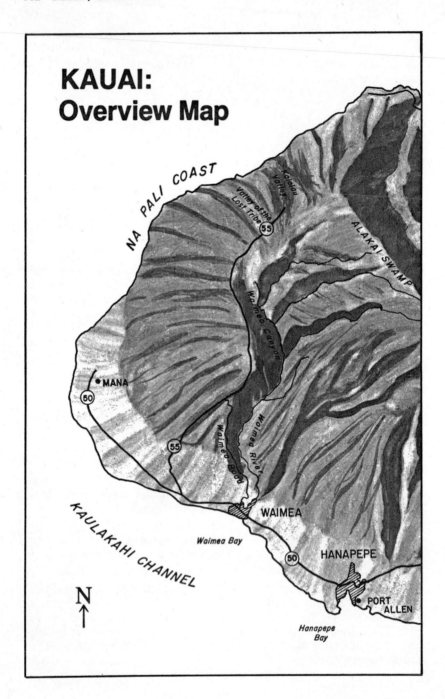

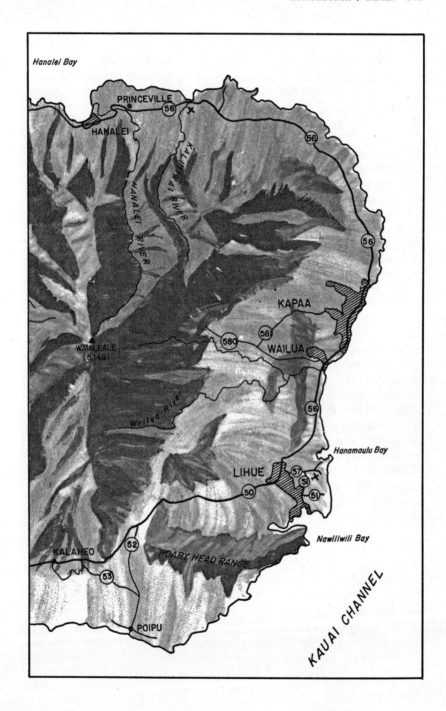

construction of condos near Poipu and Hanalei threatens to turn Kauai into the Maui of the 1990s. But the Garden Isle still offers hidden beaches and remote valleys to any traveler possessing a native's sensibility.

Historically, Kauai is Hawaii's premier island—the first to be created geologically and the first "discovered" by white men. Following Captain Cook's arrival in 1778, explorers continued to visit the island periodically. Ten years later, settlers began to arrive, and in 1820 the first missionaries landed in the company of Prince George, son of Kauai's King Kaumualii.

Kauai was the only island not conquered by Kamehameha the Great when he established the Hawaiian kingdom. Thwarted several times in landing an attack force, he finally won over Kaumualii by diplomacy in 1810.

But Kauai's most fascinating history is told by mythmakers recounting tales of the Menehunes, the Hobbits of the Pacific. These miniature forest people labored like giants to create awesome structures which still baffle archaeologists. Mysterious ruins such as the Menehune Fishpond outside Lihue date back before the Polynesians and are attributed by scientists to an earlier unknown race. Supernaturally strong and very industrious, the Menehunes worked only at night, completing each project by dawn or else leaving it forever unfinished. Several times they made so much noise in their strenuous laboring that they frightened birds as far away as Oahu.

They were a merry, gentle people with ugly red faces and big eyes set beneath long eyebrows. Two to three feet tall, each practiced a trade in which he was a master. They inhabited caves, hollow logs, and banana-leaf huts, and eventually grew to a population of 500,000 adults.

Some say the Menehunes came from the lost continent of Mu, which stretched across Polynesia to Fiji before it was swallowed by floods. Where they finally traveled to is less certain. After the Polynesians settled Kauai, the Menehune king, concerned that his people were intermarrying with an alien race, ordered the Menehunes to leave the island. But many, unwilling to depart so luxurious a home, hid in the forests. There, near hiking trails and remote campsites, you may see them even today.

Easy Living

Transportation

ARRIVAL

Visiting Kauai means flying to the jetport near Lihue or the landing strip near Princeville. Unless you're staying on the north shore, fly to the more centrally located Lihue Airport. **Aloha Airlines, Hawaiian Airlines,** and **Mid Pacific Air** operate here; **Princeville Airways** flies in and out of

Princeville. For those interested in flying direct from the mainland United States to Kauai, **United Airlines** provides regular service from the West Coast.

The Lihue Airport has a cafeteria, jukebox-blaring cocktail lounge, lockers, book stall, and flower shop. What you won't find are buses, far more useful to most travelers than books and flowers. Transportation (it's two miles into town) requires renting a car, hailing a cab, hitching, or hoofing. Cabs generally charge about $4 to Lihue. At Princeville, it's either walk or rent a vehicle from **Avis Rent-A-Car** (826-9773), which is the only rental agency in these parts.

CAR RENTALS

Across the street from the terminal at Lihue Airport you'll find a series of booths containing car rental firms. These include **Watase's U-Drive** (245-3251), **Dollar Rent-A-Car** (245-4708), **National Car Rental** (245-3502), **Robert's Hawaii Rent-A-Car** (245-4008), **Alamo Rent-A-Car** (245-8953), **American International Rent-A-Car** (245-9541), **United Rental** (245-8894), **Avis Rent-A-Car** (245-3512), **Budget Rent-A-Car** (245-4021), and, of course, America's most popular (and most expensive) agency, **Hertz Rent-A-Car** (245-3356). There are also rental companies located in resort areas like Poipu and Wailua.

Budget-priced agencies located outside the airport include **Thrifty Rent-A-Car** (245-7388) and **Tropical Rent-A-Car** (245-6988). Or if you're up for it, try **Rent-A-Wreck** (245-4755). These outfits are located in Lihue.

Several of these outfits offer lower daily rental charges, but tack on a mileage charge. This can prove economical if the car sits while you hike or camp; otherwise the mileage charge will quickly offset the low daily rate. So I usually recommend avoiding the mileage charge and just paying a standard daily fee. (See Chapter 2 for a complete explanation of car rentals in Hawaii.)

JEEP RENTALS

Rent-A-Jeep (3137-A Kuhio Highway, Lihue; 245-9622) has 4-wheel-drive vehicles. However, most Kauai roads, including cane roads, are accessible by car so you probably won't need a jeep.

MOTOR SCOOTER RENTALS

Slow but sporting, mopeds are as much a form of entertainment as transportation. I don't recommend them for getting around the island, but if you'd like to buzz around the neighborhood, contact **South Shore Activities** (next door to the Sheraton Hotel in Poipu; 742-6873).

BICYCLING

There are no bikeways on Kauai and most roads have very narrow shoulders, but the Garden Isle is still the most popular island for bicycling.

(Text continued on page 308.)

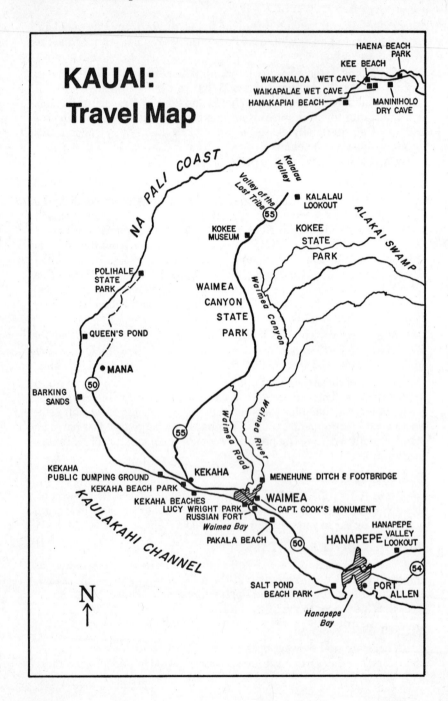

KAUAI:
Travel Map

NA PALI COAST

HAENA BEACH PARK
KEE BEACH
WAIKANALOA WET CAVE
WAIKAPALAE WET CAVE
HANAKAPIAI BEACH
MANINIHOLO DRY CAVE

Kalalau Valley

Valley of the Lost Tribe

55

KALALAU LOOKOUT

ALAKAI SWAMP

KOKEE MUSEUM

KOKEE STATE PARK

POLIHALE STATE PARK

WAIMEA CANYON STATE PARK

Waimea Canyon

QUEEN'S POND

MANA

50

BARKING SANDS

Waimea River

Waimea Road

KEKAHA PUBLIC DUMPING GROUND

KEKAHA BEACH PARK

KEKAHA

KEKAHA BEACHES
LUCY WRIGHT PARK
RUSSIAN FORT
Waimea Bay
PAKALA BEACH

55

MENEHUNE DITCH & FOOTBRIDGE

WAIMEA
CAPT. COOK'S MONUMENT

KAULAKAHI CHANNEL

50

HANAPEPE

HANAPEPE VALLEY LOOKOUT

54

SALT POND BEACH PARK

PORT ALLEN

Hanapepe Bay

N
↑

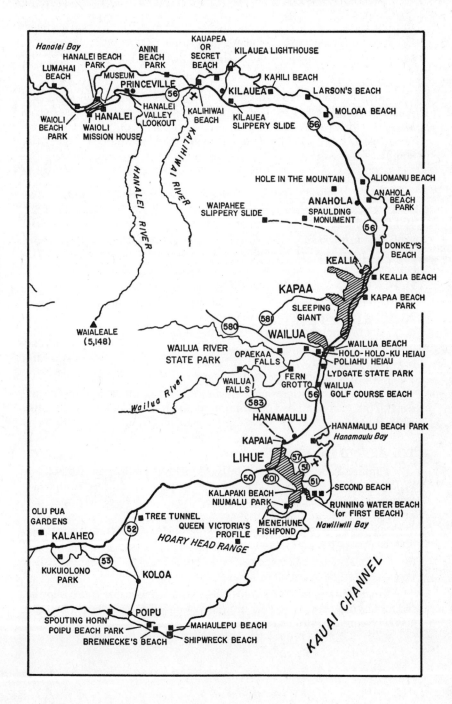

Roads are good, and except for the steep twenty-mile climb along Waimea Canyon, the terrain is either flat or gently rolling. The spectacular scenery and network of public parks make this a cyclist's dream.

RENTALS

Aquatics Kauai (733 Kuhio Highway, Kapaa; 822-9213) rents 15-speed mountain bikes as well as tandems and five-speed bikes. **South Shore Activities** (next door to the Sheraton Hotel in Poipu; 742-6873) also rents bikes. In Hanalei try **Pedal 'n Paddle** (Ching Young Village; 826-9069).

REPAIRS

The following shops do repair work and sell accessories: **Central Bike Shop** (2-2488 Kaumalii Highway, Kalaheo; 332-9122); **Kawamoto's** (1322 Kuhio Highway, Kapaa; 822-4771); and **Bicycles Kauai** (1379 Kuhio Highway, Kapaa; 822-3315). Any of these shops should be capable of supplying you with needed parts and taking care of any emergency repairs.

HITCHHIKING AND WALKING

Hitching is permitted on Kauai provided you stay off the paved portion of the road. Like everywhere else, luck hitching varies here. I had no problem going back and forth between Lihue Airport and town, but elsewhere found it slow going. In the summer there will be many extended thumbs along the road, particularly in the Hanalei area. The folks who pick up strangers are usually fellow tourists or local *haoles*.

Walking on the highways is permitted against the flow of traffic and well off the roadways, but I encountered no problem walking with traffic while thumbing.

TOURS AND DROPOFFS

Papillon Helicopters (826-6091), **Menehune Helicopter Tours** (245-7705), **Garden Island Aviation** (245-1844), and several other companies feature a whirlybird's-eye view of the island. Their aerial tours will provide you with unique glimpses of Kauai.

Na Pali Coast Zodiac Boat Expeditions (826-9371), **Hawaiian World** (826-9045), and **Blue Odyssey Adventures** (826-9033) offer zodiac boat tours of Kalalau and along the rest of the Na Pali Coast; the first outfit also provides drop-off services for hikers.

Kauai Mountain Tours (245-7224) has 4-wheel-drive tours into the mountains of Kokee State Park around Waimea Canyon. These tours can also be combined with boat and helicopter excursions.

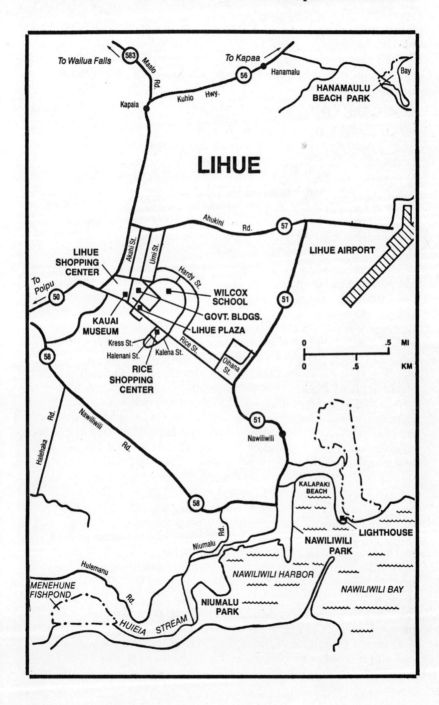

Hotels

The hotel scene on Kauai is centered around Lihue, Poipu Beach, and Wailua, with a few other accommodations scattered in the Waimea and Hanalei areas.

LIHUE AREA HOTELS

Lihue Budget and Moderate Hotels: Three low-cost facilities are located just two miles from the airport and a block or two from downtown Lihue.

At the **Tip Top Motel** (3173 Akahi Street; 245-2333) you'll find bare but clean rooms with tile floors, stall showers, and air-conditioning. The sheer size of this three-story, two-building complex makes it impersonal by Kauai standards, but I found the management to be very warm. You'll have to eat meals in the adjoining restaurant or elsewhere, since none of the rooms have kitchenettes. Budget.

Set on the same quiet street, in a courtyard shaded by lichee and plumeria trees, is the **Ahana Motel Apartments** (3115 Akahi Street; 245-2206). The clean, well-lighted rooms have a television, fan, and either a shower or a tub. Mr. and Mrs. Ah Sau Ahana, the pleasant Japanese owners, charge reasonable rates for the standard rooms as well as those with all-electric kitchens. Often, adjoining rooms can be connected, making them ideal for families or large groups. Budget.

The **Hale Pumehana Hotel** (3083 Akahi Street; 245-2106) has fifteen rooms without kitchenettes at its location in downtown Lihue. How people can fit comfortably in one of these tiny enclosures is beyond my comprehension. In addition to being slightly claustrophobic, the rooms are unimaginatively decorated and offer no view. There are fans in each cubicle, necessary because of the lack of cross-ventilation. Somewhat noisy; conveniently located; equipped with a comfortable lobby with television and wicker furniture. Budget.

The **Motel Lani** (4240 Rice Street; 245-2965), a block from the Rice Shopping Center, has ten cozy rooms facing a small patio where guests can lounge about in lawn chairs. The units are clean and comfortable, though sparsely furnished. About half are cross-ventilated; all have fans and refrigerators. This place has a noisy lobby (with television) just off busy Rice Street. Rooms with kitchenettes are hard to obtain, so you'll need to reserve these in advance. Rooms without kitchenettes are easier to book. Budget.

On a back street less than a half-mile from downtown Lihue there's a pleasant motel called **Hale Lihue** (2931 Kalena; 245-3151). Mr. Ramos, the current proprietor of the facility, rents rooms without kitchenettes and others which are equipped both with kitchens and air-conditioning.

The rooms are comfortably furnished and well-kept. There's a lobby with television plus a lovingly tended garden in the front yard. Budget.

Just around the corner, at 4271 Halenani Street, is the **Hale Ka Lani Motel** (245-6021), which has rooms with or without kitchen facilities. Dirty walls, dark rooms, and a musty corridor were the first things I noticed. Then the owner led me back to a room filled with tires and old newspapers. "This," he confided, "is supposed to be the lobby." In the world of travel, this place is the last resort. Budget.

If you have wheels or like to walk, I heartily recommend heading a mile down Rice Street to the Nawiliwili area and checking in at the **Oceanview Motel** (245-6345). You'll find it near the corner of Rice Street and Wilcox Road, beautifully situated across the street from Nawiliwili Park, and a short stroll from lovely Kalapaki Beach. Rooms are bright, blandly decorated, and carpeted. Sorry, no kitchenettes, but each room has a refrigerator. There's a small lobby plus a television room. You'll hear occasional noise from passing trucks and planes. First- and second-floor rooms rent for a little less than the larger third-story accommodations. Children are welcome, and several of the large rooms are ideal for families. Ask Spike Kanja, the feisty proprietor, to show you his fish pond. Several dozen twenty-inch carp flash their colors around the pool. The oldest, Spike claims, is over thirty years old. Budget.

For local charm consider the **Kauai Inn** (245-2720), a 48-unit country-style inn set in a secluded neighborhood. You'll find it in Nawiliwili, near Niumalu Park and the harbor. Just take Rice Street to Nawiliwili, turn right on Route 58, then left on Niumalu Road. You'll find the inn on the corner of Hulemalu Street. The rooms are decorated in a Hawaiian motif and furnished with rattan tables and chairs. Add a tropical backdrop to these corrugated-roof buildings and you have a touch of the islands at a moderate price.

POIPU AREA HOTELS

Poipu Area Budget Hotels: The **YMCA of Kauai** (2080 Hoona Road; 742-1200) will rent you a shared sleeping space for a pittance. That's mighty inexpensive for a social-hall-sized room, large kitchen, two bathrooms, and a marvelous location near Poipu Beach. You can also camp on the grounds out in back. But take note: as this book went to press, the YMCA was looking for a new location, so you might find them elsewhere on the island.

One place for people wanting to rough it or to establish a base camp is **Kahili Mountain Park** (742-9921). Facing the Hoary Head Range and backdropped by Kahili Mountain, this 186-acre domain offers an easy compromise between hoteling and camping. The one- and two-bedroom cabins come equipped with lanai, private bathroom, and outdoor shower, plus a funky kitchen. Cooking utensils and bed linens are provided. Furnishings seem a bit spartan: the cement floors are uncarpeted and the sole decoration is the surrounding mountains. Thank God for nature. At this rustic resort you can rope-swing into the swimming pond, slip into a Japanese bath, hike the nearby trails, or relax around a fire in the main lodge. The facilities include cabinettes with shared baths as well as one-bedroom and two-bedroom cabins. Cabinettes are frequently available, but cabins should be reserved several months in advance. Write to Kahili Mountain Park, P.O. Box 298, Koloa, Kauai, HI 96756. The park is three miles from Koloa town and about one mile off Route 50. Cabinettes are budget and cabins are moderate in price.

Poipu Area Moderate and Deluxe Priced Hotels: Once upon a time the island's best vacation spot was the **Garden Isle Beach Apartments and Cottages** (R.R. 1, Box 355, Koloa, Kauai, HI 96756; 742-6717). That was before the 1982 hurricane flattened the complex's beachfront cottages. Still, there are some pretty cottages left. None are on the sand, but there are small studio units across the street from the beach that come equipped with refrigerators. You'll also find one-bedroom cottages. Overlooking the ocean, these hideaways are decorated with artistic flair: oil paintings and woven pieces adorn the walls, the furnishings are bamboo, and the kitchens are modern. Moderate to deluxe.

Similarly, **Koloa Landing Cottages** (2740 Hoonani Road; 742-1470) in Poipu offers guests a choice between two studio units and two cottages. These are attractive facilities with kitchens and rent in the moderate and deluxe ranges, respectively. With their garden setting and family atmosphere they evoke a comfortable sense of familiarity.

POIPU AREA CONDOMINIUMS

Sunset Kahili Condominium (1763 Pee Road, Poipu; 742-1691). One-bedroom apartments are $61 double, two bedrooms will run $83 for one to four people. Off season they are $51 and $71, respectively.

Kuhio Shores (2525 Lawai Beach Road, Koloa; 742-6120). One-bedroom apartments are $60 for one to four people; two bedrooms, two baths, costs $90 for one to six people. On the shore, but lacking a beach.

WAIMEA AREA HOTELS

The only accommodations on Kauai's west side are the ethereal facilities in Kokee State Park and the beachside cottages in Waimea.

Nestled in secluded woods between Waimea Canyon and the Kalalau Valley Lookout are the **Kokee Lodge Cabins** (335-6061). Each of the twelve mountain cabins, varying in size from one large room to two-bedroom complexes, comes with complete kitchen, fireplace (the only heat source), and rustic furnishings. These knotty-pine cabins, 3,700 feet above sea level, are a mountaineer's dream. With forest and hiking trails all around, Kokee is ideal for the adventurer. It gets chilly here, so bring a jacket or sweater. And try to make reservations for the cabins in advance; this place is popular! If you can't make future plans, you'll have to call and hope for a cancellation or last minute reservation. Rates are the same for each cabin; some cabins sleep as many as seven people. Budget.

Waimea Plantation Cottages (Route 50, Waimea; 338-1625) is one of the most alluring and secluded facilities on the entire island. Here in a spectacular coconut grove, fronting a salt-and-pepper beach, is a cluster of 1920s-era plantation cottages. Each has been carefully restored and many are furnished with period pieces. One, two, and multibedroom houses, with full kitchens, rent for moderate and deluxe prices; maid service is every fifth day. The place is a little gem out on Kauai's remote westside. I highly recommend it.

WAILUA AREA HOTELS

Wailua Area Budget Hotels: To get any closer to the water than the **Hotel Coral Reef** (822-4481), you'd have to pitch a tent in the sand. Located on Route 56 in Kapaa, it's within strolling distance of markets and restaurants and is an excellent choice for the wanderer without wheels. A splotchy lawn leads out to a comfortable strip of sand next to Kapaa Beach Park. If you check into the old section, the rooms are a little cheaper, but don't expect the Hilton. The rooms are clean, but the only things breaking the monotony of bare walls are water streaks and paint peels. Furnishings are sufficient, but the rooms lack cross-ventilation. The new section is quite modern. Here you can enjoy a touch of wood paneling, soft beds, refrigerator, and a delightful seascape just beyond those sliding glass doors. No kitchenettes.

Wailua Area Moderately Priced Hotels: The **Kauai Sands Hotel** (822-4951) costs a little more, but it's still a bargain. This beachfront accommodation (at 420 Papaloa Road near the Coconut Plantation in Kapaa) is part of the only hotel chain in the world owned by a Hawaiian family, the Kimis. You'll find a relaxed and spacious lobby, pool well-tended lawn, carpeting, lanai, imaginative decor, and a touch of Hawaiiana, but unfortunately no ocean views.

The nearby **Kauai Beach Boy** (822-3441), a link in the Amfac Resorts hotel chain, is another extremely appealing place. Set between a white-sand beach and the Coconut Plantation mall, it's popular with swimmers and shoppers alike. There's a pool, bar, and shuffleboard courts amid the hotel's central grounds, plus a windswept lobby with adjoining shops and restaurant. For pleasant surroundings near the center of the action, it's definitely among the area's top choices. The rooms are air-conditioned and include televisions, refrigerators, and lanais. The decor is quite tasteful, and the rates, considering what the hotel provides, are reasonable.

WAILUA AREA CONDOMINIUMS

Wailua Bay View (320 Papaloa Road, Kapaa; 822-3651). One-bedroom apartments, $88 for up to four people; three-night minimum stay. Ocean view.

Kapaa Sands (380 Papaloa Road, Kapaa; 822-4901). Studio apartments, $49 single or double, $59 for an ocean view. Two-bedroom apartments, $69 (one to four people); $79 for an ocean view.

Mokihana of Kauai (796 Kuhio Highway, Kapaa; 822-3971). Studio apartments run $45 single or double. These units are supplied with a hotplate and small refrigerator. Oceanfront.

Kauai Kailani (856 Kuhio Highway, Kapaa; 822-3391). Two-bedroom apartments, $55 single or double; $60 for three or four; $65 for five people. A lot of square footage for the money. (Sleeps up to 5.) There's one catch—reservations are difficult to obtain.

HANALEI AREA HOTELS AND CONDOMINIUMS

The North Shore is short on bargains, but at **Hanalei Apartments Hotel** (Route 56, Hanalei; 826-9333) there are studio units with kitchenettes available at moderate prices. They are attractive, well-maintained rooms with woven lauhala facing on some walls, carpeting, and decorative prints. They sit amid a garden 100 yards from the beach.

At the YMCA's **Camp Naue** (P.O. Box 1786, Lihue, Kauai, HI 96766; 742-1200), located beachfront in Haena, there are dormitory accommodations at budget prices. Kitchen utensils are available but bring your own bedding. There is also an adjacent area for camping.

The only other reasonably-priced resting places around Hanalei are the condos. In the Princeville area, a few miles south of Hanalei, are several: The **Makai Club** (524-5972) has multiunit cottages from $100 double; **Pali Ke Kua** (826-9066) offers one-bedroom apartments for $60 and up; **Hanalei Bay Resort** (531-5323) features similar accommodations from $90.

Hanalei Colony Resort (on Route 56 in Hanalei; 826-6235) is the only oceanfront condominium and the most highly recommended. Two-bedroom apartments, $70 single or double; $85 ocean view; $115 oceanfront; $12 each additional guest.

Restaurants

LIHUE AREA RESTAURANTS

Lihue Budget Restaurants: Lihue is rich in low-cost restaurants. For the money, the best breakfast spot on the island is **Ma's Family** (4277 Halenani Street; 245-3142). This nondescript cafe makes up in clientele what it lacks in physical beauty. Early in the morning the place is crowded with Hawaiians on their way to the cane fields. In the world of breakfasts, this is the bargain basement. Or if you want to go Hawaiian at lunch, order a *lau lau, poi,* and salmon dish. Closed for dinner.

What Ma's is to breakfast, **Hamura Saimin** (2956 Kress; 245-3271) is to lunch and dinner. It's just around the corner, so you're liable to see the same faces lining Hamura's curving counter. When I ate there the place was packed, but I was the only *turista* around. I had the *Saimin* Special, a combination of noodles, won tons, eggs, meat, onion, vegetables, and fish cake in a delicious broth.

Lihue also has numerous take-out joints and snack bars which will satisfy you physically if not psychologically. Best bet is **Tony's Delicatessen** (2962-A Kress; 245-3244) which specializes in Japanese box lunches which are perfect for picnics. The box is actually something of a grab bag, with the contents changing daily; a typical meal would include chicken, teriyaki meat, rice balls, a vegetable dish, and hash. Open mornings only.

If you're in Nawiliwili, check out **Keoki's** (245-3260) near the Westin Kauai entrance. Keoki serves a variety of ethnic foods plus mainland standards. The **Harbor Village** across the street promises several good restaurants. This shopping complex was built several years ago, but hasn't gained a noted reputation yet. Nevertheless, the few restaurants here run the gamut from budget to bulging purse.

Lihue Moderately Priced Restaurants: For good food at even better prices, the town of Lihue is a prime spot. This is the Kauai county seat, and the center of most island business, so it contains numerous restaurants that cater largely to local folks. To the discerning diner, of course, that means you can enjoy outstanding cuisine and avoid tourist prices. Even if you're not staying around town, try to stop by for at least one meal during your Kauai sojourn.

At **The Eggbert's** (4483 Rice Street; 245-6325) you'll find more than just a clever name. Here you can create your own omelette, choosing any of 50 variations ranging from a Portuguese sausage concoction to the Vegetarian's Delight, a combination of garden delicacies including just about everything a green thumb can grow.

Judy's Okazu Saimin (245-2612), on the Lihue Shopping Center's lower level (Rice Street and Kuhio Highway), serves delicious breakfasts and lunches. *Saimin*, miso soup, and various teriyaki dishes are among the offerings. Even now that Judy has retired, this small cafe is still hard to top.

Across the street in the Haleko Shops marketplace are two cozy restaurants ideal for enjoying a quiet meal. The first (both in location and rating) is **Casa Italiana** (2989 Haleko Road; 245-9586), which features Italian cuisine in the form of veal, fresh homemade pasta, and seafood. With its open-air dining and torchlit surroundings, the Casa is simply lovely.

Step next door to **J.J.'s Broiler** (2971 Haleko Road; 245-3841), the older but smaller brother of J.J.'s Boiler Room up the coast. Potted plants and wrought-iron grillwork create a patio garden atmosphere. It's primarily a broiler menu here with beef kabob and numerous steak dishes, plus a salad bar. Dinner only.

Rather go Japanese? Try **Restaurant Kiibo** (245-2650) back in Lihue at 2991 Umi Street. The place used to be just a noodle house, but a remodeling job has changed the interior into a contemporary-style restaurant. The cuisine has also evolved. Today you'll find the lunch and dinner menu filled with yakitori, tempura, and tofu dishes as well as sushi and *sashimi*.

The **Barbeque Inn** (245-2921), at 2982 Kress Street, offers Asian dishes as well as all-American meals. Breakfasts at this comfortable establishment are pretty standard; the lunch menu changes daily and often includes seafood omelettes, Filipino plates, and curry dishes; at dinner there's steak, lobster, shrimp tempura, and scampi.

Another tourist favorite is the **Tip Top Cafe and Bakery** (3173 Akahi Street; 245-2333). You can take your pick of table, booth, or counter in this large and impersonal eatery. Breakfasts are inexpensive (and the macadamia nut pancakes are delicious). Lunch entrees are not very imaginative and have received negative reviews from readers. The dinner menu is limited, but priced comfortably. The well-known bakery serves delicious cakes and pies, plus macadamia nut cookies, the house specialty. My advice? Hit the bakery, skip the restaurant.

Down Rice Street on the shore of Nawiliwili Harbor sits the **Club Jetty** (245-4970). This cozy restaurant sports a view of both the busy harbor and the Hoary Head Mountains. There's live music later in the evening, and a Cantonese menu with a la carte plates as well as multicourse meals. They also serve steak and seafood dishes. I found the cooking adequate and the staff very friendly.

POIPU AREA RESTAURANTS

Poipu Area Budget and Moderately Priced Restaurants: "Snack bar" comes closer to describing the low-priced dining facilities here. This lovely beach area hosts no full-sized budget restaurants.

In Koloa, several miles from Poipu, there's the **Kauai Kitchens** snack bar (742-1712) next to the Big Save Market on Koloa Road. Budget.

Also in Koloa, on the road to Poipu, you might consider **Koloa Broiler** (5412 Koloa Road; 742-9122). Nothing fancy; it's a bright, airy cafe with a broil-your-own kitchen and adjoining bar. There's steak, beef kabob, *mahimahi*, chicken, fresh island fish, and hamburger to choose from. Of course the quality of the food depends on your own culinary abilities; this could prove to be Kauai's best (or worst) restaurant. The one thing you can bank on is that this family-style establishment will transform dining from a spectator sport to a way of meeting fellow chefs. Moderate.

Keoki's Paradise (Kiahuna Shopping Village; 742-7534) is a beautiful patio-style restaurant centered around a tropical garden and pond. Open for dinner only, they feature a steak-and-seafood menu at moderate cost. The setting alone makes it worth a visit.

Overlooking Poipu Beach is **Brennecke's Seaside Bar & Grill** (Hoona Road; 742-7588). Downstairs at this two-level dining spot you'll find a budget-priced snack bar serving sandwiches. The upper deck is occupied by an open-air restaurant which serves cold appetizers at lunch, then stokes the *kiawe* broiler for a dinner which includes several fresh fish dishes, steak, lobster, and seafood kebob. There's also pasta at this moderate-priced nook.

Poipu Area Deluxe Restaurants: My first choice in this ethereal realm is the **Plantation Gardens Restaurant** (742-1695) across the street from the Sheraton in Poipu. Despite rather modest furnishings, the open-air design here creates a sense of elegance. The view extends along a carefully tended cactus garden which encircles this old sugar planter's manor house. Only dinner is served; the evening menu features seafood and also offers steak, chicken, and prime rib dishes. If you'd like to dine well in a tropical garden setting, this old plantation is the perfect spot.

WAIMEA AREA RESTAURANTS

Traveling west toward Waimea Canyon and Barking Sands, you'll find the watering places decrease as rapidly as the rainfall. Most restaurants en route are cafes and take-out stands. If you're on a budget, you're in luck; if you're looking for an exclusive, elegant establishment, you'll find slim pickings out Waimea way.

Waimea Area Budget Restaurants: Hanapepe specializes in these places. Take the fork onto Hanapepe Road as you enter town. **Linda's** (335-5152) is on the left. From the breakfast menu you can order a full meal for practically nothing. At lunchtime there are sandwiches for even less, plus tasty platters. The menu changes every day, except for the beef stew, which draws folks from all around. Sorry, no dinner.

Back on Route 50 near the edge of town is the **Leeward Diner** (335-5231), a postage-stamp-sized eatery with breakfasts and lunch platters. This place is a real sleeper. When I went in it was elbow to armpit with local people. The manager told me no tourists eat there, so it may be just the place for free-wheeling adventurers.

In Waimea there's **Yumi's** (338-1731), a short-order restaurant with a rotating menu. They serve breakfast and lunch.

The only real sit-down establishment past Waimea is the **Traveler's Den II** (337-9922) on Kekaha Road in Kekaha. Even this is something of a plain Jane, but it does offer hearty breakfasts and lunches. There's an adjoining bar and a lunch menu with hot plates and sandwiches.

Waimea Area Moderately Priced Restaurants: The best restaurant along Route 50 is Hanapepe's **Green Garden Restaurant** (335-5422). Dining is indoors, but the tropical plants convey a genuine garden feeling. At breakfast you can enjoy eggs and hot cakes along with a steaming cup of coffee. The lunch menu features a broad selection of meat, seafood, and Asian platters, all priced comfortably. And for dinner the deliciously varied menu ranges from pork chow mein to rock lobster tail. I particularly enjoyed the seafood special, a platter of *mahimahi,* shrimp, oysters, and scallops. Children's portions are available.

Menehune Saimin (9875 Waimea Road, Waimea; 338-1163) is a little hole-in-the-wall with a take-out counter and a few booths. But the budget-priced dinners are excellent. Feast on teriyaki, won ton mein, beef sticks, and *saimin*.

The decor at **Wrangler's Restaurant** (Route 50, Waimea; 338-1218), as you might have guessed, is western. The old wagon wheels, dusty saddles, kerosene lanterns, and trophy horns evoke Hawaii's *paniolo* country. But the prize antiques here are the jukeboxes, which played 78's and featured tunes by Nat King Cole and Jimmy Dorsey. The food? At lunch they serve Mexican-style meals, platters, and hamburgers. For dinner there are also pork chops, steaks, and even lobster tails.

When you're up in the ethereal heights above Waimea Canyon, hungry as a bear after hibernation, you'll be mighty glad to discover **Kokee Lodge** (335-6061) in remote Kokee State Park. From the dining room of this homey hideaway you can gaze out at the surrounding forest; or step over to the lounge with its stone fireplace and *koa* bar. The breakfast and lunch menus are fairly standard with pancakes, egg dishes, and fresh fruit in the morning, and sandwiches, hamburgers, and special platters later in the day. Every Friday and Saturday they also serve dinner—a full-course affair with such entrees as teriyaki steak, Korean-style ribs, *mahimahi,* and Cornish game hen. There are also salads and special desserts, and for non-carnivores a vegetarian fettuccine dish. In addition to the bounteous fare, you'll find moderate prices and a friendly staff.

WAILUA AREA RESTAURANTS

Wailua Area Budget Restaurants: Traveling north from Lihue on Route 56, you'll come upon the **Big Wheel Snack Shop** (245-2536) in the same mall as the Hanamaulu Museum. Open from 4 a.m. to 10 p.m., it serves doughnuts, coffee, and tea.

There are short-order stands galore at the Market Place in Coconut Plantation (Route 56, Wailua). **Waldo's Chicken** (822-9572) has take-out chicken dinners. **Ramona's Mexican Restaurant** (822-5919) sells tacos and burritos. **Don's Deli and Picnic Basket** (822-7025) is the perfect stop for beach-goers. **J.J.'s Dog House** (822-9943), a poor cousin to J.J.'s steak houses, features good old American food like hot dogs and hot pastrami. The **Fish Hut** (822-1712) lives up to its name. The **Plantation Cookhouse** (822-4332) serves breakfast, lunch, and dinner, at budget prices. And **Sugar Mill Snacks** (822-9981) rounds it out for dessert. Any time from early morning until eight at night several of these stands will be open. An interesting way to dine here is by going from one to the next, nibbling small portions along the way.

The **Waipouli Delicatessen and Restaurant** (Route 56, Waipouli; 822-9311) is a small Japanese-style luncheonette owned by a delightful Asian woman.

The best hamburgers on the island are reputedly found at **Duane's Ono Burger** (822-9181) on Route 56 in Anahola. If you do a taste test, let me know the results.

Wailua Area Moderately Priced Restaurants: If it's atmosphere and a taste of the Orient you're after, reserve a tea room at the **Hanamaulu Cafe** (on Route 56 in Hanamaulu; 245-2511). My favorite is the garden room overlooking a rock-bounded pond filled with carp. Lunch and dinner are the same here, with an excellent selection of Japanese and Chinese dishes. There's also a sushi bar. Children's portions are available.

The Market Place in the Coconut Plantation (Route 56, Wailua) offers several dining possibilities in this price range. **J.J.'s Boiler Room** (822-4411) is a larger version of his Lihue broiler. J.J. really gets around. In fact, **J.J.'s Barbeque Smoke House** (822-1869) sits center stage in the Market Place. This pleasant, airy cafe runs the gamut from chicken to fish, beef to pork.

Hidden (but certainly not hiding) in the wings is the **Plantation Buffet House** (822-7714). Dim lighting, potted palms, tropical oil paintings, overhead fans—all these spell Polynesia. The surf-and-broiler menu begins in the moderate range and rises steadily. Lunch and dinner are excellent; the salad bar is the best around.

Up Kapaa way on Kuhio Highway in the center of town, there's a restaurant known to Mexican food aficionados for miles around. **El Cafe** (822-3362) draws a hungry crowd of young locals for lunch and dinner. The owners raise a lot of their own beef and vegetables, and they serve monstrous portions. If you're not hungry, order a la carte. If you are, choose from a succulent menu ranging from enchiladas to burritos to ribs. All meals can be converted to cater to vegetarians. Definitely worth checking out.

One of the loveliest dining spots hereabouts is **Kapaa Fish & Chowder House** (1639 Kuhio Highway, Kapaa; 822-7488). These creative restaurateurs have converted a warehouse into a collection of cozy rooms. Each is trimly decorated, comfortably furnished, and adorned with nautical items and an assortment of potted plants; the back room is a garden patio. The lunch offering includes fish burgers, clam burgers, chicken salad, and several Louies. For dinner there are stir-fry fish dishes, tiger prawns, calamari, lobster newburg, prime rib, steak, and chicken. Moderate.

Wailua Area Deluxe Priced Restaurants: For oceanfront dining it's hard to match the **Seashell Restaurant** (Kuhio Highway, Wailua; 822-

3632). This restaurant-in-the-round is an open-air affair resting directly above Wailua Beach. The menu is dinner only and features fresh island fish, New Zealand lobster, cioppino, steak, prawns, and prime rib.

HANALEI AREA RESTAURANTS

Hanalei Area Budget Restaurants: As beautiful and popular as Hanalei happens to be, the area possesses only a few low-priced facilities. If you've ever tried to find a place to stay here, you know how tight things can be. And the budget restaurant situation is not a whole lot better.

There are several luncheonettes: the **Hanalei Museum Snack Shop** (826-6483) has sandwiches and platters; there's Mexican food at **Papagayo Azul** (826-9442). Both are located in the center of Hanalei.

At breakfast there's an excellent spot called **West of the Moon Cafe** (Aku Road; 826-7460) that is open only in the morning. The specialties here are the baked goods—honey bran muffins, scones, coffee cakes, and other homemade delectables. They also feature a variety of omelettes and a scrambled tofu dish, served with homefried potatoes and sauteed onions. Budget.

Later in the day, stop by the **Black Pot Luau Hut Restaurant** (Aku Road; 826-9871) next door. Another low-key cafe, it offers plate lunches of corned beef or chicken *hekka*, an assortment of sandwiches, and local treats like *lau lau*, *kalua* pig, *poki*, and stir-fry. If you're feeling bold, order the multicourse luau plate. Budget.

Hanalei Area Moderately Priced Restaurants: **Tortilla Flats Restaurant & Cantina** (Princeville Center, Route 56; 826-7255) offers a tremendous variety of Mexican dishes at breakfast, lunch, and dinner. In addition to standard dishes like burritos, enchiladas, and tostadas, there are fish, shrimp, and scallop entrees.

The **Hanalei Shell House** (826-9301) in Hanalei is devoted to a small restaurant serving breakfasts complete with fresh fruit and homemade bran muffins. For lunch they serve up a pasta avocado salad, "sea sandwiches," and homemade carrot cake or cheesecake. There are also hamburgers, sandwiches, and salads. The dinner menu changes frequently, but might feature sauteed scallops, ginger beef, fettuccine, veal, and shrimp scampi. Very highly recommended.

Hanalei Area Deluxe Priced Restaurants: Hanalei dining facilities jump from one extreme to the other with few moderate-priced restaurants between. But there are three expensive establishments, located on Route 56, deserving a stretch in your budget.

At **Charo's** (adjacent to Hanalei Colony Resort on Route 56, five miles north of Hanalei; 826-6422) you'll discover the best of two worlds— oceanfront dining and good food. Owned by the renowned entertainer,

Charo, this breezy establishment sits in a secluded corner of Kauai. With tile floor, colorful furnishings, and bamboo decor, it's a great spot for drinking and dining. The dinner menu includes paella, fish Oscar, scampi, veal marsala, and prime rib. At lunch there are sandwiches and fresh fish dishes.

The **Tahiti Nui Restaurant** (826-6277) has a *luau* every Monday, Wednesday, and Friday night at 6:45 p.m. If you miss it, catch a taste of Polynesian cooking with their Hawaiian Plate, a combination of *kalua* pig, salmon, chicken, fish, *poi*, and sweet potato. And check out the bamboo-fringed lanai, or the lounge decorated with Pacific Island carvings and overhung with a thatch canopy. Best of all, strike up a conversation with Louise, the robust Tahitian who owns the place.

From the large aquarium in the foyer to the porthole windows to the Japanese fishing balls, the **Hanalei Dolphin Restaurant** (826-6113) presents an interesting aquatic decor. Built smack on the bank of the Hanalei River, this eatery offers a turf-and-surf menu which includes fresh fish, shrimp dishes, and New York steak. Open nightly from 6 until 10; no reservations are taken.

Grocery Markets

The best place to grocery shop on Kauai is at the **Big Save Markets** found throughout the island. Here you'll discover an unbeatable combination—the lowest prices plus the widest selection.

Lihue has by far the greatest number of grocery, health food, and fresh fish stores. This civic center is an ideal place to stock up for a camping trip, hike, or lengthy sojourn in an efficiency apartment.

LIHUE GROCERY STORES

In addition to the **Big Save Market** in the Rice Shopping Center (4300 block of Rice Street), Lihue also has a **Foodland** located in the Lihue Shopping Center (Rice Street and Kuhio Highway). The two are comparable in size and variety. At Big Save you do indeed save, not big, but enough to make me recommend it. It's open from 8 a.m. to 9 p.m. Monday through Saturday and from 8 a.m. to 8 p.m. on Sunday. Foodland is open from 7 a.m. to 11 p.m. every day of the week.

LIHUE HEALTH FOOD STORES

Hale O Health in the Rice Shopping Center (4300 block of Rice Street) has an excellent line of vitamins, juices, and bath supplies, plus natural foods and sandwiches.

LIHUE FRESH-FISH STORES

The **J and R Seafoods** shop, 4361 Rice Street, has fresh fish available.

LIHUE SPECIALTY SHOPS

Don't miss the **Sunshine Market** (★) every Friday afternoon in the parking lot of the town stadium (Hoolako Street) or the convention center (4191 Hardy Street). All the local folks turn out to sell homegrown produce, "talk story," and generally have a good time. It's a great place to buy island fruits and vegetables at bargain prices, and an even better spot to meet Kauai's farmers.

Love's Thrift Store (4401 Rice Street) sells day-old bakery products including delicious breads for about fifty percent off.

POIPU AREA GROCERY STORES

There's a **Big Save Market** on Koloa Road in Koloa. The store includes a dry goods section and is definitely the place to shop on the way to Poipu beach.

If you're already soaking up the sun at Poipu, you have two grocery options. **Brennecke's Mini-Mart** is conveniently situated on Hoona Road across the street from Poipu Beach Park. This mom 'n' pop business has liquor, cold drinks, and a limited selection of groceries. To increase your choices and decrease your food bill, head up Poipu Road to **Kukuiula Store** at the intersection of Poipu and Lawai Roads. This market offers prices nearly competitive with Big Save.

WAIMEA AREA GROCERY STORES

There are four **Big Save Markets** along Route 50. Traveling west from Lihue, the first is in **Kalaheo**, the next at the **Eleele Shopping Center,** in the center of **Waimea,** and in **Kekaha.**

The best place for groceries past Waimea is the Big Save Market or **Kekaha Store,** both on Kekaha Road in Kekaha.

WAILUA AREA GROCERY STORES

There's a **Big Save Market** on Route 56 at the Kapaa Shopping Center.

South of Kapaa, the **Kauai Variety Store** on Route 56 in Hanamaulu has a small grocery stock. To the north is the **Whaler's General Store** along Route 56 in Anahola. This well-stocked market is the largest store between Kapaa and Princeville.

WAILUA AREA HEALTH FOOD STORES

Ambrose's Kapuna Natural Foods, conveniently located on Route 56 in Waipouli, is a recommended shopping place for health food aficionados. At this store you should be able to locate herbs and spices, fresh fruits and vegetables, as well as other natural food items.

Considering that **Farm Fresh Produce** (Kuhio Highway and Kauwila Street) is just up the street in Kapaa, this area is the health capital of Kauai. Specializing in fresh island-grown produce, this shop is especially good for fruits and veggies.

WAILUA AREA SPECIALTY SHOPS

Cafe Espresso, at the Market Place in Coconut Plantation (Route 56, Wailua), has a good selection of coffees and teas as well as locally-preserved jams. There's also an espresso bar and an assortment of baked goods here.

WAILUA AREA FRESH-FISH STORES

Kuhio Fish Market (1390 Kuhio Highway, Kapaa) has a variety of fresh, smoked, and dried fish.

HANALEI AREA GROCERY STORES

Best place on the north shore is **Foodland** in the Princeville shopping complex just off Route 56. It's very well stocked and open from 7 a.m. to 11 p.m.

Hanalei supports one large grocery store on Route 56, **Big Save** in the Ching Young Village complex.

About four miles north of Hanalei, **Wainiha General Store** has a small assortment of food items.

HANALEI AREA HEALTH FOOD STORES

Hanalei Health & Natural Foods (Ching Young Village Shopping Center, Route 56, Hanalei) has an assortment of items.

HANALEI AREA SPECIALTY SHOPS

Banana Joe's Tropical Fruit Farm (2719 Kuhio Highway, Kilauea) has ripe, delicious fruits as well as smoothies, fruit salads, and dehydrated fruit. They can also arrange farm tours.

The Great Outdoors

The Sporting Life

CAMPING

To visit Kauai without enjoying at least one camping trip is to miss a splendid opportunity. This lovely isle is dotted with county and state parks which feature ideal locations and complete facilities. There are also many hidden beaches where unofficial camping is common.

Camping at **county parks** requires a permit. These are issued for four days and may be renewed once. You are allowed to camp four consecutive days at one county park and a total of twelve days at all county parks. Permits cost $3 per person per day; children under eighteen are free. Permits can be obtained weekdays at the Department of Finance, Parks Permit Section, 4280-A Rice Street, Lihue, Kauai, HI 96766 (245-1881). At all other times permits are issued by the Kauai Police Department, 3060 Umi Street, Lihue (245-6721). Permits from the police department are issued in person only.

State park permits are free. They allow camping five consecutive days at each site, and should be requested at least seven days in advance. These permits are issued by the Department of Land and Natural Resources, 3060 Eiwa Street, Lihue, Kauai, HI 96766 (245-4444).

The State Division of Forestry (245-4433) also maintains camping areas in the **forest reserves.** These are free; permits are available at the State Division of Forestry, 3060 Eiwa Street, Room 306, Lihue, Kauai, HI 96766. Camping is limited at each site. Check with the forest division for information.

Camping elsewhere on the island is officially prohibited but actually quite common. Local folks use discretion in selecting **hidden beaches,** marked here by (★)s, for camping, and so can you. By the way, an extra effort should be made to keep these areas clean. One of the best suggestions I've ever heard is to leave your campsite cleaner than when you arrived.

Rainfall is much heavier along the north shore than along the south, but be prepared for showers anywhere. The Kokee area gets chilly, so pack accordingly. And remember, boil or chemically treat all water from Kauai's streams. Water from some of these streams can cause dysentery, and none of the waterways are certified safe by the Health Department.

To rent or buy camping supplies and equipment, check with **Hanalei Camping & Backpacking** (Ching Young Village, Route 56, Hanalei; 826-6664). They have tents, packs, stoves, and other equipment available.

SKIN DIVING

Fathom Five Divers (Poipu Road, Poipu; 742-6991) and **Aquatics Kauai** (733 Kuhio Highway, Kapaa; 822-9422) rent both diving and snorkeling equipment. They also offer tours and instruction in scuba diving. To rent snorkeling equipment also try **South Shore Activities** (Poipu; 742-6873) and **Watersports Kauai** (Hanalei; 826-6981).

SURFING AND WINDSURFING

Summer breaks in the south and winter breaks in the north constitute the surfing scene here.

Progressive Expressions (5420 Koloa Road, Koloa; 742-6041) and **Waiohai Beach Services** (Waiohai hotel, Poipu; 742-7051) rent surfboards.

For windsurfing board rentals, lessons, or sales, try **Hanalei Joy** (3781 Kalii Place, Princeville; 826-6647), **Sailboards Kauai** (3470 Paena Loop, Lihue; 245-5955), or the **Waiohai Beach Services** (Waiohai hotel, Poipu; 742-7051).

FISHING

For deep sea fishing, consult **Alana Lynn Too** (Kapaa; 245-7446). For bass fishing in Kauai's lakes and streams contact **Bass Guides of Kauai** (Lihue; 822-1405).

OTHER SPORTS

BOATING

Kauai By Kayak (245-9662) paddles up the Huleia River to a wildlife refuge and **Luana of Hawaii** (826-9195) kayaks up the Hanalei River. For sailing tours along the coast contact **Captain Andy's Sailing Adventures** (822-7833) or **Bluewater Sailing** (822-0525).

GOLF

Westin Kauai Golf Course (Nawiliwili; 245-3631), **Kukuiolono Golf Course** (Kalaheo; 332-9151), **Princeville Makai Golf Course** (Princeville; 826-3580), and **Wailua Golf Course** (Wailua; 245-2163) provide facilities.

TENNIS

Call the **County Department of Parks and Recreation** (245-8821) for information on public courts, and the **Hawaii Visitors Bureau** (245-3971) for information on private courts.

HORSEBACK RIDING

For rides in the state forest reserve 1,300 feet above sea level try **High Gates' Ranch** (Wailua Homesteads; 822-3182). In the Hanalei area call **Pooku Stables** (Hanalei; 826-6777) for treks on the beach, to waterfalls, or a stunning view overlooking Hanalei Valley. In the Poipu area try **CJM Country Stables** (245-6666).

Beaches and Parks
(Plus Camping, Swimming, Snorkeling, Surfing, Fishing)

LIHUE BEACHES AND PARKS

Kalapaki Beach—This wide strand in front of the plush Westin Kauai Hotel is situated right on Nawiliwili Bay, a beautiful harbor. Kalapaki has an idyllic setting highlighted by the Hoary Head Mountain Range rising in the background.

Facilities: Nawiliwili Park, next to the beach, has a picnic area, restrooms, and showers. Snack bars are nearby. Be sure to check out the **Pine Tree Inn (★),** a small pavilion painted with local color.

Camping: None.

Swimming: Excellent.

Snorkeling: Fair.

Surfing: Beginner's surfing is best in the right center of Nawiliwili Bay. Right slide. More experienced surfers will find good breaks next to the rock wall near the lighthouse. Left slide. There's also good surfing on the right side of the bay. Nicknamed "Hang Ten," these breaks are a good place for nose-riding. Left slide.

Fishing: Both off the pier and near the lighthouse are good spots for mullet, big-eyed scad, *papio,* bonefish, and threadfin; sometimes *ulua, oama,* and red bigeye can be caught here, too.

Getting there: Take Rice Street to Nawiliwili Park. Enter Kalapaki Beach from the park.

Niumalu Park—This tree-lined park is tucked into a corner of Nawiliwili Harbor near a sugar-loading facility and a small-boat harbor. With neighbors like this and no swimming facilities, the park's key feature is its proximity to Lihue.

Facilities: Picnic area, restrooms, showers, playground. Two miles from Lihue's markets and restaurants.

Camping: County permit required. Tent and trailer camping.

Getting there: Take Rice Street to Nawiliwili, turn right on Route 58, then left on Niumalu Road.

Running Water Beach (or **First Beach**) and **Second Beach (★)**— Hidden along a rocky coastline between Nawiliwili Bay and the lighthouse on Ninini Point are two small sand beaches. There's good swimming and bodysurfing at Running Water Beach, named for the numerous springs which bubble out of the lava and percolate up into the sand. Second Beach is excellent for sunbathing. Since they're pretty close to civilization, I don't recommend camping at either beach.

To get there, take the road leading through the Westin Kauai Hotel property in Nawiliwili. Follow this road to the golf course clubhouse. Park and walk across the golf course in a direction several degrees to the right of the lighthouse. Second Beach can be reached by walking from Running Water Beach toward the lighthouse for about three-tenths of a mile.

POIPU AREA BEACHES AND PARKS

Poipu Beach Park—This has got to be one of the loveliest little parks around. There's a well-kept lawn for picnickers and finicky sunbathers, a crescent-shaped beach with protecting reef, and the sunny skies of Poipu. If for some reason this isn't enough, check out any of the other fine beaches in front of the Waiohai, Poipu Beach, Kiahuna, and Sheraton Hotels just west of the park.

Facilities: Picnic area, restrooms, showers, volleyball, playground, lifeguards. Market and snack bar across the street.

Camping: Not permitted.

Swimming: Excellent. The best bodysurfing on the island is at **Brennecke's Beach,** the next beach east of here.

Snorkeling: The entire area has some of the best diving on the island.

Surfing: Good summer breaks nearby in front of the Waiohai and Sheraton Hotels. Waiohai breaks are on a shallow reef, so beware. Right and left slides. Sheraton or "Horseshoe" has a fast break with a right slide. Less than a mile away, near the shorefront restaurant on Spouting Horn Road, there are summer breaks on a shallow reef. Right and left slides.

Fishing: Bonefish, rockfish, and *papio* are common. There's good spearfishing on the nearby reefs.

Getting there: On Hoona Road in Poipu.

Shipwreck Beach and **Mahaulepu Beach** (★)—If you've come to Hawaii seeking that South Seas dream, head out to these lovely strands. Here George C. Scott portrayed Ernest Hemingway in the movie *Islands in the Stream.*

Now that condominiums are crawling along the coast, more and more people are discovering Shipwreck, but Mahaulepu is almost literally a beach without a footprint. Shipwreck is a sandy, rock-studded beach ideal for swimming and fishing. Mahaulepu is a dreamy corridor of white sand winding for almost a mile along a reef-protected shoreline. Local folks camp in the ironwood grove at the far end of the beach. A lone house sits on the near end. This is also an excellent hiking area. I never made it

Hidden Beaches and Cane Roads

Strung like jewels along Kauai's shore lies a series of hidden beaches which are known only to local people. Among these are some of the loveliest beaches on the entire island, removed from tourist areas, uninhabited, some lacking so much as a footprint. For the wanderer, they are an uncharted domain, and to the camper they can be a secret retreat.

Over a dozen of these hideaways are described in the accompanying section on Kauai's beaches. Some are located right alongside public thoroughfares; others require long hikes down little-used footpaths. Most can be reached only by private cane roads. These graded dirt roads are owned by sugar plantations and marked with menacing "No Trespassing" signs. Officially the public is not permitted, and few tourists ever travel along them. But local people use cane roads all the time.

They do so with the greatest courtesy and discretion, realizing that they are on private property. They watch cautiously for approaching cane trucks, and yield to plantation traffic. Most important, they respect the awesome beauty of these areas by leaving the beaches as they found them. As one Hawaiian explained to me, the golden rule for visitors is this: "If you want to go native, act like one!"

I certainly recommend that you go native, and I can't think of a better place to do so than one of Kauai's secluded beaches.

farther east to **Hidden Valley Beach** (★), but I heard it's just a short trek east from Mahaulepu.

Facilities: None. It's a couple miles to markets and restaurants in Koloa.

Getting there: From the Poipu Beach area, follow Poipu Road east until the pavement ends and the thoroughfare becomes a cane road.

To get to Shipwreck Beach, turn immediately onto either of the two cane roads heading to the right; both lead several hundred yards to the beach.

To get to Mahaulepu Beach, do not turn off to the right. Instead, continue on the main cane road (which is like a dirt road continuation of Poipu Road). Follow this road for about two miles (even when it curves toward the mountains and away from the ocean). Numerous minor cane roads will intersect from the right and left: ignore them. Finally you will come to a crossroads with a major cane road (along which a line of telephone poles runs). Turn right and follow this road for about a mile (you'll pass a quarry off in the distance to the right), then watch on the right for roads leading to the beach. Look, all this is why it's a hidden beach!

WAIMEA AREA BEACHES AND PARKS

Salt Pond Beach Park—A pretty, crescent-shaped beach with a protecting reef and numerous coconut trees, this park is very popular with local folks and may be crowded and noisy on weekends. It's a good place to collect shells, though.

The road leading to the park passes the salt ponds which date back hundreds of years and are still used today to evaporate sea water and produce salt.

Facilities: Picnic area, restrooms, showers. Markets and restaurants are a mile away in Hanapepe.

Camping: County permit required. Tent camping only.

Swimming: Good, well-protected.

Snorkeling: Fair diving near rocks.

Surfing: There's a shore break by the mouth of Hanapepe River nearby in Port Allen. Sandy and shallow with small waves, this area is safe for beginners. Left and right slides. Along the outer harbor edge near Byrnes Field runway there are summer breaks, for good surfers only, which involve climbing down a rocky shoreline. At Salt Pond there are occasional summer breaks requiring a long paddle out. Left and right slides.

Fishing: Rockfish and mullet are the most common catches here.

Getting there: Take Route 50 to Hanapepe. Turn onto Route 543 and follow it to the end.

Pakala Beach (★)—This long narrow ribbon of sand is bounded by trees and set in perfectly lush surroundings. Surfers will probably be the only other people around. They may come out of the water long enough to watch the spectacular sunsets with you. If this book were rating beaches by the star system, Pakala Beach would deserve a constellation.

Facilities: None. Markets and restaurants are two miles away in Waimea.

Camping: Not recommended: the area behind the beach is strictly private.

Swimming: Good.

Surfing: You're at one of Kauai's top surfing spots. The incredibly long walls allow you to hang ten seemingly forever. Hence the nickname for these breaks—"Infinity." Long paddle out.

Getting there: Listen carefully—along Route 50 near the twenty-one-mile marker (two miles east of Waimea) you'll see a concrete bridge crossing Aakukui stream with the name "Aakukui" chiseled in the cement. Go through the gate just below the bridge and follow the well-worn path to the beach.

Lucy Wright Park—This five-acre park at the Waimea River mouth is popular with locals and therefore sometimes a little crowded. Despite a sandy beach, the park is not as appealing as others nearby: the water is often murky from cane field spillage. If you're in need of a campground you might stop here, otherwise I don't recommend the park.

Facilities: Picnic area, restrooms, playground. Markets and snack bars nearby in Waimea.

Camping: County permit required. Tent camping only.

Swimming: Fair, unless the water is muddy.

Surfing: Varies from small breaks for beginners to extremely long walls which build four different breaks. Surfing is best near the river mouth. Left slide.

Fishing: In Waimea Bay, for parrotfish, red goatfish, squirrelfish, *papio*, bonefish, big-eyed scad, and threadfin.

Kekaha Beaches—This narrow beach parallels Route 50 for several miles in Kekaha. Although close to the highway, the lovely white strand offers some marvelous picnic spots, but the rough surf and powerful currents make swimming dangerous.

There are numerous surfing spots along this strip; but watch out for the shallow reef.

Kekaha Beach Park—Set on a beautiful ribbon of sand, this twenty-acre park is a great place to kick back, picnic, and catch the sun setting over Niihau. Picnic facilities and restrooms; no camping; swimming dangerous. Restaurants and markets nearby in Kekaha. Fishing for threadfin. Located on Route 50.

Kekaha Public Dumping Grounds (★)—Yes, I'm serious! There's a wide sandy beach past the city dump with unofficial camping and pretty decent surfing. Just take the road which leads off Route 50 one mile west of Kekaha (there's a sign directing traffic to the dump). Follow any of the dirt roads in as far as possible. These will lead either to the dump or to a nearby drag strip. Walk the last three-tenths of a mile to the beach.

Barking Sands—This military installation is bounded by very wide beaches which extend for miles. You'll see magnificent sunsets and get the best view of Niihau anywhere on Kauai. Hot, dry weather: a great place to get thoroughly baked, but beware of sunburns. The U. S. Navy's Pacific Missile Range is located here, and the area is sometimes used for war games.

Facilities: Markets and restaurants are several miles away in Kekaha.

Camping: Check with the security guards (335-4346) at the front entrance. Unless war games are actually in progress, you can generally camp for a day or two.

Swimming: Good, but exercise caution.

Surfing: Major's Bay is an excellent surfing spot with both summer and winter breaks.

Fishing: The most common catches are bonefish, threadfin, and *ulua.*

Getting there: Take Route 50 several miles past Kekaha, then watch for signs to Barking Sands. Just past the front gate, the road goes left to Major's Bay and right to Barking Sands. Take your pick.

Polihale State Park—This wide beach blankets the coast for miles along Kauai's west end. The hot, dry weather is excellent for sunbathing, and prime for burning, so load up on suntan lotion. Great sunsets; magnificent mountain surroundings; Niihau looming in the distance. There's especially good shell collecting here at America's westernmost park.

Facilities: Picnic area, restrooms, shower. Restaurants and markets are about ten miles away in Kekaha.

Camping: You can pitch a tent on the beach under a star-crowded sky, or find a shady tree for protection against the blazing sun. This is a wonderful place to camp for a day or two. After that, the barren landscape becomes tiresome and monotonous. Tent and trailer camping allowed. State permit required.

Swimming: Good in summer; dangerous in winter and during other periods of high surf.

Surfing: Very good here and around the corner at Queen's Pond. Shore break with left and right slides.

Fishing: Bonefish, threadfin, and *ulua* are the most common game fish.

Getting there: Take Route 50 until it ends, then just follow the signs along dirt roads for about five miles.

Kokee State Park—This spectacular park, high in the mountains above Waimea Canyon, is a mecca for hikers, campers, and other outdoor enthusiasts. Sprawling across 4,640 heavily-wooded acres, this rugged country offers a unique perspective on the Garden Isle.

Facilities: Kokee has everything but a store, so come well-stocked or plan to eat at the lodge restaurant. The lodge also has a museum and gift shop. Nearby are cabins, restrooms, showers, picnic area, and hiking trails.

Camping: An area at the north end of the park has been allocated for tent and trailer camping. There are also several wilderness camps along the hiking trails. A state permit is required for non-wilderness camping.

Fishing: Excellent fresh-water angling; a state license is required, though.

Hiking: See the "Hiking" section in this chapter for trail descriptions.

Getting there: Take Route 50 to Waimea, then Route 55 to the park.

WAILUA AREA BEACHES AND PARKS

Hanamaulu Beach Park—Here's an idyllic park nestled in Hanamaulu Bay and crowded with ironwood and coconut trees. I found this a great place for picnics and water sports.

Facilities: Picnic area, restrooms, showers, playground. One mile from restaurants and the small market in Hanamaulu.

Camping:: Needles from the ironwood trees make a natural bed at this lovely site. Tent and trailer camping; county permit required.

Swimming: Well-protected bay affords excellent opportunities. Not much snorkeling or surfing.

Fishing: Common catches include bonefish, mullet, and big-eyed scad.

Getting there: Take Route 56 to Hanamaulu, then turn down the road leading to the bay.

Wailua Golf Course Beach (★)—The surfers know it as "Cemetery," but since this beach fronts the Wailua links I thought a less ominous name might be more appropriate. One of the island's prettiest beaches, the strand extends for several miles to Wailua. A dirt road parallels the beach for about a half-mile, but if you seek seclusion just start hiking north along the shore. You'll find places galore for swimming, camping, fishing, surfing, and so on.

Facilities: A small market and restaurants are about a mile away in Hanamaulu.

Camping: There are numerous spots for unofficial camping along the beachfront.

Swimming: Good; well-protected and shallow.

Snorkeling: Good diving among reefs.

Surfing: Good breaks on shallow reef.

Fishing: Best near reefs.

Getting there: Going north from Lihue on Route 56, take a right onto the road which runs along the southern end of the Wailua Golf Course. This paved road rapidly becomes a dirt strip studded with potholes. Driving slowly, proceed a quarter-mile, then take the first left turn. It's another quarter-mile to the beach; when the road forks, take either branch.

Lydgate State Park—The awesome ironwood grove and long stretches of rugged coastline make this one of Kauai's loveliest parks.

Facilities: Picnic area and restrooms. Wailua's restaurants, markets, and sightseeing attractions are all close. Nearby Wailua River State Park features sacred historic sites and breathtaking views of river and mountains.

Camping: Not permitted.

Swimming: Good, but exercise caution.

Surfing: Long paddle out to breaks off mouth of Wailua River. Right slide.

Fishing: *Ulua* is the most common catch.

Getting there: From Route 56, turn toward the beach at the road just south of Wailua River.

Kapaa Beach Park—While it sports an attractive little beach (plus picnic and restroom facilities), this fifteen-acre facility doesn't measure up to its neighbors. Located a block from Route 56 as the highway passes through central Kapaa, the park is flanked by ramshackle houses and a local playing field. Swimming and fishing fair; squidding and torchfishing good.

Kealia Beach—This strand is one of those neighbors that makes Kapaa Beach the pimply kid next door: it's a wide, magnificent beach curving for about a half-mile along Route 56. This is not a park, so there are no facilities. The one-store town of Kealia is just across the road. The swimming is good, but requires caution. Fishing for *papio*, threadfin, and *ulua*; sporadic surfing; unofficial camping at the north end of the beach.

Donkey's Beach (★)—This broad, curving beach is flanked by a grassy meadow and towering ironwoods. Favored as a hideaway and nude beach by local folks, it's a gem that should not be overlooked. The swimming and surfing are good, but remember the nearest lifeguard is a world away. Unofficial camping is common.

To get there, follow Route 56 north from Kealia. At the eleven-mile marker the road begins to climb slowly, then descend. At the end of the descent, just before the twelve-mile marker, there is a cane road on the right. Take this road; bear right and watch for Donkey's Beach on the left within a half-mile. (Since the road is now chained, you'll have to hike in from Route 56.)

Several other hidden beaches are strung anonymously along cane roads paralleling the coast from Kealia to Anahola. You should watch for them as you travel through this area.

Anahola Beach Park—A slender ribbon of sand curves along windswept Anahola Bay. At the south end, guarded by ironwood trees, lies this pretty little park.

Facilities: Picnic area, restrooms, showers. Less than a mile to the market and snack bar in Anahola.

Camping: An excellent area for tent camping; county permit required.

Swimming: Use caution because of the strong currents.

Surfing: Long paddle out to summer and winter breaks along a reef. Left and right slides.

Fishing: Good torchfishing for lobsters. Fish commonly caught include *papio*, rudderfish, *ulua*, threadfin, bonefish, and big-eyed scad.

Getting there: Turn onto Anahola Road from Route 56 in Anahola; follow the signs to the beach.

Aliomanu Beach—On the far side of Anahola Bay, separated from the park by a lagoon, sits another sandy beach. Shady ironwood trees, several roadside houses, and a picnic table dot this area, which is a favorite among locals. There's safe swimming in the lagoon, but use caution seaside. To get there, turn off Route 56 onto Aliomanu Road just past Anahola.

HANALEI AREA BEACHES AND PARKS

Moloaa Beach (★)—Nestled in Moloaa Bay, a small inlet surrounded by rolling hills, Moloaa Beach is relatively secluded, though
there are a few homes nearby. A meandering stream divides the beach
into two strands. You'll see horses grazing on the nearby bluff, and a coral
reef shadowing the shore. Good fishing; skin-diving for lobsters; swimming with caution.

To get there, take Koolau Road where it branches off Route 56 near
the sixteen-mile marker. Go one-and-three-tenths miles, then turn onto
Moloaa Road. Follow this to the end. All roads are paved.

Larson's Beach (★)—This narrow, sandy beach extends seemingly
forever through a very secluded area. Rolling hills, covered with small
trees and scrub, rim the strand. A protecting reef provides excellent
swimming and snorkeling. Good fishing. This is a splendid place to set up
an unofficial camp.

It's hard to get to, but more than worth it when you arrive. Take
Koolau Road as it branches off Route 56 near the sixteen-mile marker. Go
two-and-a-half miles to a cane road on the right which switches back in the
opposite direction. Get on this road, then take an immediate left onto
another dirt road (lined on either side with barbed wire). Don't let the
fences scare you—this is a public right of way. Follow it a mile to the end.
Hike through the gate and down the road. This leads a half-mile down to
the beach, which is on your left.

Kahili Beach (★)—Tucked away in a small cove, this beach is
bordered by tree-covered hills and a rock quarry. It's a lovely, semi-
secluded spot with a lagoon. Unofficial camping; swimming with caution;
fishing. For a spectacular view of windswept cliffs, follow the short quarry
road which climbs steeply from the parking area.

To get there, take Kilauea Road toward the lighthouse in Kilauea.
Three hundred yards past the last house in Kilauea, turn onto the narrow
dirt road which angles off to the right. Don't take the first, dead end, road;
the Kahili road is just past this. This road leads one-and-a-half miles to the
beach.

Secret Beach or **Kauapea Beach** (★)—Inaccessibility means seclusion along this hidden strand. Ideal for bird watching, swimming, and
unofficial camping.

The beach can be seen from Kilauea Lighthouse, but getting there is
another matter. Take Kilauea Road toward the lighthouse. Turn left on
Kauapea Road (which is also paved). The first road on your right (with a
gate that will probably be locked) leads toward the ocean. It's about a mile
along this road and down a very steep path to the beach. But once there
the effort will seem well worthwhile.

Kalihiwai Beach (★)— Bounded by sheer rock wall on one side and a rolling green hill on the other, this semi-secluded beach is crowded with ironwood trees. Behind the ironwoods, the Kalihiwai River has created a large, shallow lagoon across which stretches the skeleton of a bridge, a last grim relic of the devastating 1946 tidal wave.

Facilities: Picnic table. Market and snack bar are about a mile away in Kilauea.

Camping: Unofficial camping under the ironwoods.

Swimming: With caution.

Surfing: Winter breaks with right slide.

Fishing: Bonefish and threadfin are the most common catches.

Getting there: Take heed—there are two Kalihiwai Roads branching off Route 56 between Kilauea and Kalihiwai. (The washed-out bridge once connected them.) Take the one closest to Lihue. This bumpy macadam road leads a short distance directly to the beach.

Anini Beach Park—Here a grass-covered park fronts a narrow ribbon of sand, while a protecting reef parallels the beach 200 yards offshore. I thought this an ideal place for kids, the ocean is glass smooth and the shell collecting along the beach is excellent. As a result it's very popular and sometimes crowded.

Facilities: Picnic area, restrooms, shower. A market and snack bar are about two miles away in Kilauea; the Princeville shopping complex is eight miles distant.

Camping: Pleasant, but lacks privacy. County permit required. Tent camping only.

Swimming: Excellent and very safe.

Snorkeling: Excellent.

Surfing: Winter breaks on very shallow reef. Left and right slides.

Fishing: Bonefish, *papio,* and *ulua* are regularly caught here. There's also excellent torchfishing.

Getting there: Between Kilauea and Hanalei, turn off Route 56 onto the second Kalihiwai Road (the one farthest from Lihue, on the Hanalei side of the Kalihiwai River). Then take Anini Road to the beach.

Other Anini Beaches (★)—Anini Road snakes along the shoreline for several miles on either side of Anini Beach Park. Numerous dirt roads lead a short distance off Anini Road to secluded beaches. These offer the same natural features as the park, plus privacy.

Hanalei Beaches—A sandy, horseshoe-shaped strip curves the full length of Hanalei Bay. Along this strand the county has three parks:

Hanalei Beach Park, Hanalei Pavilion, and Waioli Beach Park. All have picnic areas, restrooms, and marvelous ocean and mountain views.

Camping: Tent camping permitted on weekends and holidays. County permit.

Swimming: Safe near Hanalei pier; dangerous elsewhere.

Surfing: There are three major breaks here. "Impossible" breaks require a long paddle out from the pier; right slide. "Pine Tree" breaks are in the center of the bay. "Waikoko" breaks are on the shallow reef along the left side of the bay. All are winter breaks. Surfing in Hanalei is serious business, so be careful. Early morning and late afternoon are the best surfing times.

Fishing: Crabbing off the pier at Hanalei River. Fishing for squirrelfish, rockfish, red bigeye, *oama*, big-eyed scad, *ulua*, and *papio*.

Lumahai Beach—Many people know this strand as the Nurse's Beach in the movie *South Pacific*. Snuggled in a cove and surrounded by lush green hills, Lumahai is partially protected by a reef. The swimming is good, but exercise caution. And there's fishing for *papio* and *ulua*.

To get there, watch for a vista point near the thirty-three-mile marker on Route 56. From here a crooked footpath leads to the beach.

Haena Beach Park—This grassy park, bounded by the sea on one side and a sheer lava cliff on the other, is right across the street from Maniniholo Dry Cave. It's very popular with young folks and provides good opportunities for shell collecting.

Facilities: Picnic area, restrooms, shower. Markets and restaurants are a few miles away in Hanalei.

Camping: It's an attractive campground, sometimes crowded, open to both tents and trailers, and requiring a county permit.

Swimming: There are very strong ocean currents here which make swimming impossible.

Surfing: "Cannon's" breaks on a shallow reef in front of Dry Cave. For experts only. Right slide.

Fishing: Excellent rod- and torchfishing for red bigeye, squirrelfish, *papio*, and *ulua*. Cardinal fish are sometimes caught on the reef at low tide during the full moon.

Getting there: Located on Route 56 five miles west of Hanalei.

Other Haena Beaches (★)—There are "Right of Way to Beach" signs all along Route 56 near Haena. Taking any of these dirt roads will shortly lead you to secluded strands.

Kee Beach—At the end of Route 56, where the Kalalau trail begins, you'll find this reef-shrouded beach. When the surf is gentle, swimming is superb. At such times, this is the best snorkeling beach on Kauai, with its coral reef brilliantly colored and crowded with tropical fish. A camping facility is planned here.

Hanakapiai Beach and **Kalalau Valley**—See the "Hiking Kalalau" section in this chapter.

Hiking

Trekking is among the finest, and certainly least expensive, ways of touring the Garden Isle. Kauai's trails are concentrated in the Na Pali Coast and Waimea Canyon–Kokee regions with a few others near the Wailua River. Most are well-maintained and carefully charted. For further information, contact the State Department of Land and Natural Resources (245-4444).

WAILUA RIVER TRAILS

While none of these hikes actually follow the Wailua, all begin near Route 580, which parallels the river.

Nonou Mountain Trail—East side (2 miles long) begins off Haleilio Road in the Wailua Houselots and climbs 1,250 feet to the Sleeping Giant's head at Mount Nonou summit.

Nonou Mountain Trail—West side (1.5 miles) begins off Route 581 and ascends 1,000 feet to join the East side trail.

Keahua Arboretum Trail (0.5 mile) begins two miles past the University of Hawaii Wailua Experiment Station on Route 580. This nature trail is lined with native and foreign plants identified in a field guide available from the State Division of Forestry (245-4433).

Kuilau Ridge Trail (2.1 miles) begins on Route 580 near the Keahua Arboretum. This scenic hike goes past several vista points and picnic areas.

WAIMEA CANYON–KOKEE TRAILS

Kokee State Park has about forty-five miles of hiking trails which offer treks through rugged, beautiful country. Along the mountain paths listed here, you'll discover some of the finest hiking in all Hawaii.

Alakai Swamp Trail (3.5 miles) passes through bogs and scrub rain forests to the Kilohana Lookout above Hanalei Bay. This very muddy trail begins off Mohihi (Camp 10) Road.

Awaawapuhi Trail (3.3 miles) starts on Route 55 midway between Kokee Museum and Kalalau Lookout. It leads through a forest to a vista at 2,500-feet elevation which overlooks sheer cliffs and the ocean. The trail then connects with Nualolo Trail for an eight-and-a-half mile loop.

Berry Flat Trail (1 mile) and **Puu Ka Ohelo Trail** (0.3 mile) combine off Mohihi (Camp 10) Road to form a loop which passes an interesting assortment of trees, including California redwood, *ohia,* sugi pine, and *koa.*

(Text continued on page 344.)

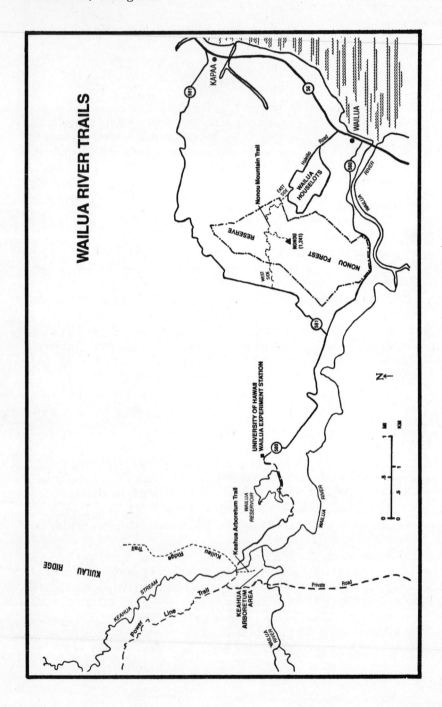

WAILUA RIVER TRAILS

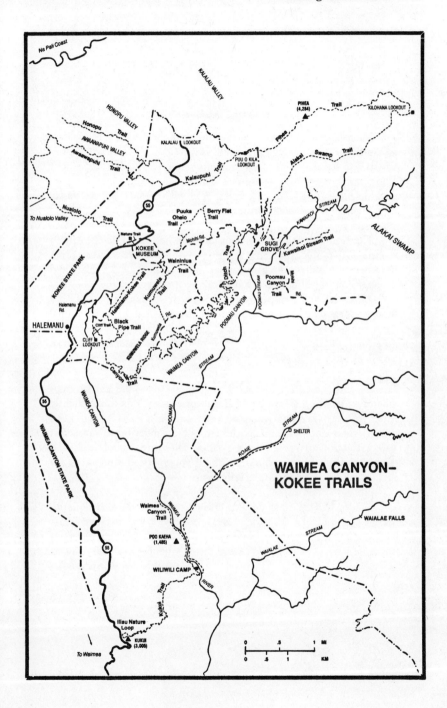

**WAIMEA CANYON-
KOKEE TRAILS**

Hiking Kalalau

Kauai's premier hike, one of the finest treks in all the islands, follows an eleven-mile trail along the rugged Na Pali Coast. This ancient Hawaiian trail to Kalalau Valley descends into dense rain forests and climbs along windswept cliffs. Streams and mountain pools along the path provide refreshing swimming holes. And wild orchids, guavas, *kukui* nuts, mangoes, and mountain apples grow in abundance.

The trail begins near Kee Beach at the end of Route 56. After a strenuous two-mile course the trail drops into Hanakapiai Valley. From here two side trails—the **Hanakapiai Valley Loop Trail** (1.3 miles) and its extension, the **Hanakapiai Falls Trail**—climb through the valley and to Hanakapiai Falls, respectively. Fringed by cliffs and possessing a marvelous sand beach, Hanakapiai makes an excellent rest point or final destination. Purists will claim you've got to "do Kalalau" to see the Na Pali Coast, but this first stop on the way to Kalalau has campsites and is an excellent introduction for day hikers.

If you bypass the side trails and continue along the Kalalau trail, you'll find that as it climbs out of Hanakapiai Valley, it becomes slightly rougher. Sharp grass presses close to the path as it leads through thick foliage, then along precipitous cliff faces. Four miles from Hanakapiai Valley, the trail arrives at Hanakoa Valley. There are several shacks and campsites here; use mosquito netting if you spend the night, as the dive-bombing mosquitoes are really fierce.

A steep half-mile trail goes up to Hanakoa Falls. Here, right in the middle of a boulder field, a friend and I managed to find an opening just large enough to pitch a tent. Campsites are rare at the falls, but if you can find one, it's well worth it. We were the only people in a valley ringed

(Text continued on page 344.)

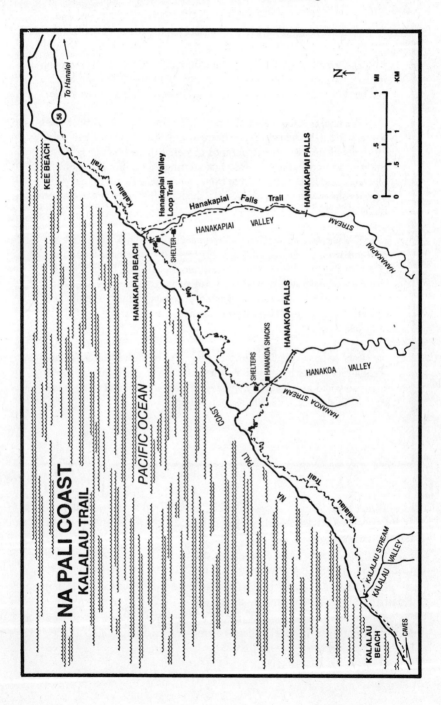

with sheer walls from which a cascade tumbled into a deep circular pool. A lot of trite statements have been made about how Eden-like Kalalau can be, but Hanakoa Falls is the closest I've been to that mythic locale.

The final trek to Kalalau, the most difficult section of the trail, passes scenery so spectacular as to seem unreal. Knife-point peaks, illuminated by shafts of sunlight, rise thousands of feet. Frigate birds hang poised against the trade winds. Wisps of cloud fringe the cliffs. The silence is ominous, almost tangible. A foot from the trail, the ledge falls away into another sheer wall which plummets a thousand feet and more to the surf below.

The narrow, serpentine trail then winds down to Kalalau Valley. A well-fed stream rumbles through this two-mile-wide vale. If you must use the water here, be sure to boil or otherwise purify it. Farther along, a white-sand beach sweeps past a series of caves to the far end of the valley. You may want to stop a while and explore the caves, but if you swim here or at Hanakapiai, exercise extreme caution. The undertow and riptides are wicked.

Kalalau has many fine campsites near the beach and hosts a colony of squatters farther up the valley. Firewood is scarce and cutting trees is *kapu,* so you'd best bring a campstove. Camping at Hanakapiai, Hanakoa, or Kalalau will necessitate a state permit.

Black Pipe Trail (0.4 mile) links Canyon Trail with Halemanu Road. It follows a cliff past stands of the rare *iliau* plant, a relative of Maui's famous silversword.

Canyon Trail (1.4 miles) forks off Cliff Trail and follows Waimea Canyon's northern rim to a vista sweeping down the canyon to the sea.

Cliff Trail (0.1 mile) begins at the end of the right fork of Halemanu Road and offers an easy hike to a viewpoint above Waimea Canyon.

Ditch Trail (3.5 miles) runs from Kumuwela Road at one end to Mohihi Road at the other. It's a rugged trail with spectacular views of forest areas and the Poomau River.

Halemanu-Kokee Trail (1.2 miles) sets out from the old ranger station. Bird watchers should especially enjoy this easy jaunt.

Honopu Trail (2.5 miles) begins on Route 55 about a half-mile past the Awaawapuhi trailhead. This poorly maintained path offers stunning views of the Na Pali Coast, including Honopu Valley, The Valley of the Lost Tribe.

Iliau Nature Loop (0.3 mile) starts along Route 55 on a short course past twenty local plant species, including the *iliau,* endemic only to Kauai. This trail offers good views of both Waimea Canyon and Waialae Falls.

Kalapuhi Trail (1.7 miles) begins at Route 55 en route to a plum grove. The plums are in season every other year. In a good year, you can enjoy both plums and a fine hike; other years, you'll have to settle for the latter.

Kawaikoi Stream Trail (0.8 miles) starts on Mohihi (Camp 10) Road across from Sugi Grove and follows near the stream through a man-made forest.

Koaie Canyon Trail (3 miles) branches off the Waimea Canyon trail near Poo Kaeha. It crosses the Waimea River and passes ancient terraces and rock walls en route to Lonomea camp, a wilderness campsite. Here you'll find a shelter and a stream chock-full of swimming holes.

Kukui Trail (2.5 miles) leads from Route 55 near Puu Kukui and descends 2,000 feet to the Waimea River. You'll encounter switchbacks along the west side of Waimea Canyon; the trail ends at Wiliwili Camp, a wilderness campsite.

Kumuwela Trail (0.8 mile) begins off Mohihi (Camp 10) Road and passes through a fern-choked gulch.

Nature Trail (0.1 mile) begins behind the Kokee Museum and passes through a *koa* forest.

Nualolo Trail (3.8 miles) starts near Park headquarters. Along the way you'll be able to see Nualolo Valley on the Na Pali Coast.

Pihea Trail (3.3 miles) offers excellent views of Kalalau Valley and the Alakai Swamp. Pihea also features a variety of birds and plant life. This trail begins at Puu O Kila Lookout.

Poomau Canyon Lookout Trail (0.3 mile) heads through a stand of Japanese *sugi* trees and a native rain forest. It begins from Mohihi (Camp 10) Road and ends at a vista overlooking Poomau and Waimea Canyons.

Waimea Canyon Trail (1.5 miles) can be reached from the Kukui Trail. It follows the Waimea River through the center of the canyon.

Waininiua Trail (0.4 mile) leads from the unpaved Kumuwela Road through a forest where ginger grows.

Travelers' Tracks

Sightseeing

LIHUE, POIPU, AND WAIMEA AREAS

LIHUE

Kauai's civic center hosts a regional library and convention center, as well as state and county offices. The **Kauai Museum** (245-6931; admission), housed in a stone building at 4428 Rice Street, is rich in Hawaiiana. This is a prime spot to learn about the history of the only Hawaiian island that Kamehameha failed to conquer.

A fascinating side trip from Lihue goes past lovely **Kalapaki Beach** and busy **Nawiliwili Harbor**, then continues to the **Menehune Fish Pond**. The pond, spread across a valley floor and backdropped by the Hoary Head Mountain Range, dates back well before the Polynesians. Legend has it that a line of gnome-like Menehunes twenty-five miles long passed rocks from hand to hand and built the pond in a single night. To get there, take Rice Street to Nawiliwili, then right on Route 58, a quick left on Niumalu Road, and finally right on Hulemalu Road.

ON TO POIPU

If you possess a Rorschach-test imagination, you'll see **Queen Victoria's Profile** etched in the Hoary Head Range along Route 50. (Need a helping eye? Watch for the Hawaii Visitors Bureau sign.) An arcade of towering eucalyptus trees forms a **Tree Tunnel** along Route 52 as the road begins its curving course to the timeworn town of **Koloa**, Hawaii's first sugar plantation began here in 1835. At nearby **Pacific Tropical Botanical Garden** (322-7361) there are tours of a 400-acre flowering paradise. Then it's on to the sunsplashed beaches of **Poipu** and out to **Spouting Horn**. Surf crashing through a lava tube dramatically transforms this blowhole into the Old Faithful of Kauai.

FROM POIPU WEST TO POLIHALE

Backtracking to Koloa, you can pick up Route 53, which rejoins Route 50. As it proceeds west, Route 50 passes the **Eighty-Eight Places of Kobo Daishi**, a collection of Buddhist shrines symbolizing man's eighty-eight sins. Unless your conscience proves overwhelming, you can walk freely among these monuments.

In Kalaheo take Papalina Road to **Kukuiolono Park** for a Japanese garden stroll and a stunning view sweeping across a patchwork of cane fields to the sea.

Back on the main road, nearby **Olu Pua Gardens** (332-8182) feature an international assortment of plant life cultivated in patterns which represent different themes. After paying an admission fee, you can stroll through this former plantation estate.

Hanapepe Valley Lookout offers a view of native plant life dramatically set in a gorge ringed by eroded cliffs. Be sure to take the fork into **Hanapepe,** a vintage village complete with wooden sidewalks and weatherbeaten storefronts. During the 1924 sugar strike, sixteen workers were killed here by police. Even today the independent spirit of those martyrs pervades this proud little town. For a sense of Hanapepe during the plantation days, drive out Awawa Road (★). Precipitous red lava cliffs rim the roadside, while rickety cottages and intricately tilled fields carpet the valley below.

The **Russian Fort,** at the Waimea River mouth, is now just a rubble heap marking a fruitless attempt by a maverick adventurer to gain a foothold in the islands in 1816. An earlier event, Captain James Cook's 1778 "discovery" of Hawaii, is commemorated with a lava monolith near his landing place in Waimea. Watch for roadside markers to Cook's monument (on the road to Lucy Wright Park) and to the **Menehune Ditch** (outside town on Menehune Road). This waterway, an extraordinary engineering feat mythically attributed to the Menehunes, has long puzzled archaeologists. As interesting as this lengthy watercourse is a nearby **swinging footbridge** which spans the Waimea River.

Next on Route 50's scenic itinerary is **Barking Sands.** These sixty-foot sand dunes reputedly make a woofing sound when ground underfoot. One local wag told me the hills got their name from tourists becoming "dog-tired" after futilely trying to elicit a growl from the mute sand. (Since the beach is on a military reservation, call 335-4346 or 335-4356 to make sure that access is open.)

Having made a fool of yourself trying to get sand to bark, continue on past the dilapidated town of **Mana** to the endless sands of **Polihale State Park.** From here you'll have an excellent view of **Niihau,** Hawaii's westernmost inhabited island. Several hundred native Hawaiians live on this privately-owned island under conditions similar to those prevailing during the nineteenth century. It seems outrageous that outsiders are forbidden to enter.

A place where you *are* permitted, and which you definitely must see, is **Waimea Canyon.** Touring the Grand Canyon of the Pacific involves a side trip along Route 55 from Waimea. As the paved road snakes along the side of this 3,600-foot-deep canyon, a staggering panorama opens. The red and orange hues of a barren southwestern landscape are splashed with tropic greens and yellows. Climbing above this ten-mile-long chasm and past the lodge at **Kokee State Park** (335-5871), the road continues to the **Kalalau Lookout.** Here Kauai's other face is reflected in knife-edged cliffs and overgrown gorges dropping 4,000 feet to the sea. Kalalau. One more spectacular scene along the way, one more reason to bring you back to this magnificent island.

WAILUA AND HANALEI AREAS

FROM LIHUE NORTH TO WAILUA

A short distance from Lihue, Route 56, the main road to Kauai's north shore, descends into the rustic village of **Kapaia.** Sagging wood structures and a gulch choked with banana plants mark this valley. On the right, **Lihue Hongwanji Temple,** one of the island's oldest, smiles from beneath a recent facelift. To the left, off Route 56, a narrow road threads through three miles of sugar cane to **Wailua Falls.** These twin cascades tumble eighty feet into a heavenly pool fringed with *hala* trees.

Return to Route 56 and follow the highway to **Hanamaulu.** Amid the old shops, a town museum houses ancient canoes and surfboards, plus relics from the days when sugar was king. Several miles farther, the **Wailua River,** Hawaii's only navigable river, meets the sea. A left just before this dramatic rendezvous leads to the Marina, where you can catch a boat chugging up to **Fern Grotto** (822-4111). I thought this a scenic but cloyingly commercial voyage.

In Lydgate State Park, where the river pours into the sea, you'll discover the rocky remains of the **Hauola Place of Refuge.** This ancient temple of refuge was a sanctuary to which *kapu* breakers could flee. Once inside its sacred perimeter, any fugitive was free.

Across the river, turn onto Route 580. **Wailua River State Park** spreads out to the left and the gorgeous **Coco Palms Hotel** sits to the right. The beautiful grounds of this plush resort include one of Hawaii's largest coconut groves. You're welcome to tour the grounds, but beware of falling coconuts! Past Coco Palms the road courses through Kauai's most historic region, the domain of ancient Hawaiian royalty. Watch for Hawaii Visitors Bureau signs pointing out the **Holo-Holo-Ku Heiau,** an ancient temple of refuge where some were saved and others sacrificed, and the **Pohaku-Ho-O-Hanau,** a sacred spot where royal women came to give birth. On the left along the hilltop rest the rocky remains of the king's house, **Poliahu Heiau,** and the **Bell Stone,** which once loudly signaled the birth of royal infants. All these places, vital to Hawaiian myth, were located along the old King's Highway, a sacred thoroughfare used only by island rulers.

For some vivid **mountain scenery** (★) continue on Route 580 past **Opaekaa Falls.** Then pick up Route 581 as it rolls through field and forest before spilling into Kapaa. En route you'll encounter **Kamokila Hawaiian Village** (822-1192; admission), a reconstructed Polynesian village featuring demonstrations of native crafts.

FROM WAILUA TO HANALEI AND BEYOND

Route 56 continues north past the **Coconut Plantation** with its sprawling Market Place shopping mall. In nearby Kapaa, rickety buildings date back to the last century. From here, there's an excellent view of the

Sleeping Giant, a recumbent figure naturally hewn out of the nearby mountain range.

Follow the direction his feet point along the highway and you'll arrive at a curving ribbon of sand known as **Kealia Beach.** Across the road, in various states of disrepair, stand the sunbleached shacks of a former plantation camp. Some of these tumbledown houses are occupied even today.

A few years ago you could reach the **Waipahee Slippery Slide** via the little enclave of Kealia. Today you'll have to content yourself with a visit to this creaky, one-store town. It seems that due to safety concerns, the natural rock slide has been closed to visitors.

From Kealia, the highway climbs and turns inland through sugar cane fields. One cane road spurs off to **Donkey's Beach** (★), a nude beach favored by local folks (see the "Beaches and Parks" section in this chapter). The main road continues through the town of **Anahola,** a small Hawaiian homestead settlement.

Beyond this tiny town, a **Hole in the Mountain** has been chiseled by the elements. Legend has it, though, that an angry giant hurled his spear through the rock.

Farther north, in somnolent Kilauea town, you'll find that Kauai's other slippery slide has also been closed. Specially designed for the movie *South Pacific*, this recreation facility proved as unsafe as its Waipahee counterpart. You can, however, still go to the **Kilauea Lighthouse.** From here you'll have the same bird's-eye view as the boobies, tropicbirds, albatrosses, and frigate birds nesting in the nearby cliffs. The lighthouse, bearing the world's largest clamshell lens, is the first beacon seen by mariners venturing east from Asia. This old lighthouse, now fully automated, sits on the northernmost point of the principal islands of Hawaii.

Once again the main highway, Route 56, offers numerous side roads to **hidden beaches** (★) as it continues on to the **Hanalei Valley Lookout.** Below this vista spreads a patchwork of tropical vegetation divided by the sparkling Hanalei River. In town, a combination of ramshackle buildings, dramatic mountain views, and curving beaches creates a mystique which can only be described in a single word—Hanalei. It's almost superfluous that the **Hanalei Museum** (826-6783) and **Waioli Mission House** (245-3202) provide glimpses of a bygone era: the entire town seems a reflection of its former self. The museum, an old plantation home, houses period pieces from the turn of the century. The mission house, built in 1836, dates even further back.

The road winds on to beaches at **Lumahai, Haena,** and **Kee,** and past several caves created eons ago when this entire area was underwater. The first is **Maniniholo Dry Cave,** which geologists claim is a lava tube but which legend insists was created by Menehunes. The **Waikapalae** and **Waikanaloa Wet Caves** nearby are said to be the work of Pele, the Hawaiian fire goddess, who sought fire in the earth, but discovered only water.

Shopping

LIHUE SHOPPING

For everyday needs and common items, try the local shopping centers. The **Lihue Shopping Center** (Rice Street and Kuhio Highway) contains a clothes shop and small department store. **Rice Shopping Center** (4300 block of Rice Street) has a few stores, including a boutique.

Even better is the **Kapaia Stitchery** (245-2281) on Route 56 in Kapaia. Half the items are designed and stitched by local women; owner Julie Yukimura's ninety-three-year-old grandmother does the crocheting. There's an array of T-shirts, *aloha* shirts, Hawaiian quilting kits, and dresses, plus stunning patchwork quilts. This is an excellent place to buy Hawaiian fabrics. In addition to the handmade quality, the prices here are often lower than in larger stores.

Kukui Grove Center (Route 50 one mile outside Lihue) is the island's largest shopping mall, an ultra-modern complex. Here are department stores, bookshops, specialty stores, and many other establishments. Though lacking the intimacy of Kauai's independent handicraft outlets, the center provides such a concentration of goods that it's hard to bypass.

Kilohana (Route 50 about two miles west of Lihue) is one of Hawaii's most beautiful complexes. Set in a grand old plantation house, it rests amid 35 acres of manicured grounds. Many rooms in this museum-cum-mall are furnished in period to recapture 1930s-era plantation life. The shops are equally enchanting.

If you can't find what you're after in Lihue, you've always got the rest of the island. Failing that, you'll just have to wait for that plane flight back to the Big Papaya, Honolulu.

POIPU AREA SHOPPING

On the way to Poipu, the former plantation town of Koloa supports a cluster of shops as well as a miniature mall. Several trendy clothing stores line Koloa Road. The mall, called **Old Koloa Town** (even though it's one of the newest developments around), houses a string of small jewelry stores, a T-shirt shop, and a photo studio.

My favorite shopping spot around Poipu has always been at the **Spouting Horn.** Here, next to the parking lot that serves visitors to the blowhole, local merchants set up tables to sell their wares. You're liable to find coral and *puka* shell necklaces, trident shell trumpets, rare Niihau shell necklaces, and some marvelous mother-of-pearl pieces. You are free to barter, of course, though the prices are pretty good to begin with. If you're interested in jewelry, and want to meet local artisans, this is an intriguing spot.

After browsing here, if you care to go from the sublime to the *tres cher*, you might consider the shops at the **Waiohai** hotel (742-9511). Located on Poipu Beach, this resort complex offers a wide selection of stores from which to choose.

Kiahuna Shopping Village on Poipu Road is a sprawling complex dotted with upscale shops. There are dozens of stores to choose from.

WAIMEA AREA SHOPPING

The Station (335-5731), on Route 50 in Hanapepe, specializes in original needlepoint designs. They are sold as kits with which you can fashion cushions, wall hangings, quilts, and so on.

The Art Hut (Hanapepe Road, Hanapepe; 245-9143), set in an old woodframe building, displays the distinguished oil paintings of an imaginative artist named Ales Sedlacek.

Bougainvilla (3900 Hanapepe Road, Hanapepe; 335-3582) has handmade teddy bears as well as clothing and jewelry. The **James Hoyle Gallery,** displaying the scintillating works of a famous Hawaii artist, is located upstairs.

Collectibles & Fine Junque (9821 Route 50, Waimea; 338-9855) has an amazing collection of glassware, *aloha* shirts, dolls, and old bottles. It's a good place to pick up antiques or knickknacks.

WAILUA AREA SHOPPING

Adjacent to the Hanamaulu Museum, in the diminutive town of Hanamaulu, are a cluster of shops selling foreign imports as well as island-wrought goods. While ambling through the stores, you might also meander over to the museum. The artifacts here reflect Kauai's early plantation days; from them you'll derive an image of the sugar industry back in the days of immigrant Chinese workers.

Positively the numbah one shopping spot on Kauai is the **Market Place** at Coconut Plantation (Route 56, Wailua). This theme mall consists of wooden stores designed to resemble little plantation houses. For decor you'll find the pipes, valves, gears, and waterwheels characteristic of every tropical plantation. This is *the* place for clothing, flowers, curios, jewelry, toys, Asian imports, T-shirts, luggage, sweets, plus leather goods, betters, and bests. If you don't want to buy, you can always browse or have a snack at the many short-order stands here. In any case, it's worth a walk through.

The nearby **Coco Palms Hotel,** that luxurious resort where Elvis Presley filmed *Blue Hawaii*, has several shops selling beautiful handicrafts. Prices are rather steep, but the quality here is superb. There are *tapa* pieces, glassware, delicate woodcarvings, intricate fishbone statuary, and an assortment of fine jewelry. And that's just on the ground floor of this two-tiered emporium. Topside you'll find a couple of clothing shops with designs for every lifestyle from island to mainland.

Rehabilitation Unlimited of Kauai (822-4975), nearby at 4531 Kuamoo Road, features bamboo and coconut items fabricated by some local disabled folks.

It's not really **The Only Show in Town** (1495 Kuhio Highway, Kapaa; 822-1442), but this eclectic antique, clothing, and art shop is the only place around where you'll find old *aloha* shirts, fur pieces, early-century cigarette packs, statuettes, and Polynesian spearheads all under a single roof.

Also stop by **My Chard'one** (1467 Kuhio Highway, Kapaa; 822-7361) up the street. This arts-and-crafts store has paintings by local artists as well as carvings and jewelry.

HANALEI AREA SHOPPING

Kong Lung Co. (828-1822) in Kilauea has a marvelous assortment of Pacific and Asian treasures and must not be missed.

Princeville is the place for exclusive shops on the north shore. The Princeville Center, located just off Route 56, is the prime spot for window browsers and big spenders alike.

Want to see what those local folks do with sewing needles? **Toucans** (826-7332), situated in this shopping complex, has some elegant designs.

In Hanalei, the **Native Hawaiian Trading & Cultural Center** contains a cluster of small shops selling jewelry, island wear, books, and knickknacks. There's also a miniature Hawaiian museum with artifacts from ancient Polynesia. **Ching Young Village** next door is a modern shopping mall which contains a variety store, clothing shops, and several other outlets.

If you're interested in homemade goods, watch for stores here, throughout Hanalei, and in other small towns along the North Shore.

Nightlife

Anyone looking to Kauai for nighttime activity has probably stepped off the wrong plane. Maui and Oahu host the hot spots in this little corner of the world. But do check out the large hotels and a few local lounges; there's bound to be something clicking.

LIHUE NIGHTLIFE

You'll find a lot of local color at the **Lihue Cafe Lounge** (2978 Umi Street; 245-6471). The drinks are cheap, the tourists are few.

The **Club Jetty** (245-4970), down in the harbor town of Nawiliwili, features live entertainment every evening from Wednesday through Saturday. There's usually no cover or minimum at this rocking seaside spot; recommended for anyone in search of a good time.

Park Place (Harbor Village Shopping Center, Route 51, Nawiliwili; 245-5775) is a disco nightclub boasting the island's largest dance floor. The motif is tropical and the club is equally hot.

POIPU AREA NIGHTLIFE

The Poipu Beach Hotel's **Mahina Lounge** (742-1681) has live music Thursday through Saturday from 9:30 p.m. The **Drum Lounge** at the nearby Kauai Sheraton Hotel (742-1661) beats out dance rhythms every night of the week. I had mixed feelings about the music, but the view from this seaside watering hole is simply spectacular.

The Waiohai hotel (742-9511), also located on Poipu Beach, hosts several plush nightspots. The **Tamarind Lounge** offers piano music; seaside at the **Terrace Bar** you can watch the moon over the water or buy a drink to go and take a stroll along the beach. To catch a more local crowd, head down to **Brennecke's Seaside Bar & Grill** (Hoona Road; 742-7588). There's no music, but the crowds are young and the views otherworldly.

WAILUA AREA NIGHTLIFE

Gilligans (4331 Kauai Beach Drive; 245-1955), at the Kauai Hilton, is a chic video disco with big crowds, big screen, and a pink marble bar. Cover.

Also check out the **Jolly Roger** (822-3451), in the Market Place at Coconut Plantation, where the music is live and the crowd even livelier. Any night of the week you can hear a medley that varies from oldies-but-goodies to country-and-western music.

There are rock bands wailing amid a cocktail lounge setting at the Kauai Beach Boy Hotel's **Boogie Palace** (822-3441). Located in the Coconut Plantation, the lounge starts rocking around 9 p.m. It's definitely worth the cover charge.

The **Lagoon Cocktail Terrace** at Coco Palms Hotel (Route 56, Wailua; 822-4921) has a torchlighting ceremony at 7:30 p.m. and dance music from ten to twelve every evening. The music is low-key, the setting is dreamlike. There's also a Polynesian show at 9:30 p.m. just across the corridor in the **Lagoon Dining Room.** You can see the show for the price of a cup of coffee.

For an early-evening drink overlooking the water, the most enchanting spot is at the **Seashell Restaurant** (Route 56, Wailua; 822-3632), situated on Wailua Beach. Sit at a table outside under the palms, order a tall, cool one, and watch the surf walk along the sand.

HANALEI AREA NIGHTLIFE

At the lovely Sheraton Princeville (826-9644)you can enjoy the views of Hanalei Bay, stop by the piano bar at the **Lime Tree Lounge,** or boogie at **Ukiyo,** an elegant video disco done in an Asian motif with Japanese masks and porcelain dragons. Located in Princeville.

Tortilla Flats Restaurant & Cantina (Princeville Center, Route 56; 826-7255) features a friendly bar but no live music.

For a tropical drink amid a pacific setting, place your orders at **Tahiti Nui Restaurant** (826-6277) or the **Dolphin Restaurant** (826-6113), both in Hanalei.

Kauai Addresses and Phone Numbers

KAUAI ISLAND

County Department of Parks and Recreation—(245-8821)
Department of Land and Natural Resources—3060 Eiwa Street, Lihue (245-4444)
Hawaii Visitors Bureau—3016 Umi Street, Lihue (245-3971)
Weather—(245-6001)

LIHUE

Ambulance—911
Barber Shop—Ikeda Barber Shop, 4446 Hardy Street (245-4983)
Books—Rainbow Books, Kuhio Highway (245-3703)
Fire Department—911
Fishing Supplies—Lihue Fishing Supply, 2985 Kalena (245-4930)
Hardware—Ace Hardware, 4018 Rice Street (245-4091)
Hospital—Wilcox Memorial, 3420 Kuhio Highway (245-1100)
Laundromat—Lihue Washerette, 4444 Rice Street
Library—4344 Hardy Street (245-3617)
Liquor—City Liquor, 4347-B Rice Street (245-3733)
Pharmacy—Longs Drug Store, Kukui Grove Center, Route 50 (245-7771)
Photo Supply—Foto Fast Kauai, 3134 Kuhio Highway (245-7881)
Police Department—3060 Umi Street (911)
Post Office—4441 Rice Street (245-4994)

POIPU AREA

Ambulance—911
Fire Department—911
Laundromat—Beside Big Save Market, Koloa Road, Koloa
Police Department—911

WAIMEA AREA

Ambulance—911
Fire Department—911
Laundromat—Menehune Center Laundromat, 9887 Waimea Road,
    Waimea
Police Department—911

WAILUA AREA

Ambulance—911
Fire Department—911
Laundromat—In Kapaa Shopping Center, Kapaa (822-3113)
Police Department—911

HANALEI AREA

Ambulance—911
Fire Department—911
Police Department—911

A Note from the Author

An alert, adventurous reader is as important as a travel writer in keeping a guidebook up-to-date and accurate. So if you happen upon a great restaurant, discover a hidden locale, or (heaven forbid) find an error in the text, I'd appreciate hearing from you. Just write to:

Ulysses Press
Box 4000 — H
Berkeley, CA 94704

Recommended Reading

Hawaii, by James Michener. Bantam Books, 1978. This lengthy historic novel skillfully blends fact and fiction, dramatically tracing the entire course of Hawaiian history.

Hawaii Pono, by Lawrence H. Fuchs. Harcourt Brace Jovanovich, 1961. A brilliant sociological study of twentieth-century Hawaii which vividly portrays the islands' ethnic groups.

Hawaii: The Sugar-Coated Fortress, by Francine Du Plessix Gray. Random House, 1972. A hard-hitting analysis of modern-day Hawaii which details the tragic effect Western civilization has had on the Hawaiian people.

Hawaiian Antiquities, by David Malo. Bishop Museum Press, 1971. Written by a Hawaiian scholar in the nineteenth century, this study contains a wealth of information on pre-European Hawaiian culture.

Hawaiian Hiking Trails, by Craig Chisholm. Touchstone Press, 1975. The best single-volume hiking guide available, this handbook provides excellent descriptions of Hawaii's most popular treks.

Hiking Hawaii, Hiking Kauai, Hiking Maui, and *Hiking Oahu,* by Robert Smith. Wilderness Press, 1977, 1978. Together these four volumes contain the most comprehensive listing of Hawaiian hiking trails.

The Legends and Myths of Hawaii, by David Kalakaua. Charles E. Tuttle Company, 1972. Written by Hawaii's last king, this fascinating collection includes fables of the great chiefs and priests who once ruled the islands.

Polynesian Researches: Hawaii, by William Ellis. Charles E. Tuttle Company, 1969. This missionary's journal originally appeared in the 1820s. Despite some tedious sermonizing, it poignantly portrays Hawaii at a historic crossroads and graphically describes volcanoes and other natural phenomena on the Big Island.

Ronck's Hawaii Almanac, by Ronn Ronck. University of Hawaii Press, 1984. Compiled by one of Hawaii's leading journalists, this handy compendium contains a wealth of information on the history, culture, geography, geology, flora, and fauna of the islands.

Shoal of Time, by Gavan Daws. University Press of Hawaii, 1974. The finest history written on Hawaii, this volume is not only informative but entertaining as well.

Shore Fishing in Hawaii, by Edward Y. Hosaka. Petroglyph Press, n.d. This how-to guide is filled with handy tips on surf-casting, fabricating your own equipment, and identifying Hawaii's fish species.

Index

About the Author

Ray Riegert is the author of five travel books, including *Hidden Coast of California* and *Hidden San Francisco and Northern California*. In addition to his role as publisher of Ulysses Press, he writes for Fodor's Travel Guides, the San Francisco *Examiner & Chronicle* and *Travel & Leisure*.

Leslie Henriques

Ray is a member of the Society of American Travel Writers and writes a weekly travel column for a Gannett chain newspaper. Currently working on a new book, *Hidden Los Angeles and Southern California*, he lives in the San Francisco Bay Area with his wife, travel photographer Leslie Henriques, and their son Keith and daughter Alice.

Also Available From

ULYSSES PRESS

HIDDEN COAST OF CALIFORNIA
The Adventurer's Guide
Ray Riegert

*T*he author of *Hidden Hawaii* explores the fabled California coast from Mexico to Oregon. San Diego, Santa Barbara, Big Sur, Monterey and Mendocino are featured. There are·also complete descriptions of the beaches of Los Angeles and San Francisco. Like the other "hidden" guides by Ulysses Press, the book comprehensively covers hotels, restaurants, shops, sightseeing spots and nightlife. Then it carries the reader a step further—leading him to secluded beaches, country inns, remote campgrounds, hiking trails and little-known points of interest. There are special sections on tidepools, surfing, fishing, horseback riding and sailing.
$10.95   348 pp.

HIDDEN MEXICO
Adventurer's Guide To The Beaches And Coasts
Rebecca Bruns

*F*rom the Pacific to the Sea of Cortez, from the Gulf of Mexico to the Caribbean, Mexico is a sparkling six thousand mile beach. This fact-filled guide covers the coastline in the most comprehensive fashion ever. It carries the reader to the fabulous resort complexes of Acapulco, Cancun and Puerto Vallarta and contains complete details on Baja, the West Coast, Yucatan and the Gulf of Mexico. In addition to information on hotels, restaurants, shopping and sightseeing, it leads the reader to an unspoiled Mexico few travelers know. There are descriptions of hidden beaches, Caribbean islands, remote fishing villages, Mayan ruins and scenic routes.
$12.95   396 pp.

HIDDEN SAN FRANCISCO
AND NORTHERN CALIFORNIA
The Adventurer's Guide
Second Edition
Ray Riegert

A major resource for travelers combing the Bay Area and beyond in search of adventure. It leads the reader to a Chinatown fortune cookie factory in San Francisco, then wanders exotic Land's End, where the city meets the sea. The book ranges Northern California from Big Sur to Oregon, stopping in shady redwood groves and quaint country inns. Then it explores vineyards in the Wine Country, pans for gold, hikes Yosemite and camps on a secluded Lake Tahoe beach.
$10.95   432 pp.

To Order Direct
Add $2 postage and handling (California residents include 6% sales tax)
Ulysses Press, P.O. Box 4000-H, Berkeley, CA 94704